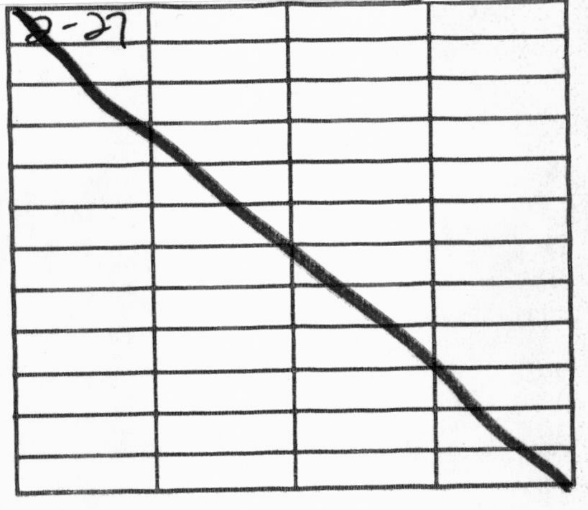
2-27

CONSTITUTIONALISM AND DEMOCRACY

CONSTITUTIONALISM *and* DEMOCRACY

Transitions in the Contemporary World

The American Council of Learned Societies Comparative Constitutionalism Papers

EDITORS
DOUGLAS GREENBERG
STANLEY N. KATZ
MELANIE BETH OLIVIERO
STEVEN C. WHEATLEY

New York Oxford
OXFORD UNIVERSITY PRESS
1993

Oxford University Press

Oxford New York Toronto
Delhi Bombay Calcutta Madras Karachi
Kuala Lumpur Singapore Hong Kong Tokyo
Nairobi Dar es Salaam Cape Town
Melbourne Auckland Madrid

and associated companies in
Berlin Ibadan

Published by Oxford University Press, Inc.
200 Madison Avenue, New York, NY 10016

Library of Congress Cataloging-in-Publication Data
Constitutionalism and democracy: transitions in the contemporay world: the American Council of Learned Societies comparative constitutionalism papers / edited by Douglas Greenberg ... [et al.].
p. cm.
Papers from a series of international conferences organized by the American Council of Learned Societies.
Includes bibliographical references (p.) and index.
ISBN 0-19-507107-7
1. Representative government and representation—Congresses.
2. Democracy—Congresses. 3. Constitutional history—Congresses.
4. Constitutional law—Congresses. I. Greenberg, Douglas.
II. American Council of Learned Societies.
JF1051.C635 1993 321.8—dc20 92-22633

4 6 8 9 7 5 3

Printed in the United States of America
on acid-free paper

Contents

VI Reflections on Constitutionalism

Contributors

Abdullahi Ahmed An-Na'im is the incoming director of Africa Watch of Human Rights Watch, New York, after serving for a year as Olaf Palme Professor of Law, University of Uppsala, Sweden. He was formerly Associate Professor of Law at the University of Khartoum, the Sudan, and Professor of Human Rights at the University of Saskatchewan, Canada. Mr. An-Na'im is a co-editor of *Human Rights in Africa: Cross-Cultural Perspectives* (Washington D.C.: The Brookings Institution, 1990); author of *Toward an Islamic Reformation: Civil Liberties, Human Rights and International Law* (Syracuse: Syracuse University Press, 1990); and editor of *Human Rights in Cross-Cultural Perspectives* (Philadelphia: University of Pennsylvania Press, 1991).

Atilio A. Borón is Founder and Director of the Center for European-Latin American Research (EURAL) in Buenos Aires, Argentina. Mr. Boron has held many teaching positions in Argentina and abroad, most recently serving as Titular Professor of the Chair of Political Theory at the University of Buenos Aires, from August 1986 to the present, and as Tinker Professor of Latin American Affairs at Columbia University, New York, in the fall of 1987.

Radhika Coomaraswamy is a director of the International Centre for Ethnic Studies, Working Committee member of the Sri Lanka Civil Rights Movement, and was recently appointed to the Presidential Commission on Youth Unrest. She is author of *Sri Lanka—Anglo American Constitutional Traditions in a Developing Society* (New Delhi: Vikas, 1984).

Jon Elster is Professor of Political Science and Philosophy at the University of Chicago, and Adjunct Professor of Economics at the University of Oslo in Norway. His most recent publications are *Psychologie Politique* (Paris: Minvit, 1990), *The Cement of Society* (Cambridge: Cambridge University Press, 1989), and *Solomonic Judgements* (Cambridge: Cambridge University Press, 1989).

Julio Faundez teaches international law at Warwick University, where he is Director of the International Economic Law Programme. His recent books include *Marxism and Democracy in Chile* (New Haven: Yale University Press, 1988), *Independent Namibia: Succession to Treaty Rights and Obligations* (Lusaka, Zambia: United Nations Institute for Namibia, 1989), and *Malvinas Hoy* (Buenos Aires: Puntosur, 1989, co-editor with Atilio Boron). He has served as legal consultant to the United Nations Centre on Transnational Corporations, the United Nations Institute for Namibia, and the International Labour Organisation. He recently advised the Government of Namibia on affirmative action legislation.

Hugo E. Frühling is a researcher at the Human Rights Program of the Academy of Christian Humanism in Santiago, Chile, a post he has held since 1984. In 1987 he held the Human Rights Chair at the Human Rights Research and Education Centre of the University of Ottawa in Canada, and prior to that was a researcher at the Inter-American Institute of Human Rights. Mr. Frühling was educated at the University of Chile and Harvard University, and received his S.J.D. from the latter institution in 1984.

Yash Ghai is the Sir Y. K. Pao Professor of Public Law at the University of Hong Kong. Until the end of 1989 he was a professor at the School of Law at the University of Warwick, in the United Kingdom. He has previously taught at the University of East Africa, Yale Law School, Uppsala, and the University of the South Pacific, among others, and has served as a legal and constitutional consultant to several governments and international organizations. Mr. Ghai is the author of numerous articles and books on public law, state-owned enterprises, race relations, and economic integration.

Eboe Hutchful is Associate Professor in Political Science at Trent University in Ontario, Canada, and Adjunct Professor at Scarborough College of the University of Toronto. He received his Ph.D. from the University of Toronto in 1973, and has taught at the Universities of Ghana, in Legon, and Port Harcourt, in Nigeria. Mr. Hutchful has researched and written on military politics, debt and structural adjustment, and the environmental aspects of the oil industry in Nigeria. He is the author of *The IMF and Ghana* (London: Zed, 1987), and of a forthcoming study on oil, ecology, and public policy in Nigeria.

Nevil Johnson has been Nuffield Reader in the Comparative Study of Institutions at the University of Oxford in the United Kingdom, and Professorial Fellow of Nuffield College since 1969. He was in the British Civil Service until 1962 and then taught at the Universities of Nottingham and Warwick successively. He has served as a part-time Civil Service Commissioner, and was from 1981 to 1987 a member of the Economic and Social Research Council. Mr. Johnson was Hon. Editor of *Public Administration* for fourteen years, and has written widely on political institutions and problems of government. He is the author of *State and Government in the Federal Republic of Germany* (Oxford: Pergamon Press, 1983); his latest book is *The Limits of Political Science* (Oxford: Oxford University Press, 1989).

Lena Kolarska-Bobinska, a Professor of Sociology, is the Director of Public Opinion Research Center, the Polish government public opinion institute. She received her Ph.D. degree from the Institute of Philosophy and Sociology, Polish Academy of Science. She advised Solidarity's group in Parliament, and was also a member of the Polish Government's Economic Council, an advisory body reporting to the Council of Ministers. The author of numerous books and articles, Ms. Kolarska-Bobinska is co-author of the "Poles" series, which analyzed changing social attitudes in Poland as reflected in polls conducted in the 1980s.

Ludger Kühnhardt has been "Privatdozent" for Political Science at the University of Bonn since 1986, where he previously was Dr. Phil. and Habilitation, and Executive Assistant for the Seminar for Political Science. From 1987 to 1989 he was the main speechwriter for the President of the Federal Republic of Germany. Mr. Kühnhardt studied history, philosophy, and political science in Bonn, Geneva, and Tokyo, and has served as a Research Associate at Harvard University's Center for European Studies. He is a 1989/1990 Senior Associate Member of St. Antony's College at Oxford University.

Daniel S. Lev is Professor of Political Science at the University of Washington. A specialist in Southeast Asian comparative politics, he has done research in Indonesia, Malaysia, and Singapore. His publications include *The Transition to Guided Democracy* (Ithaca; NY: Modern Indonesia Project, Southeast Asia Program, Department of Asian Studies, Cornell University, 1966), *Islamic Courts in Indonesia* (Berkeley: University of California Press, 1972), and essays and articles on law and politics in Indonesia and Malaysia. At present he is writing a book on the politics of legal change in Indonesia and another on the political biography of a prominent Indonesian human rights leader.

Vera Losonci is a graduate of Hunter College and Cardozo Law School. She served as clerk to the Hon. Lazlo Sólyom of the Hungarian Constitutional Court.

Mahmood Mamdani is Director of the Centre for Basic Research in Kampala, Uganda. Since receiving his Ph.D. from Harvard University, he has also served as Professor at the University of Dar-es-Salaam and the University of Michigan, Ann Arbor, and most recently at Makerere University in Kampala. Mr. Mamdani is the author of a number of volumes, among them *From Citizen to Refugee* (London: Fromees Pinter, 1973), *Myth of Population Control* (New York: Monthly Review Press, 1973), *Politics and Class Formation in Uganda* (New York: Monthly Review Press, 1976), and *Imperialism and Fascism in Uganda* (Nairobi: Heinemann Educational Books, 1983). His current interests include agrarian issues, popular movements, democratic struggles, and democratic theory.

Walter F. Murphy is McCormick Professor of Jurisprudence in the Department of Politics at Princeton University, where he is also Faculty Associate at the Center of International Studies. He has received numerous academic honors and awards, including Guggenheim, National Endowment for the Humanities, and Fulbright Scholarships. The author of many books and articles on the judiciary, comparative constitutionalism, and public law, Mr. Murphy is also an award-winning novelist, his most widely known and translated work being *The Vicar of Christ*. He served with distinction in the United States Marine Corps, retiring as Colonel in the Reserves in 1974. He has lectured widely in the United States and abroad, and is currently preparing a volume on comparative constitutionalism based on his work with this project.

Carlos Santiago Nino is a lawyer, Senior Research Member of the Center of Institutional Studies in Buenos Aires, and Guggenheim Fellow. From 1983 to 1989 he served as Advisor to the President of Argentina on constitutional reform, and was coordinator of the Council for the Consolidation of Democracy from 1985 to 1989. Receiving his degree in law from Buenos Aires and Ph.D. from Oxford University, he twice served as Visiting Professor of Law at Yale University, and is Professor of Law at the University of Buenos Aires. He is the author of numerous books and articles on legal and political philosophy and criminal and constitutional theory, and his forthcoming volume, *El constructivismo ético*, will be published in Madrid.

Samuel C. Nolutshungu is Professor of Political Science and African Politics at the University of Rochester. Born and raised in South Africa, he has also held university positions in Nigeria, Canada, and the United States. Mr. Nolutshungu has published widely, and is the author of *South Africa in Africa: A Study of Ideology and Foreign Policy* (Manchester, England: Manchester University Press, 1975) and *Changing South Africa: Political Considerations* (Manchester, England: Manchester University Press, 1982). His study, *Intervention and State Formation in Chad 1960–1992*, is forthcoming.

H. W. O. Okoth-Ogendo is the Professor of Public Law and Director of the Population Studies and Research Institute at the University of Nairobi, where he formerly served as Dean of the Faculty of Law. He is also Director of the International Planned Parenthood Federation Africa Regional Centre for African Family Studies based in Nairobi. He has held positions as visiting professor at universities in the United States and Africa, and currently acts as consultant to a number of international and national agencies, including the UN-FAO, the World Bank, the Kenyan Commission for Higher Education, and the Kenyan National Council for Population and Development. He is the author of *Tenants of the Crown: Evolution of Agrarian Law and Institutions in Kenya* (Nairobi: ACTS Press, African Center for Technology Studies, 1991) and numerous articles on agrarian reform planning, constitutional politics and human rights law, the environment, and labor.

Wiktor Osiatynski, born in 1945, holds degrees in law and sociology from Warsaw University. He has written, in Polish, fourteen books, a majority of them concerning the history of social and political thought. He has taught comparative human rights and constitutionalism at the University of Warsaw, University of Virginia, Columbia University, Chicago Law School, and Harvard Law School. Recently, he has developed, for Columbia University, a standard university syllabus on "Constitutionalism and Rights in Transition from Communism." He was an expert advisor of the Constitutional Committee of the Poland's Senate. At present, Wiktor Osiatynski is a program director at the Center for the Study of Education at the Helsinki Foundation of Human Rights in Warsaw, Poland, and a co-director of the Center for the Study of Constitutionalism in Eastern Europe at the University of Chicago Law School.

Tapan Raychaudhuri is Professor of Indian History and Civilization at the University of Oxford, and Professorial Fellow at St. Antony's College, and has taught at Oxford since 1973. A graduate of the University of Calcutta and Oxford University, he previously taught history and economic history at Delhi University, and was recently awarded the D.L.H. degree. Mr. Raychaudhuri's main area of interest is the social and economic history of India during the Mughal and Colonial period. His publications include the *Cambridge Economic History of India* (Cambridge: Cambridge University Press, 1981–1983), of which he was general co-editor, and *Europe Reconsidered: Perceptions of the West in 19th Century Bengal* (Delhi: Cambridge University Press, 1988).

Juan Rial is Director and Researcher at Peitho, Society for Political Analysis in Montevideo, Uruguay. A historian by training, his current research interest is the armed forces and society. He has presented papers on that subject, and has published widely on civil/military affairs in general.

András Sajó is Professor of Comparative Business Law at the Budapest School of Economics, and Research Director for a program on legal reaction to social problems, Institute of Law, Hungarian Academy of Sciences. He is past Deputy Commissioner for Deregulation, and a past member of the Constitution Drafting Committee for Hungary (1988–1989). Mr. Sajó's interests include legal philosophy, sociology of law, business law (economic freedom), and environmental law.

Jordi Solé Tura is Full Professor (Catedratico) of Constitutional Law on the Faculty of Law of Barcelona University, where he formerly served as Dean of the Faculty of Law from 1985 to 1988. He was a Member of the Spanish Parliament from 1977 to 1982, serving as a Member of the Parliamentary Drafting Commissions of the Spanish Constitution and Catalonia Statute of Autonomy, in 1978 and 1979, respectively. In 1989 he was elected Member of Parliament (Congreso de los Diputados) and was appointed Chairman of the Constitutional Affairs Commission of the Chamber. In 1991 he was appointed Minister of Culture of the Spanish Government.

Neelan Tiruchelvam is a lawyer in Sri Lanka. He is the Director of the International Center for Ethnic Studies, and the Director of the Law and Society Trust, both in Sri Lanka. Mr. Tiruchelvam has written extensively on constitutional law and ethnic pluralism. He is a former member of the Law Commission and the Presidential Commission on Devolution.

Klaus von Beyme is Professor of Political Science at the Institute Political Sciences of the University of Heidelberg, where he has taught since 1974. He received his training in political science, sociology, and history from Universities in Heidelberg, Munich, and Moscow, and Harvard University. He served as Professor at Tubingen University from 1967 to 1974. Mr. von Beyme was President of the International Political Science Association from 1982 to 1985, and has published widely. One of his more recent works is *America as a Model* (London: Gower, 1987).

Joseph H. H. Weiler is Professor of Law at Michigan Law School, Ann Arbor, and at the European University Institute in Florence, and is currently serving as Lady Davis Visiting Professor at Hebrew University. He is the author, *inter alia*, of *Il Sistema Comunitario Europeo* (Bologna: Il MuLino, 1985) and was director and general editor of the multivolume comparative project *Integration Through Law: Europe and the American Federal Experience* (Berlin: Wide Giruvter, 1985). Recently he has co-edited *1991: A Single European Market*? (Baden-Baden: Nomos Verlagsgesellchaft, 1988)

Introduction

The essays in this volume were originally written for presentation and discussion at a series of international conferences organized by The American Council of Learned Societies (ACLS). These conferences, which took place in Punta del Este, Uruguay; Chiangmai, Thailand; Harare, Zimbabwe; Berlin, Germany; Pecs, Hungary; and Princeton, New Jersey, were the main activities of the ACLS Comparative Constitutionalism project.

The ACLS initiated its project on comparative constitutionalism in 1987. Supported principally by the Ford Foundation, the primary goal of the project was to stimulate and broaden the study of this timely and important subject as an expression of the Council's commitment to promoting the interdisciplinary exploration of significant scholarly questions.

When the project began, it was intended to be a unique commemoration of the bicentennial of the American constitution, which was then being celebrated. The original idea was to avoid the self-congratulatory and triumphal character of so much of the Bicentennial and focus instead on the underlying ideas that have animated constitutions and their creation throughout the world. As the project proceeded, moreover, the wisdom of this initial intention was borne out by events, which eroded authoritarian regimes throughout the world with startling speed, if not finality. Indeed, the conference in Berlin occurred only a month before the opening of the Wall.

As the project developed, it became immediately clear that although the study of constitutional law and comparative government was a venerable academic subject, scholarly work on comparative constitutionalism had been both thin and superficial. The ACLS conferences thus were comparative across disciplines, cultures, and regimes, as well as through time. This focus reflected an initial premise that an effective discussion of constitutions and constitutionalism should not be the exclusive disciplinary preserve of lawyers and political scientists, but rather should involve multidisciplinary research informed by a wide range of perspectives and experiences.

The organizers of the project were especially sensitive to the need to depart from the common scholarly practice of concentrating on the American experience in constitutional study. They hoped, if it seemed appropriate in other parts of the world, to regard constitutional change as a subject that might be investigated anthropologically in its own terms and not judged by the yardstick of American experience. The goal of this project was to see constitutionalism, not just as a formal state structure, but also as a dynamic process. In this view, it is the crossroads of law and society, culture and history, economics and politics.

To accomplish this goal effectively, the project staff convened committees of advisors in each region of the world that was to be a venue for one of the conferences (Latin America, Africa, South and Southeast Asia, western Europe, and central Europe.) These committees advised ACLS in identifying the issues with the greatest significance in each region. Each committee met twice before the full conference to refine the conference agenda and suggest participants. The result was five distinct programs that focused discussion on topics of specific regional interest and relevance.

In addition, the ACLS also cooperated for each event with local organizations for substantive as well as logistic advice. In the case of Latin America, the partner organization was the Centro de Informaciones y Estudios del Uruguay (CIESU). The two cooperating institutions in Asia were the Law and Society Trust of Sri Lanka, and the Institute for Public Policy Studies of Thailand. In Africa, the local coordinator was the office of the Southern Africa Political and Economic Series/African Association of Political Science, Southern Africa Chapter (SAPES/AAPS). The John F. Kennedy Institute for North American Studies of the Free University of Berlin was the co-hosting organization for the European Regional Institute. In organizing the Pecs, Hungary institute, the Council cooperated with the Department of Sociology of Law of Eötövs Loránd University, Budapest.

Each conference was between 3 and 5 days in length. The number of participants was deliberately kept low; roughly 35–40 conferees with a broad range of professional and regional expertise were invited to attend each institute. Approximately half were drawn from the region; the rest came from other parts of the world.

Although the substantive themes of the meetings varied, the basic design was uniform. Working papers were commissioned in advance to explore each of several topics designated by the regional steering committee. These papers were then distributed to all participants weeks prior to the meeting itself, so that when the group convened, its members would have a common core of information and analysis from which to begin the deliberations. The papers were not read at the conferences, but served instead as the basis of wide-ranging discussions. It is from among these papers, subsequently revised, that the contributions to this volume were drawn.

Some themes were common to each institute, and they appear in the pages that follow. These included the nature of constitutional legitimacy; federalism and the consequences of the geographic distribution of power; religious and ethnic diversity; constitutionalism and positive rights; civil rule and bureaucracy; the role of the military in constitutional government; and the potential tension between constitutionalism and democracy.

A summary institute, held at the Woodrow Wilson School of International and Public Affairs of Princeton University, November 15–17, 1989, sought to synthesize the results of the regional meetings. It was smaller than the other conferences, and each of the participants had attended at least one or more of the earlier meetings. The meeting was primarily evaluative, but a number of the papers produced for it proved to be so provocative that they are included here.

The diverse expertise of participants in the ACLS institutes provided the intellectual depth required to stimulate exchanges on constitutionalism among academics, journalists, and public figures from around the world. Each conference included representatives of the countries in the region as well as other participants from other parts of the world. The result was an unusually rich mixture of analytical perspectives and approaches to the problem. Similarly, the more than 60 papers prepared for the conferences contained a wealth of information and such a broad view of the subject absent from the existing literature.

The papers that appear in this volume cannot begin to transmit the intellectual richness of the project. Complete sets of the working papers have been available for some time both in this country and in each region. The essays presented in this volume, all of which have been extensively revised since their original drafting, are intended instead to present a distillation of the intellectual accomplishments of the ACLS Comparative Constitutionalism project and thus to further in another way the goals that the project sought to achieve. As a group, they raise most of the important issues, utilize many of the relevant methodologies, and deal with every major region of the world.

The principles of selection applied by the editors were both simple to devise and difficult to apply. On the one hand, it seemed important to reflect the diversity of the contributions made to the ACLS project and thereby to illuminate the germane intellectual promise of comparative constitutionalism as a field of inquiry. On the other hand, an unfocused smattering of material from each of the conferences would lack analytical coherence and persuasive power.

As a result, the editors sought to steer between these two extremes by discarding the conferences themselves as an organizing principle for this volume, choosing instead to focus on a set of issues that arose everywhere and that proved to be especially compelling. The organization of this book therefore does not accord with the organization of the project from which the essays originally arose, but rather aims to recapitulate the most salient issues in a fashion that insists first on the primacy of the comparative method and second on the distinctive cultural integrity of individual polities. In the remaining pages of this introduction we have sought to highlight some of these issues and to add our own analytical gloss to them as they appeared to four American scholars whose participation in the project was among the most stimulating intellectual experiences of their careers.

Over the course of the project, it became clear that there were two dramatically differing thrusts in defining constitutionalism. The first led toward a highly formalistic view that relied principally on the structural features of constitutional documents. The second tended to regard the constitutionalism of a particular society as a dynamic process, rooted in underlying, local social realities. Despite the fundamental incompatibility of these two approaches, they repeatedly intersected analytically.

The distinction between constitutions and constitutionalism was central to the definitional problem. All of the participants understood that the questions at issue involved more than analyzing constitutional structures or texts, although several argued that in contemporary society the legitimacy of the state rests primarily on the government's adherence to the rule of law. In this definition, constitutionalism necessarily included institutions such as judicial review, due process of law, and separation of powers.

While legality and legitimacy emerged as central concepts in attempts to construct a theory of constitutionalism, the ambiguous relationship of constitutionalism to democracy was always an underlying theme. To what degree are democratic principles preconditions for constitutionalism—or necessary consequences of it? If constitutionalism is inevitably democratic, is it thus bound by the cultural and political values of western liberal capitalism?

The question of fundamental rights preoccupied all the institutes. The debates mirrored the conferees' conflicting preferences for legal formalism or sociopolitical analysis. On the subject of human rights, in particular, this took the form of a universalist argument contending with more relativistic claims. Several participants argued that there could be a single, universal standard of rights and that their protection is best ensured by means of the formal rule of law. Relativism about rights, according to this argument, is analytically indefensible and politically dangerous.

The alternative position argued that the cultural and economic diversity of everyday life makes it effectively impossible either to identify a sufficiently comprehensive core of universal human rights, or to adopt uniform sanctions that are appropriate and enforceable across cultures. Rights, like all legal concepts, are embedded in particular historical and cultural circumstances. They cannot be easily transferred from one society to another. Moreover, the relativists argued, even the most ardent advocate of a universal standard of human rights will agree that not *all* rights are universal. Analytically, therefore, it is difficult to distinguish universal rights from culturally contingent ones.

The adequacy of "the rule of law" to define constitutionalism also came in for criticism. More than one participant pointed out that the rule of law is meaningless unless one knows who makes the rules and enforces them. Underlying a commitment to the rule of law is a powerful impulse toward stability at all costs. As a result, several of the institutes focused on alternative sources of political stability, such as those that might derive from class structure and hegemonic social processes or the threat of direct and violent intervention by the military.

Most institute participants agreed that constitutional rule following, generally, and democratic order, in particular, presuppose the existence of a state and its organization of power. Thus, any understanding of constitutionalism must inevitably involve not only the "rules for making rules" but also local processes of institution building and value formation.

The question of institution building inspired discussions of democratic structures and the alternatives to them. This gave rise to a more general examination of the variety of institutional forms that constitutions establish: democratic frameworks such as parliamentarianism and presidentialism, more authoritarian models such as military regimes and one-party states, as well as others derived from oligarchical and monarchical traditions. Especially in Africa and Southeast Asia, there was insistence that the study of constitutionalism could not be restricted to the analysis of democratic institutions.

The limitations of theoretical models for a comparative understanding of constitutionalism became clearest in attempts to account for the inherently political nature of constitutionalism. Precisely because of our focus on nations in political transition, whether in the developing or more developed regions of the world, the widely shared conclusion was that constitutionalism is a dynamic, political process, rather than a fixed mode of distributing power, rights, and duties. As a result, mere structural comparisons of constitutional legal documents tend falsely to postulate a unitary phenomenon, whose actual contours are beyond the ordinary analytical tools of comparative constitutional law and comparative government, the methodological settings for most previous studies of constitutionalism.

Constitutional legitimacy thus is more often validated by political and social realities than by formal legal criteria. The general acceptance of this view prompted careful consideration of the historical and cultural forces that underlie the creation, maintenance, and decay of a variety of constitutional orders. In the developing world, ethnicity and nationhood have posed especially powerful challenges to modern U.S. and European liberal constitutionalism, which owes its existence to an historical experience quite alien, even antagonistic, to the cultures and societies of Asia and Africa, as well as some of those in Latin America. Throughout the regional institutes, individual nations and their political structures were presented as case studies, but there were very few examples of nations sufficiently homogeneous that a popular consensus on constitutional values and institutions has been easily formed. The global reality is that most societies are characterized by a pluralism that takes geographic, linguistic, religious, ethnic, and economic forms, and are finding the introduction of liberal constitutionalism a formidable challenge.

The discussions returned repeatedly to the question of whether nonliberal forms of constitutionalism, arising from local historical experience, might be sketched or imagined. Abstractly, this was not an unreasonable notion; in practice, however, it proved difficult to describe the precise form that such a constitutionalism would take. Nonetheless, the evidence from Asia and Africa, particularly, demanded consideration of complex models that organize power and create rules that are not always "democratic." The western assumption that constitutionalism and democracy are *necessarily* linked was thus repeatedly challenged almost everywhere outside the newly reforming nations of east central Europe. Yet the colonial legacies of western institutions and bureaucracies have made wholesale constitutional restructuring virtually impossible in most Third World nations. Simultaneously, however, monarchical traditions and indigenous systems of social organization continue to influence popular perceptions of governance and civic responsibility.

Many participants suggested that broad-based political socialization, generally expressed as the creation of civil society, is a prerequisite to stable constitutionalism. A theory of constitutional literacy emerged that contends that the polity must be educated about the idea of limited government before such a government can succeed. This view is based, in part, on the principle that constitutionalism imposed from above, rather than being allowed to develop from below, is actually authoritarianism, and has insufficient basis in civil society to be considered a "genuine" constitutionalism.

The form of political arrangements that might emerge from such a popular process could then coexist with traditional values, and the developing constitutionalism would not be bound by or defined by western culture. Yet even those who pursued this line of reasoning most thoroughly sometimes argued for appropriating local cultural beliefs and practices to introduce or validate concepts borrowed from the west, such as revising the doctrines of Islamic shari'ah as a way of "constitutionalizing" rights in the Islamic world. Ample evidence was cited of the same mechanism being employed in the reverse: usurping cultural values to avoid constitutional accountability. From Senegal, India, and Botswana came reports of how traditional institutions have been used to legitimize one-party states.

This led back to the question of what values one considers "constitutional": Are there preconditions for constitutionalism? Must there be a tradition of legalism? Why reform a culture at all if it is so distant from those values? In some analyses, constitutionalism may be, by definition, an imposition of western political culture on other, nonwestern societies and polities. These are exactly the questions at the center of many ongoing political struggles throughout the world. There was widespread recognition among the discussants that constitutionalism, if it is to emerge, must arise out of such indigenous political controversies, and that its final form was not necessarily predictable. As western liberal constitutionalism has developed organically over centuries from the conditions that existed in Europe and the Americas, so may other, quite different, organic forms emerge from contemporary conditions.

Attempts to manipulate this process, balancing aspirations for greater popular participation against an uncritical impulse toward governmental stability, also were analyzed. The accommodation of military elements as separate political parties, with civilian institutions regulating their budgets, as in the case of Venezuela, was cited as one such example. It is widely agreed that the power of the executive, whatever form it takes, must be limited. This, too, requires political socialization. The system of autonomous regions within a federated framework, such as the one in place in the Catalonian and Basque regions of Spain, was considered as an alternative to the situation in certain African countries where internal conflicts are frustrating the process of state formation and nation building.

The impact of both external events and geopolitical conditions on internal conditions also required extensive discussion. Imperial pressures, regional wars, and, increasingly, the demands of international funding agencies have all had a decisive impact on the course of otherwise local events. At the same time, state building and the development of new national identities are critical and self-conscious activities in many Third World countries. The pace of national development has, moreover, varied markedly. In some cases, the transition from feudalism, monarchy, and colonialism to industrialization, social diversity, and self-government has been telescoped into mere decades in comparison to the centuries over which such change occurred elsewhere.

One of the effects of this accelerated political process and intensified international economic involvement in it has been for emerging states to concentrate on economic development, frequently at the expense of the creation of organic political liberalization. The subordination of civil and human rights to the quest for economic growth is all too familiar. Guaranteeing civil and political rights may be the function of modern states in theory, but social and economic rights are more common aspirations for states in the Third World. Ruling regimes in the developing world, many of them nominally constitutional, have presented the problem as an either/or proposition: one can have food, or one can have the right to complain about the food, but one cannot have both. Sadly, in too many cases, one can have neither.

The omnipresence of externally driven change reinforces the notion of constitutionalism as a dynamic process. It also echoes repeated assertions that the essential features of the process itself are not constants. As political culture is transformed, the direction of institution building and value formation may fluctuate. Competition within and among social groups can and does erode constitutionalism, even when the formal constitutional arrangements of a particular society are designed to account for such competition.

The distillation of these varied and energetic discussions suggests an approximate definition of constitutionalism: it is a commitment to limitations on ordinary political power; it revolves around a political process, one that overlaps with democracy in seeking to balance state power and individual and collective rights; it draws on particular cultural and historical contexts from which it emanates; and it resides in public consciousness.

The work of the project isolated questions that demand further study. Throughout the meetings clear directions for further interdisciplinary investigation emerged. There is a profound need for more rigorous assessment of the historical traditions that underlie modern states, for example, since contemporary political alliances and antipathies are very often rooted in the social history of preceding generations. Here the situation of the new-old states of what used to be called eastern Europe provides a crucial case study of the persistence of earlier constitutionalist and anticonstitutionalist beliefs and behaviors.

Closely allied with this line of inquiry is one that focuses on cultural analysis. There is an organic relationship between culture and constitutionalism, one to which anthropological and sociological approaches can and should be applied. Such analyses can also contribute measurably to developing a typology of constitutional cultures, a suggestion explicitly made during the institutes.

The relationship of constitutionalism to social and economic structure was a recurrent subject to discussion. What are the economic foundations of political democracy? The repeated pattern of mass poverty and underdevelopment giving rise to authoritarian rule was frequently noted, but only partially analyzed. We need also to understand better the roles of the international economy and international institutions in both stabilizing and destabilizing constitutional governments. The same may be said for the significance of regional political and economic arrangements.

Project participants also cited the need to broaden theoretical discussion of constitutionalism. In philosophy, anthropology, sociology, and history, in particular, there are theories and methodologies, as well as accumulated knowledge, that can contribute significantly to developing a constitutional theory that responds to the sociopolitical realities of modern states. The confounding question of alternative constitutional visions can perhaps best be addressed through such a more nuanced, multidisciplinary comparative theoretical approach.

The moral values that underlie both the construction of a constitutional framework and the development of a public consciousness of constitutionalism represent another area for interdisciplinary research. Given the dichotomy revealed in the course of the project between the universalist and relativist positions, pivotal questions, such as whether there are ethical preconditions for constitutionalism, and whether international human rights law has a future, may fruitfully be addressed through this sort of analysis.

A parallel line of inquiry revolves around the related issues of state formation and nation building. Indigenous patterns of culture, along with socioeconomic stratification, distinguish the boundaries of a political map of constitutionalism. How critical is the variable of a strong and independent middle class to the development of constitutionalism? What sort of state is compatible (or incompatible) with constitutionalism? Must some specific sorts of state formation precede constitutionalism?

There were also questions raised from more practical perspectives. The role of public education in the development of political legitimacy and constitutional literacy of a pluralistic society needs to be much better understood. The evidence is already overwhelming that grass roots social movements play critical roles in the creation and stability of constitutional governments. A more careful evaluation of popular struggles can suggest ways of understanding and directing the momentum of these movements. The civic action of human rights groups, social organizations, and NGOs, as well as economic initiatives they produce, also merit study.

Several approaches are proposed in these papers to facilitate further research and its application. There are a variety of educational methods that might be developed to promote the indigenization of constitutionalism. Several observe that the knowledge gained from this sort of comparative approach has implications for the development of constructive activism involving the scholar as political actor. Some argue that comparative constitutionalism has great significance for assisting the process of adapting Western "constitutional" values, as opposed to cloning them. The dynamics of the comparative methodology itself are considered, with recommendations made that there remains a pressing need for both country-specific and multidisciplinary analyses.

A volume such as this, arising as it did from a series of conferences, incurs more debts than most. We first acknowledge the financial support of the Ford Foundation, whose generosity made the Comparative Constitutionalism Project possible. In particular, Shepard Forman, who then headed the Foundation's

Program on Human Rights and Governance, was a steady and consistent source of advice and encouragement, as were his colleagues David Arnold and Lynn Walker. We also received financial assistance from the Johnson Foundation, the Fritz Thyssen and Volkswagen Foundations, and the Swedish Riksbanken Jubileumsfond, for which we are also grateful.

Our colleagues, Walter Murphy and H. W. O. Okoth-Ogendo, not only wrote the overview essays but attended all the conferences, contributing their wisdom, knowledge, and effervescent personalities in many unexpected ways. Rebecca Nichols, now an Assistant Program Officer with the Ford Foundation, served as the administrative assistant for the project. There was not an aspect of the project to which she did not contribute. We count ourselves unusually fortunate to have had her as a colleague and friend. Susan Glassman took on the task of editing the revised papers into the polished form in which they appear here. We are grateful for her perseverance in collaborating with the peripatetic and multilingual authors to produce a volume that so vitally captures the substance and spirit of these issues.

In addition, our cooperating institutions (identified above) and their staffs in Uruguay, Thailand, Zimbabwe, Germany, and Hungary assisted both the logistical and intellectual progress of the project in a thousand important ways. We know as well that we speak for each of the contributors to this volume when we say that the more than 200 participants in the ACLS conferences, who traveled many miles to discuss the compelling issues associated with comparative constitutionalism, improved this book in ways simultaneously incalculable and indispensable.

Finally, no volume that depended so fundamentally on the editors' ability to be away from home for long periods could have been contemplated, no less completed, without the forbearance of our families. Adria, Linda-Marie, Margee, Molly, and Gracie made this entire project possible by tolerating our too frequent absences and listening patiently to our endless ruminations on a subject with which we remain deeply engaged. And with us on the road, "Mama," as she is known on four continents, lent a spirit and perspective that enlightened us all.

I

TRANSITIONS

1

Constitutions, Constitutionalism, and Democracy

*Walter F. Murphy**

Scholars no less than public officials and journalists are apt to conflate representative democracy, requiring government by popularly elected officials, with constitutionalism and its demands for limited government, then further confuse a constitution with constitutionalism. This chapter tries to untangle these concepts and analyze the product of their union, constitutional democracy.

Democracy and Constitutionalism

Democratic theory[1] is based on a notion of human dignity: as beings worthy of respect because of their very nature, adults must enjoy a large degree of autonomy, a status principally attainable in the modern world by being able to share in the governance of their community. Because direct rule is not feasible for the mass of citizens, most people can share in self-government only by delegating authority to freely chosen representatives. Thus Justice Hugo L. Black expressed a critical tenet of democratic theory when he wrote: "No right is more precious in a free country than that of having a voice in the election of those who make the laws under which we ... must live."[2]

Constitutionalism, too, enshrines respect for human worth and dignity as its central principle. To protect that value, citizens must have a right to political participation, and their government must be hedged in by substantive limits on what it can do, even when perfectly mirroring the popular will.

Democratic Theory

Although the social and economic conditions supporting a viable representative democracy are wonderfully complex, only a few formal, institutional conditions

*This paper is part of a larger study of constitutional democracy supported by the American Council of Learned Societies, the Ford Foundation, the William Nelson Cromwell Fund at Princeton University, and the Center of International Studies of Princeton University through the Boesky Family Fund.

need obtain: popular election of representatives, by universal adult suffrage in districts of approximately equal population for limited terms, to institutions that allow those representatives to govern; free entry of citizens to candidacy for electoral office; and freedom of political communication and association so citizens can be informed and can try to persuade others to join them. These conditions, of course, require a plethora of ancillary rights. Together they create a nearly open market of political ideas to allow the people to choose candidates intelligently and form groups to express common interests.

For democratic theory, what makes governmental decisions morally binding is process: the people's freely choosing representatives, those representatives' debating and enacting policy and later standing for reelection, and administrators' enforcing that policy. Democratic theory, therefore, tends to embrace both positivism and moral relativism. "The claim [for representative democracy] is most persuasively put," Michael Walzer says, "not in terms of what the people know, but in terms of who they are. They are the subjects of the law, and if the law is to bind them as free men and women, they must also be its makers."[3]

Although one can hear in democratic theory a reprise of Aristotle's claim that the people's collective wisdom will exceed that of any single person or small group, few democratic theorists assume citizens possess equal capacity to understand the options or, as a whole, will always understand the issues. Thus public policy, democratic theorists concede, will sometimes be unwise. A coherent theory of representative democracy must, however, posit that most sane adults can usually cope with political problems to the extent of being able to recognize their own self-interest, join with others who share those interests, and choose among candidates. There is a faith at work here: citizens "can, if encouraged and given the opportunity, develop the arts, the skills and habits necessary for a life of responsible deliberation and decision making."[4]

The chief check democratic theorists posit against tyranny is that the people will not tyrannize themselves. They will try to choose officials who will not enact oppressive laws and will vote out of office those who do. The "mass of citizens," Jefferson asserted, "is the safest depository of their own rights."[5] Thus democratic theory esteems popular participation not only for its positive effect of expressing individual autonomy but also for its negative effect of deterring governmental incursions into individual rights. It was because of this negative function that the U.S. Supreme Court referred to voting as "a fundamental political right, because preservative of all other rights."[6]

Because voters need to be informed to protect their interests, democrats speak glowingly about freedom of communication. As the German Constitutional Court said, quoting the U.S. Supreme Court:

> [T]he basic right of free expression is one of the principal human rights. . . . For a free, democratic order it is a constituent element, for it is free speech that permits continuous intellectual discussion, the battle of opinions that is its vital element. . . . In a certain sense, it is the basis of any freedom . . . "the matrix, the indispensable condition of nearly every other form of freedom."[7]

Yet, even in tandem, communication and voting are not sufficient for forming and expressing "the will of the people." Democratic theory also demands a right to act in concert with others. Although the U.S. constitutional text does not specifically protect a general right of association, the Supreme Court has held it "beyond debate that freedom to engage in association for the advancement of beliefs and ideas is an inseparable aspect of the 'liberty' assured by the Due Process Clause."[8] The Federal Republic's Basic Law explicitly states that "All Germans shall have the right to form associations and societies."[9] "The principle of free social grouping," the Constitutional Court has said, "distinguishes the liberal order from the system under which a people is organized from above."[10]

The constitutional texts of Canada, India, Ireland, Italy, and Japan contain similar provisions specifically protecting association along with speech and peaceful assembly. And these countries all have well developed bodies of case law interpreting these provisions to protect the specific rights involved.

Many theorists find an effective second check in the way democratic politics operates in large, diverse nations. They contend that most people have small concern for most political issues. This low level of involvement allows coalitions of minorities to form temporary alliances, trading support among themselves on different issues. These theorists claim that political cleavages are rarely cumulative, hence an interest group is not likely to be continually allied with one set of groups against another permanent coalition.[11]

Democratic theorists do not assert that these checks always protect liberty or even prevent public officials from acting independently to create public policy. Rather, they argue that, overall, such checks push public officials to mediate among interests, to broker, not adjudicate—or themselves contest in—winner-take-all struggles. In sum, officials will be wary of oppressing any group, for fear it will become part of tomorrow's winning coalition.[12] At a deeper level, democracy may cause a people to accept respect for competing interests as not only legally but, more importantly, as "itself a form of justice."[13] More specifically, professional politicians may develop a subculture that constrains them from trying to oppress minorities even when their constituents might have it otherwise.

Other proponents perceive a Rousseauian limitation: The popular will its representatives reflect must will generally.[14] A valid law cannot simply reflect prejudices against minorities by imposing burdens only or principally on them. Such a limiting principle flows from the premise that the people as a whole are sovereign and majority rule is no more than a decision-making arrangement. This principle raises interesting questions about how to determine when a law merely makes distinctions, as all complex statutes must, and when it invidiously discriminates; and who shall make such determinations, the people, their elected representatives, or nonelected officials.

Constitutionalism

Despite some basic agreements, the two theories differ significantly. Constitutionalists tend to be more pessimistic about human nature, fearing that people are sufficiently clever to oppress without hurting themselves. Constitutional theorists do not deny the importance of institutional and cultural checks but see those as insufficient. They are constantly concerned with the human penchant to act selfishly and abuse power. They want institutional restraints on substantive matters to prevent lapses into an authoritarian or even totalitarian system cloaked with populist trappings. As James Madison wrote to Thomas Jefferson:

> In our Governments the real power lies in the majority of the Community, and the invasion of private rights is chiefly to be apprehended, not from acts of Government contrary to the sense of its constituents, but from acts in which Government is the mere instrument of the major number of constituents.[15]

Whereas democratic theory turns to moral relativism, constitutionalism turns to moral realism.[16] It presumes that "out there" lurk discoverable standards to judge whether public policies infringe on human dignity. The legitimacy of a policy depends not simply on the authenticity of decision makers' credentials but also on substantive criteria. Even with the enthusiastic urging of a massive majority whose representatives have meticulously observed proper processes, government may not trample on fundamental rights. For constitutionalists, political morality cannot be weighed on a scale in which "opinion is an omnipotence," only against the moral criterion of sacred, individual rights. They agree with Jefferson: "An elective despotism was not the government we fought for. . . ."[17]

Constitutional Democracy

Although the strain between the two theories is always real and often serious, one must not exaggerate their differences. Both accept the centrality of human dignity; they differ on how best to protect that value. By limiting legitimate governmental action, constitutionalism tries to lower the stakes of politics, to restrict the risks to liberty and dignity of being a member of a political society. Democratic theory attempts to limit those risks by protecting the right to share in governmental processes.

To an extent, the two theories need each other. A majority may so restrict a minority's substantive rights and social status as to drain its formal participational rights of real effect, a danger to which constitutionalism is especially alert.[18] Constitutionalism's perils lie in its propensity to paralyze government and so create a kind of oppression: Governmental inaction, no less than action, generates costs and benefits.[19] Democracy, on the other hand, tends to respond to what elected officials perceive their constituents perceive to be societal problems.

To enjoy reasonably effective but still limited government, many countries have adopted a mix of constitutionalism and democratic theory. Most so-called democratic systems, such as those of Australia, Austria, Canada, Germany, India, Ireland, Italy, Japan, Spain, and the United States, would be more accurately classified as constitutional democracies. Each of these polities provides for a wide measure of popular political participation and simultaneously restricts the people's government by a variety of institutional means. Each tries to distinguish among powers to legislate, execute, and adjudicate, has some version of bicameralism, and includes a bill of rights. Australia, Canada, Germany,

India, and the United States use federalism to diffuse power further; and, to splinter this diffused power of majorities, the United States employs staggered elections for its legislature and indirectly elects its president. Each also authorizes politically independent judges to invalidate legislative and executive action they believe violates "the constitution."

If these institutional webs formed merely "parchment barriers," they would be important only to students of rhetoric. To think that words can constrain power seems foolish. Yet a political chemistry may turn sheets of paper into hoops of steel. First, by prescribing institutional structures and fracturing power among different offices a document can push officials, as Madison recognized,[20] to link their own interests with those of their office and jealously guard those interests against putative incursions by other officials. Further, by drawing vague divisions of authority, a document can make it likely that no set of officials can do much that is politically important without arousing the territorial imperative of other officials. Thus, a constitutional text can disperse power and protect liberty by pitting ambition against ambition and power against power.

Culture forms the second element in that political chemistry. A constitutional text that requires its officials to swear to support it can forge a moral bond. Much of the text may thus become part of the nation's customs. Children may learn about it in school as the "proper" way of politics, and later, as adults, internalize its provisions; mature citizens may come to look on it as prescribing rules for a just society; and officials may habitually put most of its command into practice. As Madison explained when he presented what became the Bill of Rights:

> It may be thought that all paper barriers against the power of the community are too weak to be worthy of attention. . . . [Y]et, as they have tendency to impress some degree of respect for them, to establish the public opinion in their favor, and rouse the attention of the whole community, it may be one means to control the majority from those acts to which they might otherwise be inclined.[21]

The Concept of a "Constitution"

Constitutionalism and democratic theory raise questions about the concept of a constitution and the relationship of any particular constitution to those theories as well as to constitutional democracy. One has to ask *what* the constitution is: What is its authority? Its functions? What does it include? How does it validly change over time?

What Is a Constitution?

What Is the Constitution's Authority?

To constitute means to make up, order, or form; thus a nation's constitution should pattern a political system. Some texts implicitly proclaim themselves to be supreme law, and many do so explicitly. Still, a document's bearing the label "a constitution" and declaring its own control over all other political acts proves nothing. We need to distinguish between the authority a text asserts and the authority it exerts.

Constitutional texts fall along a spectrum of authority. At one extreme are shams, such as those of Stalin and Mao. At the other extreme should be those whose provisions are fully operative; but no constitutional text operates with complete authority. Its description of processes may be misleading. For example, the British North America Act of 1867, which served for more than a century as Canada's principal constitutional document, asserted that the British Queen, not a Canadian Cabinet and Prime Minister responsible to a Canadian Parliament, in turn responsible to a Canadian electorate, governed. Seemingly conscientious officials may ignore or skew express commands and prohibitions: U.S. Presidents and legislators have never taken seriously their document's requirement that "a regular Statement and Account of the Receipts and Expenditures of all public Money shall be published from time to time."[22] So, too, for almost a hundred years, legislators, presidents, judges, and the mass of voters pretended that states were fulfilling their obligation under the Fourteenth Amendment to accord "equal protection of the laws" to blacks and women.

The prevalence—perhaps inevitability—of deviations from the text indicates the complex nature of a constitution's authority. Thus, when we speak of "authoritative constitutions," we are talking about those that are only "reasonably authoritative."

What Are the Functions of a Constitution?

A Constitution as Sham, Cosmetic, or Reality. The principal function of a sham constitutional text is to deceive. Lest U.S. citizens revel in righteousness, they might recall that Charles A. Beard[23] charged the framers of the U.S. text with hypocrisy, and the Conference of Critical Legal Studies[24] still so accuses the entire American legal system.[25] Whether Beard and the Critics have told the full story, they have reminded us that a constitutional document's representation of itself, its people, their values, and decisional processes is imperfect. Thus, even reasonably authoritative texts play a cosmetic role, allowing a nation to hide its failures behind idealistic rhetoric. But, insofar as a text is authoritative, its rhetoric also pushes a people to renew their better selves.

A Constitution as a Charter for Government. At minimum, an authoritative constitutional text must sketch the fundamental modes of legitimate governmental operations: who its officials are, how they are chosen, what their terms of office are, how authority is divided among them, what processes they must follow, and what rights, if any, are reserved to citizens. Such a text need not proclaim any substantive values, beyond obedience to itself; if it does proclaim values, they might be those of Naziism or Stalinism, anathema to constitutional democracy.

A Constitution as Guardian of Fundamental Rights. Thus the question immediately arises about the extent to which a constitutional text relies on or incorporates democratic and/or constitutionalist theories. Insofar as a text is authoritative and embodies democratic theory, it must protect rights to political participation. Insofar as it is authoritative and embodies constitutionalism, it must protect substantive rights by limiting the power of the people's freely chosen representatives.

The Constitution as Covenant, Symbol, and Aspiration. Insofar as a constitution is a covenant[26] by which a group of people agree to (re)transform themselves into a nation,[27] it may function for the founding generation like a marriage consummated through the pledging partners' positive, active consent to remain a nation for better or worse, through prosperity and poverty, in peace and war.

For later generations, a constitution may operate more as an arranged marriage in which consent is passive, for the degree of choice is then typically limited. Even where expatriation is a recognized right, exit from a society offers few citizens a viable alternative. Revolution becomes a legal right only if it succeeds and transforms revolutionaries into founders. And deeply reaching reform from within a constitutional framework tends to become progressively more difficult, for a system usually endures only by binding many groups to its terms.

The myth of a people's forming themselves into a nation presents a problem not unlike that between chicken and egg. To agree in their collective name to a political covenant, individuals must have already had some meaningful corporate identity *as a people*. Thus the notion of constitution as covenant must mean it formalizes or solidifies rather than invents an entity: it solemnizes a previous alliance into a more perfect union.

A constitution's formative force varies from country to country and time to time. The French, one can plausibly argue, have been the French under monarchies, military dictatorships, and assorted republics. It is also plausible, however, to contend that Germans have been a different people under the Kaiser, the Weimar Republic, the Third Reich, and the Federal Republic. In polyglotted societies such as Canada, India, and the United States or those riven by religious divisions and bleeding memories of civil war such as Ireland, "there may be no other basis for uniting a nation of so many disparate groups." A constitution may thus function as a uniting force, "the only principle of order," for there may be "no [other] shared moral or social vision that might bind together a nation."[28] It is difficult to imagine what has united the supposedly United States more than the political ideas of the Declaration of Independence and the text of 1787.

Reverence for the constitution may transform it into a holy symbol of the people themselves. The creature they created can become their own mythical creator. This symbolism might turn a constitutional text into a semisacred covenant, serving "the unifying function of a civil religion."[29] In America, "The Bible of verbal inspiration begat the constitution of unquestioned authority."[30]

Religious allusions remind us, however, that this symbolic role may also have a dark side. Long histories of bitter and often murderous struggles among Christians and among Muslims demonstrate that a sacred text may foster division rather than cohesion, conflict rather than harmony. The "potential of a written constitution to serve as the source of fragmentation and disintegration"[31] is nowhere more savagely illustrated than in the carnage of the U.S. Civil War. For, ultimately, that fratricidal struggle was over two visions of one constitutional document. The result was a gory war that wiped out more than 600,000 lives. Complicating analysis is the fact that when the blood of battle dried, the document of 1787, duly amended, resumed its unifying role.

In a related fashion, a constitution may serve as a binding statement of a people's aspirations for themselves as a nation.[32] A text may silhouette the sort of community its authors/subjects are or would like to become: not only their governmental structures, procedures, and basic rights, but also their goals, ideals, and the moral standards by which they want others, including their own posterity, to judge the community. In short, a constitutional text may guide as well as express a people's hopes for themselves as a society. The ideals the words enshrine, the processes they describe, and the actions they legitimize must either help to change the citizenry or at least reflect their current values. If a constitutional text is not "congruent with"[33] ideals that form or will reform its people and so express the political character they have or are willing to try to put on, it will quickly fade.

What Does "the Constitution" Include?

Almost every nation now has a document labeled a constitution; but to have a constitution a nation need not have a text or texts so titled. Britain, Israel, and New Zealand provide plausible examples. Nor does the existence of a constitutional document mean that any particular nation's constitution is coextensive with that text. What a constitution includes is a problem, not a datum. But where and how do we find the constitution beyond the text? Do subtexts control or mediate the text? How do we identify them? What about interpretations and practices? And what about political theories that inform and underpin the text?

The Text. The most obvious candidate is the whole text and nothing but the text. The late Justice Hugo Black[34] and former Attorney General Edwin Meese III[35] were among the more notable Americans to take that position. Such people stress the "writtenness" of the U.S. Constitution, though writtenness, literary, and biblical scholars would warn, sires as well as solves problems. Moreover, Black and Meese qualified their textualism with a commitment to "original intent" or "understanding"—additions to the text.

Less Than the Text. Anything less than the full text might seem a strange candidate, but every constitutional document drawn up in a free society is likely to reflect a bundle of compromises, necessary to obtain approval from the drafters and ratifiers but perhaps not always mutually compatible. As one solution, the German Constitutional Court has proposed reconciliation through structural interpretation:

> An individual constitutional provision cannot be considered as an isolated clause and interpreted alone. A constitution has an inner unity, and the meaning of any one part is linked to that of other provisions. Taken as a unit, a constitution reflects certain overarching principles and fundamental decisions to which individual provisions are subordinate.[36]

The final sentence also looks to invalidation, and the Court made it clear that option was also open:

> That a constitutional provision itself may be null and void is not conceptually impossible just because it is part of the constitution. There are constitutional principles that are so fundamental and to such an extent an expression of a law that precedes even the constitution that they also bind the framer of the constitution, and other constitutional provisions that do not rank so high may be null and void, because they contravene those principles.[37]

On another occasion, the Constitutional Court divided 4–4 on the validity of an amendment;[38] the Supreme Court in India has several times voided constitutional amendments;[39] and the California Supreme Court has once done so.[40] Moreover, many U.S. presidents, legislators, judges, and commentators have tried to exclude portions of their constitutional text from the canon. The Slaughter-House Cases in 1873,[41] for instance, all but expunged the Fourteenth Amendment's clause forbidding states to abridge "the privileges or immunities" of citizens of the United States. And despite frequent avowals of textualism, Justice Black could not accept the Ninth Amendment's declaration: "The enumeration in the Constitution of certain rights, shall not be construed to deny or disparage others retained by the people." Furthermore, many commentators who assert that the text's principal function is to serve as a charter for government dismiss as empty rhetoric the Preamble's statement of purposes, especially its dedication to the establishment of "Justice."

Intent of the Framers. One might claim that a text can be understood only in light of certain "understandings" and "intentions" founders took for granted.[42] To the extent that such unspoken thoughts control the text, they become a supertext. A quest for original understanding or intent raises enormous methodological, theoretical, and practical problems. After a few years have gone by, interpreters can pursue originalism only through documents, which are fraught with all the hermeneutic problems of the text itself.

Other Documents. Still other texts might have strong claims to canonicity. The Canadian Constitution Act, 1982, for example, explicitly bestows constitutional status on a number of documents. Probably most other nations have candidates with respectable pedigrees. In the United States, the two most robust would be the second paragraph of the Declaration of Independence and *The Federalist*. The Declaration justified the creation of a new nation and set out its founding principles:

> We hold these truths to be self-evident, that all men are created equal; that they are endowed by their Creator with certain unalienable rights, that among these are Life, Liberty and the Pursuit of Happiness. That to secure these rights, Governments are instituted among men, deriving their just powers from the consent of the governed. That whenever any form of Government becomes destructive of these ends, it is the Rights of the People to alter or abolish it. . . .

As the definitive statement of the new nation's basic values, so the argument goes,[43] the Declaration stands until explicitly repudiated, something neither the Philadelphia Convention nor the state ratifying conventions even suggested.

The case for *The Federalist*, essays by John Jay, James Madison, and Alexander Hamilton urging ratification of the newly drafted constitutional text, would be that those who ratified that document accepted these views as authoritative and, therefore, they form part of the original understanding.[44]

Practices and Interpretations. Some practices might become so settled as to fuse into the constitution. One would expect common-law systems, with their sensitivity to prescription, the doctrine that long and unchallenged usage confers legal title, would be hospitable to such a concept. Canadian judges, however, have been ambivalent;[45] and judges in the United States, though open to such ideas, have also recognized severe problems.[46]

Most fundamentally, governmental practice often violates the basic text or its underlying principles. Does a long violation effect a constitutional change? If "the constitution" is devoid of normative content beyond obedience to specified procedures, the answer might well be yes. If, however, "the constitution" entails normative political theory, the issue becomes far more complex. Sotirios A. Barber[47] proposes a distinction between practice, a country's history, and tradition, what the constitution's underlying theory says its people stand for. The minimum standard he would use to test a practice's legitimacy is congruence with both the document and tradition.

Interpretations trigger similar disputes. Although not every interpretation has a serious claim to be part of the canon, some interpretations meld into the larger constitution. The U.S. Supreme Court's divination of judicial review provides the most striking example.[48] As one of Court's opponents asked at the time, "Is it not extraordinary that if the high power was intended, it should nowhere appear [in the text]?"[49]

Political Theories. The case for inclusion of any theory in a particular constitution is empirical, and the mix between political theories may be complex. In the 1990s, democratic and constitutionalist theory are the prime candidates; but, in the recent past, versions of Fascism and Marxism have been successful contenders, and perhaps will be again in the future.

How Does a Constitution Validly Change over Time?

The spoken word evanesces as soon as it is uttered; the written word seems permanent. Centuries later, audiences can parse its sentences and explore its implications—thus the immense attractions of a "written constitution." Alas, even when embossed on parchment, words can suggest a variety of meanings; and readers necessarily impose their own frameworks of understanding on a text. "When the Almighty himself condescends to address mankind in their own language," Madison noted, "his meaning, luminous as it must be, is rendered dim and doubtful by the cloudy medium through which it is communicated."[50]

Moreover, language evolves. New meanings sometimes replace old; sometimes the two (or three or four) live side by side. Rules of grammar, punctuation, and syntax may also mutate. And these changes may occur at different times or proceed at different paces across a polity.

Most important, the world and people's perceptions of the world change. Framers of the German or Japanese constitutional text could not have foreseen the economic miracles that would quickly restore those devastated nations.

Thus, Japan's commitment never to maintain "land, sea, and air forces, as well as other war potential"[51] has pulsed in response to domestic demands, international crises, and pressure from the United States. Even more dramatically, the pledge of reunification in West Germany's Basic Law had by 1976 turned to de facto acceptance of two Germanys; then, in 1989–1990, reunification suddenly changed from distant dream to joyous reality.

The constitutional text of every major nation explicitly provides for its own amendment. But even a superficial glance reveals other means to change a constitution, usage and interpretation being among the most common. Furthermore, it is often difficult to tell, except in a mechanical sense, when political actors move from one of these processes to another. Officials who begin a usage may have justified their action by interpreting the text, just as those who follow an older interpretation may unthinkingly accept it as a usage. And there can be little doubt that some legislative, executive, and judicial interpretations have affected the constitutional order far more radically than many formal amendments.

It is no wonder, then, that democratic theorists express concern about "constitutional interpretation," for it is potentially both creative and enormous in effect. I am tempted to add "especially when dealing with the broad terms of most constitutional texts"; but India's experience with a finely detailed document suggests it is the capacious nature of constitutional problems rather than the generality of language that implodes creativity into interpretive processes.

Accepting constitutional change as inevitable still leaves open questions of whether some paths can lead to legitimate change and whether there are limits to valid mutation. One might argue for a hierarchy of efforts at legitimate constitutional modification, from usage to interpretation to formal amendment: the more fundamental the change, the more weighty the reasons for resorting to formal processes and the more weighty the reasons for directly involving the people themselves, as do Australia, Ireland, and sometimes Italy.[53]

The second question poses greater intellectual difficulty: Are there substantive limits to valid constitutional change? Under two circumstances, the case for such limits is very forceful. First, if the text is authoritative and specifies limits, they should be observed or changed only in accordance with the document's terms. And some texts do contain "unamendable" provisions. For example, Article V of the U.S. document forbids denying any state, without its consent, equal representation in the Senate. Article 79(3) of West Germany's Basic Law forbids amendments that would destroy the federal, democratic, or social nature of the nation, release legislation from the constitution's restraints or the executive or judiciary from those of "law and justice," lessen human dignity, or remove the right of the people to resist subversion of their constitutional order.

The second circumstance under which the case for restrictions on constitutional change is strong occurs when a constitutional text represents an agreement among a people, functions as a limitation on as well as a charter for government, states a people's goals and aspirations, and embodies normative political theory(ies). Then the very nature of the document itself may outlaw some kinds of amendment—for instance, those curtailing rights to political participation. As we have seen, some German, Indian, and even U.S. judges have directly addressed this issue: Certain principles bind those who would amend as well as those who would create constitutions in a democratic–constitutionalist mold. Provisions that violate those principles, even if lodged in the basic text itself, are void.

As applied to constitutional amendments, the gist of the argument[54] is that "to amend" comes from the Latin "emendere," to correct. Thus an "amendment" corrects or modifies the system without fundamentally changing its nature: An "amendment" operates within the theoretical parameters of the existing consitution. A proposal to transform a central aspect of the compact to create another kind of system—for example, to change a constitutional democracy into an authoritarian state, as the Indian Court said Mrs. Gandhi tried to do[55]—would not be an amendment at all, but a re-creation of both the covenant and its people. That deed would lie outside the authority of any set of governmental bodies, for all are creatures of the people's agreement. Insofar as officials destroy that compact, they destroy their own legitimacy.

This argument does not deny the legitimacy of radical constitutional reformation, but it does deny that such changes could find justification in the old text or in the compact that text reflects. Using extraconstitutional means, the people might reconstitute themselves; but it would be the people's exercising their constituent power, not the old constitution's benediction, that validates the new order.[56]

Who Is/Are the Constitution's Authoritative Interpreter(s)?

The answer to *who* has interpretive authority is seldom easy. Let us take the simplest case: a constitution that is a grant from some higher authority functions merely as a charter for government, does not incorporate normative political theory, and includes only the text itself. The document's designation of interpretive agency(ies) and the processes it outlines settles the issue. If the text does not directly or clearly address the issue, one can request the grantor to decide the matter.

A more complex case occurs where the constitution claims to be a compact among a people. Then the polity must seek a solution through interpretation, raising serpentine problems of *how* to interpret. And that reliance poses yet other difficulties: If interpretation controls the text, will that interpretation become part of the constitution?

The most complex situation occurs where a constitution is an agreement among a people, functions as a charter for and a limitation on government, expresses its people's aspirations, includes certain usages and traditions, incorporates both democratic and constitutionalist theory, and does not directly or clearly address the issue of *who.* Resort to previous interpretations, traditions, or usages might well beg questions of *whose* interpretations, *whose* usages, and *whose* assessment of traditions.

Several solutions present themselves. The first is interpretation by the people themselves: As creators of the compact, they have authority to define its parameters. Elections may allow them to do so indirectly. Jefferson advocated a more direct role: "the people of the Union, assembled by their deputies in convention, at the call of Congress, or of two-thirds of the states."[57] But "recurrence to the people" raises serious theoretical and practical difficulties, and Jefferson would have deployed a national convention only when government was deadlocked over competing interpretations. For day-to-day management, he preferred "departmentalism," under which coordinate institutions share interpretive responsibility.[58]

Democratic theorists would lodge such authority with elected officials, while constitutionalists would place it in the hands of officials more insulated from public opinion. Many texts seem to point to a constitutionalist victory. Early on, judges in the United States interpreted their document—and made that interpretation stick—as allowing them to invalidate legislative or executive action they believed contrary to its provisions. Constitution makers around the world have adopted similar institutional arrangements. Canada, India, Ireland, and Japan have vested regular courts with interpretive power, while Civil-Law nations have tended to follow the model Hans Kelsen designed for Austria after World War I: a special tribunal exercising exclusive jurisdiction within the judiciary over constitutional interpretation.[59]

Germany represents constitutionalism's greatest triumph in this respect. The Basic Law specifically establishes judicial review, vests it exclusively in the constitutional Court,[60] and protects the Court's jurisdiction against diminution even in emergencies.[61] Furthermore, in enacting the Court's primary jurisdictional statute, the Federal Constitutional Court Act of 1951, Parliament ceded the justices interpretive hegemony:

> The decisions of the Federal Constitutional Court shall be binding upon the constitutional bodies of the Federation and of the *Länder* as well as upon all law courts and public authorities.

And, in its first decision, the Court indicated it would broadly construe this broad acknowledgment of authority:

> [This] decision together with the main reasons for the decisions binds all constitutional organs of the Federation . . . in such a way that no federal law with the same content can again be deliberated and enacted by the legislative bodies and promulgated by the federal president.[62]

Britain represents almost total victory for democratic theory. Parliament is supposedly the authoritative creator, emendator, and interpreter of the constitution, restrained only by the ballot box and its collective conscience. Other officers, at least where the European Economic community or the European Convention on Human Rights are not involved, have only what interpretive power Parliament chooses to delegate.

Most constitutional democracies, however, distribute interpretive power somewhat differently. Forms of departmentalism abound. And one could make a strong case that in reality, judges are neither omnipotent in Germany[63] nor impotent in Britain. Interpreting a constitution is something executives and legislators must often do. In deciding how to draft or vote on a bill or to make an inquiry—or protest—on behalf of a constituent, legislators commonly engage in informal constitutional interpretation. Even police, in deciding if they can arrest a suspect, what they can ask, and how long the suspect can be held, are engaging in this enterprise. That some officials do so mindlessly does not alter the fact that they are doing it.

Moreover, interpretation and usage may provide for a sharing of interpretive power. Even in the United States, the Supreme Court has been reluctant to claim the role of "ultimate constitutional interpreter" as far as other branches of the federal government are concerned. It has also created the "doctrine of political questions" to mark certain areas of interpretation (such as the federal government's obligation to guarantee each state "a republican form of government") that fall outside its competence, a doctrine that has cast shadows across German and Japanese jurisprudence.[64] And judges of constitutional courts often repeat that they will usually presume legislation valid.

In addition, presidents and congresses have frequently and effectively asserted equal interpretive authority. The power to veto legislation gives the president a pulpit from which to expound his own constitutional doctrines. As President Andrew Jackson said in 1832:

> Each public officer who takes an oath to support the Constitution swears that he will support it as he understands it, and not as it is understood by others.... The opinion of the judges has no more authority over Congress than the opinion of Congress has over the judges, and on that point the President is independent of both.[65]

Congress and the president also have an arsenal of weapons to persuade the justices to change their minds. The president may refuse to enforce judicial decrees and/or Congress may decline to appropriate money for such a purpose. Congress may also repass a controversial statute to appear to meet some of the justices' constitutional objections, alter the Supreme Court's appellate jurisdiction, or increase the number of justices and so permit appointment of people with differing views. Even without such tampering, a vacancy occurs on the Supreme Court about once every two to two and a half years, allowing presidents opportunities to shape that tribunal's constitutional interpretation.

Nor are officials in other countries helpless when confronting judges. For instance, until Canada's adoption of a new constitutional text in 1982, judicial review rested only on a statute. Even now all federal courts are creatures of statutes; and what Parliament may create, Parliament may destroy. Further, while judges seldom die, they must retire at 75, thus creating vacancies ruling parties can fill with "right thinking" jurists.

Some nations have made the sharing of interpretive authority explicit. Article 34 of the Irish text vests the Supreme Court with judicial review, but Article 28, 3° excludes from this authority questions of the validity of any law "which is expressed to be for the purpose of securing the public safety and the preservation of the State in time of war or armed rebellion" as well as all acts done "in pursuance of such law."[66] Furthermore, Article 45 announces principles of social policy to guide parliament but adds that these "shall not be cognizable by any Court under any of the provisions of this Constitution."

One of the compromises necessary to secure passage of Canada's Constitution Act, 1982, makes an elegant compromise between democratic and constitutionalist theory. This text entrenched a bill of rights and explicitly lodged enforcement, under ordinary circumstances, with the judiciary. But Article 33 allows the federal or a provincial parliament, for whatever reasons, to announce that a statute "shall operate notwithstanding a provision" protecting certain fundamental freedoms and more specific rights.[67]

How Should the Constitution Be Interpreted?

This question is muddled, partly because of the inherent complexity of the interpretive enterprise itself and partly because we often conflate questions of *what, who*, and *how*—an invitation to practical as well as conceptual befuddlement.

The Who *and the* How

Who interprets affects the *how* both procedurally and substantively. If the people directly construe the constitution through referenda, less directly via special conventions, or indirectly by choosing officials who campaign on constitutional issues, interpretive processes are likely to differ vastly from those of officials insulated from the public. The literature on campaigns and elections is enormous, but it does not describe a highly informed, intensely interested electorate carefully weighing alternative solutions to complicated problems. Those studies indicate that when the people become more directly involved in constitutional interpretation, opposing sides will present alternatives in simplistic, emotional terms of "good guys versus bad buys" rather than attempt to fathom a polity's fundamental values.

Myth has it that legislators and executives are too addicted to placating constituents to interpret the constitution intelligently and consistently. There is, however, no good reason why these officials cannot carefully sift evidence and weigh arguments.[68] At minimum, they can institutionalize procedures that allow thoughtful consideration of constitutional issues. For legislators, the Italian parliament and the U.S. Congress offer models for responsible interpretation.

Each house of the Italian Parliament has a standing committee, largely composed of law professors, to report on the validity of proposed legislation. Both committees carefully scrutinize important bills and, by exercising what is almost a veto, have mooted many constitutional issues. Each house of the U.S. Congress has a standing committee on the judiciary, with its own professional staff. When an important constitutional issue arises, the committee holds hearings and invites experts, interest groups, and public officials to explain their opinions on the problem. The committee than writes a report, usually published along with a transcript of its proceedings. Together, these documents offer reasoned arguments justifying an interpretation. Sometimes they rely on, at other times distinguish, deviate from, or even attack relevant judicial opinions.

U.S. presidents often ask the Attorney General to prepare opinions on constitutional problems. Those reports are generally less comprehensively researched and less elaborately argued than judicial opinions, but usually they clearly set out the issues and justify a course of action. And, no more than legislators do attorneys general feel compelled to follow judges' leads.

Without doubt, partisanship colors these processes. But most judges are also affected by biases,[69] not toward political parties so much as toward important and controversial substantive goals. Judges, as Chief Justice Earl Warren would say, are neither monks nor intellectual eunuchs; they are apt to have deeply felt views on constitutional issues.

Where legislators, executive officials, or judges undertake interpretive tasks, the most important differences *who* makes for *how* is likely to involve substance. Obviously officials who face reelection are apt to be much more sensitive to public opinion than judges whose terms of office are fixed. But if the great temptation for elected interpreters is to equate the constitution with what they believe their constituents want the constitution to mean, the great temptation for those not responsible to an electorate is to equate the constitution with what they themselves want it to mean. These considerations lead back to the competing demands of constitutionalism and democracy, and perhaps also to the worth of preserving the two together.

The What *and the* How

Again, we begin with the simplest case: a constitution that is a grant from some higher authority functions merely as a charter for government, specifies processes without incorporating normative political theory, and includes only the document itself. There the text's designation of interpretive processes settles the matter. If the document does not clearly address the issue, grantees can request the grantor to decide.

A more complex case occurs where the constitution is a compact among a people and provides incomplete or unclear guidance about how it is to be interpreted. Then the polity must seek a solution through interpretation by one or more of its own agencies or by the people themselves and so confront that galaxy of problems associated with gleaning meaning from any text. Immediately, for instance, the old hermeneutic dilemma appears: One cannot understand any part of a document without grasping it as a whole; but one cannot comprehend it as a whole without understanding its parts.[70]

The matter of mutating language recurs. Even if it is obvious which era's language interpreters should use, it may not be apparent whose language of the time is authoritative—the technical argot of the professionals who drafted the document or the less rarified tongue of the people in whose name the text speaks. After resolving such difficulties, interpreters still must brave the problems all language presents. Then, as noted, an interpretation may become a part of "the constitution" and become the subject of further interpretation. And, because interpretation is often, perhaps inevitably, creative, problems of legitimate change resurface.

Subsidiary questions also arise: Can current interpreters "correct" earlier interpreters? To what extent should interpreters look on the text as something whose general principles rather than specific language they should adapt to new problems? To what extent should they merely apply the document's exact words—if they can determine the exact meaning of those exact words—to new situations and leave all change to formal amending processes? Should their approach be "historical" in the sense of seeking the text's meaning at a given moment or "historical" in the sense of trying to discover how those terms have developed?

This litany by no means exhausts interpretive puzzles even in simple situations. More complex problems arise where a constitution is an agreement among a people, functions as a charter for government, and also includes, or rests on, democratic theory. Initially, it might appear that the only dimension added to the previous situation would be ensuring that avenues of free political participation were truly open. If so, the actions of the people's freely chosen representatives, who followed the text's processes, would be presumptively valid.

But any operational democratic theory demands that at least two substantive elements obtain if elections are in fact free. The first involves roughly equal access to politically relevant information, expression, and association. Although a polity need not provide means for people to enjoy equal means to participate, it still cannot deny any citizen the right to equal participation nor countenance private groups' denying that right. Thus tricky issues of education, campaigns, money, and apportionment arise.

The second element involves a right to privacy. A constitution that respects the integrity of democratic theory must also respect such a right, for it is necessary to allow dissenters to formulate alternative public agenda, to organize support for their proposals, and to vote for candidates of their choice, free from retaliation. Without insulation against both government and society, dissenters would often be unable to cooperate with others to challenge views dominant in the polity.[71] Even voting, though a public act, must be done in private to be a free act.[72]

We need not troop the line of possibilities to see how infusion of constitutionalism complicates interpretation. At that point, constitutional interpretation becomes an art no less demanding than governing itself, requiring, as Judge Benjamin Cardozo said, an acute understanding of law, history, philosophy, and sociology.[73] Techniques help but can be no more useful than the interpreters' wisdom allows. It is small wonder that judges and other officials often avoid close scrutiny of what it is they are doing.

The Once and Future Polity

If a constitution aims to repress rather than liberate, to govern peacefully and effectively it still must in many respects reflect its people's traditions and history. And culling a nation's past to separate its essence from its affectations requires superb intuition as well as carefully honed statecraft. When the constitution's purpose is to keep its people free rather than to oppress them, both qualities must be present in even larger quantities; and the difficulties of the various roles that citizens and officials must play grow enormously.

Neither alone nor together does democratic or constitutionalist theory promise utopia. Both, as products of Judeo-Christian cultures, rest, however unselfconsciously, on the Torah's ancient myth: Even in Eden, when only one man and one woman were alive, human beings managed to make a mess of things. And from that primordial "fact" these theories prescribe opportunities for and limitations on self-government. They accept the inevitability of some degree of failure and the risk of total failure. Democracy is more willing to chance injuries that can flow from majoritarian domination; constitutionalism is more willing to risk harms that can flow from restricting governmental power. Both theories, however, try to mitigate those risks, to keep human inadequacy from generating tyranny, anarchy, or civil war.

The goal of constitutional democracy is not to create happiness, only opportunities for the pursuit of happiness. Thus, those who follow the path of constitutional democracy must, as Genesis put it, earn their liberty by the sweat of their brows—and by the quality of their politics.

Notes

1. Many versions of democratic and constitutionalist theories exist. The most sophisticated discussion of democratic theory is Robert A. Dahl, *Democracy and Its Critics* (New Haven: Yale University Press, 1989). See also George Kateb, "The Moral Distinctiveness of Representative Democracy," 91 *Ethics* 357 (1981); C.B. MacPherson, *Democratic Theory* (London: Oxford University Press, 1973); J. Roland Pennock, *Democratic Political Theory* (Princeton: Princeton University Press, 1979); Giovanni Sartori, *Democratic Theory* (New York: Praeger, 1965); Sartori, *The Theory of Democracy Revisited* (Chatham, NJ: Chatham House, 1987), 2 vols.; Gerhard Casper, "Constitutionalism," in Leonard W. Levy et al., eds., *The Encyclopedia of the American Constitution* (New York: Macmillan, 1987), II; Carl J. Friedrich, *Constitutional Government and Democracy* (4th ed.; Waltham, MA: Blaisdell, 1968); Carl J. Friedrich, *Constitutional Reason of State* (Providence: Brown University Press, 1957); Friedrich, *Transcendent Justice* (Durham: Duke University Press, 1964); Walton H. Hamilton, "Constitutionalism," in Edwin A. Seligman et al., eds., *Encyclopedia of the Social Sciences* (New York: Macmillan, 1930), IV; Charles H. McIlwain, *Constitutionalism* (Ithaca: Cornell University Press, 1947); J. Roland Pennock and John W. Chapman, eds., *Constitutionalism* (New York: New York University Press, 1979); Pennock and Chapman, eds., *Liberal Democracy* (New York: New York University Press, 1983); Glenn A. Schram, "A Critique of Contemporary Constitutionalism," 11 *Comp. Pols.* 483 (1979); Harvey Wheeler, "Constitutionalism," in Fred I. Greenstein and Nelson W. Polsby, eds., *Handbook of Political Science* (Reading, MA: Addison-Wesley, 1975), V; and Alan S. Rosenblum, ed., *Constitutionalism* (Westport, CT: Greenwood Press, 1988).

2. Wesberry v. Sanders, 376 U.S. 1, 17 (1964).

3. Michael Walzer, "Philosophy and Democracy," 9 *Political Theory* 379, 383 (1981).

4. Joseph Tussman, *Government and the Mind* (New York: Oxford University Press, 1977), p. 143.

5. Letter to John Taylor, May 28, 1816; Paul L. Ford, ed., *The Works of Thomas Jefferson* (New York: Putnam's Sons, 1905), XI, 527.

6. Yick Wo v. Hopkins, 118 U.S. 356, 370 (1886).

7. Movie Boycott Case, 7 BVerfGE 198 (1959), reprinted in W. Murphy and Joseph Tanenhaus, eds., *Comparative Constitutional Law* (New York: St. Martin's, 1977), pp. 528–532. See also the Schmid-Spiegel Case, 12 BVerfGE 113 (1961), reprinted in Donald P. Kommers, *Constitutional Jurisprudence of the Federal Republic of Germany* (Durham: Duke University Press, 1989), p. 378.

8. NAACP v. Alabama, 357 U.S. 449, 460 (1958).

9. Art. 9, parag. 1; parag. 2, however, adds: "Associations, the purposes or activities of which conflict with the criminal laws or which are directed against the constitutional order or the concept of international understanding, are prohibited." The Basic Law also contains the notion of "unconstitutional political parties." See Art. 21, parag. 2, and the Constitutional Court's holdings that a Neo-Nazi group, the Socialist Reich Party, and the Communist Party were unconstitutional; reprinted in W. Murphy and Joseph Tanenhaus, note 7, pp. 602 and 621.

10. Workers' Chambers Case, 38 BVerfGE 281 (1974).

11. Robert A. Dahl has done much theoretical and empirical work here: *Democracy and Its Critics*, note 1; *A Preface to Democratic Theory* (Chicago: University of Chicago Press, 1956); "Decision-Making in a Democracy," 6 *Journal of Public Law 279* (1957) (now *Emory Law Journal*); *Polyarchy* (New Haven: Yale University Press, 1971). See also David Truman's classic, *The Governmental Process* (New York: Knopf, 1955). J. David Greenstone has analyzed much of the relevant literature in Fred I. Greenstein and Nelson w. Polsby, note 1, II.

12. What has been called a "federalist theory of tolerance" for minorities may reinforce this wariness: A majority may agree that certain groups merit discrimination, but disagree about which groups are so deserving. When hostility "is dispersed, ordinary politics will moderate mass sentiments of intolerance, given the practical necessity to forge a majority on other issues." John L. Sullivan et al., *Political Tolerance and American Democracy* (Chicago: University of Chicago Press, 1982), p. 22. See also John L. Sullivan, *Political Tolerance in Context: Support for Unpopular Minorities in Israel, New Zealand, and the United States* (Boulder: Westview Press, 1985).

13. See Robert A. Dahl, *Democracy and Its Critics*, note 1, p. 164.

14. See especially Michael Walzer, note 3; and John Hart Ely, *Democracy and Distrust* (Cambridge: Harvard University Press, 1980).

15. Oct. 17, 1788; reprinted in Marvin Meyers, ed., *The Mind of the Framer* (Indianapolis: Bobbs-Merrill, 1973), p. 206

16. See Michael S. Moore, "A Natural Theory of Interpretation," 58 *Southern California Law Review* 277 (1985); and Sotirios A. Barber, "The New Right Assault on Moral Inquiry in Constitutional Law," 54 *George Washington Law Review* 253 (1986).

17. "Notes on Virginia" (1784); Andrew A. Lipscomb, ed., *The Writings of Thomas Jefferson* (Washington, D.C.: The Thomas Jefferson Memorial Association, 1903), II, 163.

18. See Stephen Holmes, "Gag Rules or the Politics of Omission," and "Precommitment and the Paradox of Democracy," in Jon Elster and Rune Slagstad, eds., *Constitutionalism and Democracy* (New York: Cambridge University Press, 1988).

19. See Cass Sunstein, "Constitutions and Democracies: An Epilogue," in Elster and Slagstad, note 18.

20. See, especially, *Federalist* No. 51.

21. Speech of June 8, 1789, 1 *Annals of Congress* 440ff; reprinted in Marvin Meyers, note 15.

22. Art. I. 9, 7. The Supreme Court has held that provision outside the reach of judicial enforcement. United States v. Richardson, 418 U.S. 166 (1974).

23. Charles A. Beard, *An Economic Interpretation of the Constitution of the United States* (New York: Macmillan, 1913).

24. See the bibliography compiled by Duncan Kennedy and Karl Klare, 94 *Yale Law Journal* 461 (1984); the Symposium, "Critical Legal Studies Movement," 36 *Stanford Law Review* 1 (1984); David Kairys, ed., *The Politics of Law* (New York: Pantheon, 1982); Roberto M. Unger, *The Critical Legal Studies Movement* (Cambridge: Harvard University Press, 1987); and Mark Kelman, *A Guide to Critical Legal Studies* (Cambridge: Harvard University Press, 1987).

25. The movement is not solely an American phenomenon. For essays by British "crits," see Peter Fitzpatrick and Alan Hund, eds., *Critical Legal Studies* (London: Blackwell, 1987); and an English scholar has written a trenchant critique: John M. Finnis, "On 'The Critical Legal Studies Movement,'" 30 *American Journal of Jurisprudence* 21 (1965).

26. Daniel J. Elazar and his associates have produced a wealth of analyses on "constitutional covenanting." See, e.g., the Symposium, "Covenant, Polity and Constitutionalism," 10 *Publius* 1 (Fall, 1980).

27. And, of course, a text may not be the result of a covenant, but imposed from above, as was initially the case with the current Japanese document, known for several decades as "the MacArthur Constitution."

28. Sanford Levinson, *Constitutional Faith* (Princeton: Princeton University Press, 1988), p. 73.

29. Thomas Grey, "The Constitution as Scripture," 37 *Stanford Law Review* 1, 18 (1984).

30. W.H. Hamilton, "Constitutionalism," note 1, IV, 256.

31. Sanford Levinson, note 28, at p. 17.

32. For justifications of this view in the American context, see Sotirios A. Barber, *On What the Constitution Means* (Baltimore: Johns Hopkins University Press, 1984); and Gary J. Jacobsohn, *The Supreme Court and the Decline of Constitutional Aspiration* (Totowa, NJ.: Rowman and Littlefield, 1986); for a bitter but confused attack, see Lino A. Graglia, "Constitutional Mysticism," 98 *Harvard Law Review* 1131 (1985).

33. Harry H. Eckstein, "A Theory of Stable Democracy," Appendix B, *Division and Cohesion in Democracy* (Princeton: Princeton University Press, 1966); and Harry H. Eckstein and Ted Robert Gurr, *Patterns of Authority* (New York: Wiley, 1975).

34. See especially Hugo Black, *A Constitutional Faith* (New York: Knopf, 1969), and his dissent in Griswold v. Connecticut, 381 U.S. 479 (1965).

35. Edwin Meese III, "Toward a Jurisprudence of Original Intention," 45 *Public Administration Review* 701 (1985).

36. The Southwest Case, 1 BVerfGE 14 (1951); Murphy and Tanenhaus, note 7, pp. 208ff.

37. *Ibid.* The Court was quoting with approval the Bavarian constitutional court.

38. Privacy of Communications Case, 30 BVerfGE 1 (1970); reprinted in Murphy and Tanenhaus, note 7, pp. 659ff.

39. Golak Nath v. Punjab, (1967) A.I.R. 1643, was the first instance. It provoked a stream of criticism—some academic—e.g., H.C.L. Merillat, *Land and the Constitution in India* (New York: Columbia University Press, 1970), but more importantly, much political. Because this, other rulings, and parliamentary opponents stymied Mrs. Gandhi's reforms, she declared a state of emergency, imprisoned opponents, and pushed through a set of constitutional amendments that reversed *Golak Naths*'s doctrine. Eventually, the Indian electorate repudiated Mrs. Gandhi's leadership; and, although rejecting *Golak Nath*, the Supreme Court found new and stronger argument for its authority and invalidated

some of Mrs. Gandhi's amendments. Kesavananda Bharati's Case, S.C.R. 1 (Supp.) (Ind.), especially the opinion of Justice H.R. Khanna; and Minerva Mills v. Union of India, [1980] S.C.R. 1789. See Upendra Baxi, *Courage, Craft and Contention* (Bombay: Tripathi, 1985); and Lloyd and Suzanne Hoeber Rudolph, *In Pursuit of Lakshimi* (Chicago: University of Chicago Press, 1987), Ch. 3.

40. Raven et al. v. Deukemejian et al., 801 P. 2d 1977 (1990), struck down part of Proposition 115, an amendment approved by voters at a referendum, because the proposal touched such fundamental issues as to constitute a constitutional "revision" rather than amendment; and the state's constitutional text required a convention for a revision.

41. 16 Wall. 36. For discussion, see Walter F. Murphy, "Slaughter-House, Civil Rights, and Limits on Constitutional Change," 32 *American Journal of Jurisprudence* 1 (1987).

42. Besides Hugo Black and Edwin Meese III, cited in notes 34 and 35, see Justice Antonin Scalia, "Originalism," 57 *University of Cincinnati Law Review 849 (1989)*, and Robert H. Bork, *The Tempting of America* (New York: Macmillan, 1990), especially Chs. 6–8. The most thorough work of this genre remains William W. Crosskey, *Politics and the Constitution* (Chicago: University of Chicago Press, 1952, 1980), 3 vols.

43. Dennis J. Mahoney makes the argument most forcefully: "The Declaration of Independence as a Constitutional Document," in Leonard W. Levy and D.J. Mahoney, eds., *The Framing and Ratification of the Constitution* (New York: Macmillan, 1987). Gary Wills, *Inventing America* (Garden City, NY: Doubleday, 1976), p. 325, makes a vigorous opposing argument.

44. For the Supreme Court's varied uses of *The Federalist*, see Charles W. Pierson, "The Federalist in the Supreme Court," 33 *Yale Law Journal* 728 (1924); and James G. Wilson, "The Most Sacred Text," 1985 *Brigham Young University Law Review* 65.

45. See especially In the Matter of §6 of *The Judicature Act*, [1981] S.C.R. 753.

46. E.g.: *Walz v. Tax Comm'n*, 397 U.S. 664, 676–80 (1970).

47. Sotirios A. Barber, *On What the Constitution Means* (Baltimore: Johns Hopkins University Press, 1984), pp. 79–85.

48. *Marbury v. Madison*, 1 Cr. 137 (1803), is usually cited as the case first asserting this principle, but it is older; see, in particular, Hayburn's Case, 2 Dall. 409 (1792) and Yale Todd's Case, decided in 1794, but not published until 1852, 13 How. 52.

49. Senator John Breckinridge, *Annals of Congress*, 7th Congress, 1st session (1802), p. 179.

50. *The Federalist*, No. 37.

51. Art. 9. See Tomosuke Kasuya, "Constitutional Transformation and the Ninth Article of the Japanese Constitution," 18 *Law in Japan* 1 (1986); Osamu Nishi, *The Constitution and the National Defense Law System in Japan* (Tokyo: Seibundo, 1987); the Suzuki Case (1952), in John M. Maki, *Court and Constitution in Japan* (Seattle: University of Washington Press, 1964), pp. 362ff; and the Sunakawa Case (1959), in Murphy and Tanenhaus, note 7, pp. 239ff.

52. Basic East–West Treaty Case, 36 BVerfGE 1 (1975); Murphy and Tanenhaus, note 7, pp. 232ff.

53. William F. Harris, II, *The Interpretable Constitution* (Baltimore: Johns Hopkins University Press, 1993), Ch. 4.

54. See Walter F. Murphy, "The Right to Privacy and Legitimate Constitutional Change," in Schlomo Slonim, ed., *The Constitutional Bases of Social and Political Change in the United States* (New York: Praeger, 1990); "An Ordering of Constitutional Values," 53 *Southern California Law Review* 703 (1980); "Slaughter-House, Civil Rights," note 41. Akhil Amar contends that popular sovereignty demands that a majority of the American people be allowed to amend their constitutional text, but he also argues that

constitutional amendments destroying democratic processes for current or later generations would be invalid. "Philadelphia Revisited," 55 *University of Chicago Law Review* 1043 (1988).

55. Kesavananda Bharati's Case and *Minerva Mills*, note 39.

56. "Consent of the people" currently functions as something of a shibboleth in many circles. Certainly it seems to be consistent with democratic theory. In fact, however, consent is a troublesome concept. Even Michael Walzer, an ardent democratic theorist, concedes there are limits to what the consent of the people can legitimate. Michael Walzer, note 3. See also Joseph Raz, "Government by Consent," in J. Roland Pennock and John W. Chapman, eds., *Authority Revisited* (New York: New York University Press, 1987); and Walter F. Murphy, "Consent and Constitutional Change," in James O'Reilly, ed., *Human Rights and Constitutional Law: Essays in Honour of Brian Walsh* (Dublin, Ireland: Round Hall Press, 1992).

57. Letter to Justice William Johnson, June 12, 1823; Lipscomb, note 17, XV, 451.

58. See Walter F. Murphy, "Who Shall Interpret? The Quest for the Ultimate Constitutional Interpreter" 48 *The Review of Politics* 401 (1986); and Walter F. Murphy, James E. Fleming, and William F. Harris, II, *American Constitutional Interpretation* (Mineola, NY: Foundation Press, 1986), Chs. 6–7. For present purposes, I exclude the final authority's being shared by the states of a federal union.

59. Mauro Cappalletti, *Judicial Review in the Contemporary World* (Indianapolis: Bobbs-Merrill, 1971); Louis Favoreu, *Les Cours Constitutionnelles* (Paris: Presses Universitaires de France, 1986); Edward McWhinney, *Judicial Review* (4th ed.; Toronto: University of Toronto Press, 1969); Murphy and Tanenhaus, note 7; Giuseppe de Vergottini, *Diritto Costituzionale Comparato* (2d ed.; Padova: Cedam, 1988); Giorgio Berti, *Interpretazione Costituzionale* (Padova: Cedam, 1988). As usual, France has gone its own way. See Louis Favoreu et Loic Philip, eds., *Les Grandes Decisions du Conseil Constitutionnel* (6th ed.: Paris: Sirey, 1991); F.L. Morton, "Judicial Review in France," 36 *Americian Journal of Comparative Law* 89 (1988); and Cynthia Vroom, "Constitutional Protection of Individual Liberties in France," 63 *Tulane Law Review* 266 (1988).

60. Arts. 93 and 100.

61. Art 115g.

62. Southwest Case (1951), note 36.

63. Under Art. 93 of the Basic Law, each house of Parliament selects half the justices of the Constitutional Court. But beyond stipulating that the justices may not, when chosen, be members of parliament or cabinet, *Land* or Federal, the Basic Law does not set qualifications for membership, the number of justices, or the length of their terms. All these, like details of the Court's jurisdiction, are left to legislative discretion. And if Parliament disapproves of the Court's interpretations, it can try, when it chooses new judges, to select people who will undo the earlier work. Furthermore, 95 percent of the Court's business comes from "constitutional complaints" filed by individual citizens—a means of access that is purely the creation of a statute that Parliament can modify or repeal. See Donald P. Kommers, *Judicial Politics in West Germany* (Beverly Hills, CA: Sage, 1976); and Donald P. Kommers, *Constitutional Jurisprudence*, note 7.

64. For Japan, see the Sunakawa Case (1959) in Murphy and Tanenhaus, note 7, p. 162; for Germany, see Kommers, *Constitutional Jurisprudence*, note 7, pp. 163–164.

65. James D. Richardson, ed., *A Compilation of the Messages and Papers of the Presidents* (Washington, D.C.: Bureau of National Literature and Art, 1908), II, 581–582.

66. The Supreme Court has narrowly construed this article. In re The Emergency Powers Bill, 1976, [1977] I.R. 159; John M. Kelly, *The Irish Constitution* (Dublin: Juris, 1980), pp. 135–141; Michael Forde, *Constitutional Law of Ireland* (Cork: Mercier Press,

1987); and David Gwynn Morgan, "The Emergency Powers Bill Reference," 13 *Irish Jurist* 67 (1978) and 14 *Irish Jurist* 252 (1979).

67. There are at least two important checks on legislative power: The first is that an exemption, though renewable, can run for a maximum of 5 years. The second is that the legislature must "expressly declare" it means to violate a constitutionally protected right—a declaration that could, at the national level, destroy a Prime Minister and his party at the next election unless they can persuade the electorate that a serious case existed to negate a constitutionally guaranteed right. At the provincial level, however, those risks may be much smaller. Quebec has not only used Article 33 to "reverse" a decision regarding rights of Anglophones to display signs in English—*Allan Singer Ltd. v. Attorney General for Quebec*, [1988] S.C.R. 790—but has also tried to protect most of its code by retroactively cloaking its regulations under Article 33. Whatever difficulties the ruling party in Quebec has experienced, popular outrage at the government's restricting the rights of Anglophones or thumbing its nose at Ottawa has not been among them.

68. See the literature cited in Walter F. Murphy, "Who Shall Interpret the Constitution," note 58, and Louis Fisher, *Constitutional Dialogues: Interpretation as Political Process* (Princeton: Princeton University Press, 1988).

69. A huge body of literature deals with judicial behavior. The most important early work was C. Herman Pritchett, *The Roosevelt Court* (New York: Macmillan, 1948). For later literature on the United States, see especially Walter F. Murphy and C. Herman Pritchett, *Courts, Judges & Politics* (2d ed.; New York: Random House, 1973), Appendix A; and Lawrence Baum, "Judicial Politics," in Ada W. Finifter, ed., *Political Science* (Washington, D.C.: American Political Science Association, 1983). For studies of judicial behavior elsewhere, see Glendon A. Schubert, Jr., and David J. Danelski, eds., *Comparative Judicial Behavior* (New York: Oxford University Press, 1969).

70. See, e.g., the Southwest Case (1951), note 36; Charles L. Black, Jr., *Structure and Relationship in Constitutional Law* (Baton Rouge: Louisiana State University Press, 1969); and William F. Harris, II, "Bonding Word and Polity," 76 *American Political Science Review* 34 (1982).

71. For fuller argument, see Walter F. Murphy, "The Right to Privacy and Legitimate Constitutional Change," note 54.

72. The College of Cardinals recognized this fact many centuries before secular nations that fancied themselves democratic. The secret ballot was not commonly used in the United States, for instance, for more than a century after the constitutional text was ratified. At that time, voting was often public and oral, causing some framers to see universal manhood suffrage as threatening to produce oligarchy. Employers could hear their employees vote and reward or punish them. Thus, those framers wanted to limit the franchise to men who owned land and could have some economic independence. Gouverneur Morris gave the clearest speech on the point—as reported by James McHenry, in Max Farrand, ed., *The Records of the Federal Constitutional Convention of 1787* (New Haven: Yale University Press, 1966) (reissued, 1987, James T. Hutson, ed.), II, 209–210.

73. Benjamin N. Cardozo, *The Nature of Judicial Process* (New Haven: Yale University Press, 1921).

2

Constitutionalism in Europe Since 1945: Reconstruction and Reappraisal

Nevil Johnson

Constitutional reconstruction in western Europe in and after 1945, and indeed such imposed reconstruction as then occurred in central and eastern Europe, took place in the aftermath of war, destruction, and defeat. These harsh constraining conditions defined to a large extent the problems and the priorities of those involved. Only in relation to its particular circumstances can we understand the character of the postwar reconstruction.

A consideration of reconstruction directs our attention to past experience; reappraisal tends to suggest different preoccupations. Of course, a process of reappraisal can itself be set into the past as an event or set of events, which makes it possible, at least in principle, to treat it on the same terms as reconstruction. But often we treat reappraisal as an exercise we undertake in the here and now. We take stock of the various reconstructions and reappraisals that have occurred, and then seek to reappraise the situation now reached in relation to our own preoccupations and concerns. This procedure inevitably involves the risk of distorting earlier experience, of seeing what has been done with its varying record of success and failure, in terms of what we might like to do or think ought to be done now and in the future. For the most part an effort will be made here to mitigate these risks by an emphasis on past experience and a consideration of both reconstruction and reappraisal in their specific historical contexts. Only toward the end of this chapter, with some attention to current challenges and broader judgments on European constitutionalism and its prospects for the future, will there be a shift to a more explicitly normative discussion.

The Circumstances of Constitutional Reconstruction at the End of the Second World War

The conditions prevalent in many parts of Europe at the end of the Second World War imposed the need for reconstruction. The war had engulfed the whole of

Europe with the exceptions of the two traditionally neutral states, Switzerland and Sweden, the Iberian peninsula where Spain and Portugal chose to remain neutral, and the Republic of Ireland, which also stayed neutral. Except for Britain, all areas experienced invasion, occupation, and the clash of warring armies. The Nazi regime in Germany first took over most of the continent, later to be driven back and defeated by the forces of the Soviet Union from the east, and of the United States, Britain and their allies from the west. The consequences of this immense conflict are in broad terms familiar enough: widespread devastation and social dislocation; the uprooting and movement of whole populations; the ruination of the economies of most countries; the actual or effectual destruction of traditional political and administrative institutions in many countries; the military occupation of Germany and Austria, and something not entirely dissimilar in eastern Europe in the wake of the decision to treat that part of continent as belonging to the Soviet sphere of influence.

Much of Europe, and especially Germany, faced a political vacuum. The perception of having to face up to the consequences of defeat was strong, not only in Germany, but to a certain extent in Italy, France, and Austria. And in eastern Europe negative images of failure and defeat burdened many of the regimes that had disappeared. Psychologically this awareness of defeat, of failure to prevent the devastation of the continent, was important: it pointed to the overriding need to devise constitutional arrangements likely to be more durable than those of 1919 and the era of national self-determination. Thus, for many societies after 1945, the reconstruction was strongly motivated by a desire to secure protection against past mistakes and, above all, to establish conditions of stability and security both within individual states and in the relations among them. The process has been characterized by one well-known political theorist as a series of "negative revolution," animated by a political theory committed to "moderation and compromise." There is much force in this judgment.[1]

The reconstruction in postwar Europe was, furthermore, decisively shaped by political events that ensured that it would take place on very different terms in the western and eastern parts of the continent. Soon after 1945, indeed portents of this change were evident even before the war ended in Europe, the alliance between the United States and the USSR fell apart. The Soviet Union made clear its determination to treat eastern Europe as the outer defenses of its empire, and to see suitably compliant communist regimes in all the countries in that area. This process of *Gleichschaltung* was not completed until 1948 when Czechoslovakia was brought firmly within the fold; indeed one potential client state, Yugoslavia, actually broke away from Soviet domination in 1948 in order to assert its independence and the right to introduce its own brand of communism. The overall effect of the Cold War and the division between east and west was, of course the reconstruction of the central and eastern European states under communist regimes. In relation to constitutionalism and genuine constitutional government they became uninteresting. Only recently has this situation changed radically as a result of the events of 1989; constitutional reconstruction has become necessary throughout eastern Europe and, indeed, made substantial progress in several states during 1990. This chapter will not, however, consider the eastern parts of Europe at all. Our concern is with the west, for only here was it practical after 1945 for serious constitutional argument to occur and real efforts made to devise regimes establishing constitutional safeguards.

We must stress another aspect of the political circumstances in postwar western Europe. There existed widespread feeling in favor of some kind of European unity, related to the recognition that Europe had suffered greatly from nationalism and its excesses, and had as a result paid a heavy price for failure to overcome its own internal conflicts. Not surprisingly, this view of past experience produced a reaction in favor of bringing the European states closer together, though a few years passed before various institutional schemes for European cooperation, integration, and union came into operation. Nevertheless, the reaction against national exclusiveness and in favor of far closer ties among the European states did have an effect on constitutional reconstruction reflected in less emphasis on national identity, a greater readiness to acknowledge the claims of minorities to special treatment, and in the sphere of interstate relations some disposition to tone down the earlier stress on untrammelled national sovereignty.

One country in Europe occupied a peculiar position in relation to the reconstruction. This was Great Britain. After the United States and the USSR, it was the most important of the victorious powers, and the only one with worldwide interests and commitments. It institutions had carried the country successfully through 6 years of war, including times when ultimate victory seemed a remote prospect. Moreover, after 1945 Britain was heavily engaged in the reconstruction process in western Europe as an occupying power responsible for large parts of Germany. Quite obviously, in these conditions there could be no question of reconstruction in Britain itself. The soundess of its institutions appeared to have been fully confirmed, and it was widely believed that the British constitutional tradition was uniquely valuable. Britain was, therefore, both a guiding hand in much of the constitutional reconstruction after 1945, and a rather detached observer of it. It was only long after the revitalization of the constitutional practices of several west European countries that it became fashionable in Britain to ask questions about the case for a reappraisal of its particular brand of constitutionalism.

Varieties of Post-1945 Reconstruction

Despite the fact that most European countries had felt the direct impact of war, there was not, after 1945, a wholesale reshaping of constitutional conditions across western Europe. The approach to reconstruction varied widely, and was influenced greatly by the degree of authority and respect enjoyed by preexisting political institutions and those holders of political office who had been driven into exile.

Undoubtedly it was in Germany (or rather in that part of it under the control of the western Allies), France, and Italy that the need for a complete rewriting of earlier constitutional documents was most decisive. In several smaller countries reconstruction was more limited in scope and consisted chiefly in a restoration and reaffirmation, sometimes with amendments, of the constitution in force before 1939; this was the case in all the parliamentary monarchies, Norway, Denmark, Holland, Belgium, and Luxembourg. Only in Belgium was there for a while some argument about the future of monarchy itself, prompted chiefly by the ambiguous behavior of Leopold III in relation to Germany during the Second World War. Eventually, this argument was resolved by Leopold's abdication in 1950 in favor of his son, Prince Baudouin.

Three other states outside the sphere of Soviet control also reverted to constitutional provisions identical with, or very similar to, those in force before the Second World War: Finland, Austria, and Greece. Greece then experienced political instability and periods of military rule right down to the establishment of the present constitution in 1975. In Austria, the constitution of the First Republic as modified in 1929 was reintroduced when the country came under four-power occupation in 1945. Eventually, nearly a decade later in 1955, the occupying powers agreed on their own withdrawal and the restoration of complete Austrian independence. By then, the Second Republic was a going concern.

Thorough-going constitutional reconstruction took place in the three largest and most populous of the western European countries: France, Italy, and West Germany. Some general comments on each of these cases are in order before we proceed to discuss more comparatively the principal components of the postwar constitutional reconstructions.

France

War had overwhelmed the Third Republic in France. A species of puppet government ruled part of the country from Vichy, claiming to be a legitimate successor to the discredited Third Republic, but committed to very different ideas of government from those held to embody the Republican tradition prior to 1940. Meanwhile, in exile and claiming a higher legitimacy by virtue of its will to continue in the war against Germany was the movement headed by de Gaulle, which in 1943 assumed the role of Provisional Government of Free France. French loyalties were torn in so many different directions between 1940 and 1945 that there was no prospect of simply resurrecting the Third Republic once the war was over. In fact, when the issue was referred to the people in 1945, the vast majority voted in favor of drafting a new constitution.

No consensus existed, however, on the kind of constitution it should be. The major party groups that emerged in 1944–1945 were in considerable disagreement with each other, and there was at that time no widespread support for de Gaulle's ideas for a constitution designed to strengthen executive authority: ironically, that appeared to some to be all too reminiscent of the ideology of the Vichy regime. There seemed to be no alternative to a return to the classical French Republican tradition. The resulting constitution was rejected in a referendum, but after amendment, secured acceptance at a second popular vote by a narrow margin in late 1946.

Conceived without enthusiasm and launched amid expressions of hostility from the opposite side of the political spectrum, the constitution of the Fourth Republic began a life that lasted only 12 hours. Indeed, it was hardly a genuine reconstruction at all. The constitution provided in effect for a revamped version of the Third Republic's institutions, with some modifications to meet the main criticisms that had been made of the Third Republic, such as that of the former Senate and its capacity to maintain a kind of conservative veto over most reformist programs. The Fourth Republic had an emasculated second chamber (the Council of the Republic), which did indeed remain more or less without influence. Above all, however, a change in the electoral system, which returned to a system of proportional representation and gave up the method of single member constituencies with elections by two successive ballots, was intended to strengthen the political parties at the expense of the largely rural conservative *notables* who had so often dominated French political life. Despite this change, the *notables* remained strong, while the parties proved incapable of effective cooperation in government, with the consequence that the Fourth Republic soon faced the reproach that the constitution had destroyed executive authority and provided no basis for the effective government of the country.[2]

Italy

In Italy the case for an entirely new constitution was much clearer. The Fascist dictatorship, superimposed on the preexisting parliamentary monarchy, had inevitably brought discredit on that form of government, though it was not a foregone conclusion in 1945–1946 that it would be replaced. After a popular vote against the retention of the monarchy, the new constitution of December 1947 provided for a parliamentary Republic. It included a programmatic commitment both to decentralization and to a wide range of welfare policies intended to promote greater social equality and solidarity within the whole society. It is in the Italian constitution that the early postwar sympathy for socializing ideals and for qualification of much of the traditional individualism of liberal political theory is most vividly stated. This is not, of course, to say that this commitment has found an equally strong expression in subsequent policies: in fact, it has not. Nevertheless, the emphasis on the social teaching of the Catholic Church continues to have a diffuse influence on the attitudes of Italian Government. Among its unintended consequences is the manner in which it works against all serious attempts to weaken the structure of vested special interests, the growth of which has been such a marked feature of the post-1945 evolution of the Italian state and economy.

Germany

France and Italy reshaped their constitutions autonomously. Germany was not able to do that. The country, divided between east and west, was subject to the authority of occupying powers. Constitutional reconstruction occurred more rapidly than most observers in 1945 would have thought possible. This was essentially a result of the Cold War, and the recognition by the United States that West German support was needed to successfully defend western Europe against threats from the east. The price of this need was the restoration of the western part of Germany as a nearly independent state, a process initiated in 1948 and completed in 1949 with the establishment of the Federal Republic of Germany and the coming into force of the Basic Law.

This new constitution, in principle a provisional foundation for the new state pending reunification of the whole country, was produced at the behest of the western occupying powers, who defined in broad terms the political requirements it had to satisfy, and whose military representatives had to approve in detail the draft constitution as it finally emerged from the Parliamentary Council in 1949. Nevertheless, one must not think that the constitution was more or less imposed on West Germany and embodied requirements alien to the German political tradition. Certain general principles were prescribed—the constitution had to be democratic in spirit and federal in form—but the manner of satisfying them in the constitution was left largely to the Germans, subject to the views expressed when the provisions of the Basic Law came forward for approval or were the object of disagreement among the drafters of the constitution themselves.[3]

Another aspect of the conditions surrounding the emergence of the Basic Law deserves emphasis. This is the fact that political activity had been revived first at the local and provincial levels of the society. By late 1946 a number of provincial or *Land* administrations were formed; the 3 years following saw a consolidation of this level of government and political life. In some instances this went as far as elaborate constitutional provisions for these new German *Länder*. The Federal Republic was built on this foundation and the constitutional provisions in some of the *Länder* served as practical models in the drafting of the new federal constitution. In other words, there was no *tabula rasa* even in the country most devastated by war and where the powers of the national political authorities had been taken over fully by occupation regimes.

Forms of Government and Civil and Political Rights in the European Reconstruction

Parliamentary Regimes

Throughout western Europe those involved in postwar constitutional reconstruction favored a parliamentary form of government. They designed the new or restored constitutions to confer full legislative authority on an elected assembly (coexisting in most cases with an upper chamber with more limited powers) responsible for installing and sustaining the political executive or Government. This structure made the Government responsible to a parliamentary assembly, which could withdraw its confidence and thus force the Government's resignation.

Essentially this system represented a reaffirmation of the institutional arrangements recommended in the classic liberal view of parliamentary government evolved in the nineteenth century. How relations between Parliament and Government then developed depended, of course, on the number, character, and behavior of political parties; those features in turn shaped by a complex range of conditions internal to each country as well as by the electoral laws in force. Where parliamentary government had previously been stable, generally it remained so after its restoration in 1945; Norway, Holland, and Denmark provide clear examples of this. These countries were so strongly committed to the negotiation of often intricate coalition agreements among competing parties and social groups and organizations, that later their mode of parliamentary government was often designated "consociational democracy," a democratic regime in which the parties mediate the interplay of numerous associations to facilitate a continuing consensus on public policy.[4]

In other countries, notably France and Italy, the record of success in operating a parliamentary regime was less persuasive. Both had multiparty systems in which internal division marked even the dominant parties (e.g., the *Democrazia Cristiana* in Italy), and many of the smaller parties had only tenuous organization and low memberships. In such circumstances the maintenance of stable coalitions tended to be difficult or impossible: internal party competition dominated political life, and parties had little or no scope for disciplining their elected representatives. A classic *régime d'assemblée* of this sort was in fact the consequence of the constitutional reconstructions in both France and Italy: governments were hard to put together and rarely endured more than a year before removal from office by movements of opinion in the assembly. This kind of executive instability was instrumental in bringing about the replacement of the Fourth Republic by the Fifth in 1958 when de Gaulle returned to power with a mandate for a new constitutional reconstruction. Italy has not experienced a comparable rejection of a parliamentary government associated with persistent executive instability: clearly, ways of compensating for the weakness of Governments have been found and, moreover, no widespread perception of an acceptable constitutional alternative exists in Italy.[5] In any society this alone can be decisive in sustaining an established constitutional tradition and its associated institutional methods.

To safeguard against a relapse into the unstable parliamentary regime of the Weimar era the West German Basic Law sought continuity in the parliamentary form of government in a number of ways and, pari passu, through a limitation on the ability of Parliament (the Bundestag) to remove governments from office without regard to the consequences. These protective measures consisted essentially in making the Federal Chancellor the sole constitutionally responsible Minister, subject to election by the Bundestag and dismissable only when that body at the same time elects a successor (the constructive vote of no confidence procedures).[6] These provisions, taken in combination with other changes such as confining the presidency to a representational role and applying electoral law conditions that made it hard for very small parties to gain representation, have undoubtedly made for executive stability under the West German constitution. On the other hand, it has to be recognized that the overall party development in the Federal Republic was, after 1949, highly favorable to the rapid establishment of consensus and the maintenance of stable coalitions. By 1953 splinter parties had largely disappeared at the national level, and after 1957, only two major parties and one minor party were represented in the Bundestag. Only since 1983 have there been signs of some loosening up of the West German party system, with four parties gaining seats in the Bundestag (one of which, the CDU, consists of two distinctive and separately organized wings). Following reunification in October 1990 there appeared initially to be the prospect of further small parties securing representation, a development that would bring nearer conditions in which, with the absence of cohesive majorities, the constitutional provisions for a "stabilized" parliamentary regime could be exposed to more severe tests than they have so far had to face. The outcome of the first early and radical modification of the stable configuration of parties established in the Federal Republic as it was before October 1990 was likely to occur.[7]

A further comment on the character of parliamentary regimes in Western Europe in necessary. None of them fully embodies the British principle of parliamentary sovereignty, though the constitution of the Fourth Republic of France came near to attributing such authority to the National Assembly as the delegate of the sovereign people. Most countries' parliaments coexist in various relationships with other institutions in a manner that qualifies their authority. The formal provisions of the written constitutions of all states (with the exception of Great Britain) limit the rights of the elected parliamentary bodies. For example, constitutional amendment is likely to involve special procedures, and sometimes a popular vote, certain conditions may be entrenched and beyond parliamentary intervention and in some cases, the most significant of which is the Federal Republic, there may be wide scope for judicial review of constitutional disputes, extending as far as the invalidation of legislation held to be in conflict with the Basic Law. Such conditions point to a more complex pattern of institutionalized checks and balances than was usually associated with classical parliamentary government. They may also help to explain why the legislative assemblies of most West European states have not found it too difficult to accept the prospect of the transfer of powers, including those of law-making, to European institutions in Brussels and Strasbourg. In contrast, a genuinely sovereign institution such as the British Parliament has found (and still finds) this process of adaptation hard to accept.

Finally, it must be stressed again that the mode of operation of a parliamentary form of government depends decisively on the configuration of parties and the manner in which they behave. It is characteristic of the post-1945 political development of Europe that parties have, on the whole, grown stronger. They have become an indispensable means of representation, they are brokers and mediators in the resolution of conflicts of interest in the society, and they are the organizations in and through which most individuals pursue a career in politics or public affairs. Exceptions can be found to these generalizations and reference will be made below to one or two of the most important. Nevertheless, in some degree all west European societies demonstrate the dominance of party as the key instrument of representation and rule in our epoch. It follows that if there are any grounds for believing that parties are no longer able to perform effectively the functions required of them in contemporary parliamentary regimes, then there is a real prospect that institutional instability and a loss of legitimacy for the constitutional provisions themselves will ensue. Such was the experience of France before 1958. I will return to this possibility in the concluding part of this chapter.

Federal Solutions

In the nineteenth century emergent constitutionalism in Europe was clearly associated with the formation and consolidation of nation states: in short, progress toward constitutional government was thought to go hand in hand with the recognition of national ties and identities. And, almost inevitably, the nation state turned out to be more or less centralized, echoing in various ways the example set by the French state after the Revolution. After 1918 the acceptance of the principle of self-determination as the basis for redrawing the political map of large parts of Europe reinforced this stress on the nation state.

These remarks indicate the relative weakness of the federal model within European political experience. There is only one long-established federation, Switzerland, unaffected after 1945 by any process of reconstruction: the Swiss confederation has unique characteristics both as a union of small states and as a political structure embodying popular vote or referendum as a key institution by which certain policy questions are resolved and the constitution itself develops.

In the postwar reconstruction only in West Germany did the federal idea play a major part. Perhaps it hovored in the background in Italy and it was reaffirmed uncontentiously in Austria with the restoration of the pre-Second World War constitution, but it was not a major issue for debate. In West Germany federation became a necessity for two reasons. First, the Allies insisted that the new constitution should be federal in character as a safeguard against an overmighty central power in the future. Second those responsible for drafting the Basic Law were for the most part firmly in favor of a federal state anyway. Political life had already been reestablished in the *Länder* or provinces of the three western zones of occupation; in addition, the earlier German experience of numerous territorial sovereignties exerted a strong pull. Furthermore, Catholic social teaching with its emphasis on the principle of subsidiariness was strong and pointed toward federal solutions. All these factors appeared in 1949 to support the case for a federal constitution as a safeguard against the abuse of power in a centralized national state.

The outcome of these considerations was that the Basic Law established a federal structure. Indeed, the federal form of state organization is declared inviolable:[8] the Federal Republic cannot abolish its own federal system. West German federalism does, however, differ in radical ways from the American model. The latter makes a sharp separation between the federation and the member states; the states are relatively autonomous in many spheres and the federal government has full charge of national policy. German federalism prefers to maintain a distinction between the functions of law making and those of execution: the *Länder* or states are chiefly responsible for the execution of the laws but also have substantial rights in the national institutions of the Federation charged with legislating and determining national policy. Consequently, the West German federal state is more closely integrated than federations built on the American pattern; it has a highly uniform legal order, a densely structured system of consultative and policy-formulating institutions, and close links between politicians and officials at the two levels of the system. A large part of the administration of services provided directly to the citizen occurs at the *Länder* level, which is virtually closed to direct intervention by the national government. A major consequence of this type of federal structure is wide dispersal of influence within the political elite: the command of resources and the possession of extensive executive responsibilities confers on politicians from the *Länder* an important role in national politics if they are disposed to perform it.[9]

No other large west European state has a genuinely federal structure. Nevertheless, the experience of federal institutions has continuing relevance for two reasons. One is that federal solutions, or arrangements pointing in that direction, may be of some significance in coping with demands for decentralization stemming from criticism of the centralized nation state. As early as 1947, certain federalizing components entered in the Italian constitution, resulting in the creation of five special regions; in the early 1970s, the pattern of regional government was extended to the whole country. Two other countries, Spain and France, have recently also moved away from the model of the centralized nation state, in Spain to accommodate the demands of special groups in the population for a measure of autonomy, and in France to experiment with a larger degree of decentralization in the management of public services than was previously held acceptable. Although these remarks represent a simplification of complex and diverse efforts to loosen up previously centralized state structures, they do serve to draw attention to one of the reasons why fully federal systems are of continuing practical relevance and interest.

Another factor sustains a concern with federal patterns of government—the slow gradual process of integration proceeding within the European Community since the founding of the coal and steel community in 1950. There has, of course, always been much disagreement about the pace and objectives of integration, but there can be no doubt about the extent to which the member states of the community have during the past 30 years become interdependent and subject to common rules and policies. Moreover, to a certain degree a centralization of powers has occurred inside the community, manifested in the central policymaking institutions of the Council of Ministers and the Commission. It does not take much imagination to appreciate that the continuation of this process of integration and of the move towards "closer union"[10] in Europe must require a strengthening of the federal idea. For in the light of the strong sentiments of national identity that exist, it is virtually inconceivable that the European Community should evolve in the direction of a superstate, a kind of projection of France or Britain on the European level. The process of integration can proceed further only if the constitutional principles implicit in federalism are flexibly adapted to accommodate diversity within the increasingly integrated and unified economy which extends across western Europe. Closer union in Europe is likely to mean at some stage in the future a confederation, probably of a loosely structured kind.

Basic Civil and Political Rights

Human rights have come so sharply into prominence during recent years that there is a tendency to judge all constitutions according to the extent to which they endorse political democracy and affirm basic human rights. This preoccupation with human rights was present in the postwar reconstruction too, but in 1945, though it seemed obvious that human freedom and dignity had to be reaffirmed, so pressing were the needs of reconstruction that few people put these matters in the forefront of practical activity. And in many countries the protection of rights simply rested with the ordinary courts (as is still the case in many). Thus, the issue of formal enforcement was not prominent.

Most of the new post-1945 constitutions proclaim in different ways a respect for basic rights. The preamble of the constitution of the Fourth Republic explicitly invokes the principles of the Declaration of the Rights of Man and of the Citizen and enumerates a range of general social entitlements. The Italian constitution contains numerous lofty references to the principles to which the state is said to be committed, ranging widely from those that affirm civil rights to those that which specify rights to social protection and indicate some of the conditions under which the economy should operate. The most powerful and concentrated statement of basic human rights occurs, however, in the West German Basic Law, the first 19 articles of which prescribe such rights and declare them to be inalienable and binding legal principles. This commitment was backed up by provisions in the constitution, which resulted in the establishment of a Federal Constitutional Court in 1951. The extensive jurisprudence of this body dealing with basic rights has created a large body of case law providing interpretations of the meaning of its constitution, unique in Europe. Indeed, only in the United States does a judicial body, the Supreme Court, play a comparable part in declaring what the constitution means and in adapting its terms to the demands now made on it.

However, the point just made about the judicialization of disputes over individual rights with constitutional protection needs to be qualified by a comment on the nature of judicial decision making in systems of law based on the Roman Civil Law tradition. In these systems judges tend to view their task as the discovery of what the law really is, as a matter of correct deductions from texts of principles to specific conclusions: in this process strictly procedural considerations play large part. This approach to the judicial function differs substantially from that found in the Common Law tradition. Here, whether in the United States with its written constitution, or in England where judges are confined to a narrower range of review, there is a stronger belief in the importance and legitimacy of judge-made law. Review is a method of adapting the law, of filling gaps, and of developing the constitution itself. This judicial review confers, actually or potentially, an important political role on judges, no matter what their status of neutrality in a party sense.

On the whole, in continental Europe the judiciary retains a narrower view of its functions. Judges are generally less inclined to embark on the kind of wide-ranging critical assessment of the meaning of terms in a constitution or law that is sometimes manifested in Common Law jurisdictions; therefore, less risk of radical political impact inheres in their conclusions. The record of the West German Federal Constitutional Court supports this view: the Court's conclusions are large in volume and extensive in range, but relatively few judgments have changed in a decisive way the quality and value of the rights protection under the constitution. One judgment that did, however, is the 1957 ruling on the joint tax liabilities of married couples which ultimately worked strongly in favor of treating men and women equally.[11]

Success and Failure in Performance: Occasions for Reappraisal

A few remarks about the record of the post-1945 reconstruction in practice will facilitate some comments on the one major "reappraisal" that took place in the 30 years between 1945 and 1975, the replacement of the Fourth by the Fifth Republic in France.

In important respects postwar constitutionalism evolved in highly favorable conditions. The popular reaction against earlier mistakes and excesses remained strong; western Europe found itself exposed to a Soviet threat and received a guarantee of its security in the shape of NATO and a commitment from the United States to defend Europe; economic recovery was rapid and went ahead with remarkable persistence over many years; there was a gradual recovery of national identities but no revival of nationalism as a destructive force making for international conflict.

These conditions promoted a rapid stabilization of the new constitutional regimes; underlying this process were two important factors. One was the relatively widespread agreement on an economic and social order resting extensively on a free market and private property, but qualified by acknowledgment of a legitimate role for public authorities in the management of the economy and the maintenance of adequate levels of employment, investment, and economic growth. The relative strength of the commitment to market methods as opposed to government intervention in the economy varied from one country to another; but nowhere was a socialized command economy accepted, just as a return to a *laissez-faire* view of the state's role was everywhere ruled out. Of equal importance was the existence in most countries of multiparty conditions in which generally the parties proved far more willing than formerly to cooperate in sustaining the constitutional order. The one great exception to this was France, where blockage in the party system eventually provoked radical changes in the regime.

The outcome, particularly in northern Europe, was that the reconstructed constitutions were successful and stable parliamentary government under coalition became the norm. It was relatively easy to find consensus in societies committed to economic growth and generous social policies intended to protect everyone in the society to the maximum extent possible against the hazards of life. Naturally, it took some time for these developments to take shape and come to fruition. By the early 1960s many saw them as the norm in Scandinavia, the Low Countries, the Federal Republic, and Austria. The same was largely true of Britain.

In the mode of parliamentary government reestablished after 1945 the parties became far more important than the parliamentary institutions themselves. As a result, parliamentary institutions have in many countries receded into the background, becoming little more than vehicles for the expression and transmission of the interests and opinions of parties. Only in one country did restored parliamentary rule prove unsuccessful, France.

France was not the only country in which a restored parliamentary regime resulted in a high degree of executive instability. Italy also encountered these difficulties, but they did not prompt any serious challenge to the form of government as such, chiefly because a single party, the *Democrazia Cristiana*, was dominant after 1947 and nearly all the parties, with the exception of the Communists, were willing to enter into coalition arrangements if necessary. The case of France was, however, different. There the parties were collectively responsible for a level of executive instability that proved a severe handicap in the effort to resolve the very difficult problems of decolonization that France then faced. Internal tensions increased and the citizens lost respect for the regime. Nevertheless, though the objective pressures were strong, it is unlikely that the Fifth Republic would have replaced the Fourth had there not been an alternative political leadership available in de Gaulle who, most crucially of all, had his own well-defined views of the kind of constitutional settlement needed in France.

The Fifth Republic, established under the constitution of 1958, embodies an unusual and so far successful compromise between a parliamentary regime and one that acknowledges an executive authority founded on popular vote. Admittedly, these different conceptions of how both to distribute authority among institutions were not clearly articulated in the original 1958 constitution, which was potentially more "parliamentary" than "presidential." The 1962 amendment in favor of direct election of the President changed that position. Henceforth, the President could claim a popular mandate and by virtue of this uphold a wide interpretation of the constitution's definition of presidential power and duties. It is true that in some degree a bicephalous executive has survived, with a prime minister dismissable under somewhat difficult terms by the National Assembly. However, with the exception of the period 1986–1988, the majorities in the Assembly and those expressed by the popular vote for the President have coincided. As a result the executive authority of the President has been extensive, and the President is widely accepted as the principal voice in government.

Along with the strengthening of executive authority there occurred a severe reduction in the authority and power of Parliament. The 1958 constitution imposed on the French National Assembly a range of procedural limitations *vis-à-vis* the Government and curtailed its legislative rights in various ways. For example, the constitution of 1958 limited substantially the legislative competence of Parliament (Article 34), conferred on the Executive wide scope for the use of administrative decrees (Article 37), deprived deputies of the possibility of proposing increased expenditure (Article 40), and imposed severe restrictions on the National Assembly's scope for proposing motions of no-confidence in the Government (Article 49).[12] Equally significant was the decision to make a parliamentary mandate and the holding of ministerial office incompatible; this decision has eased the way during the past 30 years for a high proportion of ministers to come to office from the public service. To an extent without parallel in western Europe, the constitution of the Fifth Republic has thus weakened parliamentary government; a considerable strengthening of the bureaucracy accompanied this process. This unusual attempt to reconcile what look like conflicting principles has had widespread support in France, where the Fifth Republic appears to be firmly established. But it has found relatively few admirers and no imitators in western Europe, though the model appears to have some attractions for several countries in Eastern Europe engaged since 1989 in constitutional restructuring.

The 1958 French constitution represents an effective response to an impasse created by the weakness of the executive authority. Reappraisals in very different conditions took place in the 1970s in Spain and Portugal, where the problem was how to escape successfully from the constraints of long periods of authoritarian rule, by Dr. Oliveira Salazar in Portugal and by General Francisco Franco in Spain. It is impossible here to consider in detail the constitutional changes that occurred in both countries in the period 1970–1976, and later. Portugal gradually made a transition from quasimilitary and revolutionary rule to a form of government that embodies parliamentary and presidential elements. In Spain the transition to a new constitution was complex and cautious, in part because General Franco had made transitional arrangements for the years after his death, notably by providing for restoration of the monarchy. Since Franco and his movement were not without support, the transition had to be handled carefully. The new constitution of 1978 established a constitutional monarchy with full parliamentary governmen; this constitutional structure has been remarkably effective in accommodating Spain to conditions of competitive party politics, majority rule, and acknowledgment of an extensive code of basic rights. The new constitution also provides a substantial degree of autonomy for the provinces of Spain, some of which were and are the source of demands that threaten the stability of the national state.

The constitutional reconstruction of Spain in the mid-1970s is one of the most successful examples known of an orderly transition from authoritarian to democratic rule. No doubt this success was due extensively to favorable conditions not existent 60 years ago when Spain had a larger and more mature middle class and industrial development had made substantial progress; further, the western European environment of stable democratic institutions strongly influenced a movement in the same direction in both Spain and Portugal. Moreover, both countries aspired to join the European Community; and a reasonably stable democratic condition was a precondition of membership. In January 1986 both acceded to the Community. As with Greece, which joined the Community in 1981, membership became a powerful factor that worked in favor of the consolidation of the new democratic regimes.

Contemporary Challenges and Constitutional Responses

During the past 10 or 15 years essentially three issues have influenced constitutional development to some degree in most west European countries. The first is the call for decentralization; the second is the pressure for more meticulous attention to human rights; and the third is the need to adapt to the continued erosion of the rights of the national states now within the framework of the European Community.

Decentralization

There is no single or decisive source of the call for decentralization. In Great Britain, Spain, and Italy, for example, it clearly stems from national minorities distinguished variably by language, culture, or religion from the majority of the population. In Belgium too a similar problem exists, unusual in that it takes the form of a division of the whole population into two communities distinguished from one another by language. Constitutional amendments fulfilling earlier constitutional commitments have met this demand for greater internal autonomy in Belgium[13] and Italy, the new Spanish constitution provides for a process of political devolution, while in France measures of administrative decentralization took effect without constitutional change after 1981. Even in Britain, there were in the 1970s attempts to confer a degree of political devolution on Scotland and Wales; these were ultimately unsuccessful because of adverse popular votes in 1979. Whether constitutional concessions can accommodate the demands of minorities depends, however, on the extent to which the demands made are negotiable. In the cases of Basque separatism, Corsican separatism, and Republicanism in Northern Ireland, the nature of the demands rules out a negotiated solution and agreement on acceptable constitutional amendments because the minorities in question reject entirely the state of which they are part: their objective is unilateral independence.

Human Rights

In all western societies sensitivity to human rights has grown, a process somewhat accelerated by the consolidation of institutions at the European level, notably the European Community and its body of law, and the European Court and Commission of Human Rights in Strasbourg, which operate within the framework provided by the Council of Europe and the European Convention on Human Rights (1950). As a result of these developments it is now possible for citizens and organizations to challenge their domestic jurisdictions in various ways by demanding that they apply the higher standards embodied in the provisions to which their own states have acceded. Slowly, and in a piecemeal way, something like a European jurisprudence relating to the rights of individuals and private corporate bodies is taking shape.

The domestic response to these trends is variable. France has seen since 1974 some strengthening of the Constitutional Council's powers to rule on the compatibility of proposed legislation with the constitution, and a "médiateur" now functions as a type of ombudsman to whom individuals can appeal for redress of grievances. West Germany, in contrast, thinks the protection already afforded by the procedures of individual constitutional appeal is sufficient, though modern data storage methods have motivated action to strengthen protection of individual's privacy, and several *Länder* have set up the ombudsman device. The country most seriously affected by these pressures for an extensive and meticulous interpretation of rights is Britain. The reason for this is found not so much in the abuse of powers in Britain or in real limitations affecting individual rights, but in the tensions produced by the impact of formalized principles and procedures on a constitutional tradition that is unwritten, informal, and embodies the principle of parliamentary sovereignty. So far it has been hard to reconcile these different approaches to rights protection on the one hand specific, flexible, and discretionary, and on the other general, abstract, and often inflexible. Britain has not enacted the European Convention into domestic law despite the demand for such action generated by the relatively large number of decisions by the European Commission confirming breaches of the Convention on Human Rights.

Erosion and Integration: The European Community

The third challenge is the need to adapt the nation state to ever closer integration in the European Community, an association now embracing 12 member states. So far it has been possible to achieve a large measure of economic integration without a serious clash between the Community and one or more member states, and without changes that made it obvious to citizens that they are no longer subject principally to the exclusive jurisdiction of their domestic political authorities. It is possible that the 1985 legislation on the Single Market, scheduled to become operative in 1993, will make qualitative changes necessary, though this is by no means certain. It is conceivable, for example, that the development of the Community might thereafter be arrested at a stage that could be designated economic integration by the cooperating quasisovereign states: in that event no immediate constitutional reappraisal would be necessary either by member states or by the Community as a whole. On the other hand, such an outcome to a process dedicated to "closer union" appears unlikely; the integration process has so far been dynamic, and has already affected many sectors of social life not in a narrow sense part of the economy. The urge to harmonize will remain strong, and the demand to subject the Community institutions themselves to more effective democratic control will continue. It is therefore, likely that the nation state will face a continuing erosion of its domestic sovereignty, and for that reason will need to consider seriously both its own internal constitutional adaptation to changed external circumstances, and the extent to which the Community's institutions will require changes to take account of the accumulation of powers at that level.

Reappraisal in a New Age

The constitutional reconstruction of post-1945, along with later exercises in construction and reform in western Europe, presents a series of remarkable achievements. On the surface the extent of success is visible in the diminution or absence of constitutional conflict in many states. Broadly speaking, the whole of western Eurlpe is committed to democratic government, protection of basic human rights, and the pursuit by the political authorities of a high level of economic well-being and social security. Disputes occur about how best to pursue the economic and social objectives, some arguing for more reliance on market relationships, others pressing for more stress on public service provision and regulation. But that these differences are for the most part in degree, and not of principle, has been confirmed by the revival of market-oriented economic policies in the 1980s. Far from stimulating a reinforcement of socialist doctrine, this phase has accelerated the decline of genuinely socialist arguments and proposals: the social framework for western European constitutionalism remains managed capitalism and a socially conscious market. Under these conditions the countries of western Europe do not face the challenge of a radical reappraisal of prevailing constitutional forms and methods. It appears likely that present support for a democratic political order, committed extensively to consensus, and sensitive to the individualist emphasis on the sanctity of private rights and claims, will persist.

Some features of present circumstances, however, may prompt a search for constitutional adaptation. This conclusion will present them briefly. It should be noted immediately that these issues point in different and conflicting direction, making the task of reappraisal especially difficult.

The impersonality and remoteness of governing institutions create some uneasiness, often expressed as a complaint against bureaucracy and its defects. A variety of responses is possible: one is to strengthen responsibility of the political officeholder; another is to decentralize; yet another is to widen individual participation. Arguments are put forth in many countries for all these possibilities. The crucial difficulty lies in reconciling the demand for responsive, accessible government with the imperatives of efficiency in modern large-scale social organizations. No satisfactory solution to this dilemma has been found, except perhaps in relatively small societies such as Switzerland, which are highly differentiated internally. But the creation or reproduction of such conditions is difficult and, as a rule, impossible.

There are signs of something approaching hypersensitivity in respect to individual duties, an attitude accompanied by a tendency to underrate both individual duties and collective social benefit functions. This strong emphasis on individual claims finds expression in the subjectivist and individualist premises of much modern political theory, especially that proceeding from the Anglo-American tradition. This approach renders many forms of collective action difficult or impossible, and may turn out to be a matter of particular significance in relation to the protection of the environment and similar issues, all of which have now become matters of urgency. It is difficult to tackle such problems on an individualistic basis: the environment encloses us all and its protection, along with conservation of natural resources, may well call for the acceptance of constraints currently regarded as incompatible with the standards of human freedom and economic well-being to which we aspire.

A counterforce to these two concerns is the future evolution of supranational institutions and relationships. The dynamics of economic integration have favored economies of scale, and have already resulted in a remarkable degree on concentration across national boundaries. Economic integration requires appropriate supranational institutions, and holds out the prospect of further development toward political integration in western Europe. Yet this, if it takes place, is almost certain to magnify management problems caused by remoteness and the large size of governmental institutions. Nor will it be easy to reconcile supranational needs with the stress on individual rights and participation.

There is too in relation to the evolution of the European Community an external imponderable. Profound political changes are taking place in central and eastern Europe, pointing toward democratization, protection of human rights, and rejection of the monopoly power of the state inherent in postwar communism. These changes are bound to have implications for the European Community, perhaps necessitating an arrest to its further consolidation as a political bloc sharply demarcated from its neighbors to the east.

Finally, we must recognize that stability and prosperity put at risk the quality and standing of political elites. Broadly speaking, politics as an activity has been thoroughly professionalized, becoming the specialized concern of parties and their most active members. The professional politician does, however, live under the imperatives of democratic politics in pluralist societies. This condition means that politicians can rarely offer leadership, but must give priority to adjustment, compromise and consensus formation. Whatever the practical benefits of such an approach to political activity may be, it rarely offers inspiration or commands enduring respect. Furthermore, democratic politicians who lives *off* rather than *for* politics are exposed to temptations of a material character that constantly threaten their reputation and standing;[14] the ease with which in some countries the dominant political elites vote themselves financial privileges makes them sitting targets for public disapproval. Overall, the result is that the mass electorate's opinion of the contemporary professional politician is not high, which, in turn, may increase its susceptibility to the attractions of personalities and political movements with unconventional programs that claim to stand for completely different values from those advanced by current professional party politicians.

The incidence of this phenomenon varies greatly and specific problems and circumstances influence it significantly, e.g., the level of foreign immigration. Nor is it certain that constitutional measures can usually deal with these problems. At the very least there may be in some countries a case for reappraisal of the position of the professional in politics and, more generally, of the privileges conferred on parties. To command respect, the professional politician should not enjoy too high a level of job security; equally there is no strong case for relieving parties of the need to be active in gaining and keeping members and their financial contributions. The Greeks were perfectly familiar with the descent from democracy into oligarchy. This development may be progressing in contemporary western Europe; if so, an effort of constitutional reappraisal would be justified.

Notes

1. Carl J. Friedrich, "The Political Theory of the New Democratic Constitutions," in A.J. Zurcher, ed., *Constitutions and Constitutional Trends since World War II* (New York: New York, University Press, 1955), p. 34.

2. The most comprehensive treatments of the politics of the Fourth Republic is provided in P.M. Williams, *Crisis and Comprise: Politics in the Fourth Republic* (London: Longman, 1964).

3. For a detailed account of the Basic Law see J.F. Golay, *The Founding of the Federal Republic of Germany* (Chicago: University of Chicago Press, 1964).

4. The phrase "consociational democracy" came into common currency in the 1970s, and this owed much to A. Lijphart, *The Politics of Accommodation, Pluralism and Democracy in the Netherlands* (Berkeley: University of California Press, 1968).

5. A good general survey of Italian political methods is to be found in G. di Palma, *Surviving without Governing: The Italian Parties in Parliament* (Berkeley: University of California Press, 1977).

6. Arts. 63 and 67, Basic Law.

7. The Bundestag election held in December 1990 resulted in the following distribution of votes and seats:

	% of votes won	No. of seats
CDU	36.7	268
CSU	7.1	51
F.D.P.	11.0	71
SDP	33.5	239
'Greens' + Alliance 90	1.2	8
P.D.S.	2.4	17
Others	8.1	NIL

Note that the last two of the parties gaining seats did so by virtue of special electoral provisions applying only in the former German Democratic Republic. The 'Greens' lost all seats in the old Federal Republic.

8. Art 79(3), Basic Law.

9. For a detailed account of the West German federal structure, see N. Johnson, *State and Government in the Federal Republic of Germany: The Executive at Work* (Oxford: Pergamon Press, 1983), Ch. 5.

10. The words appear in the Preamble to the Treaty of Rome, 1957, establishing the European Economic Community.

11. B Verf GE 6, pp. 55–84.

12. The provisions explicitly redefining the powers of Parliament are contained in Title V of the Constitution of the Fifth Republic. Significantly this is headed "of relations between parliament and the Government." It contains 17 Articles, many of them very detailed, all of which tend to restrict the powers of Parliament and pari passu to strengthen the position of government.

13. Constitutional amendments in 1970 and 1971 established three regions and two Cultural Councils in Belgium, these to be the basis for a considerable internal decentralization.

14. The distinction of living *for* and living *off* politics was made famous by Max Weber, notably in the 1919 lecture *Politik als Beruf* (Tübingen: *Gesammelte Politishche Schriften* J. C. B. Mohr, 1924). The distinction is drawn in many other passages in his writings on political sociology.

3

Transition to Democracy, Corporatism, and Presidentialism with Special Reference to Latin America

Carlos Santiago Nino

This chapter seeks to connect the movement toward revision of the presidentialist system of government, perceptible in several Latin American countries, with some sociostructural variables with considerable impact on the process of consolidation of democracy.[1] In particular, I intend to show that as the main threats to that consolidation of democracy are the pressures of so-called "corporative groups"—the military, the Church, the trade unions, and entrepreneurial conglomerates—it is necessary to develop mechanisms for wider popular participation and stronger political parties to counteract those pressures. Further, I want to demonstrate that those mechanisms may increase the tensions in the democratic system generated by the dysfunctions of presidentialist government. My argument will lead to the conclusion that it is necessary to modify the presidential system of government to allow for the operation of mechanisms to contain the pressures of corporations, thus amplifying the space of the democratic process.

Transition to Democracy and Corporatism

As we all know, in the past decade a wave of democratization began to move in most of Latin America, finally reaching some islands of authoritarianism such as Chile. This process is often called "transition to democracy."[2] But this phrase conceals an ambiguity: it may refer to a process of adjustment of norms or institutions to further full democratic rule of law (competition in free elections of different political parties, an independent judiciary able to enforce a bill of rights, etc.), or it may refer to a situation in which these liberal democratic institutions are in full force but political action and other measures are in process to achieve their stability through the necessary degree of consensus and social adhesion to those institutions. In general, the second sense is more applicable to the transition to democracy in Latin American countries. In Argentina and Uruguay, for instance, full liberal and democratic mechanisms are in play, although the possibility of some sort of coercive interference with those mechanisms has not vanished completely from people's minds. There are also countries in which democratic institutions still have to develop more fully: Brazil has a new constitution that provides for election of the president and Mexico is experiencing the expansion of political parties that might constitute real alternatives to the official one.

Several classifications of the processes of transition to democracy apply to those going on in Latin America. One takes into account the kind of factors that precipitate the process. These may be *endogenous* ones, such as economic hardship, social unrest, divisions among those upholding power, or *exogenous* ones, such as foreign intervention or pressures or external wars, especially a losing one. In some countries (Brazil, Uruguay, and Bolivia) the conversion to democracy was pushed by internal causes; in Argentina, in addition to the internal social and economic factors that greatly discredited and isolated the military regime, was the loss of the Malvinas war, just as the Greek colonels lost their control of the government with their defeat in Cyprus and the Portuguese dictatorship could not survive the retreat from Angola.

Another classification of processes of transition takes into account the modality of the transmission of power from the dictators to democratic authorities. The two main modes of transference of power are *force* (Venezuela) and *agreement* or *consent* (Uruguay). The case of Argentina is atypical in this respect, since the transfer of power did not correspond to either of these modes, but to one known as *by collapse*, which occurs when a regime loses the control of the situation and leaves a vacuum that is occupied by the democratic forces. Although in Argentina there was some element of consent from the military, it was they themselves who called for elections under the Constitution of the country. The fact was that they were compelled to do so by the circumstances and by the longing of the people to return to democratic rule. But there was also an element of *mistake* in the modality of transference of power in Argentina; the fact that the members of the military regime calculated erroneously about the winner of the election was not an irrelevant factor in the process of transition.

I want to argue that whatever their origins or modes, the main challenge faced by processes of transition in consolidating democratic institutions is the containment of the network of de facto power relationships that corporations weave, as they take advantage of the vacuum left by representatives of popular sovereignty. Under authoritarian rule, social groups representing particular interests carve a place for themselves after some bargaining, which includes their offer of support for the regime. Such groups are the military themselves, the religious organizations, coalitions of entrepreneurs, trade unions, and even the press. Of course, these groups resist relinquishing their power to the representatives of the people once democratic rule is established.

As is well known, there is an expanding literature about the role of corporatism in Latin American countries' social and political structures, and its connection with modes of political regimes, such as the so-called bureaucratic-authoritarianism, and with ideologies such as populism.[3] A good deal of this literature must deal with the concept of corporatism itself, whose vagueness and ambiguity are causes of many misunderstandings and spurious theoretical differences. The main ambiguity is to my mind the one provoked by the difference between the traditional and more technical use of "corporatism" (or corporativism) to refer to the phenomenon of state control of organizations and interest groups, and the use of that term, more common in the political arena, to refer to the apparently contrary phenomenon of those organizations, sectorial institutions, or interest groups acquiring considerable weight and influence and putting persistent pressures on the decisions of the state organs. Despite the fact that explicit definitions tend to emphasize exclusively one or the other meaning, I think that in Latin America the phenomenon combines these two features. Latin America corporatism is not equivalent to the Fascist institutional structure of legally sanctioned exclusive organization of interest groups (except for the close approximation of Getullo Vargas' *Estado Novo*). But neither is it true that the phenomenon that theoreticians and politicians refer to as corporatism in Latin America reduces itself to the pressures that interest groups make on political organs in every pluralist country, lobbying in favor or against measures that affect them.

The phenomenon is far more complex and includes, among others, all the above characteristics. The state does have some power over interest groups and organizations, with mechanisms that imply some measure of control over their decisions; at the same time, those organizations exert enormous pressures on legislative and administrative agencies, gaining privileges and favors of different kinds. Some of those privileges amount to a legal monopoly of the interest's representations in a way that comes close to the Fascist scheme; sometimes this monopoly gives the state important influence over the organization. Other legal or even constitutional privileges pertain to the activity with which the interests are connected, granting it protection against the working of the market or other mechanisms of expression of the preferences of the people. Of course, there are also informal ways of granting favors, which in many cases amount to sheer corruption and illegality.

This complexity of Latin America corporatism is aptly characterized as "bifrontal" and "segmentary" by Guillermo O'Donnell, who applies these labels to Latin American corporatism because it has both "statizing" and "privatist" components: it is "statizing" in respect to the element of conquest and subordination of the organization of civil society; it is "privatist" insofar as private interest groups and organizations "colonize" sectors of the public institutions. These interrelated processes lead to interpenetration; in the words of O'Donnell: "The conquering state . . . [is also a] porous state, open at numerous interstices—informal and institutionalized—to links which contain bidirectional processes of control and influence, especially with the dominant classes of civil society."[4] This bifrontality is described by José Nun in these terms:

> Now we must no longer take into account only the influence that autonomous organizations of interests may exert upon a fragmentary and basically passive

> State, but also the complex and dense practices through which the latter has a strong impact on those organizations.... This promotes a double dependency: from the State with respect to the main interest groups which define the social division of labor...: and from such groups in relation to the State insofar as it decisively conditions their activities. This double dependency generates new networks of social interaction.[5]

The segmentary aspect of Latin American corporatism referred to by O'Donnell consists in the fact that this mode of linkage between state and society works variously and has a systematically diverse impact on social and institutional arrangements according to cleavages primarily determined by social class.

This is not the place to expand on the etiology of this phenomenon, an extremely complex inquiry that must take into account the circular pattern of the causation involved, in which effects are at the same time causes of similar though deeper and broader effects. For now we suggest that some cultural components described by Seymour Lipset[6] do not seem to be alien to Latin American corporatism: the resistance, which has been part of the Spanish culture, to the internalization of universal standards based on achievement and competition, not on particularistic attachments and status; the prestige of some corporations such as the Church and the military; the pressures against general rules of behavior and evaluation—all of which lead to the intricate system of privileges and special status within which corporatism flourishes.

For our purpose, it is more important to mention how corporatism is linked with populist and authoritarian experiences in the context of Latin American political cycles. As James M. Mallory says,

> It is now evident that populism was and is based on an implicit *corporatist* image of sociopolitical organization. With the exception of Vargas, the populist preference for a corporatist solution to the pressure of modernization was seldom stated explicitly, but there seems little gainsaying that populism has always shown a high affinity for corporatist principles of organizing the relations between state and society.[7]

He adds that populism in its first phases emphasized mobilization in an "inclusionary" way, trying to broaden the set of actors in the political process while controlling them through organizations "formed, in sectoral and functional criteria thereby fragmenting their support groups into parallel primary organizational structures joined at the top by interlocking sectoral elites."[8] Similarly, Manfred Mols asserts that populism and corporatism belong to each other, or are at least in an ideal complementary relation, as corporatism is a way of controlling and containing the social strata that populism seeks to promote, thus avoiding social conflicts. Mols also makes clear that corporatism is not exclusively tied to populism but is a structural element of Latin American politics with different manifestations and cultural roots in the Spanish attitude toward hierarchical status, patronages, clientelism, etc.[9]

The interlude between this connection between corporatism and populism and that between the corporatism and the bureaucratic-authoritarian State is the social situation that Samuel Huntington called "praetorianism."[10] This is a system that combines a low degree of institutionalization with a high degree of participation of mobile social forces that penetrate the political spheres, resulting in confrontations between new active social forces and between them and the traditional establishment.[11] Malloy describes the process in several countries of Latin America in the late 1950s and from the mid-1960s until the early 1970s:

> An important aspect of the praetorianization of Latin American politics during this period was the fact that although the formal state apparatuses [sic] in the region grew markedly, this was accompanied not by an increase in the power and efficiency of the State but rather by the reverse. The continuing reality of dependence was a critical factor in the development of states that were formally large and powerful but in practice weak. Another factor was a kind of *de facto* disaggregation of the state as various particularistic interest blocs in a sense captured relevant pieces of the state which they manipulated to their own benefit.[12]

Of course, at its extreme, this process of disaggregation of the State affects also its monopoly of coercion, so that violence accompanies social confrontations.

Guillermo O'Donnell has lucidly shown how this praetorianization of Latin American politics has led to a social "impasse" in which no sector has stable domination. The way out of this impasse has been "the bureaucratic-authoritarian State, which is a system of political and economic exclusion of the popular sector and which emerges after a substantial degree of industrialization has been achieved, and also after and to a large extent as a consequence of substantial political activation of the popular sector."[13] The popular sector is excluded by abolishing its channels of participation and by controlling its organization. The bureaucratic-authoritarian state is open to other corporations, the military, in some cases the Church, and an entrepreneurial bourgeoisie, partly connected with international capital and partly protected from it by its association with the state and its enjoyment of a system of privileges and shields. This interpenetration combined with the exclusion of the popular sector is so idiosyncratic that authors such as O'Donnell have come to think of it as a special type of corporatism.

Of course, when these bureaucratic-authoritarian regimes founder and are replaced by liberal democracies, as is happening in the present processes of transition to democracy in Latin America, the previously favored groups struggle to retain as much as possible of their privileges, competing hard with the popular sector as it reenters the scene. The popular sector's return to the practical field of course overcomes its illegitimate exclusion, but often organizations claiming the privileges that the populist ideology ascribe to them reactivate corporatism.

Corporatist pressures are an important factor underlying the prevalence in Latin America of two schemes of distribution of political power. According to the first model, a cyclic instability generally exists during populist periods, praetorian, authoritarian, and sometimes liberal democratic periods, which coincides with economic cycles of expansion and retraction allowing different corporative sectors to have, in succession, access to power and to privileges, later curtailed but not altogether abolished. The second scheme exists in *conditioned democracies* that achieve stability as a result of a sort of enduring truce with corporative powers, resulting in the preservation of privileges and a limitation on the full working of the democratic mechanisms of broad public discussion, ample and alert public participation and representation, and complete independence of congress and the judiciary.

Corporatism, Popular Participation, and Political Parties

A Conception of a Deliberate Democracy

This discussion of the rough panorama of corporatism in Latin America is necessary to advance the first premise of my argument: that the main obstacle to be overcome by the process of transition to a consolidated democracy in Latin American countries is the interpenetration of corporative power relations, remnants of previous populist and authoritarian stages, within the political structure of a liberal democracy.

My second premise requires far less empirical support and appeals to the understanding of the presuppositions of the democratic process: it conceives of democracy as an organization of the process of collective discussion about the right standards on which to organize public life. It assumes that the democratic process so conceived, insofar as it respects some structural requirements of the process of deliberation and decision making, enjoys some epistemological reliability, its internal mechanisms generating an inherent tendency toward impartiality that is the mark of moral validity in intersubjective issues.[14] The premise asserts that the strengthening of the working of democracy against corporative powers requires the broadening of direct popular participation in decision making and control of governmental action, perfecting the mechanisms of representation, and strengthening political parties, which are themselves internally democratic and open, disciplined, and ideologically defined.

This view of democracy presupposes that individuals—who are basically moral persons—are its natural agents and that the freedom and quality of their intervention in the democratic process should be preserved and expanded, which is not the case when corporations intermediate. Besides, this conception of democracy as a regimentation of moral discourse presupposes that the primary objects of decision in the democratic process are, not *crude interests, but principles* that legitimize a certain balance of interests impartially. Therefore, corporations that bring people together around common interests rather than around moral views about how to deal with interests cannot be the protagonists of the democratic process.

Corporations prosper insofar as democracy departs more than is necessary from the structures of the original practice of moral discourse so that public debate grows restricted and debased, the power of the participants to influence decisions becomes unequal, and participation of the interested people narrows and weakens.

Popular Participation

Therefore, to strengthen the democratic power of common citizens against that of corporations, it is crucial to broaden and to deepen popular participation in discussion and decision. I believe that even the imposition of obligatory voting is justified as a piece of legitimate paternalism, given the problem that exists when many individuals in some sectors of society fail to vote because they are unaware of like-minded otheres, are not organized, and believe most individuals votes are of no account.[15] Another factor to consider is that the mechanisms of representation necessary in large and complex societies are prone to subversion by corporative power because representatives are subject to corruption, often blind to the interest of the people they represent when faced by the interests noisily voiced by corporations, and because the people represented are apathetic. Therefore, it is essential to widen the ways of *direct* participation of the people whose interests are at stake, by general procedures such as plebiscites or popular consultations, or by decentralizing decisions into smaller ambits in which the people concerned can affect them.

José Nun says rightly that one way to channel corporative power is to confront it with a *democratic unity* articulated through multiple forms of direct or participative democracy, which should weaken the power of elites.[16] Making the same argument primarily in reference to business corporations, Benjamin Barber asserts:

> If the corporation is not to defeat democracy, then democracy must defeat the corporation—which is to say that the curbing of monopoly and the transformation of corporatism is a political, not an economic task. Democracy proclaims priority of the political over the economic, the modern corporation rebuts that claim by its very existence. But unitary democracy [meaning one which seeks consensus by process of a cohesive identification with the community] is too easily assimilated to the unitary aspects of corporatism, with possible results that can only be called Fascistic. And liberal democracy is too vulnerable—its citizens too passive and its ideas of freedom and individualism too illusory—to recognize, let alone to battle with the mammoth modern corporation that has assumed the identity and ideology of the traditional family firm. Strong democracy (that is participative democracy) has no qualms about inventing and transforming society in the name of a democratically achieved vision and it may be able to engage the multinational corporation in a meaningful struggle. Yet the corporate society and the corporate mentality stand in the way of the idea of active citizenship that is indispensable to strong democracy.[17]

Additionally, direct participation of the population in the decisions that affect them may tend to diminish the social tensions associated with the so-called "crisis of democracy" and corporative struggles. In opposition to the recommendation of the Trilateral Commission that such crises should be countered by restraint of discussion and participation,[18] and faithful to the idea pungently expressed by Al Smith that "the evils of democracy are cured with more democracy," I think[19] that the broadening of direct participation operates as an escape valve for social pressures and helps limit them insofar as people acquire consciousness of the scarcity of the resources available to satisfy competing demands.

The Role of Political Parties

The vision of democracy as a regimented modality of discussion about moral principles in order to regulate conflicts allows us to qualify the liberal rejection of any intermediaries between the individual and the state; it is obvious that an exception is constituted by organizations that bring together people, not on the basis of crude interests, but of principles, ideologies, and moral outlooks. These are *political parties* when they are conceived of as the bearers of programs about the organization of society based on fundamental principles of political morality. They are indispensable in a modern and large society, not only because they train professional politicians who profess those principles and purport to put them in practice if duly elected, but because they exempt people from justifying their vote before each other on the basis of principles; it is enough to vote for a party that organizes its proposals on the basis of public and general principles.

Political parties are the main antibodies protecting democratic health against corporative power. Their reasons for being are exactly antithetic: to represent some particular interests in the case of corporations, and to defend principles that legitimate certain *composition* of interests from an impartial viewpoint, in the case of political parties. Therefore an inverse relation exists between their respective strengths. Juan Carlos Portantiero is acute on how a situation of inflation leads to, and is obviously caused by, a displacement of political parties by corporations:

> Perhaps the most evident institutional effect of inflationary practices consists in the perverse dialectics for democratic stability which it establishes between corporations and parties. Carrying on the hypothesis further away, we would say that, in a vicious circle which reproduces itself, the relation between strong corporations and a weak system of parties, the institutional cause of inflation, is in its turn producer of the ungovernability of the social mechanism of accumulation insofar as it blocks the possibility of elaborating consensus and replacing it by perverse and momentary equilibria.[20]

The Centrality of Parliament

The deterioration of the role of political parties in favor of corporations also involves the erosion of the importance of the natural scene of those parties: parliament. Corporations naturally prefer to exert pressures and achieve agreements in the quiet of offices than in the noisy pluralistic and more public parliamentary corridors. Of course, the administration tends to follow suit, preserving some of the practices inherited from previous authoritarian governments (for instance, the Argentinean Central Bank has powers equivalent to those that the Constitution of the country grants to the National Congress, e.g., the power to concede special lines of credit, which amount to subsidies). Of course these powers that the administration takes from parliament go with a vengeance: they put them in the hands of corporativist pressures, without the shield of a worked-out consensus with other political sectors.

However, even though the fortifying of political parties and of the parliamentary institutions contributes to protecting the democratic system from corporative power, this remains true only insofar as political parties and parliamentary bodies do not transform themselves into other corporations, developing elites with distinctive interests and prone to compromise with those of traditional corporative groups. This change occurs when parties weaken their ideological commitment, do not promote debates on essential questions of political morality, block channels of participation, operate through methods of patronage and clientelism, and resort to personalism and "*caudillism*." This situation is then reflected in parliament, by a lack of representativeness, by a discourse both ideologically vacuous and detached from the experiences and interests of the people represented, and by a general appearance of opacity and self-service.

For that reason, the strengthening of the political parties and parliament to contain corporative power requires the opening of parties to broad popular participation, the promotion of permanent political debates within them, the perfection of the internal democratic mechanism for choosing party authorities and candidates, and the openness of the management of funds. The electoral system must also combine the needs for party cohesion and ideological identity with the need for the elector to have more direct connection with the individual deputies (instead of voting for a list most of whose members are unknown.) A mixed electoral system of some sort may satisfy both needs (for instance, proportional representation with some way to express preference for or rejection of some candidates). Parliamentary procedures should also combine party discipline with a degree of autonomy of individual deputies.

Strong Democracy and Presidentialism

Methodological Remarks

After stating my first premise, that corporative political power is one of the greatest obstacles to the consolidation of democracy in Latin America, and the second, that two of the most important contributive factors to the containment of corporatism are the broadening and deepening of popular participation in decisions and control, and the strengthening of participative and ideologically committed political parties and parliamentary bodies (what, following Barber, may be deemed "strong democracy"), I am ready to defend my last two-fold premise: that strong democracy is functionally incompatible with the extreme forms of presidentialism typical of Latin American constitutions, and that when presidentialism is not accompanied by limited or conditioned forms of democracy, tensions are generated that often lead to the breakdown of the institutional system.

Before arguing for this premise, I must comment on a methodological point of great importance. There is a longstanding disagreement among philosophers, jurists, sociologists, and political scientists about the capacity of law and institutional design to influence social changes and to effect patterns of social behavior. In the field of law this disagreement can be illustrated with the paradigmatic position of two great jurists: Friedrich Karl von Savigny and Jeremy Bentham. Savigny professed a historicist conception of law, according to which the true law is found and not made; it is found in the spirit of the prople and in social customs; legislation and institutional design should be extremely cautious and follow, not promote social development. Bentham, a fervent believer in law as an instrument of social engineering, devoted his life to the writing of codes for different nations; his preaching influenced the modern conception of Parliament as an active body through which legislation can achieve social reforms.[21] In the field of political science, basically the same disagreement exists: there are currents of thought that O'Donnell[22] calls "societalist," in part influenced by Marxist assumptions that, according to him, "deny or ignore the specificity of the problem of the state as a societal factor endowed with varying but rarely insignificant, capabilities for autonomous impulse and initiative;" at the other exreme, there are "'politicist' conceptions which ascribe to the state a disproportionate weight in the causation of observed and recommended social changes." Truth seems to be here between the extremes, since it is undeniable both that the law and institutional design have on many occasions considerable impact on social developments, and that society is not a malleable material that adapts plastically to deliberate legislation, subject as it is to causal factors other than the legal.

The very subject of my last premise seems to prove the above eclectic methodological position. On the other hand, the way in which it was stated left room for the intervention of other factors, such as cultural ones, beside the legal and political. Even when true that strong democracy is contributive to the containment of corporative power, a limited democracy does not always lead to corporatism and hence to conditioned democracy in the Latin American way (this is obviously true in the case of the United States where the power of corporations is a complex phenomenon not assimilable to Latin American corporatism). On the other hand, the adoption of the presidentialist system of government is undoubtedly correlated, when conjoined with some conditions to be studied, with the recurrence of specific social effects that lead to institutional disruptions.

In this respect a study by Prof. Fred W. Riggs, prefaced by the following remark, is extremely revealing:

> One starting point for analysis might be in the proposition that some 33 Third World countries (but none in the First or Second) have adopted presidentialist constitutions. Almost universally these polities have endured disruptive catastrophes usually in the form of one or more coups d'etat, whereby conspiratorial groups of military officers seize power, suspend the constitution, displace elected officials, impose martial law and promote authoritarian rule: recent examples in Korea, South Vietnam, Liberia, and many Latin American countries come to mind. . . . By contrast, almost two-thirds of the Third World countries which have adopted parliamentary constitutions, usually based upon British and

French models have maintained their regimes and avoided the disruptions typical of all American-type systems.'[23]

Preconditions of a Stable Presidential System

Riggs undertakes to explain this connection between presidentialism and instability in Third World countries, contrasting it with the only stable presidentialist democracy, by taking into account, not environmental or contextual features, but systematic ones, that is, features of the institutional design and practices that he deems "paraconstitutional," because they are not written in the Constitution. Riggs mentions several problems of a presidentialist regime—executive–legislative confrontations, paralysis of the assembly, weakness of the party system, and the politics of the court—that have led to collapse in more than 30 such regimes outside the United States. He analyzes a number of paraconstitutional variables that explain the stability of the one and the instability of the others. Let us mention first those variables that have a direct connection with the existence of a strong democracy, as characterized in the previous section.

Riggs refers to different factors that determine the tendency for political parties to be weak and to be required to be so for the presidential system to work smoothly. One is that parties are difficult to organize and perpetuate in a cohesive way, as they must try to form coalitions prior to the elections in order to have some change of forming a majority; in a parliamentary system parties can go to elections supporting well-defined programs and try to form coalitions in parliament itself after the elections are over. A second factor (which allows presidentialism to work in the United States and involves a weakening of parties) is the lack of party discipline, which, according to Riggs, may be "a necessary condition for the success of a presidentialist regime, whereas if party discipline were enforced, the capacity of government to govern would be severely impaired whenever the president belonged to one party and the opposition party had a congressional majority." This factor is connected with another paraconstitutional feature in the United States, the electoral system based on uninominal constituencies, which affects party discipline, especially insofar as it combines with a decentralized pattern of party organization.

Another factor that weakens political parties within a presidentialist system is the effect on them of defeat in elections; many of the nonpolitical functions that parties perform in a parliamentary system cannot be carried out in a presidentialist one because parties are not tied to a more or less stable representation in Parliament, but are largely affected by the fate of their presidential candidates; when they lose, there are few incentives to remain faithful to the party. Linked to this element is another noted by Riggs. Because parties in a presidential system cannot be ideologically committed but must present broad stances and make many compromises to win support for their presidential candidates from many social sectors, they awaken little enthusiasm in voters, most of whom do not identify themselves with any party but just choose the lesser evil. In sum, the presidential system faces the following dilemma with regard to political parties. Either the parties become weaker and weaker as a result of the nature of political competition under this system—which, given some other social and cultural conditions, may make ample room for the corporations' exercise of their political muscle; or else, if some other factors operate to preserve the parties' strength, as in Argentina, they help create the tensions that are typical of the presidentialist system, blockages between the powers, exhaustion of the figure of the president, etc., which will be commented on below.

The other variable that marks the U.S. system is directly connected with the above characterization of a strong democracy: that is popular participation, particularly with the propensity to vote. Riggs is explicit about this point:

> One of the limitations of a presidentialist system of government appears to be voter apathy. Despite its long history and the apparent commitment of Americans to representative democracy, voting turnout is notably less in the United States than in virtually all parliamentary governments. We normally assume, of course, that popular participation in elections is necessary for the health of democratic institutions. However, sad to say, a low voter turnout seems to be a cost entailed by various para-constitutional aspects of a presidential system. In addition, it could even be a para-constitutional feature.... The higher the level of popular participation in voting, the greater would be the contradiction between the interests of the voting majority. The presidentialist system, therefore, works most smoothly when voting participation remains fairly low.... A conspicuous reason for the skewed distribution of voters can be found in the substance of a party platform. In order to secure the support of a majority of voters, a majority required by the arithmetic of a winner-take-all presidential competition—these platforms have to take ambiguous stands on many issues that divide public opinion. But such issues are also likely to attract the greatest interest especially of poor people.... The price for high voter turnout is lively and divisive political controversy—whereas low voter turnout is linked to apathy and indifference.... To put the negative case, mass participation is less threatening to the survival of parliamentary than of presidentialist regimes.[24]

This comment underscores a point of great importance to the comparative study of the United States' presidential system and some unsuccessful ones, such as the Argentine. In the United States the low voting turnout has a feedback effect; presidential candidates address themselves to potential voters, taking into account their common interests (possibly contradictory to those of most nonvoters) in general and vague terms that evade the possible differences; the vagueness has little appeal to nonvoters who have no reason to choose among them and who, anyway, undergo a typical "prisoner's dilemma" kind of reasoning, balancing the cost of voting against the negligible difference a vote will make. By contrast, in Argentina, for instance, a 1912 law introduced obligatory voting, which since 1916 has more than trebled the voting turnout in comparison with elections held under voluntary voting. This indicated that the middle class, mainly through Peronism, participated actively in the electoral process; those parties were at different times the only winners of free elections, permanently displacing the conservative parties that held power before 1916. Although candidates tend to be vague in their proposals and to compromise to get wider bases of support, a varying interest and even enthusiasm are preserved due in part to emotional factors, such as those involved in the Peronist–antiPeronist controversy. Rigg's suggestion about the threatening aspect of high levels of participation in a presidentialist system seems to be confirmed by the considerable political stability in Argentina prior to 1916 and the extreme instability afterward without obligatory voting. Obviously, those displaced by the results of massive voting sought other ways of acceding to power. I am not implying here, of course, that massive electoral participation is the only or even the main cause of political instability in a country such as Argentina; many other factors combine to provoke it. My only suggestion is that given certain additional circumstances, high levels of popular participation in the democratic process may contribute to that instability.

The Dysfunctionalities of Presidentialism

In other words, the two features characteristic of democracy that serve to defend it against the phenomenon of corporatism (that has arisen in Latin America due to different and complex factors) are absent in the most successful presidentialist systems in the world and there are reasons to connect their absence with its success. But the existence of strong parties and ample popular participation has the potential for the functional difficulties that are currently ascribed to the presidentialist system in Latin America.

In the first place, the presidential system of government works, as Juan Linz says, as a zero-sum game,[25] in which all that one party gains the other loses. The parties are trapped in a dynamics of confrontation for the goal of the Presidency, an indivisible position that, for a fixed and usually long period of time, controls an enormous amount of power, including that of filling innumerable public positions. This dynamic pits each party against the others, in a savage competition, for power, which may even lead to heavy bloodshed as it did in Columbia 30 years ago. These circumstances are not surprising given the fact that a big political party needs access to power to maintain its cadres of professional politicians; two or three presidential terms outside the main center of power may well be fatal for the preservation of the party.

Second, the presidential system divides the expression of popular sovereignty between the president and parliament, each of whom has a sort of veto power over some decisions of the other. When different political parties control the parliament and the presidency (a situation usually reflecting majorities that varied through time) the parties' dynamics of confrontation is mirrored in the relation between the powers of the state, leading to fights and stalemates. The United States avoids this danger as a result, as I said, to the weakness of the parties and the electoral system; the President is able to collect majorities outside the limits of his own party and to govern even when his party is the minority one in either or both of Houses of Congress. The situation is quite different in countries such as Argentina in which the traditional strength of the parties is enhanced by the discipline promoted by proportional representational. In that country several important initiatives of the present national government of the Radical Party were blocked or delayed by the opposition parties, not always by a majoritarian vote, but by parliamentary maneuvers, such as withholding a "quorum" for a session, which are sometimes addressed to obtaining unrelated advantages. The Peronist administration of the Provinces suffered the same legislative blockages. Of course, these confrontations between administration and Parliament are dangerous because in a presidentialist system the latter has no direct or indirect power to influence the course of the administration, thus the antagonism leads to complete stalemate.

In the third place, even when the parties are not seriously antagonistic, the presidential system makes it very difficult for them to collaborate in the same government, as is sometimes required in a national crisis, by an internal or external war, or by the threats of corporative power. If the main parties support the same candidate, the working of the system is affected as there is no real opposition and no prospect of a genuine alternative. If, on the other hand, the president who represents one party invites others to collaborate in his cabinet, the vote of the people who favored one party against the others seems somehow neutralized.

In the fourth place, the confrontation between the parties often leads to the political exhaustion of the President's credibility and popularity long before the expiration of his term, which usually coincides with the point of retraction of the economic cycles of expansion and retraction to which Latin American countries have long been subject. The rigidity of the term of the government in the Presidential system means the political crisis cannot be vented through an escape valve. The President often reaches a point at which, though he still has an enormous set of formal powers, he has lost credibility, popularity, and parliamentary support. The only way to replace him, other than through his voluntary resignation, would be through impeachment. Impeachments are all but impossible to carry out; they require an accusation of misconduct and a qualified majority, which implies the support of the President's party, not usually willing to commit suicide. The President himself is not generally inclined to resign; he feels that he has a mandate for the whole period and does not want to become a historical failure. In Argentina this situation occurred in 1976; several people thought that the coup could have been avoided, or at least delayed, if Isabel Peron had been removed by resignation or impeachment, or if there had been another system of government, under which she could have been confined as head of state to more circumscribed functions and an acceptable head of government appointed.

In this argument I have tried to support my third premise that the elements that may make democracy strong against corporatist pressures—wide popular participation and ideologically defined, disciplined, and broadly participative political parties—are ill suited to a presidentialist system because they generate tensions difficult to handle within it and they aggravate its inherent difficulties.

Conclusion: Toward a More Parliamentary System of Government for Latin America

My reasoning has had the following course: one of the main challenges facing the process of transition to a full consolidated democracy in Latin America is the need to overcome the entrenched network of power relations and privileges established by different corporations during earlier periods; corporations seek to preserve these power relations and privileges in the transition, generating distortions and crises, such as that provoked by inflation, that create pressures on the democratic system.

The best means to counter this corporative power is to recover a sense of a polity governed by universal and impersonal principles chosen in a process of public justification and dialogue by individual citizens, who, unidentified with any particular interests, preserve the capacity of adopting different ones. In practical terms, this requires the promotion of broad popular participation in voting, discussion, and direct decisions, and political parties organized on the basis of principles and programs, with active and participative members and with an internal democracy whose results are enforced in a disciplined way. But this kind of a strong democracy is functionally incompatible with a presidentialist system of government, which tends to weaken political parties; further, even if this weakening does not occur for diverse historical and cultural factors, the difficulties inherent in the presidentialist system—the erosion of the presidential figure, blockages between powers, the difficulties of forming coalitions—are serious and dangerous threats to the stability of the system.

This reasoning leads to an obvious conclusion: the presidentialist system of government, in Latin American conditions that include the phenomenon of corporatism, is an obstacle to the consolidation of democratic institutions. The transition to democracy would be considerably facilitated by constitutional reforms that incorporate parliamentary mechanisms.

Despite the setbacks mentioned above, many people and groups are deeply attached to the presidential system of government in Latin America. Some on the right argue for it on the basis of tradition and the widespread inclination to seek strong leaders, supposedly embedded in the Hispanic mentality. I think that these arguments are not serious enough; traditions are not above criticisms and have no automatic value, particularly when they lead to obviously evil results over a long stretch of history. It is also fair to say that the *côup d'état* is more of a tradition in Latin America than is the presidential system. As for the alleged Hispanic inclination for strong leaders, this would be in any case something to counteract institutionally rather than promote; further it is a rather dubious postulate given the easy adaptation of Spain, for example, to a parliamentary system after 40 years of a *caudillo's* rule, and the similar searches for strong leaders in the past by other nations with different traditions.

More serious is the argument of some conservatives that a parliamentary or mixed system of government would lead to unstable administrations in Latin America, given the climate of economic crisis, social strife, and political tensions. The answer to this argument is that there are mechanisms, e.g., the constructive vote of no-confidence, that considerably attenuate the risk of the collapse of governments, as has been shown in Germany and Spain. Besides, and more importantly, very often the circumstances that lead to a change of government in a parliamentary system are the same that in a presidential system lead to the exhausting of the presidential figure, to a stalemate between the administration and parliament, and to a hard confrontation between the parties, all of which often create the vacuum filled by corporative power, indirectly or through military rule.

The left also defends the presidential system. Recently the Brazilian Roberto Mangabeira Unger argued for the preservation of the presidential system in his country with some important modifications: the provision of power to the President to dissolve Congress and of power to Congress to call for a new presidential election.[26] The kernel of his argument was that only the presidential candidate is apt to break the network of power binding conservative party leaders and to mobilize the masses after a program of structural transformation. But this argument touches precisely on the main weakness of the presidential system: if there is a wide consensus on specific program and a certain man or group to carry it on, any system would work; the presidential one would only add the risk of abuses against minorities. The problem occurs when, as often happens in Latin America, there is no such a consensus. The presidential system is the least likely to promote its formation; on the contrary, it promotes dissent, even between parties with similar views, because of the struggle for the presidency. If a president with a narrow electoral base tries to enforce a program of deep structural transformation, as president Salvador Allende tried to do in Chile, he is liable to be confronted by powerful forces of the opposition and conservative groups. As Arend Lijphart has argued, a parliamentary system is more suited to govern societies in which no definite majorities exist in support of a program and a consensus has to be worked out.[27] I envisage that, for instance, in Argentina no program of deep structural transformation could be carried out without the support of the two majority parties that confront the corporative pressures maintaining the status quo, and that combined support is impossible to obtain within a presidential system. On the other hand, the progressive sector of both parties may well reach an agreement in Parliament to support a program of transformation through a collaborative government, if the struggle for the Presidency ceases.

Another possibility is a dynamic mixed system, which could both absorb some of the advantages of presidentialism without producing a deep break with tradition and eliminate its main dysfunctions.[28] A mixed system of government is one that preserves a popular elected president and divides executive functions between him, a prime minister, and his cabinet, and gives parliament some responsibility. Mixed systems can be graded along a continuum depending on the extent of the powers of the president *vis-à-vis* those of the prime minister and the degree of intervention of parliament in the formation of government.

It is possible to conceive of a *dynamic* mixed system in which the corporative real powers of the president and the prime minister would vary according to factors such as the support that the president has in parliament and in the electorate at large, the cohesiveness of his party, his personality, etc. This dynamic mixed system could be achieved if the elected president were assigned only circumscribed powers (to dissolve the lower house of parliament, to have some veto of the laws, to appoint the high nonpolitical staff of the state—judges, ambassadors and generals), and if he had discretion to appoint and remove the chief of government. This chief of government could also be censured, with some restrictions, by the lower house. This means that a president with a majority in the House of Representatives or in the electorate, despite the fact that the prime minister would control the normal functions of government, would have strong control over the main policies of government, otherwise, he would remove the prime minister.

On the other hand, if the president lost the majority support of the lower house or the electorate, he would have to take a step backward and fulfill his circumscribed but important duties, negotiating with the house the formation of a government that would have a considerable independence from him and would not compromise his responsibility.

This flexible form of government may well be suited to Latin American political-economic cycles. It is likely to have the advantages of a president backed by a strong consensus in part of the cycle, in which case the system would work like a presidential one. This system could also deal with a situation in which either no presidential candidate gathered a wide consensus or, if he did, that consensus later broke down, exhausting the popularity and credibility of the presidential figure and giving control of congress to the opposition. In this eventuality, the system would work like a parliamentary one.

The crucial advantage of a more parliamentary system would be to make the formation itself of government as responsive as possible to the consensus of society. This consensus is better reflected in parliamentary elections than in presidential ones; the former are more frequent, more sensible to the differing hues of public opinion, and more adaptable to the need of the people to express themselves in situations of cirsis. Of course, the mixed system of government allows both parliamentary and presidential elections to influence the formation of the government. That the government reflects flexibly the consensus of society enhances most of the values in the light of which a political system may be appraised. That coincidence between a government and its measures and social consensus deepens the *objective legitimacy* of the political system, under a deliberate conception of democracy; I have elaborated this topic elsewhere.[29] The fact that the government is necessarily backed by popular consensus also strengthens the *stability* of the democratic system; as we have seen, the mixed system allows for the structural transformations necessary to contain corporative power, and provides a more direct barrier against that power, constituted by a more cohesive democratic front. Finally, the correlation between the formation of government and consensus contributes to the *efficacy* of the political system; the lack of political and popular support for a government (evidenced by the last period of Raoul Ricardo Alfonsin's government in Argentina) makes it incapable of effective measures, stymied as it is by blockages, criticisms, and lack of observance of its enactments, which are the consequences of the absence of consensus.

Of course, the inability of the presidential system of government to allow for the expression of a wider consensus than that represented by the party occupying the presidency is itself the main obstacle, in many countries of Latin America, to reaching the broad agreement between the parties necessary to move away from the presidential system.

Notes

1. A different version of this paper was published under the title "Transition to Democracy, Corporatism and Constitutional Reform in Latin America," in the *University of Miami Law Review*, 44 (Sept. 1989), no. 1. I am grateful to Roberto Gargarella for his help in gathering some of the materials used here.

2. For a characterization of process of transition to democracy, see G. O'Donnell, P. Schmitter, and L. Whitehead, eds., *Transitions From Authoritarian Rule* (Baltimore: John Hopkins University Press, 1986); Juan Linz, *The Breakdown of Democratic Regimes* (Baltimore: Johns Hopkins University Press, 1978).

3. See especially the collection James M. Malloy, ed., *Authoritarianism and Corporatism in Latin America* (Pittsburgh: University of Pittsburgh Press, 1977).

4. See Guillermo O'Donnell's "Corporatism and the Question of the State," in James M. Malloy, ed., *Authoritarianism and Corporatism in Latin America* (Pittsburgh: University of Pittsburgh Press, 1977), p. 79.

5. José Nun, "La teoria politica y la transicion democratica," in José Nun and Juan Carlos Portantiero, eds., *Ensayos sobre la transicion democratica en la Argentina* (Buenos Aires: Puntosur Editores, 1987) p. 30.

6. Seymour Lipset, in "Values, Education and Entrepreneurship," F. Klaren and Thomas Bossert, eds., *Promise of Development Theories of Change in Latin America*, (Boulder, CO: Westview Press, 1986).

7. James M. Malloy, "Authoritarianism and Corporatism in Latin America: The Modal Pattern," in James M. Malloy, ed., *Authoritarianism and Corporatism in Latin America* (Pittsburgh: University of Pittsburgh Press, 1977), p. 12.

8. James M. Malloy, note 7, p. 14.

9. Manfred Mols, *La democracìa en America Latina*, trans. Jorge M. Seña (Buenos Aires: 1987), p. 97.

10. See Samuel P. Huntington, *Political Order in Changing Societies* (New Haven: Yale University Press, 1969),

11. See Guillermo O'Donnell, note 3, p. 56.

12. See James M. Malloy, note 6, p. 65.

13. See Guillermo O'Donnell, note 3, p. 60.

14. Carlos S. Nino, *The Ethics of Human Rights* (Oxford: Oxford University Press, 1991.

15. Carlos S. Nino, "El voto obligatorio," in *Segundo dictamen sobre reforma Constitucional del Consejo para la Consolidacion de la Democracia* (Buenos Aires: Editorial Universitaria de Buenos Aires, 1987).

16. See José Nun, note 5, p. 53.

17. Benjamin Barber, *Strong Democracy* (Berkeley: University of California Press, 1984), p. 257.

18. See M. Crozier, S.P. Huntington, and J. Watanuki, *The Crisis of Democracy* (New York: New York University Press, 1975).

19. Carlos S. Nino, "La participacion como remedio a la llamada crisis de la democracia," in *Alfonsin: Discursos sobre el discurso* (Buenos Aires: Editorial Universitaria de Buenos Aires, 1986).

20. Juan Carlos Portantiero, "La crisis de un regimen: una mirada retrospectiva," in the collection cited in note 4, p. 76.

21. See an account of this controversy in Carlos S. Nino, *Introduccion al analisis del derecho* (Buenos Aires: Astrea, 1980).

22. See Guillermo O'Donnell, note 3, pp. 51–52.

23. Fred W. Riggs "The Survival of Presidentialism in America: Para-constitutional Practices," 9 *International Political Science Review* 247, 249 (1988) Spanish version edited by Consejo para la Consolidacion de la Democracia, in *Presidencialismo vs. Parlamenterismo* (Buenos Aires: Editorial Universitaria de Buenos Aires, 1988).

24. Ibid.

25. See Juan Linz, "*La democracia presidencial o parlamentaria: hay alguna diferencia*," Javier Saran, trans. in the collection edited by Consejo para la Consolidacion de la Democracia, *Presidencialismo vs. Parlamentarismo* (Buenos Aires: Editorial Universitaria de Buenos Aires, 1988).

26. Roberto Mangabeira Unger, "La Forma de gobierno que conviene en Brasil," note 24.

27. Arend Lijphart, "Democratizacion y modelos democraticos alternativos," note 24.

28. See further this proposal of the Council for the Consolidation of Democracy (a multipartisan advisory body in questions of structural transformation created by President Alfonsin) in *Segundo Dictamen sobre la Reforma Constitucional del Consejo para la Consolidacion da la Democracia* (Buenos Aires: Editorial Universitaria de Buenos Aires, 1987).

29. See Carlos S. Nino, "Conceptions of Democracy and Institutional Design," in Carlos S. Nino, ed., *Transition to Democracy in Argentina* (New Haven: Yale University Press, forthcoming).

4

Constitutions without Constitutionalism: Reflections on an African Political Paradox

H.W.O. Okoth-Ogendo

In the preface to their book on public law and political change in Kenya, Y.P. Ghai and J.P.W.B. McAuslan (1970) lamented thus:

> There are so many reasons for not writing a book on the public law of an African state, not at least that much of the subject-matter of the book tends to be somewhat ephemeral, as several authors (and publishers) have found to their cost, that a book on such a topic might be thought to require some justification.[1]

Indeed, in the 1960s and 1970s, a number of authors, particularly in Nigeria, Ghana, Uganda, and Zaire, found at the end of their scholarly enquiries into the constitutional law of these states that the subject matter itself was no longer in existence!

Ghai and McAuslan noted that the problem was that most of these early enquiries tended to treat their subject matter simply as an affair of rules. Time was thus spent on the analysis of texts, cases, and whatever relevant laws were available in the statute books. As a result, the outcome of these studies as well as the discipline of constitutional law itself tended to be largely irrelevant to academic inquiry in Africa.

That "irrelevance" is perhaps most clearly evident in the absence of an authoritative or any rigorous analysis, even by social scientists, of the relationship between power and law in Africa. Much of the political science literature was mainly concerned with leadership styles and roles, elections and electoral behavior, political parties and political mobilization, etc., and did not relate these processes to the structural parameters within which they operated. Indeed, if in the decade of the 1960s lawyers tended to treat constitutions as static phenomena, in the decades of the 1970s and 1980s, scholars from other disciplines abandoned any attempt to examine African constitutions on the grounds that they bore but an obscure relation to governance and politics in the continent. But whereas there has been remarkable change in the way legal scholars now look at constitutional systems in Africa,[2] among social scientists in general, academic disregard of constitutions remains the rule rather than the exception.[3]

A number of perspectives have contributed to this distressing lack of interest in African constitutions. The first is primarily ideological and argues that the primary function of *a constitution* is to limit governmental authority and to regulate political processes in the state. This view, whose origin lies in the liberal democratic tradition, forms the backdrop of many arguments among politicians and academics about the "correct" exercise of power in Africa. According to this view, there can be no "constitutional" government unless mechanisms exist within the constitution for the supervision of these functions; further, such mechanisms must be erected on the doctrine of the separation of powers and the principle of limited government, both of which must conform to the theory that *government* itself ought, at all times, to conform to the *rule of law*.[4]

A more important factor alluded to by Ghai and McAuslan is analytical: a totally inadequate conception of law and its relationship to power in Africa. To many scholars, the idea of law still connotes the existence of a determinate rule, founded on some perspective of value (whether individualist or communitarian), that provides a basis for predicting and evaluating authoritative decisions in specified circumstances. Constitutional *law*, concerned entirely (or so it is thought) with decisions that lie in the public domain, is, more than any other body of law, expected to be basic, rational, even *fundamental*, and therefore capable of withstanding pressures generated by the vicissitudes of political life.

Political developments in Africa since Ghana's independence in 1957 have demonstrated repeatedly, however, that not only have constitutions "failed" to regulate the exercise of power, but, devastatingly, they have not become as basic as the analytical tradition scholars predicted: "few African governments have valued them other than as rhetoric."[5]

This situation has led to both a dilemma and a paradox. The dilemma is whether to abandon the study of constitutions altogether on the grounds that no body of *constitutional law or principles of constitutionalism* appears to be developing in Africa, and might well fail to do so; or to continue teaching and theorizing on the utility of constitutional values in the hope that state elites in Africa will eventually internalize and live by them. The paradox lies in the simultaneous existence of what appears as a clear commitment by African political elites to the idea of the constitution and an equally emphatic rejection of the classical or at any rate liberal democratic notion of constitutionalism.

The dilemma is, in my view, inconsequential, even false; the paradox, however, is both sufficiently manifest and intriguing to merit an examination to explain the contemporary patterns of constitutional development in Africa (or lack of them). Such an examination is all the more necessary since the paradox is essentially political, and not evidence as others think, of deliberate disregard of legal or "constitutional" processes stricto sensu.[6]

This chapter examines that paradox, its characteristics, manifestations, and developments over the past 30 years, and its implications for the distribution and exercise of power in Africa. By concentrating on what many have abandoned as a vast graveyard, we may, through a clearer glimpse of the anatomy of emerging forms and conceptions of governance in that continent, free scholars of constitutional jurisprudence from their dilemma.

Constitutions as Organized Power

The analysis of the paradox begins with a simple but important assertion: *all law*, and *constitutional law* in particular, is concerned, not with abstract norms, but with the creation, distribution, exercise, legitimation, effects, and reproduction of *power*; it matters not whether that power lies with the state or in some other organized entity. From this perspective, therefore, the very idea of law, hence of *a constitution as a special body of law*, entails commitment or adherence to a theory of organized power, as appears evident in the historical experience and shared aspirations of all societies. The fact that in some societies the exercise of power has become more predictable, and even legal-rational in Weberian sense,[7] merely records the complexity of the relationship between power and law in different contexts.

A useful model for the analysis of any constitution, therefore, is to regard it as a "power map"[8] on which framers may delineate a wide range of concerns: an application of the Hobbesian concept of "covenant"[9] as in the American constitution; a basic constitutive process, as in the Malawi constitution; a code of conduct to which public behavior should conform, as in the Liberian or French constitutions; a program of social, economic, and political transformations, as in the Ethiopian or Soviet constitutions; an authoritative affirmation of the basis of social, moral, political, or cultural existence, including the ideals toward which the polity is expected to strive, as in the Libyan constitution. The process of *constitution making*, which involves, inter alia, making choices as to which concerns should appear on that map, cannot be regarded as a simple reproduction of some basic principles that particular societies may have found operational. It is, as D. Elazar has noted, an "eminently political act,"[10] which must draw on past experiences and future aspirations. An analysis of the African constitutional paradox must start, therefore, with an examination of the *political origins of the idea of the constitution in the continent.*

The Nature of the Paradox

The precise form in which that paradox, *commitment to the idea of the constitution and rejection of the classical notation of constitutionalism*, has emerged over the last three decades requires a description.

The idea of and the necessity for a constitution appear fully established in the minds of state elites in Africa in at least two important senses. First, the constitution is an act without which the polity can have no legitimate or sovereign existence; it is of no small significance, for example, that the very first article of most African constitutions *declare* that each respective country is *sovereign*. In Africa, the idea that the constitution is "a means to demonstrate the sovereignty of the state" appears quite strong; in that sense, the constitutive value of some form of a constitution remains preeminent. It is notable that very few European and American constitutions make such declaration; sovereignty is assumed as the basis of constitution making.

Second, the idea of the constitution is firmly established as the *basic* law of the state. Since all African independence constitutions provide for some method of change, fundamental alteration, or even total abrogation (e.g., in the constitution of Swaziland 1968), *the notion of a basic law in the African context entails no element of sanctity*. What it does entail is minimum, and perhaps popular observance of the rules contained in the constitution.

The notion that a constitution is important as a basic law in the above sense underlies the amendments, the revisions, and the experimentation with non-Westminster models by civilian governments. When King Sobhuza II of Swaziland abrogated the constitution in 1973, he said that he had come to the conclusion inter alia,

> that the [independence] constitution has failed to provide the machinery for good government and for the maintenance of law and order, [and] that I and my people heartily ... desire to march forward progressively under *our own constitution* guaranteeing peace, order and good government.[11] (emphasis added)

Sobhuza was seeking a basic law more relevant to traditional Swazi values than was the Westminster constitution that brought his country into sovereign status. In 1986, the Sotho King, faced with a military insurrection, proclaimed the need for basic law (Lesotho order 1986)

> to provide for the peace, order and good Government of Lesotho until such time as a new constitution better suited to the needs of the Basotho Nation shall have been agreed.

That law formally repealed the organs of civilian government and substituted for them bodies under the nominal supervision of the King but controlled by the military.

The essence of commitment in the second sense, then, is to an autochthonous (or socially relevant) basic law. Nyerere formulated this essence forcefully as follows:

> We refuse to adopt the institutions of other countries even where they have served those countries well because it is our conditions that have to be served by our institutions. We refuse to put ourselves in a straitjacket of constitutional devices—even of our own making. The constitution of Tanzania must serve the people of Tanzania. We do not intend that the people of Tanzania should serve the constitution.[12]

This search for autochthony involves not only the rejection of external (specifically "western") institutions and constitutional "devices," but, more emphatically, the abandonment of the classical notion that the purposes of constitutions are to limit and control state power, not to facilitate it. A purely instrumental view of the purposes of constitutions, such as Nyerere's, has guided state elites' search for the formal means by which to preserve the integrity of the "constituted polity" without being embroiled in a maze of constitutional law whose function, in classical theory, is to control and supervise constitutionality.

The Origins of the Paradox

The question to ask is how did African states get into this quandary? It is my argument that the answer to that question requires a careful scrutiny of Africa's immediate past history; in particular, an appreciation of a number of historical legacies. The first legacy is the nature of legal (as distinct from constitutional) *order* that many of these states inherited at independence and perpetuated after it. Two characteristics dominated that colonial power and administration. The more visible was its labyrinthine *bureaucracy*; the other was its coercive *orientation*. Indeed, little distinction was normally drawn between the administration of those areas of public policy associated with state coercion, such as the criminal justice system or "public" order, and those that would normally be reserved to the domain of private choice, such as decision making on a subsistence farm; in both areas, control and coercion, not management and persuasion, were the hallmarks of the colonial legal order. Consequently, the sheer presence of state power in public administration, especially in rural Africa, was awesome. Without exception, independence instruments preserved that order intact as the foundation of administration in the postcolonial state; because the colonial judicial service, by and large, had administered this coercive order with Austinian particularity, its perpetuation included a heavy baggage of jurisprudence that was anything but consistent with the lofty values of constitutionalism that the new nations were expected to embrace.

The second legacy, developed fairly deliberately in the terminal phase of colonialism, was a highly fragmented political culture, which sought to institutionalize conflicts and to strengthen centrifugal forces rather than to nurture and cement national unity. Those conflicts and forces, generally organized around ancient claims, accrued rights, future demands, or matters that were peculiarly sensitive to race, religion, economy, and even geography,[13] were *essentially* divisive in character. In consequence, political parties entered the constitutional process as purveyors of irredentist ideologies, not as vehicles for the enhancement of such constitutional values as electoral sovereignty, majoritarian rule, or popular power. Fragmentation was an established style of colonial administration, known in the British sphere as "divide and rule"; in the postcolonial state it enhanced the power of the bureaucracy and gave it complete dominance over public affairs. Indeed, the effective jurisdiction of the civil service bureaucracy in many of these countries soon extended beyond the traditional confines of administration to embrace policy decisions and reformulation. It is in the effectiveness of this bureaucratic machinery, monolithic and totally controlled by the executive branch of government, that part of the reason for the decline of multiparty government and the rise of the dominant (or one)-party state is to be found. The concept of civil service neutrality that African Constitutions in many English-speaking countries provided for was thus a "dead duck" *ab initio*.

The third legacy is the economic power of the state that resulted from the interplay between the legal-bureaucratic order and a fragmented political process. Critics of African economic strategies have noted, with some justification, that the question of whether the state ought to remain the primary instrument of policy and agency in the development process always looms large. Some have even argued that the economic crisis into which the continent is currently plunged is directly related to state activity in the economy.[14]

What is often ignored is that, as in other spheres of public life, independence *expanded* the role of the state. Indeed, colonial relations of production and, in particular, the processes of expropriation and expatriation of surplus value from the colonies to metropolitan centers could have been secured only with heavy reliance on state power exerted through the civil service bureaucracy; the colonial economy was the "managed economy" *par excellence*. The effectiveness with which this strategy worked to "develop" the expatriate sector of the economy at the expense of its indigenous counterpart was clearly understood and even admired by the elites who took over at independence.

The Nature of the Constitutional State and Power Realities

The origin of the paradox also lies in the nature of the state as "constituted" by the independence constitution, which was fundamentally different from anything the colonialists themselves had devised. This was particularly obvious in English-speaking Africa, where the constituted state was based on a remarkable distrust of *centralized* power. That distrust was not founded on any clear philosophy such as, for instance, the *Hobbesian* principle of limited government; it was based almost entirely on the need to *exclude* the state (as a centralized entity) from functions it had exercised before independence.

Two aspects of the constituted state were particularly disturbing. The first was the distribution of power in these constitutions; the second was the clear tension between that distribution and the rest of the legal order. In respect to the first, instead of the highly centralized power structure that the colonial authorities had operated for more than half a century, the constituted state was erected on a fundamentally flawed and fragmented distribution of power.

In the case of English-speaking Africa, that "power map" was based on a severely modified version of the Westminster model, complete with bicameral legislatures, separation of powers, judicial review of legislative and executive action, and a Bill of Rights distilled from the Magna Charta. In the case of French-speaking Africa, that map was based on the principle of constitutional tripartism as developed in the eighteenth century by Montesquieu[15] and incorporated the provisions of the French Revolution of the Rights of Man and the Ctitizen of 1789.

Provisions were made in Mauritius, Kenya, Nigeria, Swaziland, and Zimbabwe, for the separation of powers between the head of State (the President) and the head of government (the Prime Minister), but this arrangement quickly gave way to a hybrid form of presidentialism unknown to western constitutional jurisprudence. Further, it was assumed, even though this was not expressly stated, that the constituted state would operate on a multiparty style of "democracy," an assumption derived from provisions of the Bill of Rights guaranteeing freedom of association.

What was disturbing about the power maps described above was not that they were not "democratic": *in the western liberal sense they were*. It was, first, the *rationale* for them that was the problem. Whereas institutions such as federalism (Nigeria and Uganda), regionalism (Kenya), constitutional monarchy (Swaziland and Lesotho), chieftancy (Zambia and Zimbabwe), and of course Bills of Rights have been used throughout history in appropriate contexts as the primary media for the socialization of politics and power; no such value-specific function was the reason for their presence in independence constitutions.[16] For at least a decase after independence, these institutions *essentially* were operated as mechanisms for the entrenchment of interest that had accrued by reason of the exploitative nature of the colonial process itself.

Having seen the efficiency with which control of state institutions had enabled the colonial elite to convert the "national" economy into *some kind of private estate*, the African elites regarded as sabotage any suggestion that there should be any "withering away" of state power in the domain of public (including economic) affairs. For some of these elites, control of the instrumentalities of state power was the key to development in the postcolonial state.

Another disturbing aspect of the new constitutions was their relation to the rest of the legal order. As the basic *constitutive act* provided for the continuance of the colonial legal order as the residual law of the independent state, it was necessary to ensure that a mechanism was available for the resolution of conflicts between the constitutional order and the rest of the legal order. Invariably the first or second Article of the Independence Constitution declared the former the supreme law of the land and stated that "if any other law is inconsistent with [the] constitution, that other law shall, to the extent of inconsistency, be void." The intriguing thing is that it was the rest of the legal order, not the constitutional order, that offered African elites real power and the bureaucratic machinery with which to exercise it effectively.

In these circumstances it was always tempting to "opt out" of the constitutional order, the more effectively to manipulate the legal order whenever exigencies demanded it. Indeed, the constitutional order often appeared precariously perched on the legal order and the actual power structure, without the creative and rationalizing normativity that Kelsenian positivists would have expected.[17] The potential for subverting the constitutional order through "legitimate" exercise of bureaucrative power was present, *ab initio*, and almost limitless. (It is not in the least surprising that not a single African *military* regime has forgotten to provide for the continuance "with full force and effect" of the legal order even as the constitution was being abrogated.)

The Development of the Paradox

The actual process of "subverting" the constitutional order in the sense suggested above took a number of forms. The most notorious was the *coup d'état* that did not merely involve "opting" out of the *basic law*, but often its total abrogation. Another form was a cavalier disregard of constitutional niceties and processes: the postponement of election results (Lesotho 1970), the declaration of no contest against certain election candidates (Zaire 1983), etc. The more interesting for our analysis was the move by state elites in a number of African countries to *politicize* the constitution, *initially* by declaring it a liability, and subsequently by converting it into an instrument of political warfare.

The Constitution as a Liability

The argument that the independence constitutional order was the state's most serious liability was carried to the public in the rhetoric of the need for rapid economic development. It was argued that a fragmented power structure would pose severe drawbacks to central planning, financial coordination, and the formulation of policies on important matters such as health, education, and agriculture.[18] It was also argued that the constitutional order sought to frustrate the goals of equity and faster delivery of services which the fact of independence, per se, was exposed to facilitate; by focusing mainly on the loci of power, it had failed to resolve the important ideological issue of how to locate people's expectations and aspirations within its compass and permitted the importation of "undesirable political practices alien to and incompatible with the [African] ... way of life."

The last of these arguments, although made most explicitly and forcefully by King Sobhuza II of Swaziland,[19] has been echoed in Tanzania, Zambia, Zimbabwe, Lesotho, Kenya, and the Central African Republic over the last quarter of a century.

But prosecuting that argument under the new constitutions was difficult, not least because of the severe restrictions placed on mechanisms for reconstitution. Much rhetoric was spent on exposing the absurdity of the constitutional order; for example, it was often stated, with some justification, that structuring the appartuses of the state around minority *protection* rather than majority *expectations* was inherently absurd. In Kenya and Zimbabwe, state elites succeeded in convincing "minorities" that the popular will was by no means a dangerous externality. (In Zaire, Malawi, and Zambia, minorities, including opposition parties, were simply harassed into submission.) Once that happened, as it did in Kenya in 1964 and more recently in Zimbabwe, those elites moved swiftly toward the creation of a tidier political and *administrative* landscape by removing all restrictions placed on the ability of the center to change the constitution (amendment procedures et al.!) and by making prolific use of the resulting flexibility.

The Constitution as a Political Instrument

With a tidy landscape before them, state elites then proceeded to insert new devices whose purpose was to recentralize power as it had been under colonial rule. Four main devices were used; the first was the extension of appointive and dismissal authority of the chief executive to all offices in the *public service*: civil,

military, and "constitutional," such as those of judges and attorneys-general; in 1986 Kenya joined Swaziland, Tanzania, Malawi, Nigeria, Zambia, Sudan, Ghana, Gambia, and Sierra Leone, among others, in vesting in the President the power to dismiss that officer. The second was the subjection of political recruitment at all levels (local, municipal, and parliamentary) to strict party sponsorship, the more effectively to monitor commitment to regime values. In a large number of countries including Kenya, Tanzania, Malawi, Zaire, and Zimbabwe, this particular device has led to a rapid transition toward the dominant or one-party state. In Swaziland, King Sobhuza's proclamation of the abrogation of the constitution included dissolving and prohibiting "all political parties and similar bodies that cultivated and bring about disturbances and ill feelings."[20]

The third device was the expansion of the coercive powers of the state by allowing extensive derogation from Bills of Rights wherever these were justiciable. This expansion was usually accomplished by the removal (or weakening) of parliamentary supervision of emergency powers, and then, by so subjective a redefinition of the conditions under which those powers could be invoked that any meaningful inquiry into the bona fides of any particular action was excluded. The fourth, and perhaps most interesting device, was to ensure that the constitutional order conformed to the inherited legal order; this device was often preferred whenever conflicts arose between the provisions of the constiution and those of specific legislation. The most recent use of this device took place in Kenya, where the constitution has now been amended inter alia to reflect the full complement of powers already being exercised by the police under penal and public security legislations.

As these and other devices found their places within the "constitutional" framework, so did the view that the constitutional arena, if properly controlled by the state elite, offered a more efficient and effective environment for the resolution of *political* conflicts than even the party and certainly the electorate at large. Indeed, by translating a *political* option or decision into a *constitutional* device or norm, state elites gained the added advantage of passing on the problem of enforcement or supervision ultimately to the judicial arm of government. A *run to amend the constitution* to deal with a political crisis became increasingly attractive as a method of reestablishing equilibrium within the body politic.

No doubt the original intent behind the desire to "subvert" the constitutional order in any of these ways (at least in the 1960s) was substantially above board. This intent was to redesign the state to a form appropriate to the social conditions of independent Africa.[21] In the event, however, it was not the *state* that was redesigned; it was the colonial power map that was *reconstituted.* In the course of that reconstitution, the constitutional order became not an arbiter in the power process, but a crucial element in political warfare, an instrument of and from the appropriation of power. *The Constitution lost most of its claim to being the basic law* of the land, that arbiter in the power process. State elites then revised the domain of administrative law so as to reserve to themselves full and unfettered discretion over public affairs; this was done, inter alia, by strengthening all aspects of public order law: security, meetings, police powers, processions and marches, and aspects of licensing. Thus, the coercive administrative law of the legal order continued to be strengthened even as the essence of constitutionalism was being drained from the reconstitution.

Reconstituted States

Three aspects of the reconstitutions of most African states stand out as the clearest evidence of that result. The first is the emergence and predominance of a form of imperial presidentialism, the second is a perceptible shrinkage of the political arena, and the third is the preeminence of discretion as the basis of "constitutional" power.

The Rise of the Imperial Presidency

The fusion of executive power in a *single individual* was perhaps inevitable in the historical process of redesigning the state in Africa. The fact that state elites chose to concentrate almost exclusively on the issue of power, per se, has produced a new style and mode of leadership unprecedented in contemporary history. The Nigerian writer Chinua Achebe has likened this to that of the "late-flowering medieval monarchs."[22] What I find most striking, however, is its *imperial*, not its *medieval*, character; for unlike the medieval monarchs of Europe, the African presidents do not claim any *divine* right to rule, do not demand obsequiousness from the public at large, and are, at least in point of theory, *constitutionally* subject to popular accreditation. However, the indices of imperium, the exclusive constitutional right to direct the affairs of state, are quite clear.

The first of these is the supremacy of the office of the President over all organs of government. The semblance of separation of powers that remains is, at best, of administrative significance only; indeed, the extent of administrative autonomy, if any, of the legislature or judiciary vis-à-vis the office of the President varies, in some countries, with the specific matter at issue. Although supremacy of the presidency over the legislature is usually indirect (the latter is not constituted by the former), its effectiveness is excercised through the (dominant) political party.

The second index is the immunity of the President from the legal process, civil and criminal, as long as he remains in office. There are two consequences of this immunity. The purpose, as Nwabueze has pointed out, is the protection of the dignity of the office rather than of the holder per se.[23] What is interesting, however, is the political interpretation that state elites in Africa have placed on this immunity: a President is "above" the law. He cannot be sued, nor can his decisions be challenged, in court or elsewhere. The second consequence is the protection of the President against abuse, slander, and other forms of disparagement; here the general approach both in law and practice has been that if a President is thus "above" the law, he should not be subjected to the indignity of having to seek personal redress in his own courts. Consequently, the ordinary law of libel and slander is irrelevant. The practice is to "criminalize" any utterance or conduct deemed to be disparaging to the reputation of the presidency or to its occupant; for this purpose most liberal use has been made of public order law, especially the inherited penal codes. Thus, the immunity of a President is safeguarded, and all criticism, whether legitimate or not, is censored.

The third index of *imperium* is the indefinite eligibility of a President for reelection; the reasons for it are several. The first has to do with the mystique and sanctity surrounding the public image of the *founder* president; although such figures are now few and far between, this attitude seems to have passed on to second or even third generation civilian and military leaders. The second reason involves elite perceptions of public expectations of leadership; as early as 1966, for example, the office of the President in Kenya was arguing that to be understood by the people, government must be personalized in one individual who is easily accessible, sympathetic, understanding, and authoritative.[24] An essential element of that personalization was the individual's continuity in office.

The third reason inheres in the argument that political and economic stability requires continuity in leadership *at the top.* The institutions do not matter as much as those who are ultimately responsible for the destiny of public affairs. Provisions limiting the tenure of office of the President have never been, nor are they likely to be, successful.

The fourth index of *imperium* is the high degree of paranoia that tends to surround the *exercise* of executive power in Africa, a special characteristic of military regimes, but not limited to them. This paranoia is perhaps most visible in the high attrition rate found among political functionaries and public service bureaucrats in many governments. This potential for attrition, a technique usually orchestrated from the presidency, has several important consequences: it creates tremendous uncertainty within the channels through which presidential power is exercised; it generates a concern for survival within those channels that translates easily into sycophantic behavior toward the presidency; and it identifies the presidency as the only source of final redress even for the simplest of problems. These consequences may ensure a relatively high degree of loyalty to the presidency and its occupant, but they are also the reasons why the presidency in Africa usually tends to "overreach" itself, both in political decisions and in public utterances.

The Shrinking Political Arena

The arena of politics in any country ought, at least in theory, to be open to any citizen, especially if qualified, under the law, to vote. The mechanisms for participation in that arena may vary, but it is generally accepted in all known political systems that the most important is the *political party.* The argument is that only through political parties can citizens effectively communicate their demands, articulate their interests, recruit persons qualified for elite roles including that of the chief executive, and, in general, be mobilized into action or socialized.[25] In Africa, however, the reconstitutions have recast the political parties into different kinds of instruments; instead of expanding the arena of politics in any or all of the above ways, political parties have been used to shrink it.[26]

The specific means by which this shrinkage has occurred in Tanzania, Kenya, Malawi, and almost everywhere else in Africa where parties are still an active ingredient in the political arena, are several. The primary means, however, has been through constitutional and other legal instruments that confer supremacy in matters of public policy on a single political party; the most comprehensive statement is found in Article 3 of the constitution of the United Republic of Tanzania, 1977. Seventeen Article 3 of the 1984 Constitution appears to have relaxed somewhat this comprehensive submission of the Constitution to the Party by providing, inter alia, that the party exercises its jurisdiction in accordance also, with the state constitution. Although other countries' constitutions provide merely for the existence of one political party, the effect in the political arena has been the same: once party control is appropriated by a specific elite, leadership roles will, popular sentiment notwithstanding, continue to circulate among its members until another elite takes over.

When, as often happens in one-party presidencies, the Chief Executive is also the *de jure* (or de facto) leader of the Party, the political arena may shrink even further. Skillful manipulation of the Party machinery can easily shift its entire mandate to the presidency. The presidency, rather than the Party of the citizenry at large, then becomes the instrument to define the ideology of the state, to effect disciplinary control of party rank and file, to initiate or terminate public debate on important matters of national policy, and to recruit persons considered qualified for the performance of elite roles. In countries where the Party also controls other pressure groups such as women's organizations, trade unions, or employers' associations, the shrinkage can be debilitating, affiliation implying absorption.

This power of the Party excludes the citizenry at large from any meaningful control over the conduct of government; with respect to the legislature, that shrinkage means that the electorate may be totally excluded from the determination of parliamentary (or similar assembly) membership or be subjected to a carefully orchestrated routine for that purpose. In the one-party presidencies, party membership has become essential for entry into and for maintenance of legislative roles at local and national levels; these roles can be terminated through simple expulsion from the Party. The electorate is then faced with the task, *under the supervision of the Party*, of finding a replacement. This is clearly a contest the electorate cannot win.

Discretion as the Basis of Power

The most liberal of jurists will concede that though the essence of constitutionalism may lie in the limitation of arbitrary power, "the limiting of government ... is not to be the weakening of it. The problem is to maintain a proper balance between power and law."[27]

The rise of an imperial presidency and the shrinkage of the political arena as a result of the entry of political parties in the constitutional process both point to the fact that in Africa, the issue of power and law has been resolved, for the time at least, in favor of power. Therefore the *legal* basis of executive power (if this must be found) is to be sought in the domain of administrative law, which, it is worth recalling, was and remains a complex maze of highly structured and coercive instruments. What the reconstitution added to this complex was a degree of discretion that even courts sometimes found difficult to circumscribe. Discretion as a basis of power is most visible in the ideology and operation of national or public security legislation.

The operative concept of national or public security was kept deliberately fuzzy. Such fuzziness is not only an African problem; what is peculiar to Africa is the breadth of that concept in security laws. A typical definition is to be found in Kenya's Preservation of Public Security Act (Cap. 57), which is so generous that one could say that the definition says no more than that "the preservation of public security *means* whatever the authority to invoke security powers says it is."[28] Indeed, courts in some African countries have so decided.

That breadth of definition is perhaps to be expected given the nature of the state in Africa. As J. Boli-Bennett points out, as it is the state that enacts law and determines whether that law confers sufficient power for its purposes, one must expect the state to frame the law in a manner most favorable to its proclivities.[29] With respect to public security law, the more centralized and coercive the state is, the more loosely defined will be the operative concept itself.

The most important point is that in an ever-increasing number of African countries, security powers can be and often are exercised *without* recourse to a declaration of emergency. All that is required in Kenya and Malawi, for example, is for the relevant authority to indicate by gazzette notice that *in his own subjective judgment*, sufficient grounds exist for the exercise of those powers.[30] As long as such a notice is in effect, a whole set of measures, ranging from indefinite detention without trial, restriction of movement including the imposition of curfews, press censorship, to suspension of any legislation (other than the Constitution and the enabling Act itself), may be taken; in practice, gazette notices are never withdrawn. As a result, security powers are permanently available *and* exercisable. An important consequence of this is that the boundaries between security powers, stricto sensu, and ordinary criminal law are often blurred.

Two main grounds have been used to defend this widespread use of discretionary power. The first is symbolic: the national (or public) security claim has a respectable history. Indeed, most constitutional systems and international instruments on human rights consider the power to derogate from provisions guaranteeing fundamental rights and liberties a necessity in conditions of public emergency.[31] Therefore, in retaining and strengthening this power, African elites have simply preserved a well-tested instrument. The second defense argues that as the constitution expressly permits the exercise of security powers, elites can regard that exercise as *legitimate*, however arbitrary and unnecessary it may be in particular circumstances.

The formalism with which the need for security powers is argued to the public accords well with their primary function: the strengthening of the presidency at the expense of other organs of government. Indeed, often the presidency has evaded or bypassed other branches of government by simply throwing a "security" blanket over a particular issue.

The Military and the Idea of Constitutionalism

The preceding analysis suggests that in many parts of Africa, the idea of the constitution clearly *excludes* the notion of a basic (or fundamental) law other than in a purely "constitutive" sense. Civilian regimes have reached that position in fact or in law, and more recent regimes (Zimbabwe) appear to be heading in the same direction. We will complete our analysis by looking briefly at the emerging attitude of military regimes to the idea of the constitution and constitutionalism.

There can be doubt that the *immediate reason* for the vast majority of military coups in Africa has been the failure of "constitutional" government and the desire "to wipe the political and constitutional slate clear." Some African scholars have been hailed military intervention as a "necessary tonic to decadent constitutionalism."[32] The record of military government in Africa in the last three decades with the occurrences of more than seventy *coups d' état*, does not, in my view, disclose any ground for that optimism. That record indicates only that military regimes consider he *constitutive value* of constitutions important. Virtually every announcement of suspension or abrogation of a constitution after a *coup d' état* in the 1960s was accompanied by commitment to the drawing up of a new one; these commitments were kept in some countries (Ghana, Nigeria, Sierra Leone). In the 1970s and 1980s, military rulers became even more organized; they began to suspend or abrogate only those constitutional provisions that formed the basis of their power: legislative, executive, and judicial powers, and provisions dealing with the protection of fundamental rights. The "constitutive" provisions remained virtually unscathed and survived many of changes in military and civilian government; in Uganda the 1967 document is still recognized as the constitution of the state.

The military attitude to governance appears to be no different from the civilian attitude described above. Military regimes have never been able to avoid the tendency toward an imperial presidential style; indeed, the longer such regimes have clung to power, the stronger has been that tendency. In the second place, many military rulers seem to consider their mission accomplished once they are able to "civilianize" their regimes, and assume the mode and style of those they have replaced; this development has been widespread in central and west Africa. Further, in those instances where military coups have abrogated or suspended the civilian construction, the tendency to promulgate a constitutive instrument similar to that suspended or abrogated remains strong. In short, far from wiping the political and constitutional slate clean, the militiary have only reproduced the basic power structures operated by civilian regimes. While clinging to some notion of the constitution, they have advanced the issue of constitutionalism no further than civilian regimes have.

Some Reflections

This chapter set out to examine the condition of constitutional government in Africa; what we found is a situation *in which only the idea of the constitution* has survived. The most fundamental of the functions of a constitution, at least in liberal democratic theory, to regulate the use of executive power, is clearly not one that African constitutions that have survived military intervention now perform. It is important therefore that we conclude with some reflections on what that condition means for governance in the next century.

Do Constitutions Matter?

Perhaps the first issue one should reflect on is whether constitutions really matter? In the Preface to his study of a number of Western and Eastern constitutions, S.E. Finer warns that no one constitution is an entirely realistic description of what actually happens and precious few are one hundred percent unrealistic fictions bearing no relationship whatsoever to what goes on.[33] His message is that even when constitutions are being violated, subverted, or otherwise ignored, it is important for scientists to examine them and practitioners to maintain faith in them. Constitutions therefore *do* matter. It is interesting in this respect that Swaziland, which abrogated its Independence Constitution in 1973, has had to reinstate a number of important provisions of that document over the years.

This issue becomes not whether constitutions matter, but what constitutional regime best fits the needs of particular societies? Here again Finer's observation is most apt. He says "Different historical contexts have generated different preoccupations: different preoccupations have generated different emphases."[34]

Constitutional arrangements look both to the past and to the future. Hence, although certain basic and cross-cultural functions are and should be expected of any constitution, one cannot say that a single model is good for all societies at all times. The falsity of that assumption has clearly been demonstrated in the historical experience of sub-Saharan Africa over the past 30 years. Autochthony is therefore an indispensable part of constitutional development. What appears to have gone drastically wrong in Africa is not the search for autochthony but rather the extreme disregard of constitutionalism that this process has assumed.

What Price Constitutionalism?

The more important question is: What will it take to develop a tradition of constitutionalism in Africa? Although broad agreement exists on the essence of constitutionalism, fidelity to the principle that the exercise of state power must seek to advance the ends of society, the attainment has not been an easy matter. The political history of many societies is replete with struggles for an optimal balance between the few on whom constitutions confer power and the vast majority for whose benefit it is supposed to be exercised. What is clear is that in no society has that balance been achieved through the promulgation of a constitution, per se. Nor has it been achieved simply by cultivating the "correct" attitude toward a constitution as Nwabueze suggests.[35]

More important reasons explain why that balance has not been achieved in Africa. The most important of these is the socioeconomic condition of the continent itself. That is a most dismal one. Some years ago, the Economic Commission for Africa (ECA) said, "the African region is most seriously affected by the burden of underdevelopment . . . mass poverty, unemployment, social unrest, disease, hunger and ignorance continue to plague the region."[36]

The effect of these circumstances on the politics of the constitution is that contemporary elites in Africa are preoccupied with the perfection of ways, means, and techniques of their own survival and the expansion of opportunities for private accumulation. These conditions and this preoccupation are most unhealthy for the growth of constitutionalism with any model; indeed, it is doubtful whether power, at any level, can ever be fully socialized in conditions of poverty and underdevelopment.[37]

What then will it take to develop a tradition of constitutionalism in Africa? I am inclined to the view that Africa is destined to experience struggles and disappointments similar to those through which the older political systems went before viable mechanisms for the control, supervision, and accountability of power can be developed and internalized. That may be a severe position to take; but what it says is that history cannot simply be *learned*, it may have to be *lived* as well. Constitutionalism is the end product of social, economic, cultural, and political progress; it can become a tradition only if it forms part of the shared history of a people.

Notes

1. Y. P. Chai and J. P. W. B. McAuslan, *Public L aw and Political Change in Kenya* (Nairobi: Oxford, 1970) p. v.

2. B. O. Nwabueze, *Constitutionalism in the Emergent States* (London: C. Hurst, 1973); *Presidentialism in Commonwealth Africa* (London: C. Hurst, 1974); *Judicialism in Commonwealth Africa* (London: C. Hurst, 1977).

3. Among the most recent exceptions which, in any event, is not specifically on Africa is K. G. Banting and R. Simeon, *Redesigning the State: The Politics of Constitutional Change* (Toronto: University of Toronto, 1985).

4. A. S. Mathews, *Freedom, State Security and the Rule of Law: Dilemmas of the Apartheid Society* (Cape Town: Juta, 1986); B. O. Nwabueze, *Constitutionalism*, note 2; B. O. Nwabueze, *Presidentialism*, note 2.

5. Y. P. Ghai, "The Rule of Law: Legitimacy and Governance,"[14] *International Journal of the Sociology of Law* 179–208 (1986).

6. *Ibid.*

7. D. M. Trubek, "Max Weber on Law and the Rise of Capitalism," *Wisconsin Law Review*; 720 (1972); M. Weber, *Law in Economy and Society* (Berkeley: University of California, 1978).

8. I. D. Duchacek, *Power Map: Comparative Politics of Constitutions* (Oxford: A.B.C. Clio, 1973).

9. T. Fleiner, "The Concept of a Constitution" (unpublished paper, Gainesville, FL: University of Florida, 1986).

10. D. Elazar, "Constitutional-Making; The Pre-eminently Political Act," in K. G. Banting and R. Simeon, note 3.

11. H. Kuper, *Sobhuza II: Ngwenyama and King of Swaziland* (New York: African Publishing Co., 1978).

12. J. K. Nyerere (in a speech to Parliament), reproduced in R. Martin, *Personal Freedom and the Law in Tanzania* (Nairobi: Oxford, 1974).

13. Y. P. Ghai, "Independence and Safeguards in Kenya," 3 *East African Law Journal* 79 (1967); H.W.O. Okoth-Ogendo, "Ethnicity and Constitutionalism in Kenya: A General Survey," and unpublished paper prepared for a workshop on Structural Arrangements to Ease Ethnic Tensions (Taita Hills, Kenya).

14. S. K. Cummins et al., *African Agrarian Crisis: Roots of Famine* (Boulder, CO: Lynne Rienner, 1986).

15. C. Montesquieu, *The Spirit of Laws*, trans. Nugent (London: William Cowes, 1878).

16. H. W. O. Okoth-Ogendo, "The Politics of Constitutional Change in Kenya since Independence 1963–1969," 71 *African Affairs* (1972).

17. H. Kelsen, *The Pure Theory of Law*, trans. M. Knight (Berkeley: University of California Press, 1967).

18. R. Martin, note 12; B. O. Nwabueze, *Presidentialism*, note 2; H. W. O. Okoth-Ogendo, "The Politics," note 16.

19. H. Kuper, note 11.

20. *Ibid.*

21. K. G. Banting and R. Simeon, note 3.

22. C. Achebe, *Anthills of the Savannah* (London: Heineman, 1988).

23. B. O. Nwabueze, *Presidentialism*, note 2.

24. C. Gertzel et al., *Government and Politics in Kenya* (Nairobi: EAPH, 1969).

25. G. A. Almond and G. B. Powell, Jr., *Comparative Politics: System, Process and Policy* (2nd ed., Boston: Little Brown, 1978).

26. N. Kasfir, *The Shrinking Political Arena: Participation and Ethnicity in African Politics with a Case Study of Uganda* (Berkeley: University of California Press, 1976). This concept is applied in relation to the way in which ethnicity affects political participation.

27. B. O. Nwabueze, *Constitutionalism*, note 2.

28. J. B. Ojwang, and J. A. Otieno-Odek, "The Judiciary in Sensitive Areas of Public Law: Emerging Approaches to Human Rights Litigation in Kenya," 35(1) *Netherlands International Law Review* 29 (1988); M. Ndulo and K. Turner, *Civil Liberties Cases in Zambia* (Oxford: African Law Reports, 1984); B. O. Nwabueze, *Judicialism*, note 2.

29. J. Boli-Bennett, "Human Rights of State Expansion: Cross-Cultural Definitions of Constitutional Rights 1870–1970," in Ved P. Nanda et al., eds., *Global Human Rights: Public Policies, Comparative Measures and NGO Strategies* (Boulder, CO: Westview Press, 1981).

30. B. O. Nwabueze, *Presidentialism*, note 2.

31. J. Boli-Bennett, note 29.

32. B. O. Nwabueze, *Constitutionalism*, note 2.

33. S. E. Finer, *Five Constitutions* (Sussex: Harvester Press, 1979), p. 16.

34. S. E. Finer, note 33, p. 22.

35. B. O. Nwabueze, *Constitutionalism*, note 2.

36. UNECA, *ECA and Africa's Development 1983–2008: A Preliminary Perspective Study* (Addis Ababa: 1983).

37. H. W. O. Okoth-Ogendo, " 'Human and Peoples' Rights': What Point is Africa Trying to Make?" Unpublished third Gwendolin Carter Lecture on Africa, delivered at the University of Florida, Gainesville, FL, 1988.

Additional References

A. Odinga, *Not Yet Uhuru* (London: Heineman, 1967).

S. Wiking, *Military in Sub-Saharan Africa* (Uppsala: Scandinavian Institute of African Studies, 1983).

II

HUMAN RIGHTS

5

Human Rights in Constitutional Order and in Political Practice in Latin America

Hugo E. Frühling

Historically, the constitution and the evolution of the concept of constitutionalism have been associated with the notion of limited power, especially the limitation of governmental power.[1] This evolution reached its utmost expression in the Anglo-Saxon tradition, especially in the United States, where the constitution is not only the set of rules governing the political organization of the nation, but also, and more importantly, the entity defending human rights against possible violation by the government.[2] In the Latin American tradition, it seems to us, the constitution is always the product of a political-rationalistic approach, and its objective is not so much to limit the government as to offer the latter a tool for governing society. Early Latin American history abounds in examples of the view of constitutions as extremely important documents that contributed to ensuring social rule during the first decades of the nineteenth century. In this sense, Simón Bolívar, in the Manifesto of Cartagena (1813), attributes the fall of the Republic primarily to the defects of 1811 Constitution, and in his famous speech of Angostura (1819) he tells legislators that their success is fundamental to the freedom, prosperity, and happiness of the country; without it, the country will lapse into slavery.[3] In this century, the importance given to constitutional debate in Chile in the throes of the 1920 crisis, and today in Brazil and Argentina, shows that the constitutional process is still of great political and cultural relevance to Latin America social life.

Two consequences, difficult to disregard, ensure this particular aspect of Latin American constitutional tradition. The first is that the constitution plays a central role in the efforts of the governing elite to redefine political and social order in a given period. The Constitution of Chile in 1833 is closely linked to the conservative process of institutionalization; the 1925 constitution advocates strengthening of the role of the state in the economy; in 1980, it reflects the symbiosis between neoliberal postulates in the economic field and authoritarian principles in the political sphere.[4] The Mexican Constitution of 1917 is tied to the social postulates of the Revolution, just as the Argentine Constitution of 1949 expresses the objectives of the Peronist movement. Although there are constitutions (e.g., Argentina's of 1853 or Columbia's of 1886) that outlived endless political vicissitudes, most of these texts express the great political and social changes in Latin American countries. The second is that following the republican–democratic tradition, all constitutional texts include a list of individual or social rights, but permanent rules or allowance for special circumstances often severely limit these.

Despite the ideological and political importance of contemporary constitutional law in Latin America, this analysis cannot overlook the obvious fact that the Latin America constitutional order is not very efficient, not only due to the political instability recurrent in the region, but also because of the lack of complete respect for human rights, even when the constitutionally established institutions are fully valid. The recent cases of Peru and Colombia are examples of the dramatic situations in two countries where rights, formally valid and partially applied in reality, coexist with extensive and unpunished violations of human rights.[5]

Given these facts, this chapter will follow two parallel paths. It will analyze the human rights content of Latin American constitutions, and briefly describe existing protection systems and the legal remedies available for protection; it will also discuss the practical efficacy of constitutional systems with respect to the validity of human rights. In our opinion, the content of and limitations on human rights found in certain constitutions impact negatively on the respect for human rights. All Latin American constitutions contain a constitutional system for the protection of human rights and legal mechanisms to enforce it; in practice, and with honorable exceptions, the efficacy of these protection systems is weak. The explanations for this situation are numerous and complex. We will discuss three here. In vast social sectors of the region, which should constitute the substratum of the constitutional order, exist personal relationships, cultural patterns, and values incompatible with the exercise of the citizen's rights. The entities ensuring the constitutional protection of human rights lack the autonomy or ideological audacity needed for a constitutional interpretation that would protect human rights. Latin American leadership sectors (the so-called political class) are not fully aware of the fact that a manipulative interpretation of the constitution may erode the legitimacy of the institutional order that proclaims the validity of human rights.

Constitutional Content of Human Rights

As indicated above, Latin American societies, from political and ideological standpoints, treat constitutional processes seriously, regardless of their actual validity. Even though the latter is precarious, constitutional texts do indicate the set of rights and the form of legitimate government. Power forces rarely justify their violation publicly, since they suspect, rightly or wrongly, that such justification would meet with disapproval at national and international levels.

All Latin American constitutions contain a declaration of constitutional guarantees. However, it is clear that their ideological backgrounds vary, and that the ideological, legislative, and historic processes in the various countries that gave rise to the constitutional practice of human rights protection differ. A recent treatise on the constitutional protection of human rights makes the following classification of Latin American constitutions: democratic–liberal political constitutions such as those of Costa Rica in 1949, Venezuela in 1961, Peru in 1979, and Colombia in 1886 (we would add that of Ecuador in 1986); authoritarian political constitutions of the state, represented by two examples of completely opposed political natures: the constitutions of Chile in 1980, amended to be more democratic in 1989, and that of Cuba in 1976; Liberal with authoritarian features, such as the Brazilian constitution of 1967, modified in 1969; and eclectic political constitutions namely that of Mexico of 1917.[6] This classification has its shortcomings, though it is useful because it finally explains a commonly known fact: that in this century, almost all the states of the world have adopted a catalog of fundamental freedoms and rights. The determinant factor is not its existence, but the quality and content of these freedoms and rights.[7] The only way of establishing this quality comparatively is to measure it against international human rights standards and their interpretation by specialized bodies. A comparison of all Latin American constitutions with these standards is beyond the measure of this chapter; therefore, and reserving the right of comparison with other constitutions, we have decided to concentrate an important part of this analysis on the Chilean constitution. This constitution has been valid in a country with a long institutional tradition and stability; after the institutional failure of 1973, it has followed the path established by the 1980 constitution of authoritarian origin.

Freedom and Rights Content

Not all Latin American constitutions measure well against international standards such as the International Covenant on Civil and Political Rights, the International Covenant on Economic, Social and Cultural Rights, and the American Convention on Human Rights.[8] For instance, a review of the rights acknowledged in international agreements and absent in the Chilean Constitution of 1980 (prior to the 1989 amendment) shows its ideological character; while fully supportive of a free market in the economic realm, it does not trust economic and social rights. In the political field, it maintains a restrictive view of the exercise of human rights.

Among the rights excluded or included with limitations in this constitution is the right to work, set forth in Article 6 of the International Covenant on Economic, Social and Cultural Rights (I.C.S.E.C.R.); the constitution guarantees only the freedom to work. Unrecognized is the right of the unions to form national confederations or federations; its absence is consistent with the labor law enacted by the military government.[9] Recognized in only a limited way is the right of a person accused of a crime to be presumed innocent until this guilt is proven under the law (Article 14.2 of the International Covenant on Civil and Political Rights); its Article 19 No. 3 prohibits only the legal presumption of penal liability in advance. The right to appeal condemning penal sentences to a higher court as regulated by law (Article 14.5 Covenant and Political Rights) is not included in the catalog of rights either; only after the transition to a civilian administration was the constitution amended to allow the pardon of persons condemned to death for terrorist crimes.[10] The constitution does not consider the right, established in Article 27 of the Covenant on Civil and Political Rights, allowing ethnic or linguistic minorities to enjoy their own culture and use their own language. This shortcoming is not exclusively one of the Chilean constitution. The Ecuadoran constitution, for example, ensures the use of the indigenous language in the education systems in areas where indigenous minorities are predominant; but the same is not true for their own full cultural development.

Restrictions in the exercise of constitutional rights are of two kinds: some are of a general character; others consist of the derogation of certain rights in extraordinary cases during which states of emergency are declared. The general restriction with the greatest impact in the constitution of Paraguay is its Article 71, which guarantees the freedoms of thought and opinion, only to declare immediately thereafter that the advocacy of hate among Paraguayans is not permitted, nor is class struggle, nor is the defense of crime or violence. This article of the constitution was regulated by Law 209 of 1970, which became the repressive law par excellence under the dictatorship of General Alfredo Stroessner (1954–1989).[11] This example of Paraguay reflects obvious authoritarian trends in the constitutional protection of rights. However, we must note that the liberal constitutions of other countries establish general limitations on the exercise of these rights. It will be up to the wisdom of the congresses and the attitude of the judiciaries to use these limitations sparingly in terms that do not exceed those set forth by international law. Article 46 of the 1886 Constitution of Columbia, for instance, says, "Any part of the people may assemble or congregate peacefully. The authorities may disperse any meeting that degenerates into riot or commotion or that obstructs public roads." This provision does not impose the same safegaurds as Article 21 of the Covenant on Civil and Political Rights *vis-à-vis* the authorities effecting the right to assembly. Indeed, under the covenant, such a restriction must be made by law that indicates in which specific cases a meeting may be dispersed, as well as which authorities may make that decision.

Thus, some Latin American constitutions express in their declarations of rights an authoritarian ideological approach, either by the rights they omit or because the general restrictions on the enjoyment of rights exceed those allowed by international law, or those required for peaceful coexistence. In the case of liberal constitutions, the effective protection of human rights would depend on an interpretation restricting the powers of authorities. From the political point of view, the most significant constitutional limitations of human rights are those arising from the declaration of states of exception.

Suspension of Constitutional Guarantees during Situations of Exception

The importance of the regulation of constitutional regimes of exception in many Latin American countries arises from their excessive authorization of the derogation of rights. Systematic and generalized violations of human rights accompanied the continuous application of states of exception. Although the situation was especially heated during the 1970s, abuse of states of exception in order to cope with social problems or political unrest of average importance has been a constant element in Latin American political life.[12] States of exception result in the concentration of power in the executive and in the suspension of the citizen's constitutional rights. As is known, Latin American reality widely exceeded the standards of international law. Paraguay has lived under siege (a state of?) for 40 years;[13] Chile has known various states of exception, without interruption, from September 11, 1973, to 1988; by 1986, Columbia had lived under siege for almost 30 years.[14]

International law establishes certain requirements for the legitimacy of a state of exception: a period of public emergency threatening the life of the nation; the measures adopted do not exceed those strictly necessary to respond to the needs of the situation; the measures are consistent with other obligations that the State has *vis-à-vis* international law, such as the rules governing armed conflict. Both the American Convention of Human Rights and the International Covenant on Civil and Political Rights set forth certain rights that may not be suspended: the rights to life, to legal existence, to freedom of thought, conscience, and religion, to person inviolability, and to due process of law. The International Covenant prohibits slavery and servitude.[15]

The seriousness of the continuous use of constitutional states of exception in Latin America lies in the extremely subjective interpretation of the criteria that make them admissible, a practice that rapidly erodes the legitimacy of the constitutional order. Second, the derogation of rights based on these states of exception ends up weakening the political and judicial control on the acts of the government, especially with respect to individual rights. Finally, states of exception often lead to the granting of new political functions to the armed forces, with consequences that may become extremely serious for the preservation of democracy.

Some examples prove the above allegations: the Chilean constitution of 1925, now replaced by that of 1980, established two kinds of states of exception that could be declared in cases of danger to the interior security of the State. These were the state of seige, set forth in Article 72 No. 17, which could be declared in the event of an internal rebellion or of an attack from outside, and the so-called law for extraordinary powers, originally set forth in Article 44 No. 13 of the constitution, which was applicable "when required by imperious needs of the defense of the State, preservation of the constitutional regime or interior peace."

In political practice, a state of siege was declared in situations that contained a potential danger for the country, rather than on the occurrence of a real rebellion.[16] Seemingly, the same happened with the criteria used to pass laws for extraordinary powers; careful attention was not paid to the circumstances actually occurring.

A special chapter deserves to be dedicated to the state of emergency, unconstitutionally established in Chile by Law 12.927 on "State Security," which, in its Article 31, authorized the President of the Republic to declare said state in case of war, attack from the exterior, or invasion. In 1960, by Law 13.959, a paragraph was added to Article 31 of Law 12.927, on the occasion of an earthquake, authorizing the declaration of the state of emergency in the event of public calamities. Although the purpose of the legislation (to face natural disasters) was obvious, the state of exception was repeatedly applied to face problems affecting public order, such as strikes or illegal lockouts of the National Confederation for Land Transportation. The extremely subjective interpretation of the requirements authorizing the declaration of the state of exception is not an exclusive feature of the Chilean constitutional experience. In Columbia, where the state of siege is declared after consultation with the State Council, there have been countless situations where the state of siege was maintained in force long after the disappearance of its causes. Probably the same may be said about many other Latin American countries.

A second consequence of these states of exception is that their application adversely affects the operation of the political system and has damaging effects on the institutions of congress and the courts; their declaration tends to be made without the appropriate parliamentary political control and, in most cases, their application is not duly supervised by the courts in charge of the control of constitutional supremacy.

Without going further, the Peruvian constitution in its Article 231 foresees the following states of exception: the state of emergency and the state of siege. In both cases, the Executive has the power to decree the state of exception with the agreement of the council of Ministers; congress is informed. Diego Garcia-Sayan believes that the Congress has not appropriately controlled the acts of the Executive starting from the moment it is informed about the declaration of a constitutional state of exception.[17] Article 38 of Law 23506 flatly states that the writs of *habeas corpus* and of *amparo* cannot be used to sustain judicial review of the validity of state of emergency and state of seige measures taken by the executive in accordance with Article 231 of the Peruvian Constitution.

The use and abuse by states of exception give rise to a third phenomenon that severely distorts the constitutional order; when implementing states of exception, states grant significant powers to the armed forces, or to bodies depending on them, for the preservation of internal order. Recent Latin American history demonstrates that this process undermines civil institutions. This is precisely what happened in Peru at the beginning of the insurrection of Sendero Luminoso (The Shining Path), when the Government of President Belaunde Terry created a "Political-Military Command" under Law 24.150 to which, in reality, it granted all powers and which took precedence over civil power, the political authorities of the departments and provinces declared under emergency, and over those of the Judicial Power and the Public Ministry.[18] Thus, the command was even authorized to request the firing, nomination or transfer of officials when, in the opinion of the command, they were guilty of negligence, abandonment, or absence from their functions. The replacement of civil authorities by military ones is sanctioned by Article 11 of Article 231.[19] In Columbia, the implementation of the state of siege authorized the government to issue decrees with validity of law. Under these, military courts frequently had the power to judge civilians.[20] Consequently, and for a long time, the jurisdictional competence of military courts was increased so that they could judge a larger number of crimes. Although this tendency was reversed in 1984, in the sense that military judges were allowed to judge civilians only for weapons possession and related crimes, they are still authorized to issue orders of search of the premises and of detection, following requests from military intelligence.[21]

The practice of using states of exception to restrict fundamental rights is not the cause of human rights violations. However, we must say that the road from the occasional use of a state of exception to the implementation of a true dictatorship is paved by actions, not always conscious, that by undermining the principles of the constitutional order, weaken those principles and the orders of legitimacy. Among these actions, we have mentioned the arbitrary interpretation of justifications for states of exception, the fact that congress or the judiciary fails to control their application, and the abdication of civil authority in favor of the military in the application of the powers arising from these states of exception.

Systems for Human Rights Protection

The content of human rights refers to their definition in constitutional and legal texts and to the limitations or suspensions that may affect them; protection systems are the legal and institutional mechanisms to which citizens have access when their fundamental rights are violated.

In Latin America, under the influence of the Constitution of the United States, there are constitutional systems of human rights protection. As we have seen, constitutions recognize fundamental rights; laws express and implement them. Normally, the remedies or actions available for the protection of human rights are stated in the constitution; the laws and decrees may not infringe on these remedies. Finally, the constitution itself establishes the bodies responsible for enforcing constitutional supremacy.

Perhaps more so than in other legal fields, the constitutional domain allows for different interpretations of the rules. Declarations of rights are necessarily general, which implies a high responsibility for the interpreter. In the case of the United States, this responsibility entails the question of which method of interpretation of the constitution overcomes the vagueness of the constitutional language, without granting the judges the position of nonelected legislators?[22] In a country where the process of interpreting the constitution is conducted with decision and independence by the Supreme Court, this question is of paramount importance. Many positions have been taken on this issue. They range from the emphasis on traditional interpretation procedures, which stress textual analysis and the search for the inherent intention, to those that rely for resolutiom on the legal consensus of society,[23] to those that maintain the constitutional reasoning must be simply based on moral values.[24]

In Latin America, which follows the European juridical tradition, the debate took a different direction. During the nineteenth century, a rigid approach generally was obtained, which hesitated to grant courts the protection of constitutional supremacy. As the rigid concept of separation of the branches of government lost ground, a problem arose that was somewhat more complex than that of the U.S. constitutional debate. The enhancement of the social and economic functions of the state increased the possibility of conflicts between Congress and the Executive, and engendered the need for a public body in charge of interpreting the constitution whose decisions would have mandatory effects for the conflicting parties. There was, however, resistance against the creation of courts whose rulings would decide on the constitutional validity of laws made by elected representatives. A compounding problem was that the character of constitutional interpretation seemed incompatible with the formalistic approach prevalent among Latin American jurists, hence, the interest in creating constitutional control bodies that would be more politically inclined than ordinary courts.

This complex of tensions determined a coexistence between various constitutional protection systems, dominated by the so-called diffuse model; under this model, control of constitutionality is not concentrated in a body specifically dealing with such questions, but is rather a function for the courts of various hierarchic levels. The alternative model is the concentrated one created by Hans Kelsen in Austria between the two world wars, which set up a constitutional court that had the authority to determine the compatibility of a law with the constitution, which acted in fact as a negative legislator.[25]

The Chilean case is typical of the complex process that led to the constitutional protection mechanism currently in force there. The constitution of 1925 (Article 86, paragraph 2), provided for the Supreme Court to decide the validity of a law on constitutional grounds, in the particular cases it judged or in appeals brought to its attention. The resolution of the court applied only to the particular case; the law itself remained in force. From the debate conducted in the subcommission for constitutional reform, it is clear that the reason for the limitation on the effects of the declaration of unconstitutionality was to avoid the transformation of the court into a legislative entity.[26] The Chilean political development, increasingly marred by conflicts, made evident during the 1960s the inherent limitations of the Supreme Court's ability to exercise its constitutional revision power. More importantly, the Court waived its competence to declare unconstitutional those rules regarding the procedure of issuance of the law that violated the constitution. This waiver made it apparent that a body was needed to interpret the constitution in a binding manner, to avoid major political conflicts between Congress and the President of the Republic.

In 1970 the constitution was reviewed, and a specialized constitutional justice was established, whose composition was partly political and partly judicial:[27] the new constitutional Court was granted power to resolve constitutional problems raised during the legislative process, decided on questions of constitutionality presented in international treaties presented to Congress for ratification, judge questions of constitutionality derived from decrees with force of law, and rule on other matters, less relevant to this study. The constitution of 1980, a product of the authoritarian system, created a new constitutional Court of a mixed judicial and political nature; this Court is competent to judge constitutional questions judged by the constitutional Court in existence until 1973, and other matters related to ruling on the unconstitutionality of the political organizations and parties outlawed by Article 8 of the constitution.

The Argentinean constitutional protection system more closely follows the U.S. precedent; there is no constitutional Court and the judicial power, headed by the Supreme Court, is in charge of constitutional control. This system is a disperse protection one; the control function is not concentrated and all courts may exercise it at the request of a party in specific legal cases. These rulings are valid only for these specific cases. In certain situations, an extraordinary appeal for unconstitutionality may be filed and may move to successive degrees of appeal up to the Supreme Court. Argentina has no procedure for the direct declaration of unconstitutionality, that is, a procedure whose main objective is specifically to declare the unconstitutionality of rules and acts, even though a couple of rulings of the Supreme Court allege that such a procedure can be justified jurisprudentially.

The Ecuadoran constitution of 1983 provides for a concentrated model of constitutional control. Indeed, Article 140 establishes a Court for Constitutional Guarantees to be elected by the National Congress from persons outside the Congress and from a list of three candidates drawn up by the public powers and other bodies acknowledged by the law. This Court judges constitutional claims filed by individuals and corporations for violations against the rights and freedoms guaranteed by the constitution; the Court must hear the authority or body against which the claim is made, and make observations. Article 141 No. 3 of the constitution sets forth that these observations must be obeyed by the authorities appealed against, which are subject to penalties in case of non-compliance. The Court also judges declarations of unconstitutionality *ex officio* or at request, regarding laws, decrees, agreements, rules, or ordinances. In the latter cases the court's resolutions cancel, totally or partially, the effects of the rule declared unconstitutional. The court submits its decision to the National Congress, which may derogate the rule. The Court for Constitutional Guarantees also has the power to declare a law inapplicable on grounds of unconstitutionality, granted in contentious cases to any branch of the Supreme Court, the Fiscal Tribunal, or the Court for Action under Administrative Law. The sentence is effective only for the case at hand, but it will be communicated to the Court for Constitutional Guarantees for the latter to decide on the law's possible suspension.

There are authors who support, with some reason, the creation of a special constitutional justice, different from ordinary courts and concentrated in a constitutional Court that would judge the constitutionality of laws or executive decrees and the appeals for the defense of constitutional rights.[28] The main argument seems to be that a specialized justice, based on the guarantee of human rights and with high hierarchic position in the constitutional system, would be more willing to interpret the constitution in favor of human rights and to oppose congress or the executive if necessary than would a bureaucratic judicial branch composed of career judges. To this argument can be added that a court with political compositions, although fully independent, would have better capacity to assume the juridical–political task implied in constitutional control.

In our opinion, the creation of a body to judge the appeals filed to defend constitutional guarantees does not absolutely ensure a favorable result for the protection of human rights. In certain periods of its history and in isolated cases, the Argentinian judicial power and especially its Supreme Court offered an interesting example of creativity in the field of constitutional interpretation. That is to say, a diffuse constitutional system can give perfect gurantees for the efficient protection of human rights. A second aspect to consider is that the relatively marginal position of the courts, especially supreme courts, in judging appeals related to the protection of public freedoms, could remove them from one of the most relevant juridical conflicts that society may have to face. This possibility is a negative factor for some authors who believe that it is important for judges to have contact with the most important legal conflicts of social life.[29] Finally, in countries with long authoritarian traditions and shaken by the notorious weakness of their institutions, one should wonder whether an expressly political constitutional court is indeed able to consolidate its autonomy and independence.

The protection of human rights depends largely on the institutionalization of the bodies designated by the constitutional order to protect them; obviously, the more institutional weight they carry, the stronger their ability to oppose violations of rights. However, a court of constitutional guarantees with such characteristics would have little relevance if it were not backed up by a court system willing to enforce the liability of State officials for violations of human rights, In the final analysis, the quality of the constitutional system of human rights protection does not depend on the operation of a specific institution, but on the interaction of all of them. The efficacy of a constitutional protection system also depends on jurisdictional guarantees, to which individuals affected in the enjoyment of their rights can resort. The third part of this chapter will briefly describe these guarantees in the constitutional systems of Latin America.

Jurisdictional Guarantees for the Protection of Human Rights

Latin American constitutional systems have various legal instruments to defend human rights. Enrique Haba distinguishes four fundamental types: ordinary legal instruments present in any lawsuit meant to defend interests that are not always fundamental, but that may also protect human rights; complementary legal instruments with punitive character, meant to enforce the penal liability of public officials who have violated human rights; legal instruments for constitutional control whose goal is to see that the law does not violate the constitutional scope; and legal instruments for procedural relief, specifically designed for the protection of human rights.[30] Among the latter, special mention should be made of the writ of *amparo* and the writ of *habeas corpus*.

All Latin Amrican legislations sanction the writ of *habeas corpus*. In some cases, the constitution explicitly regulates it; in others, the constitution simply establishes the bases for *a posteriori* legislative regulation. Thus, Article 18 of the Argentinean constitution states that nobody may be "arrested other than upon a written order of the competent authority"; Law 23.098 of 1984 regulates *habeas corpus* in the legislation. Other constitutions, such as that of Honduras, ensure that the *habeas corpus* action can be filed without any formality (Article 182). Article 21 of the Chilean constitution recognizes the admissibility of *habeas corpus* on grounds of any deprivation of, interference with, or threat to personal freedom and individual safety. In the legislation of various countries, a complex of guarantees surround this remedy. Among these are the principle of urgency, which must govern the action of the judge called to stop the illegal action of the authority and the inquisitive principle, since the court may, *ex officio*, order the steps that are deemed useful to obtain the desired goal. Finally, the filing of a *habeas corpus* action is free of any formalities.[31] This resource seems to be extremely weak precisely on the occassions when it is most needed: during constitutional states of exception.[32]

Besides *habeas corpus*, Latin American legal systems have a legal instrument for the general defense of human rights, frequently called *amparo*; in Brazil, *mandato de seguranca* and in Chile, writ of protection. In the latter case, which is more recent, measures affecting a series of constitutional rights cannot be reviewed by such writ.[33] Among them are economical and social rights, the right to legal defense, the right to due process, and equal protection by the law in the exercise of constitutional rights. The Chilean writ of protection applies to acts of individuals and authorities. In Guatemala, it applies to acts of the government, of the Congress in the case of acts that are not legislative, and to procedural violations committed by the Supreme Court of Justice.[34]

Jorge Mario Garcia Laguardia has analyzed constitutional jurisprudence in Mexico, Guatemala, and Honduras. He gives a partial sample of decisions on writs of *habeas corpus*, *amparo*, and unconstitutionality in these three countries. The results are not surprising, but are illustrative of Latin American reality. First, it is clear that these constitutional resources are rarely used. Second, private property is the right with the best juridical protection and the cause of most requests. Third, judges are very cautious with requests with political implications, and therefore only a minimal number of these requests prosper.[35] Studies conducted in various nations tend to support similar findings. Garcia-Sayan tells us that in the context of the nasty internal war in Ayacucho, the guarantees given by the Peruvian constitution are inoperative, partly because of the small number of writs of *habeas corpus* filed.[36] Constitutional judicial review has not been very effective in Latin America. A study on the legal profession in Colombia demonstrates that unconstitutional actions brought before the Supreme Court were fewer in number than would have been probable; the more prominent cases seem to refer to property rights.[37]

Constitutions are systems of possibilities; their rules are not always precise, the rights they foster can be limited by law, they must be interpreted by the courts in case of legal dispute, and both congress and the executive can suspend certain rights by the declaration of a state of emergency. From what we have said and from generally known facts, it follows that the operations of constitutional systems in Latin America were oriented, in general, toward a more efficient protection of human rights. What factors determined this situation in various countries of different stages of their histories? We will now explore this question.

Efficacy of Constitutional Systems for the Protection of Human Rights

Various analyses make clear that the constitutional system for the protection of human rights in Latin America has proceeded timidly. In an analysis of how Peruvian judges dealt with political cases during the validity of the 1933 constitution, Pasara shows that the courts were traditionally dependent on the political power;[38] he quotes an analysis of the use of *habeas corpus* for the defense of individual freedom between 1933 and 1970, and finds that in these political cases there is a rejection of a disproportionate number of writs of *habeas corpus*.[39] His conclusion is: "It cannot be considered an exaggeration when we say that, at least during the last sixty years, the courts did not do everything that was needed—and failed to do everything that was possible—in and attempt not only to avoid the conflict with the executive power but also to spare their mandatories any embarrassing situation that their resolutions could have caused."[40] In turn, in Argentina, where the Supreme Court played an important role in the interpretation of the constitution, political instability substantially affected its institutional weight.[41]

Despite this reality, the symbolic and political importance Latin American elites attribute to constitutional reforms is undeniable, hence, the appearance of a style of political behavior that may be called legalism, especially in countries traditionally more stable from the institutional standpoint, such as Chile. This style depends on knowledge of the rules and the rhetorical use of them as the backbone of political debate; issues of morality or efficacy are subordinate. The refined legalism, in this case constitutionalism, of Latin America is partly intended to throw a legitimate (or constitutional) cloak over institutional systems that clearly try to apply policies opposed to the values proclaimed by the constitutions. It is also, in part, the product of the Spanish tradition, especially that of the enlightened absolutism of the nineteenth century. Further, such legalism is a characteristic typical of societies that try to regulate, plan, and control unstable political relationships in highly emotional situations. As Harry Eckstein puts it, legalism can be symptomatic of an unstable and weak institutional regime.[42] L. Pye suggests that in societies with a latent threat of violence and lack of trust between elites and social groups, the law may represent a strong element of firmness and consistency in environments marred by a lack of certainty.[43]

These three sources of Latin American constitutionalism as concept and policy explain its importance, but also its weakness. Indeed, the fact that constitutionalism is part of an old cultural and political tradition gives rise to sectors interested in its survival: politicians, intellectuals, and lawyers. Its use for legitimization purpose shows that it is a socially accepted discourse that can limit the excesses of power if the powers wish to maintain the legitimacy they claim.[44] Finally, as constitutionalism is an attempt to regulate and control the uncertainties of Latin American social and political life, one hopes that its efforts to regulate effectively social tensions will be persistently maintained in the region. However, social tensions, tensions between classes particularly, and political tensions are stronger than a tradition that has difficulties in imposing itself.

In practice, adherence to the legal system and the proclamation of human rights reflect fundamental ambiguities in the prevalent political culture. Thus, we must explore the possibility of progress toward a more efficient operation of the constitutional systems of human rights protection. In this context, it is useful to identify important factors in the deterioration of the efficacy of constitutional systems.

The first significant factor that adversely affects the operation of these constitutional systems of human rights protection is the incompatibility between interpersonal relationship patterns and those inferred or proclaimed by the constitutional order. Latin American constitutions declare the equality of rights of all human beings and their ability to make these rights effective through their full access to constitutional protection mechanisms. Moreover, these constitutions assume the people's full knowledge of their content and that the isolated occurrence of human rights violations is without effect on the impartiality of the state; if violations were massive, it would be difficult to remedy them by seeking procedural relief and legal remedies.

In reality, in most Latin American countries vast social sectors have relations with other social and/or ethnic classes that are neither symmetrical nor respectful, governed not by equality but by crude domination. Moreover, violence and abuse characterize their contacts with their peers and with the dominant groups; the presence of the law as an effective regulator of social relationships is rare. The daily experience of these individuals gives no sign that their lives, concerns, and anxieties coincide with the goals and designs of the macroconstitutional mechanisms created to defend their rights. Hence, for these vast sectors of the population, legality and the state are foreign entities, distant from their problems and expectations; these groups are not aware of their rights and of the need to exercise them properly.[45] A daily look at life in the large cities of Brazil, Peru, Colombia, and so many other countries reveals a social life moving around acts and values that do not reinforce positive attitudes toward a democratic political culture: indifference toward the rules and mistrust of fellow citizens and institutions. The inconsistency between daily social relations and those regulated at the constitutional level diminishes support for democratic institutions. Consequently, the perception of the remoteness of judicial institutions grows and the latter are not used with the required frequency and intensity. Guillermo O'Donnell superbly summarizes our thoughts when he speaks of the existing socialization from Argentina and Brazil, and concludes that in both countries there is a severe lack of civic culture.[46] In one of them, it is because the political structure has authority patterns that are constantly contradicted by a society with strong tendencies toward anarchical coporatism. In the other, it is because the political structure is not representative of society

Table 5.1. Trust in Legal Institutions

Are legal decisions based on the law or on "Personal influence?"	
On the law	14%
Undecided	13%
On "influence" and money	70%
No answer	3%
What are your resources in order to avoid unjust punishment?	
Wide resources	32%
Some resources	29%
Few or no resources	32%
No answer	7%
What are your means of obtaining justice?	
Good	24%
Average	38%
Bad or none	31%
No answer	7%

and is marked by elitist authoritarianism.[47] When the pattern of social relations is not consistent with what would allow the efficient operation of democracy, the prestige and social relevance of the law suffer. Research, begun in 1964, in over 30 villages of the Peruvian countryside reveals little trust in legal institutions (Table 5.1).[48]

In a 1971 empirical study made in a shanty town of Santiago de Chile, 88% interviewed thought that there was limited access to the administration of justice. Almost 68% declared that this limited access was due to problems specific to the administration of justice, but 21% said that it was due to personal difficulties of the individual searching for justice. On the other hand, 11% of those with access difficulties said that it was due to ignorance or lack of information.[49] In all, 31% of those who thought there was not full access to the administration of justice declared that it was due to circumstances directly effecting the persons in search of justice. This is probably the main source of the failure to use the legal resurces designed to protect human rights: passivity, lack of knowledge of the law, or simply mistrust.

A second factor affecting the operation of the constitutional system for the protection of human rights is the fact that the relation between the courts and the political system developed in a way that weakened the courts.

In many Latin American countries, the courts have no independence from the political power. The influence of the executive is predominant in the nomination and promotion of judges, and the courts cannot develop an autonomy that would allow them to challenge the government successfully. Perhaps, as a consequence of this factor, the political weight of the judicial branch in certain Latin American societies is devaluated. The lack of real independence from the political power may be a by-product of the long tradition of instability, which always ends up by undermining the carreer continuity of judges who show independence. Either as a consequence of their excessive political dependence, or of the excessive bureaucracy, Latin American judicial branches were reluctant to build a constitutional jurisprudence that would augment their constitutional clout. Without doubt, this explains their weakness and the fact that the discussion regarding the "rule by the judges," which was so important in the United States, did not take place in Latin America. All this led to a loss of relevance of Latin America judges, who in many countries and in multiple situations face the inescapable reality that the main social conflicts are resolved without their participation.[50]

Chile is an alternative model of relations between the judicial branch and politics. In 1925, its professionalism was established through an agreement among the political parties that the judicial power must not be politicized. This attitude influences the Chilean judiciary in two different ways: "It allows it to develop its internal autonomy, which favors the weight of superior courts and the hierarchic principle in their midst; but it also implies a relative margination [sic] of the judges *vis à vis* the course of social life."[51] In Chile, the political stability of the years between 1925 and 1973 helped crystallize a relatively conservative and traditional ideology.

Another feature, common to the judiciary of many Latin countries, has reawakened them: their administrative inefficiency and their failure to fulfill their functions with expected speed. This perception conspires against the trust in justice and reinforces a certain cynicism regarding the institutions designed for the control of constitutionality. A recent poll (1987) conducted in Colombia by DANE (National Administrative Statistics Department) revealed that only roughly 21% of the crimes that occurred in a sample of homes in 11 cities in 1985 were followed by the filing of a suit. The inefficiency of justice is one of the most cited reasons (23%) for not resorting to courts, the most frequent reason cited (37.5%) is lack of proof.[52]

In summary then, the court's relation with politics in Latin American society, its relative lack of social relevance, and its lack of efficacy in the fulfillment of its specific functions diminish the role of the judicial power. A third factor affecting constitutional efficacy has to do with the political behavior of the political elites, which disregard the requirements and needs of the legal order, and seriously affects the legitimacy of the constitution.

In some countries, civil authorities reinforce their power through forced interpretations of the constitutional text. This behavior weakens the influence and importance of the constitution, and seriously impairs its validity and influence on the acts and values of important social sectors. An example is the interpretation of constitutional requirements for the declaration of states of exception. The wide abuse of these requirements (discussed in detail earlier in this chapter) has facilitated the concentration of powers in hands of the executive. One small encroachment on the constitution leads to another; gradually, over time, the constitution is altered without constitutional reform. In the long run, this practice often undermines the basis of authority that implements it, debilitates the political consensus that originated the constitution, and strengthens the belief of many sectors that political conflicts are not liable to regulation by law. The consensus on legality deteriorates progressively.

Conclusion

The respect for human rights depends on the appropriate operation of the constitutional system for the protection of those rights. This system, in turn, responds to two basic factors: juridical regulation and the importance and presence of juridical regulation in social life. Latin American constitutions have an authoritarian bias in regard to the content of human rights and the permanent or temporary limitations or restrictions affecting them; they do recognize rights acknowledged by international treaties; they place ideological limitations in the enjoyment of certain rights; and they grant wide and unchecked powers to the executive in the case of a state of exception. It is precisely in states of exception that most violations of human rights occur.

All Latin American countries have a constitutional system for the protection of human rights. The various constitutions contain a catalog of human rights and various mechanisms and institutions designed to protect them. Academically, none of the models for human rights protection is better than the others. What really counts is the correct operation of the institutions in charge of the control of constitutionality and the ordinary courts; only the efficacy of all institutions ensures the respect of constitutional rights.

Although more empirical studies are needed, it would seem that the constitutions' influence on social behavior patterns is not significant in many countries of the region. Nor, except in very traumatic political situations, is there frequent use of the legal remedies available for the protection of public freedoms, putting in doubt the efficacy of the constitutional systems for the protection of human rights.

Among others, three important factors influence this lack of efficacy: the first involves the lack of compatibility between the values governing the social relations of vast subordinated social sectors and those that define the full exercise of civic rights; this incompatibility results in mistrust toward juridical institutions and in the belief that they are remote from individual needs and that the legal system does not function to solve the daily needs of individuals.

The second factor is the deficient operation of the courts in their role of guarantors of constitutional rights. Either because of their excessive political dependency or bureaucracy, Latin American courts, with some exceptions, have not creatively interpreted constitutional rules to the favor of marginal social and political groups. Further, in many countries, the courts have a certain social irrelevance and are administratively and functionally inefficacious in the fulfillment of their most characteristic role.

Finally, the deliberate carelessness of the governing elites in the manipulation of the formalities established by the constitutions debilitates their impact and influence. This carelessness affects the constitutional legitimacy and the consensus on which the latter is based.

Notes

1. See for example, Carl J. Friedrich, *Constitutional Government and Democracy* (revised ed., Boston: Ginn and Company, 1950), p. 26.

2. Carl Brent Swisher, *American Constitutional Development* (2nd ed.,) Cambridge: Houghton Miflin, 1954), pp. 10–11.

3. Rogelio Pérez Perdomo, "Teroia y Práctica de la Legislación en la Temprana República (Venezuela 1821–1870)." in *L'Educazione Giuridica* [Perugia: University of Perugia, estrato (extract)], p 416.

4. Some texts describing the Chilean constitutional development are the following: Alejandro Sivla Bascuñán, *Tratado de Derecho Constitutional* (Santiago: Editorial Juridica de Chile, 1963); Jorge Maza, "Recuerdos de la Reforma Constitucional de 1925," in *La Constitución de 1925 y la Facultad de Ciencias Juridicas y Sociales* (Santiago: Editorial Juídica, 1951); Eduardo Frei et al., *Reforma Constitucional de 1970* (Santiago: Editorial Jurídica de Chile, 1970); Hugo Frühling, "Liberalismo y Derecho Duranct el Siglo XIX en Chile," in *Ensayos*, Vol. I (Santiago: Editorial Debates, 1978), pp. 7–46; Jorge Mera, Felipe González, and Juan Enrique Vargas V., "Los Regímenes de Excepción en Chile Durante el Período 1925–1973," *Workbook No. 4, Program of Human Rights* (Santiago: Academy of Christian Humanism, 1987); *Constitucion de 1980 Comentarios de Juristas Internacionales* (Santiago: Ediciones Chile y América CESOC, 1984); José Luis Cea Egaña, "Rasgos de la Experienca Democrática y Constitucional de Chile," Revista Chilena de Derecho, 14 *Chilean Law Journal* 25–35 (1987).

5. Americas Watch, "Human Rights in Colombia as President Barco Begins," September 1986, "A New Opportunity for Democratic Authority: Human Rights in Peru," September 1985, "Human Rights in Peru After President Garcia's First Year," September 1986, "A Certain Passivity: Failing to Curb Human Rights Abuses in Peru," December 1987.

6. Enrique Haba, *Tratado Básico de Derechos Humanos*, Vol. I (San José: Editorial Juricentro, 1986), pp. 190–191.

7. Félix Ermacora, "Las Cláusuals Relatives a los Derechos Humano en la Nuevo Constitución Chilena, in *Constitución de 1980. Comentarios de Juristas Internacionales*, note 4, p. 21.

8. For general analyses regarding the operation of the international system for the protection of human rights, see Jack Donnelly, "International Human Rights: A Regime Analysis," in *40 International Organizations* (1986), pp. 599 ff; in Louis Henkin, ed., *The International Bill of Rights* (New York: Columbia University Press, 1981); Thomas Buergenthal, "The Inter-American System for the Protection of Human Rights," in T. Meron, ed., *Human Rights In International Law, Legal and Policy Issues*, Vol. II (Oxford: Oxford University Press, 1984), 439–493; Cecilia Medina, "Procedures in the Inter-American System for the Promotion and Protection of Human Rights. An Overview," 6 *SIM Newsletter Netherlands Quarterly of Human Rights Protection* 83 (1988).

9. See in this respect, Peter Van Dijk, "La Constitucion Chilena a la Luz de los Compormisos Legales Internacionales de Chile en el Ambito de los Derechos Humanos," in *Constitución de 1980. Comentarios de Juristas Internacionales*, note 4, pp.34–71; Jorge Mera, "La Eficacia del Recurso de Protección en la Institucionalidad del Regiman Militar Chileno," 1 *Revista Chilena de Derechos Humanos* (*Chilean Journal of Human Rights*) 6-7 (1885).

10. Some provisions of the labor law have been amended by the new democratic government.

11. "Report on the situation of human rights in Paraguay," Inter-American Commission for Human Rights, OEA/Ser. L/V/II 71 Doc. 19 rev. 1 (1987), pp. 20–22.

12. On this topic, see Héctor Gros Espiell, Rodolfo Piza R., and Daniel Zovatto, "Los Estados de Excepción en América Latina y su Incidencia en la Cuestión de los Derechos Humanos en caso de Disturbio Interno," in Diego Garcia-Sayan, ed., *Estados de Emergencia en la Región Andina* (Lima: Andean Commission of Jurists, 1987), pp. 21–56; Domingo García Belaúnde, "Regimenes de Excepción den las Constituciones Latinoamericanas," in *Normas Internacionales Sobre Derechos Humanos y Derecho Interno* (Lima: Andean Commission of Jurists, 1984), pp. 77–111; Justo Prieto, "El Estado de Sitio como Técnica Para Amedrentar," in *Colloquium on Uruguay and Paraguay, La Transición del Estado de Excepción a la Democracia, SIJUA* (Montevideo: Ediciones de la Banda Oriental, 1985), pp. 134–139; Claudio Grossman, "Algunas Consideraciones sobre el Régimen de Situaciones de exceción bajo la Convención Americana de Derechos Humanos," in *Derechos Humanos en las Americas, Homenaje a la Memoria de Carlos A. Dunshee de Abranches* (Washington: D.E.A., 1984).

13. Justo Prieto, note 12, p.134.

14. G. Gustavo Gallón, "La Experiencia Combiana en Estados de Emergencia y la Viabilidad de su Control Internacional," in Diego Garcia-Sayan, ed., *Estados de Emergencia*, note 12, pp. 79–92.

15. Peter Van Dijk, note 9, pp. 55–62. See also, Daniel O'Donnel, "States of exception," 21 *The Review of the International Commission of Jurists* 52–60 (1978); L.C. Green, "Derogation of Human Rights in Emergency Situations," 16 *The Canadian yearbook of International Law* 92–115 (1978).

16. Thus, for example, the state of siege declared by President Carlos Ibáñez in September of 1954 was based on the danger of a possible general lockout. In this respect, see Jorge Mera, Felipe Gonzáalez and Juan Enrique Vargas V., note 4, p. 17. Regarding states of exception in Chile, Hugo Frühling, "Fuerzas Armadas, Orden Interno y Derechos Humanos," in Hugo Frühling, Carlos Portales, and Augusto Varas, eds., *Estados y Fuerazas Armadas* (Santiago: Stitching Rechtschulp Chile and Latin American Faculty of Social Sciences FLACSO, 1982), pp. 35–58.

17. Diego Garcia-Sayan, "Peru: Estados de Excepción y su Régimen Jurídico," in Deigo Garcia-Sayan, ed., note 12, p. 124.

18. *Ibid.*, pp. 117 ff. See also Patricia Valdez, "La Situación de los Derechos Humanos en el Perú," *Comisión Andina de Juristas, Boletín No. 7* (Lima: March 1985.)

19. *Ibid.*, p. 121.

20. Gustavo Gallón, note 14, p.83.

21. *Ibid.*, pp. 83–84.

22. Tom Mullen, "Constitutional Protection of Human Rights," in Tom Campbell, David Goldberg, Sheila McLean, and Tom Mullen, eds., *Human Rights: From Rhetoric to Reality* (Oxford: Basil Blackwell, 1986), pp. 15–36; R. Berger, *Government by Judiciary: The Transformation of the Fourteenth Amendment* (Cambridge, MA: Harvard University Press, 1977); M. Tushnet, "The Dilemmas of Liberal Constitutionalism," 42 *Ohio State Law Journal* 410 (1981).

23. Tom Mullen, note 22, pp.18–20.

24. *Ibid.*, p. 23.

25. Jorge Mario Garcia Laguardia, *La Defensa de la Constitución* (Gautemala: Facultad de Ciencias Juridicas y Sociales, Universidad San Carlos de Gautemala, 1983), p. 66.

26. "Official Documents of the sessions held by the Commission and subcommissions in charge of the study of the draft of the new Political Constitution of the Republic" (Santiago: 1926), p. 81.

27. Alejandro Silva Bascuñán, "El Tribunal Constitucional," in Eduardo Frei et al., note 4.

28. Hugo Pereira Anabalón, "Justicia Especializada para la Tutela de los Derechos Humanos," en *Encuentro nacional: Los Derechos Humanos al la Luz del Ordenamineto Internacional* (Archbishopric of Santiago: Vicarship of Solidarity, 1978), p. 81.

29. Jorge Correa, "Formación de Jueces Para la Democracia," mimeo, 1987 Library, Deigo Portales Law School, Santiago, Chile.

30. Enrique Haba, note 6, Vol. II; *Indicadores Constitucionales*, pp. 495–498.

31. Hugo Pereira Anabalón, note 28, p. 81.

32. Francisco Eguiguren, *Los Retos de una Democracia Insuficiente* (Lima: Comisión Andina de juristas y Fundación" F. Nauman, 1990). pp. 83–130.

33. On the remedy of protection, see Jorge Mera, note 9 and Eduardo Soto Kloss, *El Recurso de Protección, Orígenes, Doctrina y Jurisprudencia* (Santiago: Editorial Juridica de Chile, 1982).

34. Jorge Mario García Laguardia, note 25, p. 27.

35. Jorge Mario García Laguardia, "Jurisprudencia Constitucional; Guatemala, Honduras, México. Una Muestra," Anuario Jurídico Instituto de Investigaciones Jurídicas UNAM No. XIV metico (1987).

36. Diego García-Sayan, note 17, p. 119.

37. Dennis O. Lynch, *Legal Roles in Colombia* (Uppsala: Scandinavian Institute of African Studies, International Center for Law in Development, New York, 1981) p. 64.

38. Luis Pásara, *Jueces, Justicia y Poder en el Perú* (Lima: CEDYS, 1982), pp. 88–103; Domingo García Belaúnde, *El Habeas Corpus en el Perú* (Lima: Universidad Nacional de San Marcos, 1979).

39. Marcial Rubio and Enrigque Bernales, *Perú Constitución y Sociedad Política* (Lima: DESCO, 1981). p. 133, quoted by Pásara, note 38, p. 96.

40. Luis Pásara, note 38, p. 100

41. Robert E. Biles, "The Position of the Judiciary in the Political Systems of Argentina and México," 8 *Lawyers of the Américas* 287 ff. (June 1976).

42. Harry Eckstein, *Division and Cohesion in Democracy. A Study of Norway* (Princeton, NJ: Princeton University Press, 1966), p. 26.

43. L. Pye, *Burma, Politics, Personality and Nation Building* (New Haven: Yale University Press, 1962), pp. 105–107.

44. A clear example in this respect is the use of the judicial way as a means to limit human rights violations. See Hugo Frühling, "States of Repression and Legal Strategy for the Defense of Human Rights in Chile," 5 *Human Rights Quarterly* 4, 510 (1983).

45. For a theoretical analysis of the access to the legal system in Latin America, see David Trubek, "Unequal Protection: Thoughts on Legal Services, Social Welfare and Income Distribution in Latin America," 13 *Texas International Law Journal* 243 (1978).

46. Guillermo O' Donnell, "*¿Y a mi que Mierda me Importa?, Notas Sobre Socialbilidad y Politica en Argentina y Brasil*" (Buenos Aires: CEDES, 1984), pp. 44–45.

47. *Ibid.*

48. George Westcott, "La Confianza Interpersonal en el Perú. Estudio Psicosocial de Campesinos y Obreros" (Lima: ESAN, 1975), mimeo p. 71. Quoted bu Luis Pásara, *Jueces, Justicia y Poder en el Perú* (Lima: CEDYS, 1982).

49. Margarita María Errazuriz and Pura Ortiz, "Los Problemas de Justicia de los Sectores de Bajos Recursos: El Caso de Una Población Marginal," 3 *Revista Chilena de Derecho* 4–6, 214–216 (July–December 1976).

50. The concept of relevance was orally developed by Rogelio Pérez Perdomo in a

discussion held by the Human Rights Program of the Academy for Christian Humanism in August 1988.

51. Hugo Frühling, "Poder Judicial y Political en Chile," in *La Administracion de Justicia en America Latina* (Lima: Latin American Council for Law and Development, 1984), p. 118.

52. "Población afectada por la Delincuencia: Una aproximación a la Criminalidad Real." Division de Estudios Sociales, November 1986, quoted in *Universidad Nacional de Colombia, Colombia: Violencia y Democracia* (Bogotá: 1987), pp. 212–213.

6

The National Question, Secession and Constitutionalism: The Mediation of Competing Claims to Self-Determination

Abdullahi Ahmed An-Na'im

For better and for worse, the nation state[1] is now the funamental reality of both domestic and internationl political organization, and is likely to continue to be so for the foreseeable future. Yet, to think of a "nation" as a people of single ethnicity and culture, as is often, done limits our understanding of what a nation is, and forecloses the possibility of thinking realistically about the status of minorities within nations; it is very rare for the population of a nation state to consist of one nation in this sense. In the vast majority of countries, especially in Africa, the population of the nation state consist of several "nations"; a description of these entities as nation states tends to express an ideal of total national integration and unity, which may not be as desirable as it is often assumed. The nation state usually subsumes many "nations," some of whom dominate and oppress others; and the ideal integration and unity often imply the assimilation of the minority peoples (who may be, in aggregate, the numerical majority of the population of the state as a whole) into the dominant culture.

One of the most problematic aspects of constitutionalism throughout the world is the status and rights of minorities: ethnic, religious, and/or linguistic. It may be useful to see the relevant questions in terms of the principle of self-determination in order to provide some theoretical framework and to generate comparative analysis. I submit that the core issue is whether it is possible, within a unified state, to achieve mediation and resolution of the competing claims of the majority and minority (or minorities) to self-determination. If resolution is not possible in a given situation, would the minority be justified in seeking secession and the establishment of a separate nation state? The principle of self-determination can illuminate the positions of both (or all) sides, even if they are not articulated as such in political discourse.

On can also see the status and rights of minorities as fundamental rights under a domestic constitutional order. If a minority's claim to self-determination through secession is unjustified or unsuccessful, how can the collective rights of such a minority, and the individual rights of its members, be protected under the constitutional order of the particular country? I characterize this approach as the domestic or internal dimension of the right to self-determination.

It is ironic that the independent nation state, once perceived as the essential prerequisite for the achievement of the peoples' right to self-determination, is now seen by many people(s) as a major obstacle to the realization of that right. Unless the present nation states of Africa redress this situation by responding to legitimate demands for self-determination, they should expect to be treated by their peoples as colonial states to be combatted in struggles and wars of liberation.

My basic thesis is that *national unity is desirable* because it is normally conducive to greater security, political stability, and social and economic development. The economic and political interdependence of the modern world requires movement toward greater unity and integration, not toward separation and disintegration. Several successful examples of national unity built among diverse populations exist, and even the old and historically antagonistic nation states of western Europe are progressing toward greater regional unity to the best advantage of their populations. Nevertheless, *national unity should not be pursued at any cost*. The constitutional framework of the nation state must provide for equality and justice for all segments of the population, equality in sharing political power economic and social development, and the enabling of each "nation" or "people" within the nation state to maintain and develop its distinctive cultural identity. Failing that, the right to secession by an aggrieved minority may have to be granted, albeit not lightly and only as an ultimate resort. In this way, the threat of secession reinforces the obligation of the nation state to allow its population the maximum degree of internal self-determination; at the same time, the difficulty of achieving secession strengthens the cooperation of all segments of the population in building national unity.

A discussion of the issues raised by this thesis must be preceded by a brief statement of the underlying conception of constitutionalism. In my view, constitutionalism is government in accordance with a constitution that maintains a proper balance between the need of the individual for complete personal freedom and the need of the community for total social justice. Constitutionalism is committed to the establishment and maintenance of mechanisms and processes of governmental structure, economic activity, and social organization conducive to the preservation and enhancement of the life, liberty, and dignity of every person, individually and in association with others.

Historical notions of constitutionalism had their source in the need to limit the powers of rulers and safeguard individual persons and groups against arbitrary and despotic government; from this perspective, constitutionalism refers to those principles, rules, institutions, and practices that regulate the functioning of government so as to ensure the liberty and human diginity of those subject to its jurisdiction. It was realized in due course, however, that the achievements of these objectives require positive action of, as well as negative limitations on, powers of government. To my mind, therefore, constitutionalism encompasses what the state must do, as well as that it may not do, to achieve and maintain this proper balance.

This expectation of positive action on the part of the state to fulfill its proper constitutional role leads me to expect state involvement in the provision of social security and essential services, such as health, education, and housing. Traditional liberal perceptions of constitutionalism would not agree with this view, but I believe that it is supported by the underlying moral premise of liberalism itself as evidenced by the evolution of social democratic models in Western Europe.

Certain principles and practices, such as competitive representative government and separation of powers, have been successfully employed by some countries in their efforts to implement constitutionalism. Those experiences are helpful to many countries, but they should not be used as a presumption for a rigid model of constitutionalism. Under different sociololgical and cultural conditions, other methods of political and legal accountability may be more appropriate. The universal principles and institutions of constitutionalism should be adapted to the economic, political, and social realities of each country.

With this conception of constitutionalism as the context for the discussion of the issues and questions raised earlier, I begin with an overview of the principle of self-determination and its internal and external implications. Questions regarding the identification of the claimants of the right to self-determination and the options they may have for satisfying their claim will then be discussed. The final section offers an outline of a model for evaluating experiences in forging national unity out of diverse populations; we must learn from both the successes and failures of these efforts to devise a workable strategy for mediation and resolution of current and future situations of majority/minority conflicts in Africa. A workable strategy in the context of constitutionalism in Africa is proposed in this final section; this African focus does not preclude the applicability of the analysis and proposal advanced here to other parts of the world, including the developed countries of the North where, for example, the status and rights of indigenous groups raise similar issues.[2]

The Principle of Self-Determination

Self-Determination and the Nation State

"If history were a chronicle of the voluntary association and disassociation of human groups," suggests L. Buchheit, "there would be no need for a doctrine of self-determination."[3] This comment may be a useful approach to the essential meaning and moral justification of the principle of self-determination, the collective manifestation of the universal human need to identify with a group and to have control over one's fate. If a person were free to associate with or disassociate from a group, and the group as a whole were free to associate with or disassociate from other groups, then both the individual amd collective needs for self-determination would be satisfied, making any discussion of the nature and scope of a "right" to self-determination redundant. But life is never that simple: neither the individual nor the group can have such freedom in the absolute and unfettered sense. *To maximize this freedom in practice is, in my view, one of the most vital functions of constitutionalism.* This chapter, however, is concerned with the collective aspect of self-determination, particularly in the context of the modern nation state in Africa.

The moral justification and the political force of the principle of self-determination are linked to the notion that government should be based on the consent of the governed: that people have a right to associate freely into an entity organized to govern itself, thereby giving expression to "the consent of the governed."[4] People need not, and do not in fact, belong to a single entity or group; they belong to different entities or groups for different purposes. Moreover, not all functions of government need be vested in a single entity. The right to self-determination can be satisfied through a variety of entities exercising different functions of government. Much of the confusion surrounding the meaning and implications of the right to self-determination is due to the conception of the right as vested in a single entity, a "nation," which constitutes the nation state.

In common usage, the term "nation" is used interchangeably with the term "political state," thereby assuming the desirability, or even the inevitability, of identifying the political state with a nation unified by common culture. This leads to two contradictory approaches to the nation state.[5] The ideal of the identification of nation and political state encourages the state to make the facts fit the ideal, regardless of the rights or liberties of those citizens who do not belong to the majority or dominant "nation" within the nation state; this line of thinking denies the possibility of a multicultural state, thereby justifying governmental action to accelerate the process of cultural assimilation as a means of legitimizing the state by unifying its cultural and political identities.

The same line of thinking supports the contradictory view that every culture must be a state in embryo. Minorities who are oppressed through the majority's tendency to assimilate them find in that tendency justification for seeking to break away and form their own nation state. Once they achieve their own statehood, two sources of further tension and conflict may arise. First, the population of the new state may demand that people who constitute part of their "cultural nation" who happen to be citizens of another state be allowed to join the new state. Second, minorities within the new state may also be oppressed by the new majority, and demand their own right to self-determination.

I suggest that the conflict between these contradictory approaches to the nation state can be avoided if the right to self-determination is preceived as exercisable *within*, as well as through, the nation sate. The "nations" or peoples constituting the Nation of the nation state need not challenge and overthrow that state to satisfy their right to self-determination. Nevertheless, it must remain conceivable that such challenge with a view to establishing a separate nation state may be justified under certain circumstances.

The International and National Dimensions of Self-Determination

As the collective manifestation of the powerful individual desire to have control over one's affairs and to ensure one's economic and social well-being, the political idea of self-determination must be as ancient as organized human society itself; as a doctrine of international law, it is a recent and somewhat controversial principle.[6] Although external self-determination, in the sense of liberation from traditional colonialism, is firmly established and largely achieved, internal self-determination within existing nation states, and against what might be called "local colonialism," remains problematic, especially in the African context.

Because states are traditionally taken to be only "proper" subjects of international law, self-determination has generally been thought to be realizable only through the establishment of nation states for the people claiming the right. According to this view, only "a state or the community of states forming the United Nations [or the Organization of African Unit] can seek performance of a state's obligation to accord self-determination to its people, not the people of that state... What is involved here in terms of international law is the international obligation of a state and not the right of its people."[7]

Leading scholars maintain that this is an inaccurate, or at least a dated view of the subjects of international law;[8] it will be shown, self-determination is now firmly established as a human right of "peoples," not states. I believe that peoples within a nation state are entitled to assert their rights to self-determination against the states, and I adopt D.B. Levin's formulation of the position under national law:

> When a nation exercises its right to self-determination, form[s] an independent state, voluntarily remains in a multinational [multicultural] state or joins another multinational [multicultural] state, its right to the free determination of its further internal political, economic, social and cultural status passes to the sphere of state law of the state to which the nation now belongs. But this holds good only as long as the conditions on which the nation became part of the given state are not violated by this state and as long as the nation's desire to stay within it remains in force, and it is not compelled to do so by coercive means. As soon as one of these phenomena occur, the question again passes from the sphere of state law into the sphere of international law.[9]

An existing nation state should normally have the opportunity to honor its obligation to guarantee genuine self-determination to all its peoples, both minority and majority alike. A variety of constitutional devices, including appropriate internal arrangements regarding the autonomy and self-governance of its constituent parts in some situations, can fulfill this obligation. Under international law, a state may make whatever internal constitutional and structural arrangements it deems fit, so long as the state as a whole continues to be capable of exercising its rights and honoring its obligations in relation to other states. Thus, acceptance of the above-mentioned restriction of nation states' right to self-determination does not preclude internal arrangements that give aspects of the substance of self-determination to various peoples within the state while maintaining the sovereign unity of the state for the purposes of international law.

Self-Determination as a Human Right

Although the Charter of the United Nations provided for the right of peoples to self-determination,[10] the 1948 Declaration of Human Rights did not recognize it as a human right; this omission was rectified in subsequent human rights treaties. The right to self-determination is now firmly established as a human right by virtue of Article 1, common to both the International Convenant on Economic, Social, and Cultural Rights and the International Covenant on Civil and Political Rights.[11] The right is expressed in this common Article 1.1 as belonging to "all peoples," so that they can "freely determine their (political status and freely pursue their economic, social and cultural development." Furthermore, Article 1.2 of both covenants provides that States party to either Convenant "shall promote the realization of the right of self-determination, and shall respect that right, in conformity with the provisions of the Charter of the United Nations."

The African Charter on Human and People's Rights of 1981 not only affirms, in Article 20.1, the right of "all peoples" to "the unquestionable" and inalienable right to self-determination," but also specifies some of the implications of that right in a number of articles.[12] This is particularly significant for our purposes here because, as a document drafted and adopted by all of the members of the Organization of African Unity, the African Charter on Human Peoples' Rights should carry political and moral weight all African states, regardless of whether they are legally bound by this Charter through formal ratification.

Despite its formal recognition as a human right, the right to self-determination needs further specification before it can be implemented in practice. For example, the formulations of self-determination as a human-right in the Covenants and African Charter contain significant elements of ambiguity. Though attributing the right to "peoples," none of these human rights instruments addresses the question of whether this right is exhausted or satisfied by the achievement of independence from colonial rule and the establishment of a nation state, or whether the right continues to exist within the framework of such a state.[13] Is it reasonable to deem a "people's" right to self-determination exhausted with their incorporation into a nation state, even against their will or without consulting them? And if they were consulted and did consent to being so incorporated, at the initial formation of the state or at a subsequent stage, will a people have no right to self-determination regardless of what happens to their status and rights within the nation state?

If a people's right to self-determination does persist within a nation state, its scope and implications remain uncertain. How can such a right be satisfied short of secession? Does it ultimately extend to justifying secession? Under what circumstances? Who are the "people" entitled to self-determination, whether through secession or other means short of secession? In other words, what constitutes the "self" of self-determination, and how can it be identified? What is the scope of the "determination" to which that self is entitled, and how can it be realized?

Some scholars and the delegates of some governments at international fora cite these ambiguities in support of the view that it is not appropriate to think of collective rights, such as self-determination, as human rights;[14] other scholars accept the possibility of developing collective or "solidarity" human rights while sounding strong warnings against the abuse of this new concept.[15] A third group of scholars maintains that it is meaningful and constructive to speak of collective human rights.[16] As T. van Boven pointed out, opponents of collective human rights "are inclined to take predominantly legalistic approach to human rights in the sense of legally enforceable rights. Leading instruments, such as the ... Universal Declaration of Human Rights and the African Charter on Human and Peoples' Rights, are more than legal instruments. They are also instruments of liberarion .... The struggles for human rights and people's rights are not only settled in the courts but also and *perhaps more decisively in political fora*."[17]

I concur with van Boven's view of collective human rights. I believe it is desirable to think of some collective rights, such as the right to self-determination, as a human right because of the power of the idea of human rights and its utility in political discourse. Such *collective rights are an essential framework for realizing most human rights of the individuals*; individuals are the direct beneficiaries of collective rights, and, further, cannot exercise most of their traditional human rights except as members of a collectivity. I also believe that it is possible to formulate and implement such collective rights in a meaningful way. In so doing, valid differences between individuals and collective human rights must be recognized; it is particularly important to identify the claimant of the collective right, the entity against whom the right is held and the means of satisfying the right in any given case.

The Claimants and Respondents of the Right to Self-Determination

Who Has the Right to Self-Determination and Against Whom

The charter of the United States, the two Covenants, the African Charter of Human and Peoples' Rights, and other Principles of International Law Concerning Friendly Relations,[18] speak of "peoples'" right to self-determination. It can therefore be said the international law recognizes this right belonging to peoples and not states; it can also be said that the underlying assumption of these instruments is that people are represented by their states in the international arena. In other words, whereas people are the holders of the right, *states are the entities charged with the obligation to ensure the satisfaction of the right at both the domestic and international levels*. For this interpretation to be acceptable, people must have some recourse should the state fail to honor its obligation. Before elaborating on this aspect, the notion of "people" as holders of the right to self-determination must be clarified.

Neither the U.N. Covenants nor the African Charter define the term "people"; drafters of international instruments sometimes prefer that a central concept or term be defined by subsequent practice and jurisprudence rather than impose their own definition. For example, the International Law Commission declined to define "state" in its draft Declaration of the Rights and Duties of states, preferring the term to be interpreted in accordance with international practice.[19] Nevertheless, we must here attempt a working definition of the term "people" for the purposes of the present discussion.

According to Y. Dinstein, peoplehood can be seen as contingent on two separate elements: an objective element of being an ethnic group with a common history, a cultural identity, and a subjective element indicating itself as a people.[20] I. Brownlie defined "people," in terms of a core of meaning, for the purposes of applying the principle of self-determination.

> This core consists in the right of a community which has a distinct character to have this character reflected in the institutions of government under which it lives. The concept of distinct character depends on a number of criteria which may appear in combination. Race (or nationality) is one of the more important of the relevant criteria, but the concept of race can only be expressed scientifically in terms of more specific feature, in which matters of culture, language, religion and group psychology predominate.[21]

These and similar definitions of the term "people" emphasize the attributes of commonality of interests, group identity, distinctiveness, and a territorial link. As R. Kiwanutka notes, "It is clear, therefore, that 'people' could refer to a group of persons within a specific geographical entity (e.g., the Alur of Uganda or the Amandebele of Zimbabwe) as well as to all the persons within that entity (e.g., Ugandans or Zimbabweans)."[22]

In mentioning these attributes in a report prepared for the U.N. on the right to self-determination, Aurelieu Cristescu stated that a people should not be confused with ethnic, religious, or linguistic minorities whose existence and rights are recognized in Article 27 of the International Covenant on Civil and Political Rights.[23] This distinction does not appear to me to be valid; it seems to have been prompted by the author's conception of self-determination as achievable only through the establishment of a separate state. I submit that an ethnic, religious, or linguistic minority are a "people" entitled to its right to self-determination, within an established state or through secession under certain circumstances.

Another approach to defining a "people" that focuses the last point is one that distinguishes a people from their state.[24] Again, Kiwanuka: "This view, by separating the people from their state, does for collectivists what civil and political liberties do for individuals. It seeks to reserve a certain amount of political and economic space for peoples qua peoples. This space, or peoples' sovereignty, becomes critical where the interests of the people and those of the state diverge."[25]

One of the objections to the recognition of collective rights as human rights is the alleged uncertainty of the entity against which such rights are to be asserted. Provided that it is appreciated that the term "rights" is used in a broader sense than mere "legal" rights enforceable in a court of law, I can see no particular difficulty in this regard because all rights are activated and asserted against the source of challenge, denial or threat, be it the nation state of the same people, another people within that state, any other state, and so forth.

The Manner of Exercising the Right to Self-Determination

The vast majority of the new nation states seem to think that the right of their populations to self-determination has been satisfied through the achievement of formal independence from colonial rule;[26] in particular, African states have individually and collectively resisted claims for secession by various peoples as a means to achieving self-determination.[27] This resistance is perhaps understandable because, given the arbitrary boundaries drawn by colonial powers at the time of independence, almost every existing African state risks complete disintegration if the integrity of its international boundaries is questioned. The states fear that if the right to secede and establish an independent state is granted to one people within a state, other peoples might claim similar treatment, leading to dismemberment of the existing state, and probably to its total disintegration. Moreover, since another part of the same people who are demanding secession from an existing state may be within the boundaries of a neighboring state, granting the demand of the first part may encourage the other part to demand to join their people, thereby threatening the territorial integrity of the neighbouring state as well.

Another realistic consideration involves the political and economic viability of any proposed new state.[28] From the political point of view, tribal and ethnic diversity in Africa makes it almost certain that the territory of the proposed secessionist state would include minority groups who could feel threatened by the dominance of the majority group;[29] these groups could create political difficulties similar to those that led to demands for secession by the majority group from parent state in the first place. Ethnic or other identity of the population of a given territory does not necessarily mean that such territory could support an independent state in material terms; conversely, the secession of one part of an existing state could diminish, or even completely eliminate, the economic viability of that state.

Although these considerations may present a powerful argument against the realization of the right to self-determination through secession and the establishment of an independent state in some cases, arguments, explained below, in favor of secession under appropriate circumstances can override them. Moreover, the above arguments do not necessarily apply to alternative arrangements short of secession. I would therefore suggest that each situation be considered in light of some general criteria for the validity of claims for secession; if secession appeared justified in a given case, the principle of self-determination would require granting secession and recognizing the new state; where secession is clearly not justified, or is at least of doubtful validity, it may be appropriate to consider alternative arrangements for satisfying claims for self-determination.

Justification of Secession

When may secession be justified? This question is deliberately formulated in this way because, as is clear from the following formulation of possible criteria for judging the validity of claims for secession, each element of the ultimate decision is open to a variety of interpretations, rendering it vulnerable to criticism and rejection by one side or the other. It is therefore imperative that those claiming, or called on to adjudicate among competing claims to self-determination, try to see the issues from both (or all) points of view. The next section will address the circumstances and mechanisms of the "adjudication."

Because there are competing policy arguments with corresponding conflicting evidence of state practice, both in favor and against self-determination through secession,[30] the following criteria have been suggested for judging the validity of claims for self-determination: (1) the degree of internal cohesion and self-identification of the group claiming self-determination, (2) the nature and scope of their claim, (3) the underlying reasons for the claim, and (4) the degree of deprivation of basic human rights for the people in question.[31] The higher the degree of the internal cohesion and self-identification of the people, the greater their historical claim to separate identity; the more they are deprived of their basic human rights under their present "nation" state, the stronger would be their case for secession.

This analysis, in my view, is consistent with a reasonable interpretation of the Declaration of Principles of International Law Concerning Friendly Relations and Cooperation among States in Accordance with the Charter of the United Nations.[32] This Declaration is one of the most authoritative international pronouncements; it "codifies" the relevant principles of international law and addresses the issues in the postcolonial context. Although this Declaration affirms the principle of the territorial integrity of existing states, it does not make it absolute. Principle (e), paragraph 7 of the Declaration reads as follows:

> Nothing in the foregoing paragraphs shall be construed as authorizing or encouraging any action which would dismember or impair, totally or in part, the territorial integrity or political unity of sovereign and independent States *conducting themselves in compliance with the principles of equal rights and self-determination of peoples as described above and thus possessed of a government representing the whole people belonging to the territory without distinction as to race, creed or color.*

As clearly indicated by the words I have italicized, the territorial integrity or political unity of existing states is guaranteed only when the state in question respects the equal rights and self-determination of the people subject to its jurisdiction.

Other considerations for judging the validity of claims for self-determination exist. First, the people seeking secession must not only constitute a clear majority in a geographical unit that is capable of sustaining an independent state in economic and political terms, but due regard must be given to the status and rights of other minorities within the region. The establishment of the new state by a previously oppressed minority should not create problems of self-determination for others within the new state.

Second, it should be considered whether it is appropriate for a strong minority capable of achieving secessions to do so and leave other minorities within the existing nation state vulnerable to greater oppression. It may be better for all concerned for the stronger minority to remain within the existing state and struggle for the protection of the rights of all minorities than selfishly to seek an answer to its own problems through secession, abandoning other minorities to a worse fate. After all, although political independence, when justifiable and achievable, may be a right, it is not an imperative duty.

Finally, it should be recalled that external factors may strongly influence, if not effectively decide, the situation one way or the other. The establishment of Bangladesh in 1971 may serve as an instructive example of how external forces can make secession possible. V. Nanda demonstrated how Bangladesh's claim to secede was helped along by specific circumstances: the physical separation of East from West Pakistan, the total domination and brutal suppression of the former by the latter, the nature of the ethnic and cultural differences between the populations of the two parts, the disparity in their economic growth to the disadvantage of East Pakistan, the electoral mandate to secede, and the viability of both regions as separate entities.[33] Nevertheless, It is extremely unlikely that the secession of Bangladesh would have materialized except for the fact that the "humanitarian" intervention of India presented both West Pakistan and the international community with a *fait accompli*. In contrast, the insufficiency of external sponsorship contributed significantly to the failure of the Biafran bid for secession from Nigeria in the late 1960s.

The Circumstances and Mechanisms of Mediation

Observers may reasonably differ on the relative significance of each element in the circumstances that "legitimized" and effectuated" the secession of Bengladesh, and on whether any of them is present in sufficient magnitude in any given situation; the participants in a majority/minority conflict will normally disagree more drastically in their evaluation of these elements. Moreover, in the heat of confrontation and historical antagonism, their perception and discourse about the issues and considerations will no doubt be seriously influenced and distorted by passionate and irrational components of concrete situations. It must also be noted that perceptions and discourse about these matters are played out in a world of local and international power politics. These complicating factors are relevant to both the internal dynamics of perception and discourse and the processes of mediating and adjudicating between competing claims to self-determination.

A theoretical argument must recognize the presence and power of the irrational components of these situations. The irrational can be at least as influential as the rational in shaping the attitudes the position of participants in a conflict, diminishing each's willingness and ability to appreciate and deal with the attitudes and positions of the other side. Without such appreciation little chance for compromise exists, and the use of force to "subdue the enemy" becomes almost unavoidable. This situation is the antithesis of the constructive scenario of dialogue and peaceful mediation of competing claims.

A hypothesis for peaceful adjudicating must also take account of the realities of regional international power politics and their impact on the participants in the conflict. Majority/minority conflicts often attract involvement of outsiders, who deliberately exploit the conflict to further their own self-interest. The case of Bangladesh cited above is a clear illustration of the sometimes decisive impact of external factors. Nevertheless, it is the attitudes and positions of the participants in the conflict that provide opportunities for external interference and exploitation.

Without understanding the power of the irrational and the role of power politics, I maintain that it is useful to make the sort of theoretical argument I am advancing. The irrational components of the positions of participants can be overcome only through a clear explanation of the consequences of those positions and exploration of realistic alternatives of them. I believe that participants to a conflict would usually prefer a peaceful settlement of their dispute, and can be brought to an appreciation that dialogue and negotiation can achieve that end; the fact that each side to these conflicts usually claims this to be their position supports my thesis, and can be used by mediators to induce the parties to negotiate. As indicated earlier, the framework for negotiation and mutual compromise is the ultimate threat of secession, on the one hand, and the difficulty of achieving secession, on the other.

The logic of the theoretical exposition of the issues presented here can promote the willingness to negotiate; it should not be difficult to devise the necessary mechanisms and safeguards. International and regional organizations, such as the United Nations and the Organization of African Unity, or other mutually acceptable mediators, can provide or devise the forum for negotiations. If needed, the personnel of these organizations or other third parties acceptable to both or all sides of a conflict can then act as mediators or facilitators of dialogue and negotiation. I submit that the willingness to negotiate, and the prospects of a successful peaceful resolution of majority/minority conflicts, will be greatly enhanced by appreciating that the substance of self-determination can be achieved through means short of complete secession.

Internal Self-Determination

Assuming that secession is either undesirable or unattainable, (or until that is the case), much can be done at the internal domestic level to guarantee the legitimate collective rights of minorities within an existing nation. What are these minorities and what are their legitimate collective rights?

It should first be recalled that we are concerned with the collective rights of peoples, are briefly defined above, and not any random or transitory group of people. Its historical link and subjective identification make a group into a people. In usual practice, the group of people with whose collective rights we are concerned are referred to as "ethnic, religious, and/or linguistic minorities." Space does not permit elaboration of each of these features of identity, but we must clarify the term "minorities" in the following ways.

With the glaring example of the Republic of South Africa, it should be clear that the sociological minority is not necessarily the political majority. Even when the minority is a numerical one, and ethnic, religious, or linguistic group may be a majority in the state as a whole and a clear majority within a specific region or district, with the countrywide majority constituting a minority in that region or distric. When these districts enjoy a high degree of autonomy, it is the rights of the countrywide majority that have to be protected qua minority rights in the specific area. It may therefore be appropriate to speak of protecting the collective rights of ethnic, religious, and linguistic groups in general.[34]

We must also avoid lumping all minorities, whether sociological or political, together; different models or regimes may have to be developed to fit the situations of specific minorities, depending on their demographic composition, affiliations, and preferences.[35]

With respect to the rights of these minorities, we are concerned with the collective human rights to be "afforded to human beings *communally*, that is to say, in conjunction with one another or as a group, people or a minority . . . The group which enjoys them communally is not a corporate entity and does not possess a legal personality. The nature of these human rights require, however, that they shall be exercised jointly rather than severally."[36] Although there is often an individual dimension to the rights in question, that dimension derives its significance for our purposes because of its implications to the collectivity; discrimination on the grounds of race, religion, or language is usually experienced by individual persons. Without minimizing in any way the gravity of such discrimination to the individual, I wish to focus here on the implications of such discrimination for the people or minority to which that individual person belongs, that is, on the collective right to be protected against such discrimination.

According to the Permanent Court of International Justice, the predecessor of the present International Court of Justice, the international system for the minorities between the two world wars had two objectives: to achieve complete equality between the nationals of the state regardless of race, religion, or language, and to ensure for the minority (or minorities) suitable means for the preservation of their racial peculiarities, traditions, and national characteristics.[37] The Court perceived these two objectives as interlocked; no true equality would exist between the majority and minority if the latter were deprived of the means of preserving its special characteristics.

A contemporary authoritative formulation of the rights of minorities is Article 27 of the International Covenant on Civil and Political Rights:

> In those States in which ethnic, religious or linguistic minorities exist, persons belonging to such minorities shall not be denied the right, in community with the other members of their group, to enjoy their own culture, to profess and practice their own religion, or to use their own language.

The African Charter on Human and Peoples' Rights contains a member of detailed provisions relating to the rights of peoples, which presumably apply to minorities within nation states. Article 22, for example, provides that

> 1. All peoples shall have the right to their economic, social and cultural development with due regard to their freedom and identity and in the equal enjoyment of the common heritage of mankind.
>
> 2. States shall have the duty, individually or collectively, to ensure the exercise of the right to development.

These formulations suggest that strict adherence to the "melting-pot" concept, presumed to be prevailing in the United States and other countries with high immigration rates, may defeat the right of minorities to preserve their separate identity.[38] However, such separate identity has to be balanced against the equally legitimate claims of national integration. In other words, ways must be found for reconciling the two competing claims, countrywide cohesion and integration, and diversity of radical/ethnic, religious, and linguistic identities.[39] Whether through formal federalism or some other form of regional or functional autonomy, the basic objective is to afford the minority (or minorities) *equality* in political participation and economic and social development at the national level and *equality* in pursuit of cultural identity. If these objectives are achieved, neither subjective motivation nor objective justification for secession will exist because the secession is not an end in itself, but a means to these objectives. The precise formula may vary from one situation to the other, but the basic criterion is the *golden rule of reciprocity*: one should place the self in the position of the other person; whatever the self expects or demands must be conceded to the other person. Once this fundamental appreciation of the nature of the legitimate collective rights of minorities is achieved, the appropriate constitutional measures can easily be articulated and implemented.

Strategy for Mediation of Conflicts in Forging National Unity

No given formula for forging national unity exists that should be automatically applied by others. The first point to note is the importance of clarity about the meaning of national unity. As emphasized above, national unity is not necessarily cultural unity; cultural diversity is seen as desirable and compatible with national unity. I believe that an appropriate degree of cultural unity is most likely to evolve naturally over time through the processes of education and social and economic interaction, but it should never be forced through coerced assimilation into the dominant culture. Coercion breeds resentment and resistance; respect for cultural diversity induces a sense of solidarity and vested interest in genuine and lasting national unity and integration.

To assess experiences with the forging of national unity, I would therefore apply the dual criteria of the maintenance of national unity with the encouragement of cultural diversity. Categorical judgments are unlikely to be valid or particularly constructive: impediments to making an objective categorical judgment include the difficulty of ascertaining the lack of verifiable and reliable information, and the emotional, and therefore controversial, nature of the issues. The time frame of the experience is also problematic; one must also consider how long the elements of the above-mentioned criteria have been satisfied in a given case, and how long they are likely to remain in a state of equilibrium. It would be useful to learn from the experiences of various countries what is conducive and what is counterproductive to the forging of national unity as defined here; in so doing, it would be important to extrapolate from the details of each country some general principles and guidelines applicable to other situations.

Although the established states of Europe and North America have had rather favorable conditions for forging national unity, these states continue to experience problems with the rights of minorities. When their constitutional models were adopted by Third World countries (e.g., India, which enacted extensive constitutional provisions for minority rights in an effort to anticipate and preempt likely causes of ethnic, religious, and/or linguistic conflicts), such conflicts nevertheless arose in practice. One should not conclude therefore that national unity, as defined above, cannot be achieved. The key to a successful creation of national unity, in my view, is the ability to mediate among the various segments of the population and reconcile competing claims to self-determination.

I suggest a dual strategy for this mediation and reconciliation, one at the domestic national level and the other at the regional or international level. The failure of reconciliation at the domestic national level may lead to civil wars, which are likely to have serious consequences for the security and stability of neighboring and other states. Domestic conflicts therefore usually implicate other states, despite demands for, or pretense to comply with, the principle of nonintervention in the domestic affairs of other states.

The Domestic Level Strategy

Assuming the desirability of maintaining the national unity and territorial integrity of existing African states, the primary level of action should be at the domestic national level. Many economic, social, structural, and other factors are relevant at this level, but I will confine my remarks to the constitutional aspects.

Internal self-determination can be realized through the operation of the three interrelated and mutually supportive principles of empowerment, participation, and accountability. Contemporary experience seems to support this view. The population at large, and each segment or group thereof, must be empowered to articulate and demand their individual and collective rights; such empowerment is developed through popular participation in all facets and levels of the processes of government. To maintain the effective empowerment of the people, the mechanics and processes of accountability of all elected and appointed officials must be established and implemented; this accountability, in turn, will be sanctioned by the empowerment of the people and their participation. In terms of constitutionalism, these principles of empowerment require the establishment and maintenance of a strong constitutional order, not merely a formal constitution. A constitutional order includes institutions of political participation and accountability and balanced and carefully worked out governmental structures, judicial organs, and so forth: it provides for and effectuates a decentralized system of government that allows the various peoples the maximum degree of autonomy compatible with national unity and territorial integrity of the state; and it articulates, verbally and institutionally, collective and individual rights and ensures their effective implementation.

But no constitutional order can provide these guarantees unless it enjoys genuine legitimacy among the population at large; nor can the constituent aspects or institutions of the constitutional order play their role without such legitimacy. Legitimacy provides the political will that supports constitutional institutions and sanctions their functioning. For example, an independence judiciary is one of the primary mechanisms for safegaurding individual and collective rights; as African experiences clearly show, no judiciary can function without the support of an enlightened and effective public opinion.

To achieve and maintain legitimacy for the constitutional order, the whole population must be educated and socialized into safegaurding and implementing it. Political accountability is the essence of any constitutional order; no political regime can maintain power without the cooperation, or at least the acquiescence, of the population. If the populace realizes that it has the ultimate political power, that it can exercise that power by withdrawing its cooperation, or refusing to acquiesce, even the most brutal dictatorship can be terminated. Such realization develops only through education, literature, the arts, and all other means of communication among the whole population, especially rural and nomadic peoples who constitute the vast majority of the population in all African states.

Mediation Strategy

Realistically speaking, those who control the machinery of the state are far more likely to be responsive to political and other forms of pressure than to ethical considerations or abstract notions of justice and higher interests. The domestic constitutional order outlined above will have a better chance of success if it is supported by international political accountability and economic pressure on offending governments and majorities. It is in the best interest of the international community to impress on national governments that they cannot get away with denying their own populations internal self-determination; such denial leads to conflict and civil war, which endangers the vital interests of other states, increasingly independent regionally and internationally. No civil war can be relied on to remain within the boundaries of any state. The fundamental choice facing the international community is a simple one: ensure the satisfaction of peoples's right to internal self-determination or risk the widepsread conflict and war that might result from demands for secession.

In advocating a more active role for the international community, I am *not* advocating direct, *unilateral* intervention in the internal affairs of other countries. Unilateral intervention would probably be counterproductive and prejudicial to the interest of all parties, including those of the oppressed minority. I am suggesting concerted and coordinated efforts at mediation and influence through *multilateral action of regional and international organizations*, such as the United Nations and the Organizations of African Unity, to achieve and maintain internal self-determination for all the peoples of each country. Peaceful collective international support for the mediation and reconciliation of competing claims to internal self-determination is the most effective way to preempt military, or other aggressive, intervention by other countries. Nevertheless, I would not deny an oppressed minority their right to external self-determination through secession if all efforts to achieve internal self-determination fail.

Conclusion

This chapter utilized the principle of self-determination as a theoretical framework for discussing issues of constitutionalism in relation to the status and rights of minorities. This approach is useful because I believe that the collective rights of minorities are integral to the rights of individuals and worthy of protection as such. Collective rights should therefore be protected under domestic law even where existing national constitutions do not recognize them as such. Further, I maintain that states are charged with the international legal obligation to protect the collective rights of minorities; in my view, the right of "peoples" to self-determination (in the above-cited provisions of the Charter of the United Nations, the two Covenants, and the African Charter of Human and Peoples' Rights) means internal self-determination for minorities at the domestic level, as well as the right of colonized people to formal political independence.

Moreover, I argue that the underlying logic and moral rationale of traditional decolonization cannot end by the achievement of formal independence. As colonized people(s) are entitled to the self-determination of formal independence from a colonial power, so they should be entitled to self-determination through secession from the new independent state if they are denied internal self-determination. In this way, the international legal right of minorities to secession can arise if they are denied internal self-determination at the domestic constitutional level.

But to have an international legal right to secession does not mean it is necessary. My primary concern is to avoid secession. I perceive my argument for the possession of this right as a necessary means for *avoiding* its exercise by guaranteeing internal self-determination through appropriate constitutional means. As indictaed earlier, the combination of an ultimate threat of secession and the difficulty of its achievement is the incentive to all parties to a majority/minority conflict to develop and implement the necessary constitutional mechanisms to achieve substantive internal self-determination for all segments of the population. Self-determination can be achieved within the nation state through varying degrees of regional and local autonomy which guarantee meaninfgul political participation and equitable economic and social development while allowing the various peoples of the county to preserve their cultural identity.

Emphasis should be placed on the essence and substance of self-determination rather than the political form of a nation state.

National unity is desirable, because it is normally conductive to greater security, political stability, and social and economic development. In my view, however, national unity should not be pursued at any cost and certainly not at the cost of achieving personal liberty and economic, political, and social justice for all segments of the population, or at the cost of securing collective and individual rights. These legitimate aims must be protected under the constitutional order of the state. A right to secession should be maintained for use as a last resort when all efforts at establishing the appropriate constitutional order have failed.

I have set forth my view of constitutionalism in the introduction to this chapter and indicated the main features of a suggested model for achieving internal self-determination. Here I wish to emphasize that the constitutional balance between the need of the individual for complete personal freedom and the need of the community for total social justice must apply to every individual and every community within the state, without discrimination on grounds of race or ethnicity, religion, and/or language. Further, each country must adapt the general principles and institutions of constitutionalism to its own circumstances and, although there must be flexibility about the forms and structures of constitutionalism, there can be no flexibility with respect to its substance of individual and collective rights and justice for all. The principle of self-determination, external and internal, utilized in the above discussion, is a shorthand reference to the substance of constitutionalism in the modern world.

Notes

1. For a brief history and meaning of the term nation state, see Alfred Cobban, *The Nation State and National Self-Determination* (London: Collins, the Fontana Library,1969), Chs. II and VII.

2. See, for example, Hurst Hannum, "The Limits of Sovereignty and Majority Rule: Minorities, Indigenous Peoples, and the Right to Autonomy," in Ellen L. Lutz, Hurst Hannum, and Kathryn Burke, eds., *New Directions in Human Rights* (Philadelphia: University of Pennsylvania Press, 1989), p. 3.

3. Lee C. Buchheit, *Secession: The Legitimacy of Self-Determination* (New Haven: Yale University Press, 1978) p. 3.

4. Harold S. Johnson, *Self-Determination within the Community of Nations* (Leyden: A. W. Sijthoff, 1967), pp. 25–30.

5. Alfred Cobban, note 1, pp. 108–109; Rupert Emerson, *From Empire To Nation* (Cambridge, MA: Harvard University Press, 1960), p. 299.

6. Michla Pomerance, *Self-Determination in Law and Practice* (The Hague: Martinus Nijhoff, 1982), pp. 1–13, 72–76. There is a useful select bibliography in this book on pp. 130–138. See also sources cited in Ved. P. Nanda, "Self-Determination under International Law: Validity of Claims to Secede," 13 *Case Western Reserve Journal of International Law* 257–280 (1981), notes 8 and 9 on 259.

7. S. Prakash Sinha, "Self-Determination in International Law and Its Applicability to the Baltic Peoples," in A. Sprudz and A. Rusis, ed., *Res Baltica* (1968). pp. 256–257, as quoted in Lee C. Buchheit, note 3.

8. G. Ezejiofor, *Protection of Human Rights Under International Law* (London: Butterworth, 1964), pp. 15–32; H. Lauterpacht, "The Subjects of International Law," 63 *Law Quarterly Review* 438–460 (1947); 64 *Law Quarterly Review* 97–119 (1948).

9. D. B. Levin, "The Principle of Self-Determination of Nations in International Law," *Soviet Year Book of International Law 1962* 45–48, p. 46.

10. Articles 1.2 and 55 of the Charter of the United Nations.

11. The International Covenant on Economic, Social, and Cultural Rights was adopted by the General Assembly of the U.N. on December 16, 1966 (Annex to G.A. Res. 2200, 21 GAOR, Supp. 16, U.N. Doc. A/6316, at 490); and entered into force on January 3, 1976. The International Covenant on Civil and Political Rights was adopted by the General Assembly of the U.N. on December 16, 1966 (G.A. Res. 2200, 21 GAOR, Supp. 16, U.N. Doc. A/6316 at 52); and entered into force on March 23, 1976.

12. The African Charter was adopted by the Organization of African Unity on June 27, 1981, and came into force in October 1986.

13. On this controversial question see, for example, Rupert Emerson, "Self-Determination," 65 *American Journal of International Law* 459–475, 463–465 (1971).

14. See, for example, Paul Sieghart, *The International Law of Human Rights* (Oxford: Clarendon Press, 1983), p. 368; Jack Donnelly, "Human Rights, Group Rights, and Cultural Rights," *Universal Human Rights in Theory and Practice* (Ithaca: Cornell University Press, 1989), pp. 143–154.

For misgivings by some delegates at the U.N. about the appropriateness of including the right of peoples to self-determination in the Covenants, see Annotations on the text of the draft International Covenants on Human Rights in U.N. Doc. A/2929, chapter V, paras 4 and 8–10.

15. See, for example, Philip Alston, "A Third Generation of Solidarity Rights: Progressive Development or Obfuscation of International Human Rights?," 29 *Netherlands International Law Review* 307–322 (1982).

16. Yoram Dinstein, "Collective Human Rights of Peoples and Minorities," 25(1) *The International and Comparative Law Quarterly* 102–120 (1976); Theo van Boven, "The Relations between Peoples' Rights and Human Rights in the African Charter," 2(2–4), *Human Rights Law Journal* 183–194, 191–192 (1986).

17. Theo van Boven, note 16, pp. 191–192. Emphasis added.

18. Declaration on Principles of International Law Concerning Friendly Relations and Co-operation Among States in Accordance with the Charter of the United Nations, G.A. Res. 2625 (XXXV 1970), adopted by the U.N. General Assembly without a vote on October 24, 1970. 25 U.N. GAOR (No. 28), 121, 123–124, U.N. Doc. A/8028 (1970).

19. See, 1949 *Yearbook of the International Law Commission,* 289.

20. Yoram Dinstein, note 16, p. 104.

21. Ian Brownlie, "The Rights of Peoples in Modern International Law," 9 *Bulletin of Australian Society of Legal Philosophy* 104 at 107–108 (1985).

22. Richard N. Kiwanuka, "The Meaning of 'People' in the African Charter on Human and Peoples' Rights," 82:1 *American Journal of International Law* 80–101, 88 (1988).

23. A. Cristescu, *The Right to Self-Determination, Historical and Current Development on the Basis of United Nations Instruments,* para. 279, U.N. Doc. E/CN. 4/Sub. 2/404/Rev. 1 (1981).

24. This is the approach adopted by the Universal Declaration of the Rights of Peoples (the Algiers Declaration of July 4, 1976), a populist document adopted by a group of Lawyers, economists, politicians, and men and women in liberation struggles. For the test of the Declaration see Antonio Cassese, ed., *UN Law/Fundamental Rights: Two Topics in International Law* (Alphen aan den Rijn, The Netherlands: Sijthoff & Noordhoff, 1979), p. 219. This book also contains commentary and discussion of the Declaration by two of its authors, Francois Rigaux and Richard Falk, pp. 211 and 225, respectively.

25. Richard N. Kiwanuka, note 22, p. 81.

26. Harold S. Johnson, note 4, pp. 51–53. A few states have expressed a wider view of self-determination. See, for example, comments of the representatives of Belgium and the United Kingdom during the 1987 secession of the U.N. Human Rights Commission. E/NC. 4/1987/SR. 10, at 4; and E/NC.4/1987/SR. 13, at 8–9. It seems very doubtful, however, that even those states would allow their own minorities, such as the Scottish or Welsh peoples, of the United Kingdom, to secede if that were the wish of those minorities.

27. Rene Lemarchand, "The Limits of Self-Determination: The Case of the Katanga Secession," 56 *American Political Science Review* 404–416 (1962); Umozurike O. Umozurike, *Self-Determination in International Law* (Hamden, CT.: Archon Books, 1972), pp. 186–187, 230–235; Onyeonoro S. Kamanu, "Secession and the Right of Self-Determination: An O.A.U. Dilemma," 12(3) *The Journal of Modern African Studies* 355–376 (1974); M. G. Kaldharan Nayar, "Self-Determination Beyond the Colonial Context: Biafra in Retrospect," 10 *Texas International Law Journal* 321–345 (1975); S. K. N. Blay, "Challenging African Perspectives on the Right to Self-Determination in the Wake of the Banjul Charter on Human and Peoples' Rights," 29 *Journal of African Law* 49–55, 147 (1985). See also O.A.U. Charter, articles 2(1) (a) and (c) and 3(2) (3) and (5). In O.A.U. Res. AHG/16/1 (1964) the Assembly of Heads of States and Governments "declares that all Member States pledge themselves to respect the frontiers existing on the achievement of national independence." For the text of this Resolution see Ian Brownlie, *Basic Documents on African Affairs* (Oxford: Clarendon Press, 1971), pp. 360–361.

Numerous constitutions of African states reiterate the unity and indivisibility of their territories. See, for example, Article 4 of the Angola Constitution and Article 2 of the Senegal Constitution. See also A. Blaustein and G. Flanz, eds., *Constitutions of the Countries of the World* (Dobbs Ferry, NY: Oceana Publications 1971).

28. On the problems posed by the creation of ministates, see T. Frank and Paul Hoffman, "The Right of Self-Determination in Very Small Places," 8 *New York University Journal of International Law & Politics* 331–386 (1976).

29. For example, some of the equatorial tribes of southern Sudan might feel threatened by the dominance of Nilotic tribes in a separate state in present day southern Sudan.

30. Ved P. Nanda, note 6, pp. 263–274; and Onyeonoro S. Kamanu, note 27, pp. 356–362.

31. Ved P. Nanda, note 6, pp. 275–278; and Onyeonoro S. Kamanu, note 27, pp. 360–362.

32. This Declaration was adopted unanimously by the General Assembly of the United Nations in its twenty-fifth session. See, generally, C. Don Johnson, "Toward Self-Determination—A Reappraisal in the Declaration on Friendly Relations," 3 *Georgia Journal of International and Comparative Law* 145–163 (1973).

33. Ved Nanda, "Self-Determination in International Law: The Tragic Tale of Two Cities—Islamabad (West Pakistan) and Dacca (East Pakistan), 66 *The American Journal of International Law* 321–326 (1972).

34. Yoram Dinstein, note 16, p. 112.

35. See the example of various minorities within Poland and other European countries between the two world wars discussed by Yoram Dinstein, note 16, pp. 112–117.

36. Yoram Dinstein, note 16, pp. 102–103. Emphasis added.

37. *Minority Schools in Albania* (AB/64) 17 (1935).

38. Josef L. Kunz, "The Present Status of the International Law for the Protection of Minorities, " 486 *American Journal of International Law* 282–287, 282–283 (1954).

39. For an excellent analysis of the experience of the United States in this regard see Kenneth Karst, "Paths to Belonging: The Constitution and Cultural Identity," 64(2) *North Carolina Law Review* 303–377 (1986).

7

European Courts and Human Rights

Ludger Kühnhardt

Using the perspective of political science, not of law, to explore the idea of European courts and human rights in the context of Europe as a political concept and reality, we will trace the historical roots of the human rights issue as embedded in the process toward the integration of Europe, begun after World War II. This chapter deals with the impact of the European Court of Human Rights and the European Court of Justice on the protection of human rights in Europe. A comparison of these two court systems in the perspective of their respective political framework, background, and intentions will allow us to analyze the possibilities and limits of these diverging human rights approaches launched by the Council of Europe and by the European Community.

The evaluation of the human rights competence, goals, and impact of each court and its political institution will lead to a proposal that human rights instruments that exist on a supranational level can encourage the political, intellectual, and ethical unification of Europe. The existing supranational court structure in Europe will remain insufficient to this purpose if reduced to a mere judicial-functional purpose or applied only to a limited part of the continent. Therefore, we will question how these limited human rights instruments can be catalysts to the process of moving toward a European constitution. The chapter concludes with the assumption that the process of the advancement of human rights on the supranational level must be related to the search for a European constitutionalism and European identity in order to gain substantial results and progress.[1]

The Integrating Quality of Human Rights

Human rights are an expression of the ethos of freedom. A portion of the intellectual heritage of Europe, their metapolitical justification lies in natural law, which considers them inalienable moral rights. In their classical formulation—John Locke's "life, liberty and property"—they refer to the relationship between a state and the individual; though considered prelegal, they can be realized and protected only within the constitutional structure of the nation-states. "Invented" as a negative means of protecting the individual against its state, their progress has been closely related to the course of constitutionalism in Europe and North America since the eighteenth century. Today, their fulfillment has become the ultimate positive moral justification and legitimacy of democratic state power, and their validity has an international character as a moral program, if not as a global reality.

Since the promulgation of the Universal Declaration of Human Rights through the United Nations on December 10, 1948, the debate on human rights has been a feature of the international order and of global politics. The experiences have been ambivalent and various; assessments differ about the global standard of human rights protection, about diverging interpretations of human rights in different cultures and by varying ideologies, and about the political implications of human rights protection. One conclusion seems consensual: where human rights are violated, criticism of the offending political system increases from within or by foreign voices, and tends to delegitimate the system. Human rights protection also has a unifying function for societies and states alike; it supports the acceptance of a constitutional system, if such can prove that it serves the purpose of protecting human rights. The liberal pluralistic Western democracies share this experience.

It is possible to view human rights protection through theories of integration. Some such theories emphasize values and ideals as tools to build understanding and consent as necessary prerequisites for the creation of a community and its institutions. Rudolf Smend, one of the theoreticians in this field, relates the many expressions of values and willpower, of action and reaction—the permanent dynamisms of a society—to the legal values represented in the constitution and protected by it. The highest courts of a system, according to his theories, should fulfill the task of integrating the diverging, heterogeneous processes and profiles of social realities. The courts would be able to do so only if consensus could be reached on the ultimate values, and if strong authority and the power of implementation were bestowed on them.

It remains open to argument whether human rights and legal processes to protect them can help achieve a higher level of integration outside the structure of existing nation-states, with all their integrating forces to support this effort. The supranational bodies in Europe, the Council of Europe and the European Community, now have experience in the field of human rights. Three hypothesis may be drawn from this debate: first, the system of human rights protection in Europe has contributed to the moral legitimacy and intellectual identity of the ambition for the supranational integration of Europe; second, the protection of human rights on a supranational level depends strongly on the independence, strength, and competence of the instruments established to support the rights of the individual; third, the long-range process of human rights systems in their European dimension remains related to, if not dependent on, the unresolved efforts to create a better constitutional legitimacy for the process of European integration (e.g., rights efforts of the European Parliament embracing the new democracies of Central and Southeastern Europe).

The Human Rights System of the Council of Europe

The first conceptual ideas about the European supranational role of human rights protection and its relevance for the process of regional integration date back to the European perspective of some of the resistance movements during World War II. Human rights protection served as a point of orientation for their actions and hopes, and simultaneously as a central element in their concepts for a European postwar order. Human dignity and freedom, the respect for the individual, and social responsibility for the weaker segments of the society—these were some of the most fundamental human goals during and against the darkest years of the twentieth century. These norms found their way into reality: the first postwar conference of European Federalists promulgated a program of action in Hertenstein on September 21, 1946. The envisaged European Union was called on to achieve a "Declaration of European Citizen Rights," based on the respect of fundamental human rights and freedoms; the first European Congress, held in The Hague between May 7 and May 10, 1948, demanded in its political resolution a "Charter of Human Rights" to be respected by the members of a forthcoming European Federation, and the creation of a court capable of imposing the necessary sanctions to implement the ideals of the charter. In November 1950, the 15 Foreign Ministers of the Council of Europe signed the European Convention for the Protection of Human Rights and Fundamental Freedoms (ECHR), which came into force in 1953. Since then, 25 states have signed the Convention, including Hungary and Czechoslovakia in 1990.

The European Convention (ECHR)

The European Convention for the Protection of Human Rights and Fundamental Freedoms guarantees, for the most part, civil and political rights: the right to life, liberty, and security; freedom from inhuman or degrading treatment, slavery, servitude, and forced labor; the right to a fair trail; and freedom of conscience, of speech, and of assembly. Section I of the Convention spells out most of the basic civil and political rights contained in the Universal Declaration of Human Rights of 1948, though generally in more detailed form, because the convention gave them the binding force of law. This Convention is now the most relevant supranational human rights protection in Europe, and the most advanced and ambitious global instrument for the protection of the individual on a supranational, regional level. Its position is due to its most important and original feature, the system it established for the protection of human rights, under which any individual of any of the signatory states had the right to sue any against any breach of the convention in any of the signatory states or by any of the signatory states.[2]

The Convention created two bodies to ensure the implementation and protection of the rights it guaranteed: the European Commission of Human Rights and the European Court of Human Rights in Strasbourg. The primary function of both is to deal with charges brought against the states who are party to the convention by other states or by individuals. Under Article 24, any state who is party to the convention, may refer to the Commission any alleged breach of the provisions of the convention by any other member state. Under Article 25, the Commission may receive charges from any person, nongovernment organization, or group of individuals claiming to be the victim of a violation by any state who is signatory to the convention. This application depends on the willingness of the state to recognize the competence of the Commission to receive such applications; such declarations may be made for a specific period, and may be renewed. All states party to the convention, with the exception of the latest members San Marino and Finland, have made such declarations, in most cases for a limited period of time. All states party to the convention but three (San Marino, Finland, and Turkey) have also recognized under Article 46 the compulsory jurisdiction of European Court of Human Rights.

Innovations under Articles 24 and 25

Under the control of the Secretary General of the Council of Europe, the Convention institutes a certain form of the reporting procedure. Most important, however, are the innovations under Article 24 and Article 25 of the convention. These surpass the traditional standard of international law. A state presenting an application under Article 24 need not *prove* itself, even indirectly, a victim of the alleged violation of human rights. The general premise of the convention is that all states party to it have a collective interest in the maintenance of human rights. The guarantee created by the convention is likewise a collective guarantee, not based on subjective rights or on reciprocity. This is an entirely novel category of human rights protection as compared to all other international or supranational instruments that exist today for the protection of human rights.

Article 25, which allows for the direct right of action of any individual against his own or another state before an international organ, is an even greater and more revolutionary innovation. It elevates the individual to the status of a subject of international law. This reflects the farsighted and courageous quality of the founders of the European Convention for the Protection of Human Rights and Fundamental Freedoms and remains a noteworthy event in the history of international law and international relations. It hints at the fact that the adversarial breach between the two concepts of sovereignty, state sovereignty and popular sovereignty, might be overcome wherever serious endeavors are taken to do so.

The Commission and the Court

The function of the European Commission of Human Rights, as of the European Court of Human Rights, is "to ensure the observance of the agreements undertaken" by the signatory states (Article 19). The formula is very broad, but the functions of the Commission as well as of the Court are clearly defined and limited. They are to examine the admissibility of applications by individuals under Article 25 or states under Article 24; to establish under Article 28 the facts of the admissible case and to place itself at the disposal of the parties in order to reach a friendly settlement (if such a settlement can be reached, the case is closed); and to draw up, in the absence of a friendly settlement, a report on the facts and to state its opinion whether there has been a breach of the Convention.

Most applications out of more than 12,000 submitted have never met rejection by the Commission as inadmissible on various grounds specified within the Convention: e.g., the complaint was incompatible with the context and the rights referred to by the Convention; domestic remedies had not been exhausted; and the complaint was "manifestly ill-founded" [Article 27 (2)].

The final decision on an admissible case that has not resulted in a friendly settlement rests with either the European Court of Human Rights or the Committee of Ministers. The Commission's report, which is transmitted to the Committee of Ministers, contains only its opinion as to whether the Commission found proof for a violation of human rights; it is not legally binding. Within 3 months of the transmission of the report, the Committee of Ministers (which normally endorses the Commission's opinion without any fresh investigation of the complexity of the case) either makes a final decision or refers the case to the Court. If the case is referred to the Court, a new stage in the procedure begins. The judgment of the court, if taken, is binding and final. In the European Court of Human Rights, the Commission and the state concerned are represented, but the individual applicant is not. This is one of the formal lacunae of the system of human rights protection under the auspices of the Council of Europe.

Effect of ECHR Judgments

The impact of the judgments under the provisions of the European Convention for the Protection of Human Rights and Fundamental Freedoms is difficult to judge. The Convention does not provide for sanctions to impose its decisions. It can, however, exert a political and public pressure of some importance. Publicity as a means of moral pressure forced the Greek Generals on 1967 to leave the Council of Europe; only after returning to democratic rule in 1974, did Greece reenter the Council and again accept its human rights instruments. In other cases, particularly with respect to human rights violations in Turkey, the system of the Council of Europe has proved insufficient because it cannot overcome state sovereignty, the ultimate border line blocking the imposition of internationally acknowledged human rights standards.

The common human rights standards expressed in the convention reflect "that European states make up a culturally identifiable unit and their like-mindedness had meant easier agreement on what are considered to be basic human rights."[3] This is the normative analysis; the overall impact of the human rights system of the Council of Europe on the national protection of human rights differs. The convention is not national law in all member states (notable exceptions are Great Britain, the Scandinavian countries, France, and Switzerland); the Court established under the convention is not an isolated element, but an integral part of the general approach and intention that the Council of Europe has chosen to pursue.

The legal literature finds the most important effect of the instruments and judgments of the Convention to be the self-binding consequences for the signatory states. The effects of the system under the European Convention for the Protection of Human Rights and Fundamental Freedoms are mainly indirect: its decisions have led to changes in the legal processes of a condemned member state; the convention and the decisions of its organs support a standardized interpretation of the *Ordre public* and a harmonized interpretation of open legal terms and situations; and the human rights problem has been debated on a new, higher constitutional and political level. This is particularly true in the case of Great Britain, where the convention has inspired a debate on whether the country should introduce a "Bill of Rights," with no results so far.

The Greek and the Turkish cases do show that the Convention has little, if any power to prevent a country from violating human rights per se, or to encourage it to return to democratic standards of rule by simple means of the Convention's existence and good-will. In the final analysis, the ground must be laid within a given society and a given state on which to pursue a political course in accordance with the human rights standards set forth by the Convention. The Convention is a certain challenge to state sovereignty in the field of human rights protection: it sheds much light on the ongoing existence, perseverance, if not arrogance, of state sovereignty, particularly in cases of conflict with the individual.

Possibilities and Limits

Some other questions have to be raised in connection with the possibilities and limits of the human rights system established under the Council of Europe: to what extent can the Convention be considered the nucleus of an overall European human rights system? Would the human rights standard of the Convention be endangered if Eastern European countries, who are currently going through a remarkable process of domestic reforms, would apply for membership in the Council of Europe and hence in its human rights instruments? Or would such a membership rather increase the possibilities for human rights advancement in Eastern Europe due to the pressure that the Convention and its organs could exert?

The European Convention for the Protection of Human Rights and Fundamental Freedoms expresses the highest quality of integration so far reached in the context of the Council of Europe; in all other areas, the methods of the Council remain limited to interstate coordination. Yet it must be asked how much does the individual citizen of Europe know about the provisions and the spirit of the Convention?

Outside of Europe, at least some people are aware of the provisions of the Convention: the American Human Rights Convention of 1978 refers indirectly in the preamble to the European Convention for the Protection of Human Rights and Fundamental Freedoms by stressing the usefulness of regional approaches to human rights protection. They could also be helpful in specifying the idea of universal human rights.[4]

The Convention can certainly live up to this hope, primarily because its standard of human rights protection has not been relativized or reduced compared to the standard set forth in the Universal Declaration of Human Rights from 1948. To the contrary, the Convention has sharpened and tightened the United Nations definitions and notions of human rights. Thus, it serves the freedom of the individual, which cannot be said about some tendencies in other regional instruments for human rights protection, notably in Africa, where the collective right to self-determination, peoples' rights, are being put on an equal footing with individual rights, thus reducing the relevance of the latter in the context of the modern nation-state and its monopoly of power.

The Human Rights Dimension of the European Community

A comparison of the Council of Europe's and the European Community's respective efforts for the protection of human rights leads to mixed results. On one hand, the Council of Europe has framed farsighted instruments for the protection of individual human rights: on the other, it has not been able to create a version and vision for a political Europe. The Council remains more a club than a living experience for the citizens of Europe. The European Community has a different record. Though, it lacks a specific human rights perspective and program, it has developed into a stable, visible community that truly affects the lives of the citizens within its member states. It has achieved a high level of economic integration and looks for means to strengthen its political role and identity. Although the human rights dimension played an important role during the direct postwar years as a point of orientation for the future course of European integration, the Rome Treaties of 1957, which gave birth to the European Community, do not refer to human rights in a specific sense. And yet, it would be incorrect to conclude that the Rome Treaties fail to hint at individual legal positions and reduce the concept of the European Community to a mere functional one. The individual legal positions under the Community are, however, confined to the sphere of economic self-realization. The "Four Freedoms," today revitalized on the concept of the Common Market to be achieved by 1992, can well be interpreted as indirect economic rights of the individual: freedom of labor and of capital, of services, and of trade. However, they refer to the European Community citizen as a market citizen, not as a political citizen.[5]

The only institution of the European Community that can, independent of political consensus among. the member states, develop the community law through court decisions is the European Court of Justice in Luxemberg. As early as 1963, the Court stressed that the creation of the European Economic Community constitutes per se a new legal order in international law; in a limited sense, states have revoked parts of their sovereignty in favor of the Community that, by way of its legal processes, should grant rights to the individual citizen of member states. This self-interpretation of the Community's ethos refers unwittingly to the integration theories mentioned above. The primary legitimacy of the community derives from its competence to establish an efficient economic reality of integration, accepted by all its participants. The more fundamental source of legitimacy, however, depends on the degree of loyalty that the citizens of the member states express toward the community. This loyalty will be as high as the individual's perception and realization of its nominative quality. In other words, the more clearly the European Community can demonstrate its role as protector of the rights of the individual by means of progress in the economic and political integration among the member states, the greater will be the appreciation and support of it. The European Community in search of basic rights—this formula describes the requirements as well as the ambitions and activities of the community in this area. Various strategies have been suggested to advance with this task.

The European Court of Justice

The most pragmatic solution favors human rights protection through legal processes, encouraging the European Court of Justice to extend and to strengthen human rights protection through its decisions. The debate on this approach has been ample and diverse. It embraces highly optimistic as well as more skeptical voices.[6]

Since the late 1960s, the European Court of Justice has used basic rights as the criteria of legality for acts of the European Community, compensating in some sense by doing so, for the democratic deficit of the Community. This deficit is due to its lack of a constitutional basis and its Parliament's failure to meet the national standards of democratic competence achieved in the individual member states. Through its decisions, the European Court of Justice has protected against community acts that violate basic human rights, provided general standards for the unification of the Community's legal order, and, one hopes, strengthened the identification of the citizens with the European Community.

The European Court of Justice, however, is limited to the field of economic and social rights. Its casuistic principle makes the Court a flexible institution, but has fallen short of establishing a more systematic and detailed human rights instruments, such as the European Convention for the Protection of Human Rights and Fundamental Freedoms under the Council of Europe. In various cases, the European Court of Justice has relied on provisions under the European Convention. Critical observers argue, however, that only in four cases has the Court declared the Convention, or a provision of it, to be of immediate assistance in the determination of the case. And only in one case did the Convention alone have relevance for the Court's decision. "The development of fundamental rights within the Community has not therefore been dependent on the ECHR. It is suggested that the European Court could have developed fundamental rights to the same position as present purely relying on constitutional provisions of the Member States as guidelines."[7]

Beyond the casuistic approach of the European Court of Justice, two other ways have the potential to develop a broader human rights formula within and for the European Community: the creation of a European Bill of Rights and the accession of the European Community to the European Convention for the Protection of Human Rights and Fundamental Freedoms.

A European Bill of Rights

The pursuit of a European Bill of Rights would primarily serve a political and psychological course. Those who favor it argue that it could help harmonize human rights standards in Europe and strengthen the moral legitimacy of the European Community. At the same time, the implementation of this approach would provoke problems relating to the very democratic deficit of the European Community deplored today: who would be able to claim competence and legitimacy for drafting such a Bill of Rights: The European Parliament, the Commission in Brussels, the Court of Justice, or the Council of Ministers, representing the individual member states of the community?

One advantage of a European Bill of Rights could be its ability to include both liberal political rights and participatory rights. Such a Bill could anticipate and encourage the necessary process toward a European constitution. Given the fact that basic rights are the heart of any constitution, one might expect a revival of the debate on a European Bill of Rights in the course of an intensified discussion on ways of realizing a European constitution. Unfortunately, such a development does not seem politically feasible in the foreseeable future.

Among the arguments against a Bill of Rights is the one that could be interpreted as a sign of mistrust of the European Convention for the Protection of Human Rights and Fundamental Freedoms and could dilute the efforts directed toward the human rights system of the Council of Europe. Why develop a second set of human rights provisions not all that different from the first one, and more limited in scope? To differ only to differ?

The European Community and the ECHR

A more realistic, concrete debate involves the possible accession of the European Community to the European Convention. The Commission of the Community proposed this accession in a memorandum on April 4, 1979.[8] The European Parliament has debated the question several times in a positive, encouraging way. No result has been achieved so far and in some countries, most notably (no surprise) in Great Britain, fear was expressed that the European Convention after integration into the binding EC system could interfere too strongly in the domestic legal processes. Even supporters of the accession are skeptical or reserved in some respects; for instance, they reiterate that by all means the European Court of Justice must remain the only legitimate body to interpret Community law, thus calling into question the competence of the European Court of Human Rights. But one cannot have the cake and eat it too.

The whole debate seems to be more confusing than helpful. In some sense, the democratic countries of Western Europe appear to be victims of their success in the field of human rights protection and of intense sensitivity to the issue of human rights that made them develop various approaches and suggestions. They have created courts and committees and invented ways and means, but they are obviously not fully able to coordinate, let alone integrate, all of them in a convincing, harmonious way.

This inability has evidently to do with the diverging realities of the different bodies for European integration. To put it sharply: the Council of Europe has established interesting innovations for the protection of human rights, yet it lacks the inner character to act as the nucleus for the advancement of a solid and plausible political architecture of the continent. Whether this will change in the years to come remains to be seen. So far, the Council of Europe has not been able to provide for a constitution of Europe that would include human rights provisions or even a Bill of Rights. In the past, the Council of Europe had even sufferred the failure of some of its member states to live up to the standards of democratic freedoms and human rights provisions that are the clearly expressed notion and hope of the Council. And yet, it remains true that the human rights instruments it has shaped remain of interest and importance for the cause of human rights in a global sense.

The European Community, on the other hand, possesses no human rights concept as such and carries the burden of a democratic deficit. However, it has proven its stability as a community of strong democracies. Its parliament, insufficient as it is compared to the democratic level of those within the individual member states, pursues an active human rights policy, for example, with regard to Eastern Europe and in its relation with the developing world.[9]

Thus we must live with confusing, or at least ambivalent realities, with a complex structure of human rights protection. Instead of complaining about its lack of clarity and cohesion, we might as well be advised to take this situation as an opportunity and an asset. This seems at least to be the position of the European Parliament. On January 19, 1989, it lauded the European Convention for the Protection of Human Rights and Fundamental Freedoms, the European Court of Justice, and the constitutional processes within the various member states as combined elements of a "European human rights system." This system, fully developed and applied, could, according to the European Parliament, support the development of other regional systems for the protection of human rights.[10]

Unlike the United Nations System for the protection of human rights, regional endeavors can indeed provide for better means of protection, provided they include truly binding provisions. The argument in favor of regional instruments for the protection of human rights is often supported with reference to the advantage of a better cultural and political adaptability. This, however, is a most delicate and ambiguous argument. It might serve the purpose of human rights protection to reflect on positive reactions to and consequences of regional experiences with specific legal processes to protect human rights. But once it encourages deviations form the international standard of human rights, it can easily lead to ethical relativism in the name of regional identity and cultural heterogeneity. This eventually would certainly not serve the course of global human rights protection, but would inevitably create diverging standards of values and notions, of strategies and criteria to protect the dignity of the individual.[11]

European Human Rights Protection and European Constitutionalism

The implications of the European court system's protection of human rights are several. The degree of human rights protection in Europe depends in the first place on the quality and stability of a democratic nation-state. It is here, within the confines of the existing nation-states of Europe, that human rights will be tested as a living reality, and may be challenged as protection of the individual against the state. The protection of human rights becomes the ultimate moral criterion used to judge and justify the legitimacy of a political order. For their protection and implementation they do require juridical support and legal processes; in this sense, they depend on independent courts, which have a mandate to protect them. The supranational courts in Europe do play a supporting role in the overall process of human rights protection among and within the democratic countries of western Europe, but they cannot gain strength and legitimacy by themselves. They remain dependent for their functional relevance on the institutions that have given birth to them; their strength and legitimacy can only be as strong as that of their "mother institutions," the Council of Europe and the European Community. Finally, it is not the court system as such that is key to the stability of human rights protection in Europe, but the degree to which the court system is integrated into the supranational order of democratic legitimacy and functional efficiency.

In Europe and North America, the structure of human rights protection has been related to the constitutional structure of individual countries. On the national level, the advancement of the constitutional order and of human rights protection have gone hand in hand until they reached a stage of political and juridical marriage. It is open to historical proof whether such an amalgam of human rights processes and constitution building can be achieved on the European level—and on which level. The current European system of human rights protection is impressive but not necessarily because of the performance of the European courts. This impressiveness may not even be due to Europe's current quality of institutional integration: it may reflect the quality of the European democracies, their governments, and their citizens to implement their laws.

Countering the sober political realism of the day, we will conclude with an optimistic, if not visionary outlook. We should reflect on strategies to encourage the rapid progress toward a European constitution. This constitution could embrace human rights provisions as the ultimate expression of a European identity and integrational legitimacy. And it could provide for substantial legal processes to protect them, including a European constitutional court for which the current European Court of Human Rights could serve as the nucleus. Such a development could truly go beyond the current double standard that exists with the Council of Europe and the European Community and could bring about a qualitative leap toward a supranational European human rights system that would be both democratically legitimized and legally coherent.

Common sense reminds us that there is a long way to go before such a vision can become reality. The problem is all the greater when we look beyond the boundaries of the European Community (EC). It is no longer possible to seek an European identity and to develop a European constitution without looking to the whole of Europe. The end of Communist regimes means that we have entered a new phase of history. The challenges are difficult and will be influenced by reemerging precommunist phenomena, such as nationalism in the Balkan peninsula. The ways to surmount these challenges are not yet clear and the end of this phase is not yet in sight, but history has given all of Europe a new chance.

Hungary and Czechoslovakia have already joined the Council of Europe and signed the European Convention for the Protection of Human Rights and Fundamental Freedoms. Other countries will follow. During the 1990s, some of the new democracies of central eastern Europe, namely Hungary, Czechoslovakia, and Poland, will inevitably join the EC, stabilizing their democracies and their economic transformations, as was the case with Spain and Portugal in the 1980s. The European Community is the only relevant, workable and powerful European institution and the eyes of the new European democracies look to it.

The Council of Europe and its human rights documents will be instrumental in bringing the present gap between the countries of central, eastern, and western Europe and facilitating the full-fledged integration of a new Europe, of a real European Community. The process of extending the boundaries of Europe begun by Hungary and Czechoslovakia cannot continue without a simultaneous deepening of the European Community. The EC needs a democratic, human rights-based constitution as an anchor for its current member states and as a standard for the other European democracies. Human rights have a catalytic funcion on the moral and political dimensions to shape and hasten the necessary process of the integration of a new Europe. The historic changes in Eastern Europe should give us optimism to hope for fresh impulses from that part of the continent.

Notes

1. For the historical development of human rights, see Gerhard Oestreich, *Die Idee der Menschenrechte in ihrer geschichtlichen Entwicklung* (3rd ed., Berlin: Duncker & Humblot, 1969); Louis Henkin, *The Rights of Man Today* (London: Steven & Sons, 1979).

2. Ralph Beddard, *Human Rights and Europe*. A study of the machinery of human rights protection of the Council of Europe (London: Swat & Maxwell, 1973); Francis G. Jacobs, *The European Convention on Human Rights* (Oxford: Clarendon Press, 1975); Jochen Abr. Frowein and Werner Peukert, *Europäische Menschenrechtskonvention* (Kehl: Engel, 1985); Klaus Dicke, *Menshenrechte und europäische Integration* (Kehl: Engel, 1986); Franz Matscher and Herbert Petzold, *Protection Human Rights: the European Dimension* (Köln: Heymann, 1988).

3. Ralph Beddard, note 2, p. 1.

4. Jochen Abr. Frowein, "Die Europäische und die Amerikanische Menschenrechtskonvention," *Europäische Grundrechtezeitschrift*, Vol. 7 (Kehl: Engel, 1980), pp. 442–449.

5. A. Glen Mower, Jr., "Human Rights in Western Europe: Progress and problems," 52 *International Affairs* 235–251 (1976); Hermann Mosler, Rudolf Bernhardt, and Meinhard Hilf, eds. *Grundrechtsschutz in Europa* (Berlin: Spranger, 1977); Jochen Abr. Frowein, "Die Europäische Gemeinschaft auf der Suche nach Grundrechten," in Robert Bieber et al., eds., *Das Europa der zweiten Generation*, Band II (Kehl: Engel, 1981), pp. 727–738; Rudolf Hrbek, "Menschenrechte in einem souveränen Europa." in Johannes Schwartländer, ed., *Menschenrechte und Demokratie* (Kehl: Engel, 1981), pp. 41–62.

6. Meinhard Hilf, "Der Gerichtshof der Europäischen Gemeinshaften als Integrationsfaktor, dargestellt anhand der Rechtssprechung zu den Grundrechten," in *Die Grundrechte in der Europäischen Gemeinschaft. Schriftenreihe des Arbeitskreises Europäische Integration* (Baden–Baden: Nomos, 1976), pp. 23–34; Ingolf Pernice, *Grundrechtsgehalte im europäischen Gemeinschaftsrecht. Ein Beitrag zum gemeinschaftsimmanenten Grundrechtsschutz durch den europäischen Gerichtshof* (Baden–Baden: Nomos, 1979).

7. Nigel Foster, "The European Court of Justice and the European Convention for the Protection of Human Rights," 8 *Human Rights Law Journal* Parts 2–4, 245–272, 271 (1987).

8. Memorandum betreffend den Beitritt der Europäischen Gemeinschaften zur Konvention über den Schutz der Menschenrechte und Grundfreiheiten (Luxembourg: EG Kommission, 1979)

9. Klaus Dicke, note 2, pp. 202 ff.

10. Europäisches Parlament, 1988–1989, Protokoll der Sitzung vom 18 (January 1989) PV 52 II, PE 129. 733, Part II (Strasbourg: Europeane Parliament Document) 26 ff.

11. Ludger Kühnhardt, *Die Universalität der Menschenrechte. Studie zur ideengeschichtlichen Bestimmung eines politischen Schlüsselbegriffs* (München: Olzog, 1987); Karl-Josef Partsch, "Vor- und Nachteile einer Regionalisierung des internationalen Menschenrechtsschutzes," in *Europäische Grundrechtezeitschrift*, Vol. 1–2 (Kehl: Engel, 1989). pp. 1–9.

8

Social Movements, Constitutionalism, and Human Rights: Comments from the Malaysian and Indonesian Experiences

Daniel S. Lev

Constitutionalism

Like other complex ideologies, constitutionalism is often obscured by a haze of mythology that makes it difficult to deal with realistically. Believers cannot help but see in it an end to a thousand vices and the source of as many virtues. But uncritical enthusiasm, without pause to examine assumptions, complicates any effort to understand clearly what is at issue. Before turning to constitutionalist claims in Indonesia and Malaysia, therefore, it may be useful to begin with a few premises.

What exactly do we mean by constitutionalism? Rather than take for granted that we share an understanding of it and risking the intellectual abuse that accompanies such terms as "development" or "modernity" or those grand obscurantisms "East" and "West," I want to sketch the meanings that inform this discussion. As I use the term here, "constitutionalism" implies that political process, with or without a written constitution, is more or less oriented to public rules and institutions intended to define and contain the exercise of political authority. At the core of constitutionalism is legal process. The point should not be exaggerated beyond the capacity of any state to represent the genre. For the centrality of law and legal process does not mean that nothing else counts. The influence of economic interests, elite leverage, and popular values all matter in every society, contrary governing principles notwithstanding. But constitutional regimes necessarily foster a common appreciation of, or orientation to, legal rules and the general principles that underlay them.[1] This orientation depends not only on appropriate institutions and roles, but on the widely accepted myth that legal process is efficacious and that its principles are eternally valid.

By contrast, religious, aristocratic, military, or charismatic regimes, whatever their constitutional or other overlay, imply quite different orientations with other institutional arrangements and legitimating ideologies. If the going myth is that law counts, people will use law to the limits of its assumed capacity to get things done. But if a god or gods alone provide, then priests will exercise authority. If the understanding of politics suggests that powerful men get things done, then patron–client relations are likely to prevail. The analytical problem is to ascertain in any society what exactly are the most sensible means, or mix of sensible means, of reaching objectives. Within society most people understand this implicitly, and those who object to the prevailing means, for whatever reasons, may try to change them if they can.

Historically, the rise of constitutional regimes has had to do with hemming in the state and confining its managers. Constitutionalism, a slightly higher abstraction than the rule of law or *rechtsstaat*, hence means little more (nor less) than the limited state, one in which official political power is surrounded by knowable laws whose acceptance transforms power into *legally* specified legitimate authority. In Weberian terms, constitutionalism grows out of the rational–legal form of domination, and is no less a means of political domination than any other. It may be a peculiarity of constitutionalism, however, that it presupposes at least a distinction, perhaps an antithesis, between state and society, without which there is little reason to make rules of the state.

Understood in this way, constitutionalism, like any other structure of state/society relations, is a matter of the distribution of power and authority. All organizations, including the state, are fundamentally coercive, their responsibilities ranging from subtle pressure and approving acquiescence to frank brutality and reluctant surrender. Political orders may be distinguished by how they apportion coercive power and legitimate authority, and what instrumentalities are differentially available to state institutions and social organizations to enforce their wills or to defend themselves from one another. The more power available in society, the more likely something like a "constitutional" order may exist. The more power available to the state, the more likely it is that a constitution, if it exists, will be beside the point. Constitutionalism is meaningless without resources of power, in some form, both to achieve it and sustain it.

There is, however, nothing particularly compelling or inevitable about the constitutional republic. The view that constitutionalism represents the natural course of history, morally superior at that, is an ideological conceit that should have dissipated long ago but, like other such myths, has infinite staying power. Far from inevitable, the demand for constitutional definitions of state authority grows from identifiable changes in economic and social structures that are likely to extrude new conceptions of group interest and political value.[2] Without such transformations, it is hard to conceive the source of serious pressures for change at all. The most fundamental of changes is that in class structure, for the emergence or expansion of a social class causes tension as those who belong to it seek security and advantage by redefining political, social, and economic rules to accommodate themselves. Historically, constitutionalism has been the peculiar ideological haven of the middle class that could not claim an inherently legitimate right to govern but were dissatisfied with their lack of regular access to and influence over those who did govern.[3] Persuasive evidence from around the world now suggests that this pattern remains fairly constant.

The social movements I have in mind are largely the product of new or growing middle classes, whether the groups they encompass are or are not self-consciously "middle class," bent on reordering state and society to their own purposes. The nature of middle-class ideologies in search of serviceable change is that their appeal cannot be restricted to middle-class interests alone. Although royalty and aristocracy naturally claim restrictive rights, justified by birth, and religious hierarchies are blessed by heaven, middle-class groups, lacking innate legitimacy, have no choice but to generalize the appeals to all who own property or to all citizens or even to all humanity. It is in this connection, in part, that human rights have become so prominent in the repertory of reform ideology now. I do not mean to imply that human rights appeals are no more than politically instrumental, but they do have to be understood in terms more complicated than those of the Universal Declaration. In some ways, human rights today serve precisely the same ideological purpose as natural rights did in Europe a few centuries ago, which may help to explain (only partially) why the political "rights" of the Universal Declaration remain generally more prominent than the social and economic "rights."

Because the political contentions that bracket constitutionalist demands are local matters, fed by local issues, interests, values, and historical circumstances, the outcomes (constitutionalist or not in whatever measure) are comprehensible essentially only in local terms. Neither constitutions nor constitutionalism can be transferred. The point should be obvious, but is often obscured by proprietary claims to the correct model.[4] The dimensions of French constitutionalism are not altogether clear to Americans or to Japanese, the Indian or Norwegian cases seem odd anywhere else, and so on, because the political compromises worked out historically, the tacit social and economic agreements made along the way, the play of local habit and values and cultural assumptions, the ways in which change proceeds, are all taken for granted at home but are unfathomable away.[5] Without an understanding of the conflicts that go on in state and society, and between the two, of the ways in which power is generated and authority actually exercised, of the values and ideologies that inform political structure and behavior, we cannot comprehend constitutionalist (or any other) movements as they have evolved. We are left puzzled, for example, by the apparently cavalier attitudes of the constitutionalist French toward constitutions, or the strong patrimonial edge to Japanese practice, or the reverence in which Americans hold their constitution without bothering much to read it, or by any of the institutional outcomes along the routes of change anywhere.

Finally, it should go without saying but usually does not, constitutionalism is not the obvious solution to many of the most serious, compelling problems that humanity has to deal with. It does not eliminate economic poverty, or social discrimination, or political abuse, or the incompetence, greed, or stupidity of political leadership. For all these miseries the only sensible solutions remain relevant knowledge, clearly articulated ideology, and effectively organized power in whatever kind of political structure exists.

Indonesia and Malaysia provide a useful contrast of constitutionalist movements that demonstrate this complexity. In both countries, and one can argue also in Thailand, the Philippines, and Korea for neighboring examples, nothing less is happening than contests over the shape of the state, over who will dominate its resources of power, and by what conditions of authority. In both countries persistent struggles over the way in which state authority is exercised has produced a subtle transfiguration in, and considerable tension over, the conception of state/society relations. These struggles have been initiated and sustained by groups with an interest in protecting themselves against the state and in gaining access to it.[6]

Indonesia and Malaysia arrive at these struggles from distant poles, though the social strata involved have been similar. In Indonesia the effort has been to establish a *negara hukum*, an Indonesian version of the rule of law, against the will at present of a powerful military-based regime: in Malaysia the objective has been to defend and strengthen a working constitutional order against undermining forces. Although in Malaysia state organization lends a conservative advantage of sorts to constitutionalist groups, in neither country have political balances favored the constitutionalist argument.

Indonesia: In Search of a Negara Hukum

Following the revolution (1945–1950) it seemed that Indonesia had established a secure constitutional system, complete with a parliamentary government explicitly predicted on rule of law principles. As in many other former colonies, this system lasted only briefly, about 7 years. As in many other newly independent states, the pattern of system change thereafter moved through an intense period of patrimonialism—Soekarno's Guided Democracy—and on to military rule after 1965.

Constitutional Failure

Why did parliamentary government fail? The basic reasons anticipate later debates about reform. For one thing, formal constitutional and political structure excluded and could not satisfy the many new groups whose energies were liberated by the revolution.[7] Most important was the army, which overthrew both the parliamentary system and Soekarno. But there were socially mobilized others who found no ready satisfaction, practical or symbolic, in the institutions of the parliamentary state. Moreover, the party system articulated deep ideological cleavages in the country, precluding consensus on fundamental issues, for example, the place of Islam in the state, and sapping government authority. President Soekarno and army leaders held the parties responsible for weakening the state and, in early 1957, during a period of regional crises that eventuated in open rebellion in 1958, overthrew government in favor of central political roles for Soekarno as charismatic leader-in-chief and the army under martial law.

But there were also more subtle and intractable reasons for the failure of the constitutional regime. Hindsight makes it seem clear that the regime rested on the surface of an unsupportive environment that the parties had inadequate time and imagination to make more friendly. The essential middle class was too small and substantially constituted of ethnic Chinese, cultivated in the colony as a prosperous but vulnerable ethnic island. Power in the private economy belonged still to the Dutch, until 1957, and to the ethnic Chinese, not to ethnic Indonesians who controlled the state.

Institutionally, the colonial, national, and local bureaucracy, the skeleton of state, survived the colony and remained better suited to purposes of colonial supervision than to those of an independent parliamentary regime that needed to mobilize popular political support. Elsewhere I have suggested that of the two sides of colonial government, a liberal legal one intended for Europeans and a patrimonial–bureaucratic one intended for Indonesians, it was the latter with which independent Indonesia made do.[8] A significant instance of the problem is the *pamong praja*, local arm of the Ministry of Interior, a prototypical colonial institution fashioned around the functions of control and extraction. Revolutionary leaders had left it in place. By the time Parliament got around to subordinating the *pamong praja* to elected local councils, in Law 1/1957, it was too late. The law was rescinded by the Guided Democracy regime, which set about strengthening the state according to the only model its leaders knew intimately, that of the colony.

Indonesian constitutionalism gave way in part because its appeals were fundamentally weak, but even had they been stronger the audience for them was small. Against its offer of procedural justice according to legal processs, dissatisfied groups demanded varieties of substantive justice—nationalist justice, Islamic justice, economic justice, social justice—that were incomparably more compelling. Unable to manage serious regional crises and frightened by what seemed to be revolutionary challenges from Islam on the one hand and Communism on the other, parliamentary leadership collapsed in early 1957, surrendering to the superior authority of Soekarno and the incontestable power of the army.

Guided Democracy drew on sources of legitimacy that had nothing to do with constitutionalism, whose symbols were ignored as irrelevant and even contrary to the integrity of Indonesian history. Unapologetic nationalism, the search for an Indonesian identity that would exorcise the curses of colonialism, the demand for a dignified place in the world, politics as mobilization and adventure and risk, the revival of the spirit of the revolution—all submerged the duller appeals of constitutional process. Soekarno contemptuosly swept aside the separation of powers so important to lawyers and political liberals, and, under pressure from the army, prorogued the Constituent Assembly, dumped the liberal parliamentary constitution of 1950, and by decree restored the strong presidential constitution of 1945. But the 1945 Constitution itself stood merely as a symbol of the revolution without much further effect. Political and bureaucratic institutions reoriented themselves around the magnetic Soekarno, who rose self-consciously as a patrimonial phoenix to embody the spirit of this nation on the move.

While Guided Democracy was rationalized by appeal to what its elite imagined to be the traditions of precolonial Indonesia, particularly old Java, what shone through the strained rhetoric was the outline of the Indonesian side of the colonial state. The strong state that emerged (and endured) during these years rested on the precedent of colonial institutions—the *pamong praja* not least—and the repressive techniques they had generated. Institutional controls all but disappeared, allowing uninhibited leeway. Bureaucratic corruption deepended, judicial corruption took root, and abuse of power became common. Legal process became peripheral to the discretionary authority that flowed through officialdom. One result, however, was that law began to be taken seriously, as ideology and as practical reform, by all those disadvantaged by anything else.

When Guided Democracy collapsed in a huge pool of blood after an attempted coup in October 1965, one of the louder claims in the din that followed was for the restoration of the *Negara hukum* (*rechtsstaat*), a constituional state informed by the rule of law. *Negara hukum* has remained a major symbol of critical reform. It was not to be, for the army, having supervised the obliteration of the Communist Party, presently asserted its political prerogatives, brushed off such civilian allies against the old regime as Islamic and student groups, imposed a tight grip on existing political institutions, and created the New Order. Soekarno's appeal for a reborn Indonesian spirit was dropped in favor of "economic development," but his successor, General Raden (now President) Suharto, while insisting that legal process would be restored, had no intention of relinquishing authority or subjecting it in any way to institutional control. Consequently, legal process not only remained corrupt, but grew more so, as the state bureaucracy, now the instrument of the military, became the essential but miserable and expensive route to most ends. No less was this true of the judicial system, whose political loyalty and services to the regime were compensated in the currency of opportunity to extort additional income.

Support for Legal Reform

The formal legal system, then, could not be used for purposes of reform, any more than it could be under Guided Democracy, for it remained fundamentally the government's instrument of control, not a means of access to state authority. But the legal process itself became the object of reform. For the first time in the independent state, the *Negara hukum* became a primary source of serious ideological contention, the starting point of challenge and criticism of the New Order state. From the late 1960s onwards private lawyers, students, intellectuals, journalists, and others persistently raised issues of official abuse and corruption in the judiciary and in the general bureaucracy. Though there was little practical effect, despite some statutory reforms, an ideological agenda took form.

Why should legal process have become so central an issue? In part, demands for legal reform were an obvious response to the legal abuses of Guided Democracy and the New Order, but this alone does not illuminate much unless we know who has pressed the case for the *Negara hukum*. The sources of support are several. Religious minorities, for example, see in law some protection from majority Muslims, who themselves hope for protection from the state itself. Ethnic and regional minorities expect from strong legal emphases a guarantee of opportunities equal to those of the heartland Javanese who control the state and its bureaucracy. Upwardly mobile students assume that legal process will allow their merit to shine through the ascriptive connections of others. Most such groups, basically political outsiders, are outspoken proponents of a constitutionally organized law-state.[9]

So are others who are more usefully conceived as elements of a middle class that has expanded impressively behind the economic growth stimulated by New Order policies. Characteristically, these are urban groups more or less solidly grounded in the private economy, not only businessmen but private professionals, as well as the normal run of intellectuals, academics, and students who increasingly seek more autonomous social and political space for themselves and both access to and insulation from political authority. One should not generalize too easily about them, for they are socially, politically, and ideologically fragmented and ambivalent in their attitudes toward power. Yet except for those with directly advantageous channels to the regime, they do share considerable doubt about the beneficence of the government and an interest in imposing controls over it. From such groups reform organizations have drawn at least tacit support, enough so to make the government think carefully before simply stomping them out.

These groups are part of the evidence for an emergent ideological tendency, not entirely new but more substantial now, that favors institutional controls over political power and the legitimation of private preserves of public life. Other evidence exists in the new writing, since 1966, on private rights against state authority, in persistent complaints against corruption and abuse of authority, and in the organization of private associational life.

This last point is especially significant. Since the 1970s a number of NGOs have appeared, self-consciously NG, committed to diverse reforms and by implication to reworking a political order over which, at present, they have no control and shallow influence. The very existence of these organizations represents a public argument and a social statement about the separation of state and society and the legitimacy of privately mobilized public efforts, in rural development, in environmental affairs, in intellectual work, or in legal reform.

The most relevant of these NGOs for our purposes is the Legal Aid Bureau [Lembaga Bantuan Hukum (LBH)] established in 1970, the first of the major new activist NGOs and something of a model for others that followed. It was sponsored by PERADIN, the Indonesian Advocates Association. Private lawyers are a particularly important group in the history of constitutionalism, not because they are responsible for it or even all that essential to its evolution, but because thay become the most articulate rationalizers of constitutionalist ideas, in which they have a direct interest. Moreover, the private legal professions, like other private professions, tend to represent the interests and influence the attitudes of their clienteles. In Indonesia professional advocates, who suffered economically and ideologically under Guided Democracy, became the most fervent promoters of rule of law ideas in the New Order. And when it became clear that the New Order would not differ politically and institutionally all that much from the old, they prepared in effect for a longer struggle by creating the LBH.[10] Thereafter the profession itself went through a transformation, growing with the economy to 10 or 15 times its 1965 size of only 200 or less nationwide, and diversifying and stratifying as never before. Private lawyers by and large lost active interest in reform in proportion as their incomes rose during the next two decades. But the LBH remained and grew from a Jakarta office into a national foundation with a dozen branches in the major provinces. Its success, moreover, initiated a legal aid movement in the late 1970s, with scores of active organizations around the country.

Legal aid, the LBH particularly, represents a highly sophisticated constitutionalist movement. Not limiting itself to formal legal assistance, it has conceived its work more broadly as the cutting edge of political, social, and even cultural reform. Law to the LBH is both means and end ideologically, but part of the end has to be understood as a state surrounded by political and institutional controls. Legal assistance to indigent clients is the daily work of the LBH offices, but it is only the base of a much larger effort—"structural legal aid"—that extends to the representation of peasant and labor interests, social–legal and political criticism, lobbying pressure reform, defense in political trials that also provide a forum for political and legal commentary, and promotion of human rights.

Legal assistance apart (thousands of cases but inevitably far less than the need), how effective politically has the legal aid movement been? As always, the answer is mixed, with apparent successes that do not mean much and evident failures that obscure significant change. Its pressure (along with that of the professional advocacy) helped to produce important statutory reforms in criminal procedure, for example, but government enforcement of them has been unimpressive.[11] Nor obviously have the LBH and its partners achieved the constitutional transformation of the regime that remains militarily controlled and, at will, coercive. Yet the LBH has contributed substantially to the development of an ideology of political, constitutional, and legal reform, built around human rights emphasis, that has drawn considerable support and is likely to endure. The support, however, has not been equally consistent among all groups; nor has the LBH been able to persuade its audience on all important issues. It did not persuade many that the death penalty was wrong or that the killing of troublesome "delinquents" by military death squads was morally and legally abhorrent. Nevertheless it has elaborated an ideological grid that is put to constant use against government abuse.

Key elements in the political ideology of Indonesian legal aid include the related ideas of a *negara hukum*, an independent judiciary with powers of judicial review, and human rights. The implications of the *negara hukum* as an

Indonesian version of the rule of law are self-evident, but the emphasis on autonomous courts and human rights merits comment. The demand for an independent judiciary in part responds to the reality that Indonesian courts are politically bound, their judges civil servants like any other with responsibility for implementing the will of the regime. Autonomous courts, many assume, will be more responsive to society and less corrupt because they are less dependent on political protection. In addition, however, the political significance of courts lies in their symbolic link to the suprapolitical idea of "impersonal" law, their separability from political authority and their potential as a means of confining that authority.

They represent the institutional promise of control. The emphasis on human rights does the same ideologically, inscribing a circle of inviolability that limits political authority by defining what it cannot do. The universality of human rights claims has the additional advantage of linking reformers to a worldwide movement that lends external support and legitimacy. The LBH and related organizations have often raised issues of social and economic rights as well, but their essential focus has been on legal process as the only effective means by which other objectives are likely to be easier to achieve. By implication, it can be argued, social and economic rights also impose limits on political authority by prescribing what must be done.

The New Order and Reform

The New Order administration has made only symbolic concessions to demands for reform; it has relinquished none of the effective power or authority at its disposal. The control lines of the bureaucracy and the legal system, including the civil judiciary as well as the security apparatus, are all securely tethered at a point within easy reach of state leadership, backed by an army fully entwined structurally and ideologically with the state. As yet there is no compelling reason for regime leaders to make far-reaching concessions. Even so, a choppy dialogue with reformers goes on from which an outline of state ideological defenses can be ascertained. These defenses are paradoxical and increasingly strained. While maintaining that authoritarian supervision is necessary for the sake of "development," that is, economic and social change largely modeled on industrial Europe, North America, and Japan, they condemn reformers who promote human rights for importing "western" values. Such arguments ought not to be dismissed because they seem hypocritical or because leaders with enough power can say anything they like. Partially, at least, they reflect a genuine understanding, derived from local history, of the responsibilities and prerogatives of authority. With this understanding reform ideology must contend.

The issue of "western" origins of constitutionalist and human rights values requires special comment because of its influence and appeal. While the charge is in one sense true, it is little more consequential than cultural borrowing anywhere. What is critically important, however, is that the search for principles and their adaptation and elaboration are locally determined. The source of ideological conflict over the definition of state authority is not the imported idea per se but the rise of domestic social groups whose interests and visions demand change.

It bears repeating that neither legal aid alone nor the wider NGO movement in Indonesia has generated enough power to compel state leadership to concede or compromise towards genuine constitutional reforms. Political power, resting firmly on a military–bureaucratic alliance, remains quite differently oriented. But ideologically the idea of constitutionalism has been solidly entrenched, fed in part by memories of the parliamentary years but also by the interests of influential social groups in a more restrained, accountable, and accessible political system. The idea is likely to persist and to sustain a long struggle, without final outcome but with many compromises, adjustments, and adaptations in a recognizably Indonesian political evolution.

Malaysia: In Defense of Constitutionalism

The Malaysian contrast with Indonesia is striking and easier to take for granted than to explain. Why should a constitutional order have maintained itself so long after Malaysia became independent in 1957? Why has legal process remained so prominent? Why have political leaders been willing, generally, to accept legal definitions of their authority?[12] And if any of this can be explained reasonably, how then to analyze recent challenges to constitutionalist patterns and habits?

The Malaysian constitution succeeded, to put it too simply, because it was fitted to a solid structure of political power, the Alliance, now the National Front (Barisan Nasional), which had every interest in making it work. Elsewhere in Southeast Asia, Indonesia, Burma, the Philippines, and (from time to time) Thailand, the more usual case was the reverse: attempts to squeeze recalcitrant patterns of political power and organization into artificial constitutional arguments failed. In Malaysia, however, the emergence of ethnic parties in the late 1940s, the United Malay National Organization (UMNO), the Malaysian Chinese Association (MCA), and the Malaysian Indian Congress (MIC), and the creation of the Alliance Party coalition among them in the early 1950s, preceded both the development of a suitable constitution and independence.[13] The conservative elite in charge found the constitutional arrangements, and therefore constitutionalism, congenial.

They were equally comfortable (and by training often familiar) with the legal system, whose continuity from the colony significantly adumbrated the constitutional order. The courts were strong and respected, staffed by able judges supported by a small but growing and influential private legal profession. To some political tastes, the government was unmeasured in its dealings with opposition. During the Communist insurgency (1948–1960) the British had promulgated a Sedition Act and the Internal Security Act, among other similar politically repressive laws, which the independent state found useful as well against dissidents of any other sort. There were other political abuses, often matters of "normal" politics, which some Malaysians found morally objectionable and dangerous precedents but not necessarily profound threats to constitutionalist norms.[14]

The NEP Social Change in Ideology

The presidential threat to Malaysian constitutionalism has always been the possibility that the ethnically delicate political compromise on which it was based might collapse.[15] But when serious ethnic riots broke out in May 1969, the Alliance elite adapted quickly to repair the dikes, establish a New Economic Policy (NEP) intended to redress economic imbalances (to give the Malay population a fairer share of economic advantages), *and* maintain the constitutional arrangements and legal process that lent state leaders comfortable legitimacy and seemed a reasonable means of avoiding persistent violence. The memory of the 1969 crisis served to contain ethnic tempers, to justify the NEP, and to make legal process appear convincing in view of the alternatives.

Yet a more subtle challenge to constitutionalism was gradually generated by the NEP itself. Although government favor for Malays created anxiety and tension among the ethnic Chinese and Indians, the 1970s and 1980s were prosperous years that spread a great deal of wealth around the higher echelons of all three ethnic groups. In some respects (not all, by any means), it was a successful "developmental" effort that did promote new economic opportunities for Malays. It did not achieve the redistributive targets that had been set for the period of twenty years initially agreed upon, but from 1970 onwards more Malays than ever before took up entrepreneurial and professional roles, breaking the colonial mold into which ethnic relations has been cast. A specific and relevant indicator is that the proportion of ethnic Malay private lawyers rose from less than 5% in the early 1960s to more than 16% (and rising) in the mid-1980s.[16]

The NEP naturally strengthened the state, vesting more authority in central bureaucratic and political institutions; it also produced a growing, ethnically mixed social middle stratum that was likely at some point to question state prerogatives. State/society balances changed and became more complex as both sides of the divide grew stronger and as the private sector became more conscious of a divide. Private groups gradually demanded more space, political and social elbow room, against the government's firm insistence on the priority of public authority.[17] During the early 1980s, in response to the increasing salience of private associations critical of public policy, the Government imposed restrictions through a revised Societies Registration Act that classified some organizations as "political" and, by implication, subject to controls. The result was a landmark battle in which private associations, for the first time, collaborated publicly in political protest, forcing the Government to make a few symbolic concessions.[18] Similarly, the Malaysian Bar Council, grown larger and younger with new recruits, grew increasingly critical of the Internal Security Act and of the Government's quickness to amend the constitution. The Government responded by imposing restrictions on the Bar Council.

By the 1980s these crises, along with a few others, had evidently produced among private groups a heightened political consciousness, a sense of their own privateness and perhaps even of the existence of a civil society; this new consciousness sharpened state/society tensions, generating criticism of public policies and reinforcing demands for more effective controls over public institutions. In this ideologically arable ground new NGOs founded in the late 1970s took deeper root. Among them was Aliran, a reform organization that self-consciously addressed a cross-ethnically conceived middle class constituency. Despite its limited size and resources, Aliran developed remarkable influence as a source of social and political commentary. Its vision of Malaysian society presupposes less emphasis on ethnic cleavage and much more on economic and social equality, controls over the exercise of executive authority, and human rights.[19] With a difference of accent, Aliran's social and political outlook is much like that of the LBH; the groups behind it are, by and large, similar to those that support the legal aid movement in Indonesia. Aliran also shares with the LBH a burden of government resentment and antagonism.

Political Crisis, Constitutional Crisis

At about the same time, in the mid-1980s, and from the same impetus of socio-economic change, the keystone of Malaysian political structure, the ethnically composed National Front, began to come unhinged. The MCA went through a debilitating crisis resulting from challenges to older style leadership by newer professional and entrepreneurial elements. UMNO, led now by Prime Minister Datuk Mahathir Mohammed, confidently helped out, but soon began to show signs of a similar crisis that broke out openly during the last few years. Mahathir's accession to leadership marked a break in the history of Malaysia's political elite, for as a medical doctor, he was the first non-aristocrat and nonlawyer to lead party and government. Whether or not his own constitutionalist commitments are weaker than those of his predecessors, he has been more distant than they from the premises of the political order they helped to create and more inclined to use political resources inherent in the ethnic assumptions of national political organization. It is this willingness to resort to ethnic claims above all that has most deeply threatened Malaysian constitutionalism, for ethnicity as an offensive or defensive appeal to substantive justice is perfectly capable of displacing the procedural priorities of constitutional government.

Late in 1987 the government itself, intentionally or not, set off an ethnic crisis over the staffing of Chinese schools that became the pretext for a coup from within, one whose unwinding consequences made for a major crisis in the grand tradition of constitutionalist conflicts. In October the Police Special Branch, under authority of the Internal Security Act, suddenly arrested over a hundred political figures, including Chandra Muzaffar of Aliran, several Members of Parliament, and others from various parties and groups critical of the Mahathir administration. The justification was the necessity of heading off ethnic violence, which might have been more convincing had more of the detainees been involved in ethnic issues. Although within months most of the detainees were released, though others waited much longer, the effect of the arrests was to cast a pall over political opposition and criticism of any sort. All but government-related newspapers were closed at the time of the arrests, when allowed to publish again they were obviously subdued. The law had not been violated (the ISA, after all, like sedition acts generally, makes it unnecessary to violate the law) but its spirit had been badly abused.

The next step in the crisis, in 1988, was a direct attack by the Mahathir government on the judicial establishment, which in Malaysia stands at the symbolic center of constitutional doctrine and values. There is no space here to discuss the issues fully, but in essence the government undertook successfully to remove the Lord President of the judiciary and other justices whom the Prime Minister believed to be lacking in pliability or sympathy.[20] What stood out in the political smoke was Prime Minister Mahathir's determination to concentrate more authority in executive hands and to subordinate the resources of the legal system to the government's will. The ultimate rationale was the preeminent necessity of serving the Malay community, along with keeping racial harmony, maintaining stability, and promoting "development."

The furor eventually settled, but this crisis has not yet really ended. Prime Minister Mahathir won the battle and the additional advantage of a public now disinclined to risk government displeasure. But the crisis may have the effect of consolidating the views of private groups around issues of political and institutional control, constitutionalist issues. Aliran, the Bar council, and others did not stop protesting, and educated Malaysians from all ethnic lines were at best startled by what had happened. According to one source (in a personal communication), the number of subscriptions to *Aliran Monthly* rose impressively from October 1987 to October 1988, which is evidence of increased interest in the perspective that Aliran offers. (The government has refused Aliran permission to publish in Malay, confining its influence to those who read English, but many in the Malay middle-class subscribe.)

What this means, of course, should not be interpreted too simply. Some who were upset quietly adjusted to the new conditions, and others who did not like the conditions may see commercial or other advantages in a stronger government. Yet constitutionalism in Malaysia also has ideological support from a now substantial middle class that will continue to produce pressure to restore and reinforce constitutional balance.

Constitutionalism and Human Rights

Different as they are, the Indonesian and Malaysian cases nevertheless manifest similar patterns of institutional and ideological conflict. In these contests between public and private power, Indonesian and Malaysian reformers have emphasized legal process, judicial institutions, and human rights. Each point suggests a slightly different limit on the exercise of state power by shifting the sources of legitimate authority—from personal or group influence to law, from executive offices to courts, and (in some measure) from local political doctrine to transcendent values.

The Malaysian concern to defend judicial autonomy and the Indonesian effort to establish an independent judiciary derive from exactly the same concern, which has less to do with the capacity of courts to accomplish much than with the wish to reduce the concentration of power in executive institutions. Inherently the weakest of political institutions, judicial authority nevertheless seems to promise access to and some control over the state; and it is, of course, linked to legal process, the one means, short of adequate power, by which private social interests can begin to lay claim to equality with state interests. Similarly, the defense of human rights, an appropriate response to abusive government treatment of citizens, also fashions an ideological lever against the state by prescribing areas impervious to discretionary political and bureaucratic power.

By now these arguments are planted ideologically and likely to survive because they make sense to groups with staying power.[21] But to focus on these issues alone is mistaken from any point of view concerned with something more than political transformation towards the "modern" (i.e., European model) state. It is worth asking whether constitutionalism represents the most significant struggle going on.

The conflicts I have dealt with in Indonesia and Malaysia, not unusual elsewhere, may be conceived as discourses over state/society relations, more or less serious arguments between different visions of (and interests in) state organization and social structure and the passage between them. Yet it is too easy to accept such discourse as merely about the organization of state. Because constitutionalism is largely a middle class project, with significant but limited objectives, debates over it tend to diminish those economic and social issues of greatest importance to underclass (and underrepresented) majorities. Such reform groups as Aliran and LBH make powerful cases for social equality and economic redistribution, but there is good social reason to suppose that their audiences are less interested in these claims than in priorities of political change.

Human rights broadly conceived in terms social and economic as well as political constitute at once a more serious and less attainable objective than constitutionalism, but, for all that, provide a better balanced and more rigorous standard. No constitution by itself can guarantee political rights, let alone social and economic justice. The most that can be said is that the peculiar distribution of political and social power that produces constitutional regimes here and there also provides the means by which some groups, more than others, can look out for themselves. But it requires little acuity to notice that, other things being equal, groups without power fare little better in constitutional than nonconstitutional regimes. It is important to understand the advantages of constitutionalism for pursuing political, social, and economic change. But it is equally important to recognize that the human rights (however we conceive them) of the poor are vulnerable in all types of political order.

Which returns us to a premise argued earlier in the paper: that resolution of the key issues of constitutionalism *and* human rights depends on a favorable distribution of mobilized political power. Ignoring this elementary proposition reduces constitutionalism and human rights both to the stuff of dreams.

Notes

1. I borrow the notion of "orientation" from Max Weber. See the discussion in Max Weber, in Günther Roth and Claus Wittich, eds., *Economy and Society*, Vol. I, (Berkeley: University of California Press, 1968), pp. 217 ff.

2. If we take seriously the study of constitutionalist evolution, moreover, we must take equally seriously the study of constitutional decay. It is no less important to understand how constitutional structures fall apart than to understand how thay come together. This is one reason for examining the Malaysian case along with that of Indonesia in this chapter. But it is equally a reason for examining venerable examples in Europe and North America, not only the failed Weimar but others that now seem secure in constitutional cloaks but may not be.

3. See Michael E. Tigar and Madeleine R. Levy, *Law and the Rise of Capitalism* (New York: Monthly Review, 1977); Franz Neumann, "The Change in the Function of Law in Modern Society," in Franz Neumann, ed., *The Democratic and Authoritarian State* (New York: Free Press, 1957), pp. 22–68. Also, significantly, Barrington Moore, Jr., *The Social Origins of Dictatorship and Democracy* (Boston: Beacon Press, 1966).

4. This is evident, I think, in Roberto Unger's *Law in Modern Society* (New York: Free Press, 1976). The more one studies his concept of "legal order" the more it looks like the United States case. Americans (or admirers of American constitutionalism) may be more prone than most to suppose that there is only one genuine model and that all others are somehow lacking.

5. Though not fully relevant to our concerns here, Mary Ann Glendon's recent *Divorce and Abortion in Western Society* (Cambridge, MA: Harvard University Press, 1988) nicely demonstrates the kinds of local cultural and ideological influence to which we ought to pay careful attention in studies of constitutional order. More to our point, see also, for examples, Otto Kirchheimer, "The *Rechtsstaat* as Magic Wall," in Kurt H. Wolff and Barrington Moore, eds., *The Critical Spirit: Essays in Honor of Herbert Marcuse* (Boston: Beacon Press, 1967), pp. 287–313 and Alexander Pekelis, "Legal Techniques and Political Ideologies: A Comparative Study," 41 *Michigan Law Review* 4, 665–692 (1943).

6. Some of the ideas and material in this chapter have been developed in earlier essays: Daniel S. Lev, "Judicial Authority and the Struggle for an Indonesian Rechtsstaat," 13 *Law and Society Review* 1 37–71 (Fall 1978); "Colonial Law and the Genesis of the Indonesian State," *Indonesia* 40 57–74 (October 1985); *Legal Aid in Indonesia* (Monash University Centre of Southeast Asian Studies, Working Paper No. 44, 1987); "Intermediate Classes and Change in Indonesia: Some Initial Reflections," in Richard Tanter and Kenneth Young, eds., *The Politics of Middle Class Indonesia* (Monash University Centre of Southeast Asian Studies, 1990), p. 44; "Human Rights NGOs in Indonesia and Malaysia," in Claude E. Welch, Jr. and Virginia A. Leary, eds., *Asian Perspectives on Human Rights* (Boulder, CO: Westview Press, 1990), pp. 142–161.

7. See Herbert Feith, *The Decline of Constitutional Democracy in Indonesia* (Ithaca, NY: Cornell University Press, 1962); G. McT. Kahin, *Nationalism and Revolution in Indonesia* (Ithaca, NY: Cornell University Press, 1952); Benedict O'G. Anderson, *Java in a Time of Revolution* (Ithaca, NY: Cornell University Press, 1972); Harold Crouch,

"The Trend to Authoritarianism: The Post-1945 Period," in Harry Aveling, ed., *The Development of Indonesian Society* (New York: St. Martin's Press, 1980), pp. 166–204.

8. See Daniel S. Lev, "Colonial Law and the Genesis of the Indonesian State," in note 6.

9. See Daniel S. Lev, "Judicial Authority and the Quest for an Indonesian *Rechtsstaat*," and the sources cited there, note 6.

10. On the LBH, see Daniel S. Lev, *Legal Aid in Indonesia,* and the sources cited there, note 7. The original idea for the Legal Society came from the Jakarta advocate, Adnan Buyung Nasution, who asked PERADIN to sponsor it. Over some opposition from more conservatively inclined private lawyers, the senior members of the organization pushed the proposal through.

11. See ICJ, *Indonesia and the Rule of Law: Twenty Years of 'New Order' Government* (London: Francis Pinter, 1987), passim.

12. Despite the obvious counterexamples—Burma, the Philippines, and Pakistan among them—there may be something to the analysis that common law structures are slightly more conducive than those of constitutional civil law to constitutionalist evolution. But the issue, though worth mention, requires more discussion than we have space for.

13. See inter alia Khong Kim Hoong, *Merdeka! British Rule and the Struggle for Independence in Malaya, 1945–1957* (Kuala Lumpur: INSAN, 1984) and K. J. Ratnam, *Communalism and the Political Process in Malaya* (Kuala Lumpur: University of Malaya Press, 1967).

14. On the Malaysian constitution, which has been taken more seriously and therefore generated more serious commentary than is true of constitutions anywhere else in Southeast Asia, see Tun Mohamed Suffian, H. P. Lee, and F. A. Trindale, *The Constitution of Malaysia: Its Development: 1957–1977* (Kuala Lumpur: Oxford University Press, 1978), of which there may be a later edition. Also Tan Sti Data' Haji Mohamed Salleh bin Abas, *Constitution, Law and Judiciary* (Kuala Lumpur: Malaysian Law Publishers, 1984). Salleh Abas succeeded Tun Mohamed Suffian as Lord President of the Malaysian judiciary, but he became the key figure in the judicial crisis of 1988 and was dismissed.

15. Ethnicity is basic to Malaysian politics. For one very useful introduction to its complexities, see S. Husin Ali, *Kaum, Kelas dan Pembangunan: Malaysia* (Ethnicity, Class and Development: Malaysia.) (Kuala Lumpur: Persatuan Sains Sosial Malaysia, 1984).

16. In mid-1984, of a total of 1708 practicing lawyers in west Malaysia 829 (48.53%) were ethnic Chinese, 551 (32.25%) ethnic Indian, and 278 (16.27%) ethnic Malay. (The ethnic origins of 50, or 2.92%, were either European or could not be ascertained from their names.) These distributions were compiled from the 1984 Legal Directory of the Malaysian Bar Council.

17. For a trenchant analysis and critique of the political values of the Malaysian governing elite, see Chandra Muzaffar, *Protector?* (Penang: Aliran, 1979).

18. See Gurmit Singh KS, *Malaysian Societies: Friendly or Political* (Kuala Lumpur: Environmental Protection Society Malaysia and Selagor Graduates Society, 1984).

19. For the range of Aliran views, see *Aliran Speaks* (Penang: Aliran, 1982).

20. On the judicial crisis see *Aliran Monthly*, which has published documents and verbatim accounts along with critical commentary, and Tun Salleh Abas (with K. Das), *May Day for Justice* (Kuala Lumpur: Magnus Books, 1989).

21. By using the term "ideology" throughout this chapter I have tried to emphasize the self-conscious ideational concerns of those engaged in struggles for political and social change and to deflect discussion away from the less tractable dimensions of "culture." It

is important, however, to keep in mind that conservative interests have the advantage of familiar political values and historical experience in arguments against change. In both Indonesia and Malaysia, as well as elsewhere in the region, ideological evolution has encompassed criticism of traditional political culture. See, for Malaysian examples, *Aliran Speaks* (Penang: Aliran, 1982), passim, Chandra Muzzaffar, *Protector?* (Penang: Aliran, 1979), and *Whither Democracy* (Penang: Aliran, 1978). For Indonesia, see inter alia Adnan Buyung Nastion, *Bantuan Hukum di Indonesia* (Legal Aid in Indonesia. Jakarta: LP3ES, 1981) and T. Mulya Lubis, *Bantuan Hukum dan Kemiskinan Struktural* (Legal Aid and Structural Poverty. Jakarta: LP3ES, 1986).

III

PLURALISM AND NATIONALISM

9

Uses and Usurpation of Constitutional Ideology

Radhika Coomaraswamy

On January 2, 1988, the second executive president of Sri Lanka took his oaths of office. From the sacred octagonal of the Dalada Maligawa (the temple of the Buddha's tooth), in the presence of the Buddhist clergy, he swore to uphold and defend the Constitution of Sri Lanka. The president paid traditional obeisance to the relic, and to the clergy. His speech, however, reflected the cirsis of our times, the problems of pluralism, of constitutional liberties, and of geopolitical realities. The event was of historic significance because the president, whose origins in other than the traditional elite, was ritually reenacting the legitimation rights of the ancient kings, in whose day he would have been denied access to the inner sanctum of the temple.

Political Legitimacy

It is the proposition of this chapter that, like the inaguration ceremony of the Sri Lankan President, political legitimacy has two sources in the South Asian societies of India, Pakistan, and Sri Lanka: the legitimacy derived from a liberal constitutional order and the legitimacy attached to political forces of nationalism and ethnicity. The two sources of legitimacy are in constant tension; the dialectic conflict between them is responsible for much of the ideological conflict in these societies. Both are "used and usurped," either to push forward political reform or to engage in political repression. The process varies depending on the issue and the circumstance.

For the purpose of this chapter, the term "constitutionalism" will be used broadly, in both its ideological sense and imply a process and style of decision making specific to the genre of constitutions drafted in the Anglo-American tradition of jurisprudence. Although they vary in substance and although many of the provisions in South Asian Constitutions have been taken from socialist constitutions, this chapter assumes, perhaps mistakenly, that these constitutions have a similarity of tradition, style, and interpretation that reveals their origins in a liberal, social democratic political order. Each of these terms, "liberal," "socialist," and "democratic," have been and can be the subject of long discussions, although the bitter conceptual debates belie the fact that they are drawn from similar political traditions coming out of postenlightenment Europe. In the South Asian context, constitutionalism has been enhanced by these traditions, which, precisely because of their source, share a similar crisis of confidence; they are not considered legitimate, and are not widely accepted as the only means of conducting political life. This illegitimacy then unites them in a common struggle; that illegitimacy rooted in eighteenth and nineteenth century European humanism is the similarity on which this analysis begins.

In today's world, with the exception of the United Kingdom, the source of legitimacy for liberal democratic values is a written constitution. In India and Sri Lanka, the source itself has been subject to repeal, reenactment, and an extraordinary number of amendments. This fact leads one commentator to state that the use of constitutions in these societies is "instrumental" for those who actually capture state power.[1] Therefore, constitutions and constitutionalism in South Asia cannot be seen as fundamental law but as a process in which the values of the constitution are mediated by realities of power and social antagonism.

The transfer of power in South Asian societies after the era of British imperialism saw the transfer on paper of the institutions of parliamentary democracy. Within a decade, Pakistani society experienced the strengthening of the executive presidency and the growth of military dictatorships. In Sri Lanka, three decades witnessed three constitutions, each drafted by a different government. Successive Indian governments in three decades of existence amended the constitution 50 times. Clearly the sense of a constitution as "fundamental law" has yet to emerge as a settled consensus, accepted by all shades of political opinion. The process has begun but it may still take some time for the constitutions to become accepted social contracts.

Liberal scholarship in these societies has taken the constitution as granted and then spelled out the enormous evidence of situations and contexts that violate the basic tenets of any liberal constitution. If one adopts this line of reasoning, the picture is very clear; constitutions in South Asia are formal pieces of paper, whose basic provisions, such as fundamental rights, are rarely observed. However, what is also interesting but rarely analyzed are the ways and means in which liberal democratic values are transformed by the contexts of cultural nationalism and economic and social underdevelopment. This process has openly perverted liberal values. In certain creative instances, and in specific areas, experiments have resulted in what may be termed a "genuine legitimacy" for liberal values.

State and Civil Society

Religion

In attempting to understand the growth and evolution of constitutionalism in the South Asian context, it is important to keep in mind the distinction between the state and civil society. In the west, the forms of the state naturally evolved from the conflicts and struggles of civil society. In South Asia there is a fundamental disjuncture between society and state. A set of factors conditioned by liberal norms and, more fundamentally, by traditional practices and discourses themselves altered by contact with western colonialism motivate civil society. No pure tradition or religion has been left untouched by modern values. Such traditions are the illusions of romantic conservatives. An imperative other than that of constitutional change governs the transformation of these traditions to meet modern needs. For example, Gananath Obeyesekere points to the new developments in Buddhist practices in Sri Lanka that meet the exigencies of a modern society. The modern wedding ceremony for Buddhists and Hindus now is modeled on the 40-minute sacrament that is the Christian rite.[2] Other new rituals transforming the nature of Buddhist religiosity make it central to the political and social life of a modern Sri Lanka. This impulse does not come from international constitutional traditions; the dynamism draws its sustenance from the energies of civil society. The result of all these changes in civil society has been to strengthen the hold of religion and religious values on modern Sri Lankan life.

The development in some ways runs counter to the tenets of secularism, and to the concept of the separation of state and religion, the bases of liberal constitutionalism. Every public function, political or otherwise, begins with a symbolic gesture inviting the blessing of religion.

The Courts and Tradition

The distinction between state and civil society is vital to an understanding of the parameters within which a liberal ideology functions in South Asian society. It is easy to engage in a sterile constitutional analysis of the words of constitutions, and their interpretations in different situations. But the more important question is: what cases actually come before the courts? Is it not more likely that the average South Asian will go to the mediators from headman, priest to astrologer, in civil society, to resolve conflicts rather than an open court with alien procedures.[3] Other systems of mediation and consultation are often preferred to the present courts of law. Further, the lack of access skews the presentation of issues that are of interest to constitutionalism in these societies and has an incontrovertible class bias. An empirical analysis of cases that came up in early years in India and Sri Lanka shows the importance of such constitutional provisions as the right to property and freedom of speech. In Sri Lanka the most litigated clause is the equal protection clause; Sri Lankan civil servents use it to protest against dismissal, transfers, and political victimization.[4]

Some major changes occurred in the 1970s and the 1980s. Liberal democratic values, no longer merely a "passive inheritance" from the British, have become an active tool of political and social accountability. Examples of this change are the growth of social action litigation in India, the shift in the language and the discourse of political opposition against military dictatorship in Pakistan and in Sri Lanka, and a slowly growing judicial scrutiny in such areas as freedom of speech and criminal procedure. These changes cannot all be called revolutionary, but liberal values are not only longer valid as "scraps of paper"; they have become active, albeit in association with other values, interests and struggles peculiar to the South Asian context.

Uses of Constitutional Ideology

Judicial Activism

The 1970s and 1980s saw the innovative use of constitutional ideologies in the South Asian context. Perhaps the most innovative of these developments was the phenomenon of Social Action Litigation in India. Many articles analyze the implications of this litigation in South Asia. Upendra Baxi, not usually known for adulatory positions, writes that "The Supreme Court of India is at long last becoming, after thirty-two years of the Republic, the Supreme Court for Indians."[5] It is his argument that the Indian courts, reacting to the special reality of India, have evolved a strategy for dealing with collective rights especially those related to economic and social justice. In many hallmark decisions the Supreme Court raised social welfare legislation and practices of the executive to the level of constitutional issues deserving of constitutional scrutiny.[6] They relaxed the procedures of the courts to allow for open letters by those who would normally lack standing in the courts of law and they introduced commission-style evidentiary procedures to allow for more complex fact finding. All this was made possible by the Indian Constitutional provisions that guarantee and protect human dignity. In this way, the Supreme Court dealt with the rights of construction workers, untouchable leather workers, women in remand homes, under-trial prisoners, pavement dwellers, bonded labor, etc.[7]

The spirit of judicial activism in these areas was contagious, spurring lawyers to take up cases hitherto unknown in Anglo-American jurisprudence. The demonstration effect may have spread into other more traditional areas such as freedom of speech. In the famous Doordharshan case, the Indian Supreme Court held that the state media, by editing the views of a legal activist on a particular case, distorted her presentation and violated her freedom of expression. The case is a hallmark one and goes further than do western cases on point, in which the rights of viewers or participants in media activity are not as protected as are the rights of the press industry.[8]

In Pakistan, the ideology of constitutionalism came into sharp focus when women activists used it creatively in protesting against the Hudood ordinance, which brought in "Islamic" justice for crimes such as adultery and fornication. Modern consciousness about the rights of women, especially in Pakistani society, combined with a particular legal tradition of interpretation within Islam led to victories in many famous causes. One of these involved a blind girl, raped by a landlord and later convicted for adultery by the lower courts; the conviction was reversed on appeal by the judges.[9] In many such cases, courts have used discourse associated with Anglo-American constitutionalism to make the law less harsh in implementation.

Against Government Excesses

Politically, the ideology of constitutionalism is especially powerful against authoritarian regimes. Benazir Bhutto's victory in Pakistan and the reintroduction of Parliamentary democracy was in fact the victory of constitutionalism over dictatorship. The only other political alternative in Pakistan also poised to confront dictatorship is the discourse of Islamic fundamentalism.

In Sri Lanka, the values of constitutionalism fought the excesses of a government in power for 11 years. The manifesto of the opposition party, firmly committed to these values, set constitutional reform as its major platform. Constitutionalism also functioned in a very unusual situation to give power to the minorities as part of a political solution to Sri Lanka's ethnic conflict. The thirteenth amendment to the Constitution, introduced after the Indo-Lanka Accord, attempted to bring about some form of political settlement to the raging ethnic conflict. The amendment introduced a system of "devolution" of power to the regions, an action long resisted by the Sinhalese majority and constantly demanded by the Tamil minority. The arguments in favor of the amendment stressed that the amendment was made in the spirit of the democratic values that underlie a constitutional order, i.e., the ability to increase participation of the people at the grassroot level.[10] The arguments against the amendment were made in the same western-style court of law, but were in favor of values and standards alien to modern liberal constitutions; the most strongly presented argument stated that such a scheme of devolution not only endangered the unity status of the Constitution but would put political power in the hands of a hostile minority, naturally resulting in the destruction of Buddhist relics and Buddhist institutions in Tamil areas. The assumptions of the Court about the nature of the "other" ethnic minority living in its midst was based on the perceptions of the Sinhalese majority. This type of blatant bias is unusual in modern Anglo-American jurisprudence. The court was evenly divided and many of the judges opposed to the amendment adopted the argument of the opposition. The amendment was passed, after a technical point relevant to a particular judge was remedied; thus a bare majority of the court supported the amendment.

The dissenting judgments will provide interesting reading for those who believe that South Asian judges are "apolitical" and imitative of western discourse. These judges accepted arguments never placed before any constitutional court in the Anglo-American tradition of jurisprudence because they felt that the country and religion were threatened.

A brief excerpt from the petition of the opposition will give some sense of this kind of thinking.

> Apart from other consequences, the loss of control over Buddhist shrines and places of worship some of them of great antiquity and held in veneration by the Buddhists of the country, which are scattered in these two provinces .... The virtual handing over of these places of historic and religious importance to persons culturally alienated from Buddhism is an abrogation of the duty to ... protect and foster the Buddha Sasana.[11]

The legal notion of persons who are "culturally alienated" is quite a new invention for Anglo-American jurisprudence. In this case, the values of constitutionalism challenged by the ideologies of nationalism and ethnicity only barely managed to survive in the highest court of the land, firmly rooted in and committed to the values of a liberal constitutional order.

Political Reform

The ideology of constitutionalism has also furthered political reform, both in government and as a mobilizing force, in the last four decades. In India, constitutionalism in the form of social action litigation has been most successful in economic and social areas where the state has not lived up to the standards that it has set for itself. This is especially true in India regarding legislation with respect to caste, class, and women. As we have seen, the ideology of constitutionalism has also been important as a language of protest against military regimes and authoritarian governments. Benazir Bhutto was elected the first women head of an Islamic state because she mobilized the country using the discourse of constitutionalism, fair play, and democratic values; in this context, constitutionalism as a commitment to a type of public decision making that lessens the arbitrariness of the executive has often been the only common rallying cry of diverse political groupings. It is important to note, however, that constitutionalism as substantive ideology (as opposed to commitment to process and procedural style) does not have a monopoly on dissent. Marxism, nationalism, ethnic chauvinism, and religious fundamentalism are some of the alternative discourses competing for ideological legitimacy in many South Asian societies.

The Conservative Opposition

It is also important to note that when some of these progressive reforms were introduced through a creative use of constitutional ideologies, the negative reactions came from diverse sources. In India lawyers and interest groups committed to a more conservative interpretation of constitutionalism preferred the mechanical interpretation of the rule of law postulated by positivist scholars to social action litigation.[12] From within the tradition, those who laid claim to constitutional legitimacy and who put forward the argument that the judiciary should not legislate, that plain meaning interpretations should prevail, and so on, challenged the progressive use of constitutional ideology. Bitter debates ensued, but within the accepted framework of the Constitution. As we have seen, the reaction to the women's struggle in Pakistan and to the thirteenth amendment in Sri Lanka did not come from an alternative tradition of interpretation within the ideology of constitutionalism but from an alternative discourse altogether—the discourse of nationalism, ethnicity, and religious fundamentalism, which placed the preservation of national ethnic and/or religious identity as the primary political issue of importance.

Usurpations

Sri Lanka: Procedural Manipulation

Usurpations of constitutionalism can be said to take place when groups use constitutional ideas and processes for partisan political ends or to prevent progressive reform inherent in the spirit of the constitution, although not stated. South Asian societies have seen many examples of these usurpations and such actions by the executive have contributed to the illegitimacy of Anglo-American traditions and constitutions on these societies.

A key example is the use of the amendment process in Sri Lanka. It is clear that since the drafting of the 1978 Constitution, the party in power has used the amendment process to gain tactical advantage. The first amendment put in place the legal provisions that allowed for the deprivation of civic liberties of Mrs. Sirimavo Bandaranaike, the leader of the opposition party.[13] The use of a constitutional amendment to neutralize politically the opposition does not help to sustain the legitimacy of the constitutional order. The second amendment provides for the expulsion of members from a political party. Expulsion leads to the loss of a seat, if, after a Select Committee inquiry, the majority, of the House seeks to expel the member. Although in written form this appears fair (i.e., the House is the judge of its members), in real terms it means that government MPs who cross over will lose their seats, but opposition MPs will not; they can in fact cross over and strength the government.[14] The second amendment was enacted to provide a tactical advantage for the government in power. The third amendment gives the President the right to determine the time of the presidential election; in most other presidential systems, the time for election is generally fixed for a period. In a parliamentary system the government can choose the time of elections. The president of Sri Lanka now has this electoral advantage.[15] The fourth amendment provides for extension of the life of the first parliament and was introduced after the referendum of 1982. It does not even couch itself in any general democratic language; it merely states that the life of the first parliament is extended. By focusing on a national electorate, it deprived citizens of the choice of their local representatives. It also entrenched a four-fifths majority beyond the life of the present parliament.[16]

These amendments unabashedly serve the tactical advantage of the government. Some of the other amendments to the Sri Lanka Constitation of 1978 have been antidemocratic in substance; their purpose was to weaken accepted democratic safeguards. The sixth amendment, for example, banned separatist movements; whole parts of it were supposedly modeled on Indian legislation along similar lines. But again, despite the form, the real effect of the amendment was to remove the representatives of the Tamil-speaking areas of the north and some parts of the east: it put an end to any from of democratic opposition from those troubled areas, in effect, removed them from accountability and from participation in the mainstream democratic process.[17] The tenth amendment removed the safeguards against the extension of emergency powers after 90 days without a two-thirds parliamentary majority, which the ruling party itself had built into the Constitution.[18]

In Sri Lanka, the courts have a means to curtail the amendment power of Parliament. Certain entrenched provisions relating to the basic structure of the Constitution require a referendum to overcome. The courts have been reluctant to call for a referendum on any particular amendment. The general reluctance of the judiciary to interfere with the decisions of the executive has been noted by many scholars;[19] since 1987, after the major crisis facing the country, the courts appear to have become more independent. Yet, that the judges are appointed by the executive and have to retire at an early age may be factors inhibiting their independence. As others have pointed out, however, the process for removal of judges is cumbersome and Indian courts with similar provisions have in fact asserted their independence in a very significant way.

The history of the amendment process in Sri Lanka clearly reveals that the constitutional process may be used for partisan political ends and has no inherent safeguard against abuse. If used craftily, it may in fact clothe an arbitrary process with a facade of constitutional legitimacy. These tactical maneuvers by political parties have led to a great deal of disillusionment with the democratic process and with the ideology of constitutionalism.

India: Substantiative Manipulation

Not only procedural manipulation leads to the usurpation of constitutional values. Manipulation of the substance of the ideology of constitutionalism can have the same effect. This is particularly true about a right such as the "right to property" in the Indian Constitution.

When the political concept of constitutionalism gained currency in the eighteenth and nineteenth century, the right to property was seen as a fundamental right, to be protected by a democratic constitutional order. Though Rousseau and the tradition of French constitutionalism may not have recognized the right to property, the Anglo-American tradition from its inception, based on the philosophy of political reformers such as Locke, established the right to property as a fundamental right. These rights found their way into the Indian Constitution as articles 19 and 31, and they become two of the most litigated clauses in the first twenty years of Indian independence.

The forty-fourth amendment, introduced in India after the election of the Janata Government in 1977, removed property as a fundamental right and reduced it to the level of a legal right.[20] This act of Parliament was a result of three decades of litigation and conflict over the right in the courts of law, which was one of the main issues of litigation before the Indian Supreme Court in its early years.[21] The very first amendment to the Constitution itself resulted from the controversy over the Bihar Land Reform Act of 1950; landlords and propertied interests challenged the Act stating that it violated their right to property.[22] The fourth amendment to the Constitution also dealt with property and the right to compensation. The notorious twenty-fifth amendment, which attempted to remove judicial review in certain instances, also involved the right to property. Legal challenges by interested parties met every attempt by the government to change by the legislation the structures of economic power. At the same time the government used the power of eminent domain to divest hostile groups and parties. The issues concerning property rights were so central to the constitutional process in the 1950s and the 1960s that until the 1970s and the advent of social action litigation, the law, the judiciary, and the courts were often identified as the bastions of conservatism, the protectors of privileged interests.

Constitutionalism, especially in the 1950s, may have been perceived by the general public and politicians using populist rhetoric as the ideology allowing the middle class to challenge progressive economic and social welfare legislation. The executive and the legislature positioned themselves as "the voice of the People"; the executive portrayed the Constitution and the courts, during times of crisis, as the brakes on social change. These characterizations had tragic consequences. They allowed the executive to discredit the ideology of constitutionalism as spelled out by the courts and to engage in populist acts. Sometimes, such as in the cases of declaring emergencies and dealing with political opponents, the courts and liberal ideologues often found that they did not have the legitimacy with which to challenge successfully the arbitrary acts of the executive. Identified with the property rights of vested interests, the constitutional process was not trusted by those who wished to challenge the repressive political acts of the executive. In fact until the very last years of the emergency in India, progressive social reformers saw the constitutional process as defending vested interests against progressive legislation in the one hand and deferring needlessly to the executive in times of political repression on the other. They identified the process as being against social justice and for political repression. It was perhaps the worst period for constitutional development in South Asian societies and may be said to have spanned the regimes of Indira Gandhi in India and Sirimavo Bandaranaike in Sri Lanka.

Ironically, since the right to property was so often involved, those with property were often the ones capable of translating their grievances into the discourse of constitutionalism; some of the more interesting developments in Constitutional law came out of these cases. In 1973, the Supreme Court decided *Kesavananda vs. Kerala* involving the twenty-fifth amendment's attempt to remove judicial review in certain types of property cases. A divided court spelled out the innovative doctrine of "Basic Structure," i.e., that the legislature cannot amend the Constitution so as to change its basic structure. The court argued that removing judicial review of acts that affect fundamental rights was to transform the basic structure of the Constitution.[23]

The court's position has subsequently met with a great deal of skepticism from progressive groups in these societies as the activism appeared linked to the right to property. But, in a follow-up case in which Mrs. Gandhi attempted to vindicate her electoral seat by taking away the judiciary's right of judicial review of an election petition filed by her opponents, the court responded more fully and expanded the doctrine beyond the right to property.[24] The case heralded the showdown between Mrs. Gandhi and the judiciary, leading to confrontation and impasse. Since her defeat in 1977, the executive and the judiciary have attempted to respect their separate spheres.

Substantive Constitutionalism

What the right to property cases show us most clearly is that constitutionalism as a substantive ideology can suffer from many of the same problems that the doctrine of substantiative due process suffered before the U.S. courts. In this connection it should be recalled that the doctrine of substantive due process was initially used to protect the employer's contract as a fundamental right by preventing the setting of a minimum wage and by limiting workers' rights.[25] In the 1960s U.S. lawyers used the same doctrine to promote and foster the civil rights of blacks and women. Similarly the Indian court's activism in the early years involved the right to property. By the 1980s, its activism and intervention was on behalf of economically underprivileged groups. In both instances, a doctrine of usurpation changed with time into a doctrine of use. This protean quality of judicial activism makes lawyers and scholars hesitant to put forward strategies for judicial intervention.

Few people would not find offensive the usurpation of procedural aspects of Sri Lankan Constitutional law. The more difficult area remains that of substantive constitutionalism: when does a court intervene, with which doctrine, for whom, and at what time in a country's historical evolution?

Many scholars, such as F.A. Hayek,[26] in analyzing the U.S. due process provisions, have argued that constitutionalism should be seen in its narrowest sense with emphasis on process not principles. They would prefer that substantive issues be resolved by the legislature and the executive. In developing countries, however, this passive inheritance as part of a general transfer of laws from British colonial tradition may be a luxury that we can ill afford. We need substantive but principled intervention in areas of democratic life that are threatened by legislative and executive arbitrariness; these areas therefore require special scrutiny by the courts. Such intervention based on judicial review of state action may naturally be reserved for areas like fundamental rights. However, even within that sphere, rights such as the right to property raise political questions. Which fundamental rights require greater protection? Should they all be treated equally? What are the guidelines that courts should follow to evolve a strategy of intervention?

The answer must surely begin with the development of a constitutional doctrine that attempts to argue for the greatest constitutional scrutiny of fundamental rights in cases affecting the most vulnerable sectors of society who have no *access* to other recourse. There have been some attempts to devise such doctrines in courts of law with regard to discrete and insular minorities. John Hart Ely, focusing on access, argues for that kind of approach to civil rights in the United States, that is, state action relating to access to democratic process must have a higher level of constitutional scrutiny.[27] But a more radical doctrine ensuring access not only by judicial scrutiny but through the enactment of special laws may have to be developed to cope with the realistic constraints of South Asian societies.

Political Challenge and Constitutionalism

For a long time, lawyers and political scientists saw development in Third World societies as a linear process. Until recently, for many of us, the challenge to mainstream politics in these societies came either from the discourse of socialism, Marxism, or a more radical tradition within liberalism, drawing from the experience of social democratic forces from around the world. The debates amog intellectuals in the first two decades since independence polarized along these lines, and assumed that history and people's aspirations would always move toward greater democracy, equality, and tolerance. Questions related to how the rate of social change could be acclerated but nobody seriously questioned the nature and direction of social change.

In South Asia, especially in India and Sri Lanka, there has always been a third discourse, its source in the Gandhian tradition of politics.[28] Many understood Gandhi as sharing the essential humanism at the base of universal theories such as liberalism and socialism, but wanting that humanism couched in terms and in cultural symbols with relevance and meaning for the vast majority of South Asians. The essential values of freedom, dignity, and social justice could have meaning only if they related to the actual reality of South Asian society. The introspection and self-awakening that nationalist leaders like Gandhi fostered in India were imitated by leaders throughout Asia. The anger and energy engendered by this were powerful in the struggle against colonialism. In the postcolonial era, however, the political forces generated by this self-awareness often broke away from the humanistic source and became autonomous ideologies, fostering ethnic chauvinism, religious fundamentalism, and cultural exclusiveness.

Toward a Genuine Legitimacy: Indigenous Constitutionalism

What are the implications for constitutionalism of the predominance of this culture-specific alternative discourse in South Asian political and social life? What happens when social change is not necessarily within the spirit or even the framework of the liberal, democratic values spelled out in the constitution? How should the legal system respond? For many, such as the lawyers who were involved in litigation with regard to the thirteenth Amendment in Sri Lanka, there was nothing but despair as they saw constitutionalism, both mainstream and progressive, being swallowed up by primordial politics, whose emphasis on nation was accompained by bitting contempt for process and rationality in public decisionmaking. Others view the current impasse as a challange from which may emerge a constitutionalism with a "genuine and authentic legitimacy" in the South Asian context.

Social science literature[29] has always been skeptical about the terms "genuine" and "authentic," as these terms have often been catchwords for political messianism, especially for culturally intolerant forms. They are often artificial constructs fostering discrimination against "culturally alien" groups, migrant communities, and assimilative folk culture. But at another level, it is possible to see the call for authenticity, not as an end in itself, but as a call for a process in which the institutions of government and the law begin to interact with existing social processes in a creative and innovative manner so that an indigenous jurisprudence evolves. Social action litigation in India is one such example, but such experimentations are still too few and far between. Moreover, recent Indian decisions that move away from social action litigation point to the fact that the constitutional system can take such activism only in fits and starts, the inherent conservatism of the legal process requires a period of consolidation after a period of growth.

How then can constitutionalism acquire "genuine legitimacy" in South Asia? One must recognize the inherent strength of a constitutional process—its potential for evolution and growth. None of the other ideologies prevalent in South Asia today is as committed to so specific and detailed a process of nonviolent decision making; most of the other ideologies pursue substantive values, and are near Kautilyan of Machiavellian in their philosophy about the political process. The strength of the constitutionalism as an ideology is that it spells out the ways and means of resolving conflict, of electing representatives, of making and implementing public decisions, and of reconciling interests and rights in a systematic and open manner. No indigenous ideology in South Asia that has gained currency as a dominant political force has such a comprehensive project for consultation, compromise and conflict resolution. The political processes represented by the architects of indigenous ideology were either dynastic, religious, or tribal and not one of them was designed to cater to the needs of the modern nation-state.[30]

To survive and grow as an important aspect of political life, constitutionalism must develop internal processes relevant to the actual struggles taking place in South Asian societies. The involvement of constitutional processes in elite concerns and in elite rights, such as property, lessens their legitimacy in the society at large. If, in the coming years, the processes of constitutionalism were to be attached to issues of poverty, political repression, social justice, regional backwarness, etc., it would be more likely that constitutionalism would enhance and enrich the democratic process in South Asian societies. Success will depend on a younger generation of lawyers, born in the postcolonial period, who have in some way managed to integrate values drawn from Asian civil society with the modern political demands for democracy and constitutionalism. The use of constitutionalism in the furture cannot be restricted to that of a watchdog for an errant executive. Its uses must be extended to become active and dynamic, to protect values by the use of language, discourse, and doctrine that have some resonance in South Asian reality.

Notes

1. N. Tiruchelvam, "The Making and Unmaking of Constitutions—Some Reflections on the Process," 8(2) *The Ceylon Journal of Historical Studies* 19–24 (1977).

2. See generally R. Gombrich and G. Obeyesekere, *Buddhism Transformed: Recent Religious Changes* (Princeton: Princeton University Press, 1989), p. 447.

3. See G. Obeyesekere, "The Goddess Pattini and the Parable on Justice," in the Punitham Tiruchelvam Memorial Lecture (Colombo, 1983), p. 32.

4. See R. Coomaraswamy, "Sri Lankan Judiciary and Fundamental Rights: A Realist Critique," in N. Tiruchelvam and R. Coomaraswamy, eds., *The Role of the Judiciary in Plural Societies* (London: F. Pinter 1987), p. 107.

5. See U. Baxi, "Taking Suffering Seriously," note 4, p. 32.

6. I. M. Chaqla v. P. Shiv Shankar (1981), 4 SCALE 1975.

7. See P. N. Bhagawti, "Social Action Litigation," in note 4, p. 20.

8. See Doordharsan Censorship case writ no. 1980 of 1986 (New Delhi).

9. NLR 1985 SD 145 Safia Bibi.

10. Petition on behalf of the Citizen's Committee for National Harmony and the Movement for Inter-racial Justice and Equality S.C. Application no. 14/15 of 1987.

11. Petition on behalf of the SLFP SC Application no. 7/8 of 1987.

12. See generally the writings of H. M. Seervai, *Constitutional Law of India*, Vols. ii and iii (Bombay: N. M. Tripathi, 1975–1976).

13. First Amendment to the Constitution of the Democratic Socialist Republic of Sri Lanka, 1978, 1979.

14. Second Amendment, February 1979.

15. Third Amendment, August 1982.

16. Fourth Amendment, December 1982.

17. Sixth Amendment, August 1983.

18. Tenth Amendment, August 1986.

19. See R. Coomaraswamy, "The Sri Lankan Judiciary and Fundamental Rights: A Realist Critique," in note 4, pp. 107–130.

20. Forty-fourth Amendment to the Indian Constitution, January 1978.

21. See, e.g., *Golak Nath v. State of Punjab*, 1967 S.C. 1 1643.

22. See *Sankari Prasad Singh Deo v. Union*, 1952 S.C.R. 89.

23. *Kesavananda v. Kerala* 1973 Supp S.C.R. 1.

24. *Indira Nehru Gandhi c. Raj. Narain*, 1976 S.C.R. 1.

25. *Lochner v. New York*, 198 U.S. 42 (1905).

26. See F. A. Hayek, *Law. Legislation and Liberty* (1979).

27. See J. H. Ely, *Democracy and Distrust: A Theory of Judicial Review* (Cambridge: Harvard University Press, 1980).

28. See Ashis Nandi, *The Intimate Enemy: The Self Under Colonialism* (New Delhi: Orient Longman, 1983).

29. For a particularly bad source see S. Goonetileke, *The Crippled Mind* (London: Zed, 1979).

30. See B. Anderson, *Imagined Communities* (London: Verso, 1984).

10

Social Movements and Constitutionalism: The African Context

Mahmood Mamdani

Are human rights a western invention? Is the very conception and accompanying notion of constitutionalism a legal process that sets definite limits on the exercise of political power, specifically inventions of the seventeenth-century enlightenment philosophers, and ideological products of the French and the American revolutions? And thus, is any talk of human rights in Africa tantamount to a mechanical import of a western bourgeois ideological conception without the struggles and the relations that gave rise to it in the first place?

Without the experience of sickness, there can be no idea of health. And without the fact of oppression, there can be no practice of resistance and no notion of rights. "Nothing sensible or pertinent can be said about human rights," writes the philosopher Paulin Hountondji:

> if one ignores this daily, universal fact of revolt. Only those aware of rights infringed and dignity flouted can be indignant. Only by remaining silent about this commonly experienced fact, or by considerably reducing its implications, is it possible to make human rights an invention of Western culture.[1]

With oppression, and Europe had no monopoly over this phenomenon in history, there must come into being a conception of rights. This is why it is difficult to accept the idea, even in the case of Europe itself, that no notion of human rights existed prior to seventeenth-century enlightenment philosophy. True, one can quote Aristotle and his ideological justification of slavery as evidence that the idea of human rights was indeed foreign to the conscience of the ruling classes in ancient Greece. And yet, did anyone—as Hountondji rightly asks—question the slaves? Given what we know today of slave revolts in antiquity, can we assume that these revolts in no way shaped the thinking of slaves, and give rise to a conception of rights tending simultaneously to legitimate their revolt and to undermine the legitimacy of their masters' practices? Or, given that the victims' discourse on this question has not survived, must we not assume the opposite?

Does this mean that Europe made no original contribution so far as human rights is concerned? No, it does not. What was unique about enlightenment philosophy, and the writings of the French and American revolutions, was not a conception of human rights, but, as claimed by Hountoundji, a discussion of these in the context of a formally articulated philosophical system:

> It thus produced, not the thing, but discourse about the thing, not the idea of natural law or human dignity but the work of expression concerning the idea, the project of this formulation, explanation, analysis of its presuppositions and consequences, in short, the draft of a philosophy of human rights.[2]

The sociopolitical context of this *systematic* interrogation of the conception of human rights in Europe was the transition from feudalism to capitalism. It was the context of the emergence of the individual, from submersion under a variety of forms of social bondage through the medieval period to the status of a person juridically free.[3] This emergence was a phenomenon that went hand in hand with the development of a social space defined by contractual relations between juridically free individuals, a process that Hegel characterized as the emergence of "civil society."

And yet, to talk of a "western tradition" is necessarily to indulge in a degree of ideological mystification. For the "western tradition" was neither homogeneous nor consistent. It varied from one geographic location to another and from one historical period to another, and also from one social class/group to another. Its contradictory character reflected internal struggles.[4] Is it then surprising that what has been handed to us in the colonial world as "the western tradition" is none other than the standpoint of the dominant classes in the west? For that very reason, it is that dominant tradition that we need to interrogate critically and analytically.

Some Remarks on the Western Tradition and Contemporary Africa

De Tocqueville remarked on the difference between the American and the French democratic traditions, underlining the contrast between democracy as a stabilizing and conservative force in the United States, and as a revolutionary and destabilizing force in France.[5] What de Tocqueville termed "democracy in America," however, was the core of republican thought and practice in the United States, a body of thought that in fact evolved in contradistinction to popular conceptions of democratic practice.

A central concern of the mainstay of that republican thought was in fact to place legal limits on democratic political practice, in the process separating law from politics, seeking to keep political questions out of the courts and legal questions out of politics. The point was to set parameters on *popular sovereignty*, and thus on the right of the majority to transform society, by the *rule of law*, which formulated the inviolable rights of the minority in reference to that majority, or of the individual in relation to the political (state) power. The dominant conception of the rule of law forbade the majority from appropriating the property of the minority. This contradiction is expressed in the language of rights, between *natural rights* to transform society and *vested rights* that remain judicially enforceable; or, in the language of the law, as a contradiction between the public law model based on the *rights of the citizen* and the private law model based on the *rights of property*.[6]

Whereas in western Europe the rule of law was seen as a check on an arbitrary and capricious royal power, in the U.S. tradition it emerged as a limitation on popular sovereignty. The point is that the historical routes to the rule of law and a concept of constitutionalism are several and contradictory. The terrain of constitutionalism has never been and cannot now be an uncontested one. Surely, a conception of the rule of law that arose in response to arbitrary state power was potentially part of the agenda of movements anchored in popular social strata. On the other hand, an alternate concept set the rule as a limit on the exercise of popular sovereignty, particularly as it affected the right of property. It is in this sense that I hope to show that the discourse on human rights and constitutionalism in contemporary Africa should not be seen as a settled issue.

Africa and the Politics of Human Rights

The politics of human rights in contemporary Africa bears a strong resemblance to the politics of independence in Africa after the Second World War. In only a decade after Ghana's independence in 1956, most African countries could claim independent statehood and a seat at the United Nations. "We have *won* independence," celebrated the nationalists. "This flag independence was *granted*," retorted the crities from the left. Both claims contained a grain of historical truth. The rush of independent statehood for dozens of African countries in a short space of a decade was the outcome of the confluence of two contradictory factors: antiimperialist struggle from below, and interimperialist rivalry above, finding expression in rapidly organizing national movements for independence; between the old colonial powers (Britain and France in particular) who monopolised access to the continent's resources and markets and the United States, which called for an "Open Door" to these assets.

Behind the present emphasis on human rights on the continent, too, there stand different and contradictory forces, external and internal. Once again, their significance can be understood only through an analysis that relates the global to the local situation. In a global context, the emphasis on human rights is clearly an ideological and political initiative with a strong American flavor, whose immediate background was the defeat of U.S. imperialism in Indochina, and of Portuguese colonialism in Africa in 1975. The result in Africa was to unleash a sharp rivalry between the super powers, particularly over Portugal's former African colonies, but generally over southern Africa.

A human rights emphasis summed up the new U.S. offensive in a new situation.[7] *Ideologically*, human rights had a dual significance. In the post-Soweto tempo that marked developments in the period that followed the independence of the Portuguese colonies, the emphasis on human rights was an attempt to replace the discourse on power with one on rights. The historical significance of this should be clear if we realize that power is to popular sovereignty as rights are to the rule of law. It was thus a rearguard action that sought to substitute the discourse of reform for the discourse of revolution. For the fact is that apartheid can be dismantled and the agenda for human rights realized in South Africa without a transfer of power from the minority to the majority.

In relation to those countries where the Soviet Union was beginning to be the dominant military and political influence, such as Ethiopia, the emphasis on human rights made for a sharp and relevant ideological critique of Soviet practice. It highlighted the fact that Soviet talk of social rights was not an attempt at build on and thus enrich the minimal foundation of political rights, but was in fact a demagogic attempt to displace any discussion of political rights. For the fact was that Marxism on the African continent was no longer simply an ideology of struggle; in the Soviet version, it was also now a state ideology. As such, Marxism was no longer formulated around a conception of class struggle, but around "the primacy of productive forces," in the process redefining socialism as the development of productive forces minus the class struggle. In the Soviet conception of Africa's future, there was room neither for democracy nor for human rights; and this much the new U.S. offensive on human rights highlighted effectively. The human rights offensive also had an important *political* objective, of particular significance in southern African situation. In context where the balance of forces was rapidly changing, it was an attempt to reorganize the ruling bloc from above , to prune its worst elements and to bring into its fold the most palatable sectors from the popular movement. The point was to effect a transition from above that would reform but not replace the existing power bloc, while at the same time paralyze and cut off embryonic revoultionary initiatives. Therefore, the strategy was adopted in, for example, Zimbabwe and Sudan to preempt revolutionary developments, although such political initiatives were not confined to the African continent. Emphasis on a democratic transition from above has characterized the U.S. response to a number of potentially revolutionary situations: the Philippines and South Korea in Asia, Haiti in the Caribbean, and above all, of course, in South Africa.

Does this mean that the human rights movement is in reality an imperialist Trojan Horse? No! It is in reality a contested terrain. For the fact is that the political situation on the African continent is extremely uneven, exhibiting sharp contrasts, potentially revolutionary situations, and situations where repression threatens to stabilize. The significance of reform movements cannot be the same in both contexts. In the former, reform may be the cutting edge of a political program designed to undermine revolutionary initiatives; in the latter, the struggle for reform could just as easily be the opening phase of a struggle against the forces of repression.

But even in South Africa, no revolutionary struggle can gather steam if it proceeds by way of denouncing the agenda of human rights and the rule of law. The point is to struggle toward a definition of the agenda of human rights and the rule of law that will not displace the discourse on power and popular sovereignty, but will lead to it. To do so, of course, is impossible without arriving at an idea of rights that derives from a concrete conceptualization of the wrongs on the continent. This analysis shall focus on four issues: the organization of the state (both colonial and postcolonial) in relation to the peasantry; the significance of the discussion of rights for migrant labor; the emergence of new social groups, workers and middle classes, and the specificity of their struggle in the sphere of rights; and finally, the question of the rights of groups, particularly of political minorities.

The State and the Peasantry

The colonial state in Africa was sharply divided between the colonizers and the colonized; and, except in settler-dominated Africa, between urban and rural areas. The state that confronted the European population in the towns and cities was organized along liberal bourgeois lines. It was structured with a clear demarcation among the administrative, the judicial, the legislative, and the executive, respecting the principle of division and balance of powers, so crucial to the practice of rule of law. In the nonsettler colonies that existed in most of east and west Africa, this liberal colonial regime was gradually extended through a series of reforms, which were responses to a serious of struggles, to immigrant minorities (of Indian and Lebanese origin mainly), and then to native middle classes.

There was, however, nothing liberal or bourgeois about the organization of state authority in the rural areas. The state power that originally confronted the entire "native" population, and later, the mass of the peasantry, was organized along prebourgeois lines. Power was fused in the person of one individual: the chief. It is the chief who enumerated the property of the peasant, assessed the tax, collected it, heard his appeal if the peasant felt he had been unfairly assessed, arrested him in case of failure to pay tax, jailed him on arrest, and released him on expiry of the term of arrest. Although presented ideologically as a continuation of "traditional" precolonial authority on the continent, any examination of the division between clan and administrative authority in most precolonial African state systems reveals this claim to be hollow.[8]

This personalized and fused political authority was not an oversight, or just a detail of the colonial system. It was in fact the heart of it, since it was the seat of a series of extraeconomic relationships through which the peasantry was systematically exploited. The I.M.F. notwithstanding, the exploitation of the peasant occurred only in part through market relationships. The rest (which could often account for a larger share of the surplus appropriated from the peasantry), was the result of a galaxy of relationships that required an element of force to be implemented and to be reproduced: forced crops, forced sales, forced contributions, forced land enclosures, and forced labor.[9] In many parts of Africa, including the so-called radical states of Tanzania, Ethiopia, and Mozambique,[10] one could argue that this state of affairs has deteriorated. Under the guise of ideological purification and the superiority of moral incentives, what has occurred is an intensification of the extraeconomic exploitation of the peasantry; state authority is now redefined as state-party authority, and its on-the-scene representative is called a "cadre," instead of "chief." But then, in a context where socialism itself has been divorced of any democratic content and redefined as a strategy for economic development, the result could be none other.

The same dual organization of state authority—one rural, confronting the peasantry; the other urban, dealing with the rest of society—could be seen in the organization of the ministerial structure in the capital city. The service ministries of health, education, transportation, etc., usually took responsibility for services in the urban areas only. A clear distinction existed between education for the peasantry (primary) and for the propertied state (postprimary), as between health for the peasantry (prehospital) and for the propertied (hospital), and between rural roads (feeder roads) and the main arteries; the functional ministries directed their resources to services for the urban population and the propertied classes. Services for peasants and administration over them was fused in a single ministry, usually known as the Ministry of Local Government in independent Africa and as the Ministry of Bantu Affairs in apartheid Africa. The point to note is that state organization in independent Africa is a structural continuation from the colonial period.

Is it then surprising that almost every rebellion in rural Africa had, if not as the principal target than one of its targets, this personal embodiment of fused state authority: the chief? Were these not demands for democracy? For dismantling this system of *informal* apartheid? In such a context, the state apparatuses in the rural areas need to be reorganized so that there is a clear division of powers among the legislative, the executive, the judicial, the administrative, and the coercive, as well as a system of built-in safeguards and checks. Such reforms can only lead in the direction of democracy for the peasant majority, and hence help to bring to an end their extraeconomic exploitation. Furthermore, where a widely supported movement results in such, then it is bound to give rise to a definition of powers with a strong popular content. For example, are disputes to be settled by legal professionals in courts or by the peasant community? Given that nowhere in Africa (except Ethiopia) was land private property in the precolonial period, notions of community control over land and of community adjudication of land issues are deeply rooted in popular culture. To take another example, are public officials (judges and magistrates, police and administrative chiefs) to be popularly elected or administratively appointed? Are they to be popularly accountable through a system of mandates and popular recall or responsible to an administrative hierarchy? In a nutshell, is the system of checks and balances to be purely administrative, or primarily popular?

My point is that we must not confuse the general with the particular in the implementation of reforms. In the present context of Africa, a general movement toward constitutionalism and the rule of law that calls for a reorganization of state structures so as to institutionalize the principle of the division and check of powers must be welcome as a step toward democratization. But it cannot be assumed that a legal system operated by legal professionals will ensure that the rights of the peasantry are protected, since this will depend on the balance of political forces and the nature of the process that leads to this reform. In other words, the actual institutional guarantee for the defense of rights will depend on how the question of power is settled.

The State and Migrant Labor

When the "rosy dawn" of capitalism broke over the African continent, millions of Africans were shackled in the New World, just as many thousands of Asians landed as indentured labor on African shores. Later, in pursuit of cheap labor either for settler farms or for the mines, colonial labor policies reorganized the economic life of entire regions and nationalities as labor reserves. Migrant labor built the sinews of settler capital in both the north and south of the continent. Even in the west and the east, where settlers in agriculture were an exception, the economic life of inland communities was often reorganized around migrant labor that supplied the labor needs of commodity agriculture closer to the coast. Africa, it may be said, is the original home of migrant labor.

If we superimpose on the geographic outlines of these economic processes the political map of independent Africa, we begin to get some idea of the contradiction between the economic and the political realities of the continent. In the history of state formation in Africa, its notorious balkanization, the key event is not the partition of the 1880s but the independence of the 1950s and 1960s. For the simple truth is that the continent that imperialism conquered in the 1880s was not a political unity, it was a collection of diverse political groupings, from stateless communities to principalities and kingdoms. The political thrust of colonialism, like that of most formal empires, was to centralize. The real slicing up of Africa took place at independence, the moment of transition from formal to informal rule.

It is with the second partition of Africa—"independence"—that the significance of cross-border migrant labor became enormous. Entire communities now migrate to labor as "noncitizens" in foreign territories: the Bourkinabe in Ivory Coast, the Ghanaians in Nigeria, the Rwandese in Uganda, and a whole string of border nationalities inside South Africa. Add to these labor migrants the swelling number of refugees on the continent, in some cases the result of "destabilization" promoted from the outside (e.g., refugees from Mozambique in Malawi), but in other cases the result of deliberate policies by a state to disenfranchise a section of this own population (e.g., Burundese refugees in Tanzania). Today, Africa is said to host over half the refugee population of the entire world, and the trend shows no sign of subsiding.[11] In some countries, such as Malawi, refugees have come to number as many as a seventh of the total population, and are now the most vulnerable pool of cheap labor available.

What is the connection between cross-border migrants and refugees? Both are either an actual or a potential source of cheap labor and both share the status of "noncitizens," a status tantamount to being without rights under the law. Refugees are a potential source of cheap labor, and migrant laborers are potential refugees. Both are equally vulnerable, since both are without rights under the law.

These vast and growing groups of producers on the continent are caught between the proverbial devil and the deep blue sea. Perceived notions of "rule of law" have little relevance to their position as the "rule of law" is said to govern mainly relations between citizens and the state. On the other hand, prevailing conceptions of citizenship in Africa are carried over from modes of thinking shaped by precapitalist social realities: thus, the right of citizenship is often seen as principally a birth right, an extension of the principle of clan right by birth. But where there is a radical rupture between the place of birth and the place of work, should rights derive wholly from the fact of birth and not from the contribution of labor? Should it be possible for states to hold at ransom large sections of their resident working population under a "noncitizen" status, and then to expel them when expedient, as with the Ghanaians in Nigeria, and the Rwandese in Uganda?

The State and the Middle and the Working Classes

The Southern Cone is that part of Africa most pregnant with revolutionary possibilities today, but the demand for rights is central to the struggle of oppressed strata, classes, and groups in the rest of Africa. A dominant characteristic of this struggle is a distinction between rural and urban protest. Thus, from the Ivory Coast and Senegal on the west coast to Kenya and Zambia in eastern Africa, what has come to be known as the "democratic movement" is primarily an urban affair. It is a movement whose thrust is shaped primarily by the activity of middle and working classes.

The human rights activity of these classes is specific, shaped in each instance by concrete historical experience. Both the nature of its demands and its varying perspectives elude easy generalization. I shall try and underline this point by contrasting the rights activity of middle and working classes in contemporary Uganda.

In the 1980s, broad sectors of the middle classes rallied around the demand for free expression, concretely formulated as a call for press freedom. More than the right to form political parties, it was this right for a free press—for independent sources of public information and for a public forum for a public discussion of public policies—that caught the imagination and organized the energies of broad sectors of the middle class in their struggle for rights. Why was there not a similar enthusiasm for the defense of the right of political organization?

Because large sectors in society, and not only in the middle classes, have come to understand politics as a profession, not as a popular political activity; as a profession, it is seen as a way of making one's living and of looking for an opportunity to enrich oneself when possible. Political parties are thus seen as associations of professionals called politicians, which make a clear distinction between their own corporate interest and that of their members on the one hand, and the interest of their constituencies on the other. In normal times they excel in building ever larger constituencies through demagogic appeals to high principles or broadly held prejudices; when it comes, however, to situations of confrontation between state authority and their constituencies, these politicians are naturally loath to risk their future careers in the name of some vague and higher general principle. Such, in brief, is the cynicism with which broad sectors of the middle class view the standard careerism and the occasional opportunism of politicians of different stripes. No wonder that a demand for the right of political party activity has a far narrower audience within middle-class circles than does any call for press freedom.

What is the historical experience of both the press and political parties that gave rise to such a judgment? An active press came into being in Uganda after the fall of the Main regime in 1979, when a loose coalition of diverse parties and groups, called the Uganda National Liberation Front (UNLF), ruled the country. At the time, effective power lay in the hands of the Tanzanian army, which had defeated the Main forces in an interstate war; the government machinery was run by different factions of small exile groups, each group turning to the press and to recruiting armed militias in preparation for the next round of battle. Thus, the press freedom of the UNLF days was a sign of the reality of a political vacuum, of a postponed confrontation, not a historical gain of any sector of society.

Press freedom did become the stuff of political struggle in the coming period. As guerilla war raged in the countryside, the urban middle classes rallied around broad sectors of the intelligentsia in a struggle for more information and more discussion. This struggle developed through the press, through institutions of higher learning (including the university), and through the schools. For the urban population, the opposition political parties could offer little by way of resistance beyond an occasional press conference. But, newspapers, like *Weekly Topic* and *Munasi*, magazines like *Forward* and university-based forums like *Mawazo*[12] became the fora of public criticisms of the regime and a public discussion of the necessity for an alternative to dictatorship. Following the Lutwa coup of July 1985, the military regime imposed a military censor on the press, and important sections of the press, led by *Weekly Topic*, openly and publicly defied the censor, becoming the spearhead of urban middle-class resistance to the military dictatorship. With the victory of the guerilla struggle in 1986, it was this press that became the first effective barrier in the path of hegemonic tendencies within the ranks of the guerilla movement. For the fact was that press freedom was not the gift of government from above; it had in fact been won through struggle from below. In the late 1980s, Uganda and the Sudan had the freest press in eastern Africa.

Notwithstanding the widely held middle-class view that the purpose of agitation for the "right of organization" is to further the narrow career interests of professional politicians, the long struggle of many workers in the area of rights centered on the "right of free and autonomous associations"; as a result, the trade union movement has also helped to check hegemonic tendencies within the new ruling circles in Uganda. The occasion for this development was a reform introduced by the leading element, the National Resistance Movement (NRM), in the broad coalition of political parties that governs the country. The reform earmarked certain seats in the new legislative body for interests that had been disregarded in the past: women, youth, and workers. When the NRM proceeded to determine the manner in which these seats would be filled, the National Organization of Trade Unions (NOTU) objected to the announced method of electing workers' representatives on the grounds that it would undermine its own integrity. The NRM conceded this right to NOTU.

In contrast, the women and the young people lacked the organizational capacity to defend their autonomy, and did not challenge the NRM proposals, which went into effect. The outcome is worth reflecting on. One woman is elected to represent each district by its counsellors; as the latter are predominantly male, it is not at all clear why the person so chosen should be considered a women's representative, except to underline her gender! The youth's representation was settled by forming, under the initiative of the NRM, a national youth organization that would elect youth representatives to the legislature.

The same reform for special representation in the legislature has had opposite effects for the groups concerned. For women and youth, the reform comes as a gift from above, not as a right struggled for; it will probably tend to create a set of women's and youth's "representatives" beholden to the ruling power who would most likely function as that power's representatives to women and youth. For workers, in contrast, the same reform takes on the shape of a concession, a right extended as a result of a successful struggle. Women and youth representatives were incorporated into the ruling system; workers representatives won a recognition of autonomy.

It is worth noting that the tendency for regimes in Africa to want to monopolize organizational initiative, and the corresponding denial of the right of self-organization to social groups, has usually been expressed in the language of radical politics, as a call for "national unity" against "imperialism" externally and "sectarianism" internally. However, the extent to which this tendency has prevailed has depended not just on the aspirations of ruling powers but also on the organizational strength of popular classes in society. Contrast, for example, the experiences of Libya and Egypt. In both countries, a coup against a foreign-backed, quasimedieval monarchy took on the dimensions of a national rejuvenation. The antiimperialist credentials of both postcoup regimes combined with an antidemocratic orientation that denied social groups the right of independent self-organization. Despite this similarity in the origin and orientation of the Nasser and the Qaddafi regimes, the results of the two coups were hardly the same. In Egypt organized sectors of middle and working class stood for the right of self-organization and checked hegemonic tendencies within the military; in Libya, hardly any effective check on the militarization of society existed. The capacity of a victorious political movement to transform itself into a hegemonic force that denies all other sectors of society the right to organize autonomously, can also be seen in Tanzania and Ethiopia. By contrast, we can see in Egypt,

Uganda, and the Sudan the capacity of important sectors of urban society (middle and working classes) to stand for the right of self-organization.

Ironically, the capacity of popular classes to defend their rights is often at its weakest in countries where the political (state) power has been reorganized as a result of a protracted armed struggle. For the very fact of an armed struggle is evidence of both the limited development and the organizational weakness of sectors of the so-called "civil society." A successful armed struggle is more likely to exacerbate than to militate this contradiction: for to be successful, it must bring together the best of the elements from various social sectors; yet on victory, the armed struggle reorganizes the state, and only then develops an agenda for social change. If this reorganization is combined with a perspective that sees in democratic demands nothing but a demand for "bourgeois" rights, nothing but fresh evidence of "counterrevolution" rearing its ugly head under new conditions, it is likely to leave popular sectors in society even weaker than before. Mozambique ought to be a warning. There, the democratic phase of the national revolution was cut short, and the dynamizing groups dissolved when, through an act of sheer will, the Front for the Liberation of Mozambique (FRELIMO) passed a conference declaration "transforming" "national front" into a "proletarian party," and the state power into a "proletarian dictatorship."

The Question of Group Rights

In the dominant liberal tradition in the west, the theory of rights derives from an opposition between the individual and the state,[13] and focuses on the individual, not the state. This emphasis may be the result of the experience of western state formation in which "nation-state" with relatively homogenous cultures were created when multinational states (really empires) broke up into a number of nation-states. This is one reason why the liberal tradition contains little theorization of groups as intermediaries between the individual and the state.

The lack of interest in groups has tended to harden in the colonial setting for two main reasons. The first lies in the very nature of colonial ideology, which presented the western, secular, enlightenment tradition in universalistic terms and tried to delegitimate all cultural and ideological tendencies among the colonized by characterizing them as particularities and backward—thus tendency to see all group identities and ideologies (e.g., "tribalism," "fundamentalism") as nothing but uncritical carryovers of "tradition," rather than as identities and perspectives created through a contemporary social and ideological confrontation. A second factor of consequence has been the colonial tradition of statutorily defined groups, either racial or ethnic, as the basis of community (residence), or work (job reservation and renumeration), or provision of services (schools, hospitals), or political processes (elections, constituencies). The colonial practice in relation to groups has thus tended to exhibit a sharp duality: on the one hand, outright cultural genocide and denial of the legitimacy of any identity other than that defined by the dominant "western" tradition; on the other, a statutory recognition of frozen identities defined more or less as anthropological artifacts rather than as living cultures with internal tensions and contradictions, and possibilities of growth and decay.

From this historical context arises the need to rethink the question of groups rights. These include those defined by the NRM as "historical minorities" (groups such as women and youth who, no matter how large or small, have been historically oppressed), and cultural groups (whether ethnic or religious). Bearing this identification in mind, let us return to the dominant "western tradition," which can now be seen to comprise two strands: the "North American" strand addresses the question of historical minorities, whereas the "European" perspective focuses much more on cultural groups. North American discussion on "affirmative action" have little to say about the right of cultural groups; and European constitutional thought is relatively silent on this question precisely because it assumes that the right of a cultural group ("nation") to "self-determination" is ultimately none other than the right to form its own state.

The extremely disruptive effect of the transfer of this European notion to African soil needs no emphasis. On the one hand, any demand for the right of a cultural group tends to turn into a "secessionist" call; on the other, every claim to safegaurd "national unity" begins with the denunciation of any demand for the right of cultural groups. Could not the agenda of group rights turn out to be no more than a modern formula to divide and rule the continent, thereby accelerating the balkanization of Africa into a number of Bantustans? Would it not be, as best exemplified by the South African situation, a way of denying the existence of a majority based on communality of interest by splitting it into a number of minorities, sanctified as separate primordial groups? Alternately, would not the claims to safegaurd "national unity" in the face of such tendencies turn out to be, as in Ethiopia or Zaire, no more than ideological fig leaves hiding the brutal character of centralizing dictatorships on the continent?

Does the answer lie in a shift from the "European" to the "North American" tradition, in redefining the core content of group rights from the right of self-determination to the twin right of nondiscrimination and equality?

Lest we give in to this temptation, let us anchor ourselves in African realities. The question of group rights has an added significance in Africa precisely because of a dramatic tension between the history of state formation (the political history of countries) and that of social transformation (the social history of peoples). Nowhere else have so many integral nationalities been so casually sliced up and scattered into the political domain of surrounding states, and nowhere else have surrounding communities been set in motion to labor in neighboring countries. Is this not reason to take a fresh look at what is common to both strands of constitutional thought in the west, the fact that the discourse on rights is simultaneously about citizenship, before we accept the North American baby along with the western bath water?

Conclusion

It is better to sum up with a series of questions that tend to open the inquiry rather than to try and close it prematurely.

As a political movement, constitutionalism is a contradictory phenomenon, both a limitation on popular sovereignty and popular movements imposed from above and an achievement of these very movements won from below. As a historically evolved mode of thought, it is shaped by a cultural and class context, which often finds expression in its unstated assumptions. To take as our starting point the historical realities of Africa is none other than to query these assumptions in light of our conditions.

In the radical rupture between the history of state formation and nation formation that is the African context, are liberal notions that derive rights as an attribute of citizenship liberating or limiting? Do we follow liberal practice that treats "noncitizens" or "national minorities" as hostages within the boundary of a "nation-state," a minority whose humane treatment makes sense only as *realpolitik* because a state is likely to have its own "nationals" as a minority on the other side of the border? Or do we query the very relevance of the notion of a "national minority" in a context where most African states are multinational, and few have a "national majority," and thereby question the very root of liberal thought for which the very discourse on rights is a derivative of the discourse on citizenship and the state?

This is why theoretically we must resist a textbook posture toward the question of constitutionalism. In so doing we allow for a variety of historical contexts in which different social forces may push for similar conceptions, and for different outcomes of constitutional struggles. We would, for example, allow for the possibility of a democratic movement that may not necessarily be bourgeois and constitutionalist movement that may not necessarily be liberal!

Notes

1. Paulin J. Hountondji, "The Master's Voice—Remarks on the Problems of Human Rights in Africa," reprint (Republic of Benin: National University of Benin), p. 320.

2. *Ibid.*, p. 323.

3. The transition and the process are analytically captured in Karl Polanyi's seminal work, *The Great Transformation* (Boston: Beacon Press, 1957).

4. Thus, the "rights of man" so closely identified with the French Revolution were opposed by a "new version of the rights of man and citizen" proposed by Robespierre, who appealed directly to "the poor class... of sans-culottes," defining property as a "social" rather than a "natural" right. See David P. Jordan, *The Revolutionary Career of Maximilien Robespierre* (Chicago: University of Chicago Press, 1985), pp. 126–127, 142.

5. See Alexis de Tocqueville, *Democracy in America* (New York: Random House, 1945) and *The French Revolution and the Old Social Classes* (New York: Random House, 1955).

6. For an excellent analysis see Robert Meister, "The Logic and Legacy of Dred Scott: Marshall, Taney and the Sublimation of Republican Thought," in *Studies in American Development*, Vol. 3 (New Haven: Yale University Press, 1989), pp. 206–211.

7. In the learning process through which the United States moved from disorganizing retreat in the years following the defeat in Indochina to an ideological and then political

offensive, Andrew Young played a central role. Young pointed out to U.S. ruling circles the country's strategic weakness *vis-à-vis* the Soviet Union, and that in Africa the United States stood outside the camp of "liberation," that it could neither speak the language of "liberation" nor boast closeness to any "liberation movement." Young also taught that the revolutionary language of MPLA and the Cubans not withstanding, there was no better effective protector of U.S. oil interests in Cabinda than the same MPLA and the Cubans! Young, in other words, taught U.S. ruling circles both to modernize their demagogy and to see through modern demagogy. Although he paid professionally for being a few steps ahead of official thinking, subsequent developments have confirmed that his point of view was not lost on his employers.

8. See, *Report of the Commission of Inquiry into the Local Government System in Uganda* (Kampala, Uganda: 1988), pp. 12–13.

9. See Mahmood Mamdani, "Extreme but not Exceptional: Towards an Analysis of the Agrarian Question in Uganda," *Journal of Peasant Studies* (London: Frank Cass, January 1987), pp. 191–225.

10. See Bertil Egaro, *Mozambique: A Dream Undone. The Political Economy of Democracy, 1975–84* (London: Zed Press, 1988); Dessalegn Rahmato, *Agrarian Reform in Ethiopia* (Trenton, New Jersey: Red Sea Press, 1985); Andrew Coulson, *A Political Economy of Tanzania* (Oxford: Oxford University Press, 1982).

11. See Inodep (an N.G.O. working in development education), and Mink (the International Nkrumahist Movement), *Africa's Refugee Crisis: What's To Be Done?* (London: Zed Press, 1986). The authors come from Cimade, founded during World War II to help displaced persons.

12. The first three were created in the post-Amin era. *Mawazo*, on the other hand, had been a relatively tame university-based journal in the 1960s that ceased publication in the Main era. When revived in 1983, each biannual issue of *Mawazo* was prepared for by a conference attended by diverse strata from the city population, university academics, secondary school students and teachers, workers, and civil servants.

13. See Rajni Kothari, *The State Against Democracy: In Search of Humane Governance* (New Delhi: Ajanta Publications, 1988).

11

The Theory of the State in the Third World and the Problematics of Constitutionalism

Yash Ghai

The purpose of this chapter is to try to provide some explanation of why it has proven so hard to establish constitutionalism in many developing countries, but particularly in Africa.[1] I attempt this principally by examining the nature of these states and their specific international context, and drawing implications for a system of governance from this analysis. I point to the specificity of the contingencies of governance in these countries by discussing the conditions and ideologies that produced and now sustain constitutionalism or the rule of law in the west. There is a danger in this method of drawing unwarrantably sharp contrasts, and of romanticizing the western experience. I hope I can avoid this danger by focusing on those features of the Third World state that both distinguish them from and ally them to the western states. The primary assumption underlying my approach is that to understand the dynamics and function of constitutionalism, one has to uncover its social and economic bases, and thus transcend the formal boundaries of the law. Legal theory needs to be enriched by sociological perspectives and enquiry.

Although in the writing of this chapter I have drawn greater inspiration from Marx than from Weber, I have used a dichotomy of Weber's (legal–rational/patrimonialism) to elucidate one of my principal points. It is well known that the notion of the rule of law is associated with a mode of nomination and legitimation, the rational–legal, that Weber regarded as central to the development and functioning of the modern state. The authority of state actions is founded in the law, which also provides the basic framework for the institutions and the operation of the state. No one is above the law, which is itself purposive and rational, the product of human deliberation. The principal instrument of the state is the bureaucracy, recruited on the basis of merit and expertise. Its neutrality and impartiality are ensured through an independent method of recruitment and promotion as well as by fidelity to the law. The constitutions of most Third World countries promulgated on independence conformed to this pattern, establishing the supremacy of the constitution, the neutrality of the public service, and the independence of the judiciary.

Patrimonialism is a different mode of domination. It is a form of personal rule, which does not tolerate opposition. Administration is based on the total power and discretion of the ruler. The bureaucracy is an extension of his household, and to which he delegates its powers. Officials owe their appointments to his trust and goodwill. There is no clear separation between the private and public spheres of the ruler. He is above the law, as are his officials, and dispenses justice; petitions to him for clemency and generocity substitute for legal writs. The ideological superstructure of such domination is the goodness, generocity, and concern of the ruler for his people. He is the "father of his people," "the father of his nation."

I argue that in many Third World countries the trend has been toward the patrimonial form of rule and away from the rational–legal. I offer some explanation of why this shift has occurred. The rational–legal model (as well as its accompanying ideology) is not completely superseded but coexists with the patrimonial. The trend has fundamental implications for constitutionalism and the status and role of rules.

The Absence of the Rule of Law

It is unnecessary to argue that on the whole the record of most Third World governments on human rights is dismal. Overwhelming evidence of the gross violations of law on the part of governments and officials; arbitrary and capricious exercises of power are frequent; there are many detentions without trial (and occassionally torture of detainees); massive direct or indirect censorship is obtained and it is difficult to exercise the right of association if the government does not like the officials or the purposes of the association; succession to office is seldom the result of elections; judiciaries are weak and some are compliant. One person or one party rule dominates the political system of most of these countries. The denial of human rights is part of the wider spectrum of undemocratic and authoritarian rule.

There is, in other words, despite occasional outward forms of liberal constitutional guarantees and institutions (mostly remnants from the period of decolonization), an absence of constitutionalism and the rule of law. By these terms I mean a constitutional system in which the powers of the government and the legislature are defined and limited by the constitution, which enjoys the status of fundamental law, and by which the courts are authorized to enforce these limitations through various forms of judicial review that can be initiated at the request of any party that feels aggrieved by the law or executive action. The authority for executive action, even that of the president, must be based on laws; this does not preclude the vesting of discretionary powers in executive authorities, but the law must establish the purposes for which discretionary powers may be exercised, and the actual exercise of the discretion must be fair and reasonable. In general, the law must provide for the equal treatment of all persons.

So defined, the rule of law is synonymous with democracy; indeed in historical terms it preceded democracy. It is sometimes argued, even now, that democracy, based on the principle of majority rule, is incompatible with, or at least is in tension with, the rule of law, premised on certain closures of legislative and executive action. On that bases the rule of law is attacked for its conservative bias, and is contrasted witn the dynamic mission of democracy. This is not the place to debate these issues, particularly on the consequent question of whether the priority in the Third World, particularly Africa, should be democracy or the rule of law; my own view is that modern notions of the rule of law have become suffused with democratic values and practices and that, in the contemporary African situation, the rule of law, far from being threatened by democracy, cannot be sustained without it. For the present, my purpose is narrower, to understand why it has been so difficult to establish a system of domination and administration that operates primarily through rules that define the scope, purpose, and procedures for the exercise of public power, and to explain the social forces behind the constitutional forms of these states.

Various explanations have been offered for the absence of the rule of law and constitutionalism in Africa: the colonial heritage of authoritarian government, the engagement with the international economic system, the low level of development, the pull of ethnicity, the immaturity and greed of its leaders, and people's lack of consciousness of rights. No doubt there are elements of truth in these explanations but they do not go anywhere near the heart of the matter; and do not significantly help us to understand why it is so difficult to achieve or fight for human rights in Africa. I will argue that neither the substance nor the ideology of the rule of law is necessary to governments and their economic systems in Africa, and that an understanding of its role can be complete only if we pay attention to the processes of accumulation and reproduction in Africa and to the central role of the state in them.

Roots of Constitutionalism

Constitutionalism, with its constituent concepts of the secularization, nationalization, separation, and limitation of public powers emerged in Europe as part of the bourgeois revolutions. The overthrow of temporal papal authority was engineered to bolster emerging national monarchies in Europe. The nationalization of power was necessary to advance the cause of national bourgeoisies in search of mercantilism. The other roots of constitutionalism are the need of capitalism for predictability, calculability, and security of property rights and transactions. Capitalism required the conversion of serfs into wage earners and the expansion and consolidation of national markets, thus compelling the alliance of the bourgeoisie with the monarchy against feudalism. Capitalism also required the limitation of the arbitrary or discretionary powers of the monarchy (or the centralized state) against the intervention in property and contractual rights.

The concept of general rules was particularly well suited to these aims. Generality of rules prevented both discrimination and arbitrary action (important for competitive capitalism); it prevented the subordination of the judge to the legislature in specific disputes, at the same time it put a curb on judicial adventurism; and generality, with its connotations of rules for the future, ruled out the retroactivity of law. It is, however, not so self-evident that individual entrepreneurs and capitalists want general and equal conditions of competition. A monopoly maximizes profits and capitalists expend considerable energies and other resources to secure a monopoly for their firms or special protection for their industry. On the other hand, once special rules are permitted for these purposes, the possibility of state favoritism (and indeed of corruption) opens up, and this is bad for capitalism in general. Indeed, part of the movement for general rules was reaction to special privileges and monopolies accorded in royal charters and instruments of incorporation. There is considerable tension between the needs of capitalism in general and the desires of individual enterprises or sections of industry, which different modern states resolve in different ways.

The rule of law or constitutionalism reached its apogee in the nineteenth century. This came about not only because the capitalism of that age was still competitive, but also because the propertied class had achieved political dominance. This class exercised its dominance essentially through the autonomous and decentralized economy, the state merely providing the framework for it. It enabled a relatively neat separation of public and private spheres. It may indeed be a condition for the rule of law that there is a significant congruence of economic and political power. Since the nineteenth century the rule of law has certainly receded from its high water mark, for a variety of reasons: the political need to accommodate new economic and social interests (especially those of the working class); the broadening of the franchise; the internationalization of capital and the rise of multinationals and other corporate groups (diminishing the importance of state representative institutions as policy makers); periodic economic crises that invited state intervention in the economy, leading to a copenetration of the state and economy and undermining the regime of general rules through discretion, discrimination, and a larger role for the state. Notwithstanding these changes, it is still possible to talk of constitutionalism in the west, a search where possible for generalized rules (which in Europe has undoubtedly received an impetus through the capitalist orientation of the Treaty of Rome), competitive political systems, independent judiciaries, etc.

The continuing imperative of the rule of law is closely connected with its other major function—the ideological. Both Marxist and liberal scholars agree that the dominant ideology of the liberal economic order is the rule of law. There is little doubt that it is a powerful means for the legitimation of western regimes, and their rulers carefully cultivated it. It hides the way in which power is exercised in these societies; giving the impression of pluralism and competitive political systems, responsive to new interests and change; and it emphasizes the primacy of representative and judicial institutions, thus mitigating the appeal of radical politics. Following Marx's analysis of the masking functions of legal concepts and relationships, Nicos Poulantzas argued that legal ideology serves the interests of capitalism by procuring the economic isolation of individuals by emphasizing their separateness and autonomy, and hiding the dominance of one class over another by notions of equal and free citizens "unified in the political universality of the state/nation." Capitalist legal ideology reinforces the notion that human beings are free and equal, and that the processes of the law, particularly its application, are autonomous and impartial. The appearance of the neutrality and autonomy of the law is possible because the primary form of subordination or unequal relations is not the law but social and economic forces that rely on equal and neutral legal concepts and rules to achieve that effect.

But because of the very power of this ideology, overt behavior inconsistent with it is likely to raise questions about the exercise of power. In this way the ideology does act to restrain official excess and to secure to some extent the liberties and freedoms of citizens. For although in its origin the rule of law had little to do with democracy, political freedoms, or social justice (and was indeed an instrument of class rule), through the years the concept has broadened to encompass those notions, particularly by the extension of the franchise and the recognition of certain social and collective rights. The rule of law in the Weberian sense of traditional-legal administration of a system of rules is in itself unlikely to inspire loyalty. At first its appeal lay in its connection with the market system considered both efficient and just, and more recently with its connection with the welfare state. An essential basis of contemporary western constitutionalism is a social compact between capital and labor under which the market system is accepted within the context a welfare state, designed to mitigate the worst social consequences of the market and to ensure to a reasonable standard.

Decolonization, Constitutions, and New Politics

For a variety of reasons, countries emerging from colonial rule did so with constitutions closely modeled on those of the west. Whether they provided for parliamentary or presidential systems, they separated powers and personnel, diffused power through federal or regional devices, limited the scope of legislative and executive power by human rights, and separated religion under the state. A variety of devices protected minorities, and judicial review safeguarded the supremacy of the constitution. During the early years of decolonization, there was great faith in the ability of constitutions to settle the problems of new nations; later, considerable cynicism set in, and few, even those who participated in its preparation, believed that constitutional settlements made at independence would endure. Only a handful of countries still have the constitution they adopted on independence; yet, despite political vicissitudes in which military or other authoritarian regimes replaced democracy, aspirations for the return to the constitutional values of the independence period for the resolution of their problems animates the peoples of these countries.

Athough it appears unfair to condemn them as utopian, one must question the feasibility of western models for most developing countries. Western constitutions (and constitutionalism) assume settled political and economic conditions and a broad consensus on social values (as is obvious from the readiness with which they are willing to suspend substantive and procedural legal guarantees when faced with a crisis, such as terrorism). The constitutions themselves created neither the conditions nor the consensus, although they consolidated and reinforced them. Constitutionalism represented the victory of particular groups and classes; but the victory itself was often the result of violence, exploitation, and repression.

In the developing countries the constitutions were expected to carry a much heavier burden. They had to foster a new nationalism, create a national unity out of diverse ethnic and religious communities, prevent oppression and promote equitable development, inculcate habits of tolerance and democracy, and ensure capacity for administration. These tasks are sometimes contradictory. Nationalism can easily be fostered on the basis of myths and symbols, but in a multiethnic society they are often divisive. Traditional sources of legitimacy may be inconsistent with modern values of equality. Economic development, closely checked and regulated during colonialism, also threatens order and ethnic harmony, as it results in the mobility of people and the intermingling of communities in contexts where there is severe competition for jobs and scarce resources. Democracy itself can sometimes evoke hostilities as unscrupulous leaders prey on parochialism, religion, and other similar distinctions.

The burden of constitutional tasks was, moreover, compounded *au fond* by the nature of Third World polities, different in crucial respects from the west. Although often attended by violence, the growth of the state in the west was more organic than it was in the Third World where it was an imposition. The state dominated the economy and was instrumental in shaping it; in the west the state reflected the economy. The political factor was consequently more important. Political power is harder to control because civil society is weak and fragmented, itself the result of colonial practices (which have proved congenial to new governments). The state in the west enjoyed relative autonomy from international forces, which facilitated indigenous control over society and enabled a degree of diffusion and institutionalization of power. The Third World state owes not only its genesis to imperialism, but even contemporary international economics and politics condition its very nature and existence. Hardly in control of its destiny, such a society finds it hard to institutionalize power on the basis of general rule, any more than it can resist encroachments on rights and democracy engineered by the more powerful states and corporations. At the time many Third World states moved into independence, the tools of coercion were easily available, which made them careless of cultivating the consent of the ruled.

The ideology of constitutionalism has only the slenderest appeals to the rulers or the ruled in the Third World. Legitimacy comes from other sources, and some of these sources are antithetical to the rule of law. Closely associated with independence was the ideology of modernization and development, in whose name state structures were strengthened and their writ expanded. People appear to regard the promotion of development as the primary task of the government; and the governments, for their part, justify the aggregation and concentration of power (and dismiss debates on human rights) on the imperatives of development. Closely connected ideologies proclaim the supremacy of the party, reaching in some countries levels of deification, or, more frequently, the sanctification of the leader. A major characteristic of many Third World (especially African) countries is the personalization of power in the president (increasingly the equivalent of the European monarch in the seventeenth and eighteenth centuries, the starting point for the search for the rule of law). Constitutions and laws are tailored and bent to the hegemony of the leader; out of his overriding legal powers grows a kind of charisma (even if fear is a major constituent of it), in a neat reversal of the Weberian transition of legitimacy from charisma to law.

Another important source of legitimacy, more significant in Asia than in Africa, is religion, of which the most influential has been Islam, the world view of many of its adherents being dominated by religion. Their religious belief underpins their self-identification and locates them within a community. The Islamic revolution in Iran inspired Muslims in many other parts of the world to establish a state based on Koranic principles. Islam makes no distinction between the temporal and the spiritual, and provides a complete system of philosophy and life. In many ways the resurgence of Islam is a reaction to unequal development as well as to the dominance of western influence in many Third World countries. As with other religious movements, it is in a significant measure a response to the tensions and uncertainties of modernization, the concentration and secularization of public power. But these lead to the theocratization of power, with less rather than more democracy.

If the rule of law as an ideology is unimportant, it will come as no surprise that it is also unimportant in it substantive aspect. In most developing countries, whether the economic system is a species of capitalism or socialism, general norms play a secondary role. Both kinds of economy are essentially administered economies, where the license is the king and discretion is the norm. The role of the state in extracting resources from the countryside and foreign institutions and dispensing it domestically is crucial. Capitalists seek the embrace of the governments, and concentration of state and capital is extensive and complex. Markets themselves are the creation of governments, whose leaders, not having a secure base of their own in the production of distribution process, are fearful of the free play of economic forces. Multinationals accept that bargains have to be struck with the government and concessions negotiated. Key prices are regulated and controlled. The administered economy is compatible with generalized norms operating autonomously. But more fundamentally, it is the character of the state and the nature of the process of accumulation in most Third World countries that undermine constitutionalism.

State and Accumulation

There has been considerable debate on the nature of the state in the Third World. The general agreement seems to be that the role of the state is important to the process of accumulation and reproduction; disputes rage, however, over who controls the state and the protection of which class is its primary responsibility, as well as over its precise strength vis-à-vis civil society. Without going into this controversy, I will refer to the main characteristics of the state necessary to my argument.

The relationship between the state and the market is problematic. Colonialism unleashed market forces but it did not establish a genuine market. An important role for the state (especially in Africa), for both economic and political reasons, is the articulation of the diverse (capitalist, cooperative, and subsistence) modes of production, which compels restraints on market forces.

Another reason why the market must be checked involves the fact that those who accede to political (state) power have at best an insecure base in the economy, which is dominated by foreigners or immigrants. Political leaders cannot therefore allow the market to become the primary agency for integration or allocation, at least not until they have secured dominance over it. In the initial period, they use state resources to establish this dominance (i.e., it becomes in Habermasian terms "the steering mechanism"). This and the previous points make evident the interest of political elites in strengthening institutions and extending their reach (to minimize their accountability).

The use of state resources involves essentially what one may call primitive accumulation, which takes primarily the form of exploitation of the peasantry, and also the workers. Compulsory state marketing channels and other forms of state enterprise are frequently used for the former; serious restrictions on trade union rights are necessary for the latter. As the state is the primary instrument of accumulation, corruption is endemic, woven into the very fabric of the appratus of the state. The pressures toward corruption arise not only from economic greed, but also from the imperatives of political survival, since the primary basis of a politician's support is generally not the party or another political platform, but clientalism, sustained by regular favors to one's followers. Public control and accountability over that apparatus are unacceptable; resistance on the part of the exploited is met principally by coercion. The state therefore becomes authoritarian and irresponsible in terms of its public accountability.

The authoritarian character of the state is its dominant feature. Constant threats to the political hegemony of the ruling group lead to their intolerance of independent centers of authority or power. As the state seeks the total subjection of the civil society, it permits autonomy only where it is functional to its own purposes. The greater the role of the state in accumulation, the less the scope for social autonomy. The right of association is a first casualty, and with it the weakening of the will and capacity of groups in the civil society to resist the encroachments of the state. Civil society in any event is fragmented and dispersed, and in that sense it is possible to talk of the overdeveloped state. Unlike the development of the state in Europe, it did not grow out of civil society, but was imposed from above as a bureaucratic device. In one sense the weakness of the civil society may give the appearance of strength to the state, but in the west at least the capacity of civil institutions to exercise various forms of disciplinary control over their members lightens the task and increases the capacity of the state. Indeed, the form of delegation implicit in institutional disciplinary control itself makes possible the rule of law.

Although the state has the strength to subjugate civil society, its capacity to direct the movement of society is weak. Society's submission is sullen and resentful; frequently its only resistance is evasion of state *diktats* and withdrawal from its domain. Because the submission is forced through coercion (coercion that appears to become easier daily with the new technologies of weapons and torture), it is precarious, and political adventures can overthrow a regime without resistance from the people. Indeed it may be the only way to change governments, for the insecurity that governments feel leads them to repress legitimate opposition. Because many political leaders are involved in primitive accumulation, and a strong or organized peasant or worker opposition does not yet exist, class identification is weak; politicians in power tend to rule directly and to share power with as few others as is compatible with maintaining their hold on the government. These societies lack the equivalent of Poulatnzas' governing class to mediate the differences between the different factions of the "ruling class." In these circumstances, coups, which are merely transfers of power among the political elites, are common.

The fluidity of class relations and the lack of cohesion among the dominant classes (compounded by ethnic divisions) lead to and almost require a dictatorial head of government, which in one sense represents the extension of the charismatic leader of the national struggle and inherits the constitutional powers designed for him. By appearing to symbolize the new nation and standing above ethnic and other factions, he seeks legitimacy for the government. He may have the potential to coordinate and harmonize the interests of the leaders of ethnic and class factions, but few leaders have filled this role. Fears of their own economic vulnerability and ethnic consciousness fostered by politics of clientalism prevent them from guiding by example or rising above factionalism. Unable or unwilling thus to assert moral authority, presidents seek wide and untrammeled powers (including detention without trial) and vast patronage. The consequence is a type of court or patrimonial politics, characterized by sycophancy, intrigues, and factions. Those who are in his favor, or seek it, glorify and pay homage to him in public. Criticism of the president is treated as treason. Access to the president becomes more important than rules; he himself claims and is generally acknowledged to be above the law; the law is what he says it is (and he is not wanting in intellectuals who would rationalize these claims for him). Both repression and bounty become selective. But because there is a limit to the favors he metes out (which are not out of his own patrimony but that of the state) and he has to rely heavily on repression or threats of it, his position remains precarious, and the political system unstable.

External factors aggravate the instability of the government. The Third World state has limited autonomy from the international economic and political system, heavily dependent as it is on it for economic and military aid and for trade and technology. Frequently a vassal of a big power, it can be held to ransom by international capital. The political fortunes of the country and, in particular, the prospects of democracy are not always within the control of its people or government. An influential school of thought has ascribed the rise of authoritarianism in Latin America to the collusion among its bureaucrats, propertied classes, and foreign capital, as their interests converged on the maintenance of public order, repression of labor, and the encouragement of foreign investments and technology. In Africa too, it is possible to point to the difficulties of establishing democratic regimes due to the impact of foreign intervention, whether it be the destabilization politics of South Africa and the United States in Mozambique and Angola, or the support to authoritarian regimes (frequently supplied by armed coercion) as in Zaire, Malawi, and Ethiopia. Foreign powers (and capital) have no principled attitude toward democracy; they are guided by their own interests, and rarely do these necessarily lie in the support for democracy. It is easier for them to deal with governments that can disregard popular or worker pressures.

The role of constitutions and laws in these situations becomes totally instrumental, unmediated by autonomous processes and procedures. Law itself becomes a commodity that only the state may mobilize and manipulate. Governments think it dangerous to allow dominated groups any purchase on the law, except as part of careful stage management. Limitations on the powers of government itself are inconceivable, as, on the whole, are challanges to the government to enforce human rights.

Conclusion

Decolonization ushered in constitutions based on notions of the constitutionalist state, underpinned by the primacy of the law, which has to be the principle mode of domination. Drawing on Weber's notion of rational–legal domination, one may say that the system was to be characterized by impersonal authority defied and limited by the law; there was to be a clear separation of the private and the public aspect of the leaders of the government. The law was to be exercised by a neutral (and largely independent) bureaucracy recruited on grounds of qualifications and experience; public office was to be a public trust, not a personal benefice; the bureaucracy was to be purposive by pursuing national goals; it was to be accountable for the manner in which it exercised its powers. An independent judiciary was expected to supervise the system.

What has emerged from instruments designed for legal rationality and domination is a patrimonial state, with highly personalized authority; state property scarcely separated from the ruler's personal assets; the conversion of the bureaucracy into and extension of the presidential household; the undermining and occasional discrediting of the judiciary so that justice is seen to flow from the president, personal petitions to him replacing writs under the law as means to vindication, redress, and mitigation. Celebrations of the goodness and greatness of the president (equally mandatory in the public and private sectors) replace other forms of legitimacy.

On must, however, be careful not to push these Weberian parallels too far. Weber, although reluctant to commit himself to an evolutionary scheme, had envisaged the progression from patrimonialism to the rational–legal state, with the growing purposiveness and rationality of the law and state institutions. What we have been examining is the rapid emergence of a patrimonial state on the legal foundations of a constitutionalist state, some transformations secured through formal amendments of the law, but a great deal through the manipulation, trivialization, and disregard of the law.

Whether one can move again to a more formal, law-constituted polity is an open question. There is no inevitability in my model that represents a certain conjuncture of social and economic forces that may well change in the future. The collapse of colonialism promoted latent divisive tendencies, but its structures nourished an authoritarianism. Perhaps there is no straight route from colonial legality to constitutionalism; perhaps it must pass through a new process of state building. The Latin America experience, where there is now a resurgence of democracy and the rehabilitation of human rights, shows the contingency of authoritarianism. In certain situations it may well be that the costs of suppression outweigh the gains from it. Circumstances may so change that the vested rights of the dominant class (and interests of foreign states and capital) are better served through a democratic than an authoritarian polity. The forms of development generated through authoritarianism frequently give rise to their own contradictions, for instance, the development of a propertied and professional middle class that values democracy and human rights for pragmatic and ideological reasons. Nor are authoritarian regimes sheltered from the winds of change that blow through other countries. The collapse of communist regimes in eastern Europe and of authoritarian capitalist regimes in Latin America gives hope that the vocation of our times may well be democracy and human rights (although it is just well to temper our optimism by reminding ourselves that dissatisfaction with one form of authoritarian regime does not necessarily lead to a democratic order).

Note

1. I would like to thank the Ford Foundation for a research grant that facilitated the preparation of this chapter.

12

Constitutionalism and the Nationalist Discourse: The Indian Experience

Tappan Raychaudhuri

In India the colonial state, with its representative institutions and written constitutions, encountered after 1919 a nationalism bent on dismantling the system of which that constitutional structure was an integral part.[1] Indigenous politics in general and nationalism in particular were inevitably drawn into the constitutional processes in their encounter with the imperial power. But in the crucial phase of the political developments that led to decolonization, the involvement of mainstream nationalism in constitutional experiments was the result of reluctant and ambivalent decisions. Almost until independence itself in 1947, nationalism's ostentible posture was one of rejection; involvement in the representative institutions was seen as a tactical measure, part of a wider strategy for the achievement of independence. Although the interchanges with the Raj inevitably focused attention on the degree of devolution to be demanded, these interchanges all occurred within the framework of perceptions that emphasized the overwhelming necessity for persistent agitation outside, and generally in opposition to, the constitutional order. Even the 1928 effort to devise a draft constitution for an independent India was partly in response to a British challenge that the Indians were incapable of agreeing on a constitutional future. In short, constitution making was in no sense central to the nationalist discourse in India. It is essential to recognize in this context that Indian politics was never a monolithic structure and that nationalism was but one element in its complex structure. Indian nationalist consciousness, contrary to popular perceptions formed by the post-1920 developments, was intensely loyal to British rule. Being subjects of an empire on which the sun never set was a matter of pride and joy.

Ambivalent Constitutionalism in Nationalism

Despite the necessarily unconstitutional agenda of militant nationalism in India, the ideology and expectations around which that movement had developed were informed by a concern for constitutionalism and liberal democratic values. The self-conscious expressions of nationalist ideology and its programs assured constitutional rights to be "natural" objects of political aspiration; until the Gandhian mass agitations of 1920, the methods adopted to attain these goals were also predominantly constitutional. It would, however, be a mistake to assume therefore that constitutionalism was *the* or even *a* central theme in the nationalist discourse.

The central strand in post-1920 nationalism, structured around Gandhi's leadership, had little faith in constitutional methods as a possible means for the attainment of its goal of political independence. Only a minority of genuine patriots such as Tej Bahadur Sapru or Muhammad Ali Jinnah, worried by the likely consequences of open confrontation with the Raj, continued to stand by the ideal of "legitimate" agitation (i.e., political pressure considered permissible by the colonial masters), and devolution of power in stages.

The reasons for this half-articulated and uncertain involvement with constitutionalism are to be found in the very length of the history of nationalism in India. Long before the emergence of militant programs for the attainment of independence, the western-educated intelligentsia developed perceptions of their social identity and the public good that can only be described as elements in a burgeoning national consciousness. That consciousness, developed within the framework of authoritarian rule, accepted with enthusiasm as a benign dispensation at least until the middle of the nineteenth century and subsequently as a mildly grievous misfortune from which there was no early prospect of deliverance. In both phases, and until the articulation of militancy in the 1890s, the central themes in the nationalist discourse were not political. They concerned issues such as the type of education, western or oriental, to be supported by the state, the condition of middle class Hindu women [first, *suttee* (widow-burning) and later, widow remarriage], socioreligious reform, which had as one primary object the rebuttal of criticisms by the ruling race, and literary effort aimed inter alia at creating worthwhile vehicles for a national culture. Later, the nationalist agenda proposed a reconstruction of national life, whose central point would be the restructured individual, a patriot, strong in body and mind, dedicated to the service of the motherland in a spirit of self-abnegation and firmly rooted in the culture of India, or rather its Hindu component. These restructured individuals were to cooperate to achieve social welfare, especially a better life for the downtrodden, and the protection or recapture of the vantage points of national life: modern economic enterprise, education, rural reconstruction, and the like. Acceptance or rejection of constitutionalism was equally irrelevant to these objectives. Where public concerns did have distinctly political implications (criticisms of the executive or charges of discrimination in the administration of justice and public appointments), they were hardly ever pressed on the government until the 1970s in any manner, constitutional or unconstitutional. Criticism long remained just that: patterns of protest with no expectations of relief, articulated by the press and on public platforms.

Yet the social classes who collaborated with the functioning of the colonial state—the bureaucrats, western-educated professionals, landowners and commercial entrepreneurs, beneficiaries of the newly established *pax Britannica*—initiated constitutional endeavors as early as the 1820s. Their appeals to the constituted political authority for intervention in social matters in the "public" interest were actions without precedent in India's precolonial past. The style and assumptions of these appeals implied an understanding of the constitutional process and an acceptance thereof. These appeals for the abolition of *suttee* or for regulation of tertiary education, represented a discontinuity with the tradition of social autonomy that had precluded any state intervention in matters affecting social conduct. The beginning of constitutionalism was thus linked to an acceptance of colonial intervention in these areas of life. Those who rejected this intervention developed a psychological resistance to the constitutionalist approach to problems of public life itself. The tradition of social conservatism, manifest in the opposition to the law prohibiting *suttee*, resonates with that rejection. As those who favored state intervention in such matters adopted the methods of constitutional agitation, petitions, public propaganda, and so on, the conservative opposition to these methods implied a rejection of public activities that was sanctioned by the colonial ruler and that facilitated their intervention in social life. Constitutionalism under colonial rule came to be associated with a betrayal of a tradition of social autonomy. Here are the roots of a debate eventually resolved in the era of militant nationalism in favor of extraconstitutional endeavors. But, as discussed below, even that rejection was never entirely unqualified.

Constitutional Elements in Early Nationalism

The beginnings of constitutionalism as one element in the nationalist discourse, however, can be traced back to the earliest signs of a modernist consciousness in the subcontinent. When Raja Rammohan, the pioneer of modernism in India, protested to the Governor-General against the expulsion of an English editor from British India in 1823, he appealed to the principle of freedom of expression. His was a constitutional rather than a libertarian argument. When he described the Reform Bill of 1832 as a triumph of justice for all mankind, he also implied that it was an achievement of the parliamentary system. A further, and somewhat unexpected, expression of his interest in the contents of constitutions was his faith in republicanism. He found it rather absurd that a people as civilized as the English should find monarchy an acceptable institution. He was also the first public figure in India to think of legislation as a lever of social change; he supported Governer-General Betinck's proposal for the abolition of *suttee*. The fierce debate on this issue had implications for future attitudes toward the constitutional processes themselves. For underlying these attitudes were the harsh facts of colonial domination. Hence, the indigenous political consciousness associated constitutionalism with collaboration, which became increasingly unacceptable.

Activities clearly identifiable as political developed to a large extent outside the sphere of governmental influence. The first political associations in Bengal, Bombay, and Madras, formed as early as the 1850s, were fora for the expression of opinions and propagation of ideas and pressure groups on the government to secure particular concessions and redress and as a platform to express public grievances. These early associations, merged in 1876 into the Indian Association, were in a sense the first focal points of constitutionally oriented political activity. Though in no way involved in the machinery of government, and hence the "constitution" of the day, their purpose was "legitimate" agitation. Despite the increasingly sharp criticism of the colonial regime, very few among the western-educated appear to have questioned the legitimacy of that regime or even its fundamentally beneficial character. As one famous publicist, Dadabhai Naoroji, put it, there were "un-British" elements in the governance of India, especially in the ecomonic sphere; if these aberrations were brought to the attention of the British public through peaceful "constitutional" agitation, things would be set right in due course. In pursuit of this goal, Naoroji actually contested a seat in the British Parliament on a liberal ticket, and won (1892). A similar enterprise on the part of Lalmohan Ghosh, actively supported by Gladstone, had failed (1883). Another Indian, Bhownagree, was elected to the British Parliament on a conservative ticket. These endeavors represent the apex of the constitutionalist program. But the multiple critiques of the regime in the press and from the public platform were also constitutionalist in outlook so far as they did not question the basic legitimacy of the British rule.

Extraconstitutionalist Elements in Early Nationalism

As early as the 1860s, strident voices were questioning that legitimacy directly or indirectly. Such questions implied a rejection of the limits imposed on political activity by the colonial rulers and hence of constitutional agitation defined by them as legitimate. The *Amritabazar Patrika* spoke of the tyranny of Englishmen and declared that thousands of Bengalis were ready to lay down their lives to end it. Indian magazines described and extoled the patriotic virtues of the Italian and Irish revolutionaries. When Vasuden Balwantrau Phadke in Maharashtra organized an armed rebellion to overthrow British rule, *Amritabazar Patrika* reported his deeds in detail; many read of them with admiration. At least one secret society was founded in Calcutta for the political liberation of India by violent means. Though this romantic endeavor produced no action whatever, it anticipated the outlook of Indian revolutionary terror.

Until the early 1890s, however, protests and petitions considered permissible by the colonial rulers were the dominant features of nationalist activity. All other forms of political activity and expression were exceptions so far as the politicized Indians were concerned. But legitimate protest itself was acquiring a militant edge and a language far removed from constitutional dialogues. When Surendranath Banerji, a pioneer of nationalist agitations, launched his campaign against the reduction in the age for admission into the Indian Civil Service (a measure that was to the disadvantage of the Indian candidates) his style was that of reasoned discourse aimed at removing a discriminatory rule. But his rhetoric, as well as the response of the thousands who came to hear him, suggested a revolutionary upsurge rather than a peaceful, constitutional agitation. The

Indian National Congress (INC), established at the initiative of Alan Octavian Hume, a retired English civilian anxious to prevent any reenactment of the great rebellion of 1857 and to create a way to express and contain Indian grievances within the limits of acceptable criticism, was *non grata* to government within 3 years of its foundation. Votes of loyalty to the British Crown remained a feature of its annual sessions, but its resolutions, especially on economic matters, were implicitly opposed to Britain's long-term interests in the Indian empire. The INC, which had the blessings of the Viceroy himself when it was founded, soon acquired a radical element that had little stomach for constitutionalism within the colonial set-up.

Mass Politics

Recent research has focused on a dimension of political awareness to which constitutionalism was totally irrelevant—that of mass politics. The induction of the masses into a broad anticolonial struggle in the Gandhian era, and of the underprivileged among the Muslims into the movement for attainment of Pakistan did not invoke any constitutionalist ideology unless one stretches a point to claim that all struggles for self-determination are in essence a demand for constitutional rights. Such a proposition would be obviously incorrect because a struggle for autonomy can result in many types of political order, including dictatorships. That the masses had their areas of autonomous political consciousness has been established by historians contributing to *Subaltern Studies*. That consciousness was conspicuously unattached to any form of constitutionalism.

It is important to explore the nature and implications of this disjunction for it fed into and reinforced other exceptions to constitutionalism in the development of indigenous politics in India. It needs to be emphasized at this point that the developing political processes in South Asia encompassed multiple challenges to constitutionalism from a variety of sources, even after it had been accepted as the basis for the future polity or polities in South Asia. Extraconstitutional programs, and, more importantly, attitudes and ideologies underlying them, have been in continuous tension with constitutionalism in all phases of indigenous politics in this region in modern times.

The tradition of mass politics in colonial India was marked by a pattern of acquiescence *vis-à-vis* the colonial state and the established social order the greater part of the time. Acquiescence, however, did not mean acceptance; the popular interpretations of the social and political reality that held the masses in subjection were constructed around deep-seated resentments, programs of resistance, and millenial dreams. The great rebellion of 1857, in which the agrarian masses joined sections of the dispossessed political elite in one gigantic effort to overthrow the colonial regime, was a unique event in the history of India. Its uniqueness has not been adequately emphasized in the relevant historical literature; never before had the Indian masses attempted to change the political order on a subcontinental scale. Their positive purpose was to restore the political system of the defunct Mughal empire. In short, neither the purpose nor the method of the great rising was in any way linked to modern political concerns. This point is relevant, because there is a marked continuity between the motives that inspired the masses in 1857 and their understandings of the Gandhian era. The purpose in both cases was the replacement of a political authority perceived to be unjust by an order expected to fulfill their hopes. This continuity is most marked in the case of the Khilifat component of the first sustained agitation led by Gandhi for the attainment of *Swaraj* (political autonomy) in 1920–1922. The Muslim divines at the forefront of that movement were the direct ideological descendents of their 1857 counterparts who had appealed to the masses in the name of the Islamic faith and portrayed the alien ruler as the enemy of both Hindus and Muslims. The Khilafat noncooperation movement, as interpreted to the Muslim masses, appealed to very similar sentiments.

Again, though the great rebellion was unique in terms of its scale and articulated purpose, continual agrarian and tribal rising in virtually every part of the country marked the history of colonial India. These were inspired by perceived disruptions in the moral economy and millenial dreams, and perhaps by a measure of xenophobia as well. The agrarian and tribal elements who participated in the Gandhian movements often interpreted his message in very similar terms. Arguably, the real continuity with tradition in Gandhi's movements is to be sought in this area of popular perceptions rather than in the anticipations of *ahimsa* (nonviolence) in the Vaishnava or Jain tradition or the saintly life of the Mahatma. These facts emphasize the strong extraconstitutional element in nationalist politics, especially where the masses were involved in it. The induction of the masses into a modern political struggle drew on premodern patterns of consciousness. Even where Gandhian ideology was entirely innovative, it was not concerned with initiating the masses into constitutional politics, a point discussed in somewhat greater detail below.

Indian Nationalism

This may be the appropriate point to comment briefly on the nature of Indian nationalism itself. General theories on nationalism in the Third World have offered diverse opinions as to its origins and nature. From Eli Kedourie's ascription of a totally negative, derivative, and xenophobic character informed by a sense of inadequacy in relation to the pace-setters of civilization in western Europe, to Benedict Anderson's explanations emphasizing creole revolt against metropolitan privilege or the educated colonial's sense of shared experiences and interests, we indeed have a bewildering array of "models." Necessarily, no particular historical experience fits into any one of these empty boxes.

It would, however, be correct to say that nationalism and its antecedent ideologies in India surely began with the urban intelligentsia who shared an educational–cultural experience, similar economic and career aspirations and frustrations, and a growing awareness that there were many others like them scattered through the subcontinent. The "imagined community" we know as the Indian nation began in this way. Such imaginings, soon reinforced by an awareness of the past partly based on orientalist scholarship, had no preordained hostility to the colonial regime. That hostility was generated by the experiences of frustrated aspirations aggravated by racial slights. Nationalism in India, as in many other parts of the world, also had its component of demonstration effect. The politicized Indian had been taught to admire patriotism as a virtue, told repeatedly by his colonial mentors that it was no part of his country's tradition, which was a matter for shame, and had learned through his readings into history that people in other lands had sacrificed their lives to attain the honorable state of independence. Even if British rule was perceived to be a blessing, the absence of independence was a state of disgrace, a symbol of degeneration. The contemporary struggles in Greece, Italy, and Ireland were studied with admiration and as object lessons. National liberation was perceived as a part of a nobler endeavor to achieve the ideals that had inspired the French Revolution. Constitutionalism in any form was not part of these multiple sources of nationalist inspiration; its only sources in the Indian context were the exchanges with the colonial authority and an admiration for the British political system, overt and universal at one point and less openly admitted later; the constitutional developments of the colonial era, which defined the formal structures of the postdecolonization successor states, were an integral part of that admired system.

"Cambridge Thesis"

The historians of indigenous Indian politics, often described as the "Cambridge Writing School" (a description they do not accept), have a very different understanding of the relevance of constitution and constitutionalism in the context of colonial India. They have interpreted the political process in India in terms of networks of interest competing for shares of power and resource doled out by the Raj to secure collaboration and loyalty. As both political aspirations and the cost of government reached increasingly higher levels, the colonial power created representative institutions to accomodate the rising aspirations and to lower the costs. The process began at the local level where nominated or elected representatives of very limited constituencies began to discharge some of the responsibilities entrusted to paid officials until then. Local networks of interest began to compete for shares in this effective authority. Those who lost out in the competition, the "have-nots" of power, began to challenge the credibility of the concessions. The agitations stopped at the point where it was realized that the government could be pushed no further and all parties settled down to work within the limits set by the ruling power until the next round of constitutional initiatives.

A second argument in this hypothesis also emphasizes the constitutional structure. According to the Cambridge historians, this pattern of collaboration and competition was deeply involved with the structure of government or the constitution of the colonial state. To gain local ends, say at the level of the district or subdivision, the most effective pressure one could put on the government was at the provincial level. By the same logic, pressure on the central government was the most effective means of gaining provincial ends. The structure of indigenous politics was hence based on the imperatives of the constitutional structure. The networks of local interest formed alliances encompassing entire provinces, while the provincial networks for identical reasons were drawn into countrywide alliances. The national organizations thus reflected the constitution of the colonial state. And, as already noted, the constitutional initiatives of the government shaped the dynamics of the indigenous politics.

Critique of "Cambridge Thesis"

This analysis of Indian politics under the Raj is criticized primarily because it attaches too little or no significance to the phenomenon of nationalism, and explains the struggle for independence itself as an agenda of the "have-nots" of power seeking a larger share of the loaves and fishes that the colonial government could be expected to distribute. Further, it plays down the relevance of class or ethnicity in shaping indigenous politics, seeing ethnicity itself as a creation of the colonial state for practical purposes: the Muslims or non-Brahmin identity acquired political significance only when the government recognized such categories as the basis for distributing share in power and resources. These aspects of the thesis are indeed questionable.

The abiding value of the "Cambridge thesis" lies in the explanation it provides of the structure and dynamics of collaboration on which the colonial state was based. The constitution of that state is shown to have a centrality in the indigenous politics of collaboration. Collaboration, one must remember, was the dominant fact of indigenous politics until 1919; until that year nationalism itself did not preclude collaboration. Insofar as the "Cambridge thesis" is correct, the collaborationist dimension of Indian politics, nationalism included, was focused on the constitution and hence constitutionalism. The truth of this contention is evident in the style, method and even the stated objectives of early nationalism in India. The political associations were formed on the British model (the exceptions to this pattern are discussed below) with constitutions, rules of procedure, and articles of association. Parliamentary procedures were followed in electing officials, discussing issues and adopting resolutions. Considerable enthusiasm met Lord Ripon's decision (1883) to allow Indian representation on the local bodies, a measure described as the grant of local self-government. The continuous involvement of the Indian National Congress (until 1920) in the politics of the corporations, municipalities, and district boards does suggest the importance of local interests, even in nationalist organizations.

What is more relevant to the present discussion is the fact that nationalist politics in colonial India, until 1920, got deeply involved in constitutional organizations and maneuvers. Its early demands, from 1885 to 1919, necessarily focused on an extension of the Indian share and the representative principle in these institutions. The early resolutions of the Indian National Congress were not ideological manifestos or statements of long-term goals centered on nation building; they were specific demands for more seats on the legislative bodies, for increased Indianization of the bureaucracy, and for frameworks of policy that would protect and stimulate Indian industry and rescue the peasant from dire poverty. When representative Indians were first admitted into the legislature in 1909, to meet their rising aspirations, the issues debated in nonofficial forums were brought into the orbit of the official bodies. There is very little explicit discourse on the theme of constitutionalism in nineteenth-century nationalist writing, which touched on every aspect of public life, but the assumption that a democratic constitutional system was the legitimate object of political aspirations and that its denial was the *raison d'être* for the assault on colonialism is evident in all relevant action. Constitutionalism becomes a subject of debate only on the question of the method to be adopted to achieve an independent constitutional democratic state. To repeat, collaboration within the framework of the constitution was the dominant fact of indigenous political activity. Until the 1890s, such opposition as feebly emerged from time to time was also within the same limits. Only criticism in the less "responsible" section of the press, i.e., periodicals that attacked alleged acts of injustice and racial discrimination in often intemperate language, and were seen as irresponsible by the rulers, and the expression of discontent from the underprivileged masses occasionally crossed those limits.

Tensions: Nationalism and Constitutionalism

Nationalism's Alternative Agenda

Nationalism was also developing an alternative agenda, outside the realm of organized politics. Its chief expressions may be described as rudimentary movements, aimed at fostering national consciousness: the Society for the Promotion of National Feeling, Nabagopal Mitra's multiple initiatives all of which had the word "national" as a qualifying adjective, or the Servants of India Society in Bombay; these were nation-building efforts that accepted the fact of colonial rule, not always enthusiastically, but functioned outside the scope of its constitutional framework. Arguably, as the urban intelligentsia and the collaborating classes generally had less and less reason to feel contented within the colonial order, such movements, (assuming at times the shape of religious reform, e.g., the *Arya Samaj*) and the "irresponsible" vernacular press had greater appeal for the political elements than the more orderly and institutionalized expressions of indigenous politics. Militant nationalism of the 1890s, however limited in scope, was rooted in this impatience with constitutionalism. Later, under Gandhian leadership, this stream of disaffection was joined by another and far more powerful one, expressed as mass militancy. Neither had much faith in constitutionalism. Arguably, nor had the man who led the struggle for independence, though the contingencies of colonial politics forced him from time to time to get involved in constitutional dialogues with the British and the other elements in the political arena of his days.

Adoption of extraconstitutional methods was inevitable in a colonial situation, which also induced a measure of indifference and even skepticism regarding the constitutional processes initiated by the Raj.

Other Nationalist Rejections of Constitutionalism

Other forces within the nationalist front also rejected constitutionalism during the phase of mass militancy. The Noncooperation—Khilafat movement (1920–1922), the demonstrations against the Simon Commission, the Civil Disobedience movement (1930–1934), the Quit India movement, and even Gandhi's individual *satyagahara* (1939) were intended either as revolutionary actions aimed at overthrowing the existing order or acts of defiance questioning its legitimacy. Even though the ultimate object of these actions was the establishment of a state based on liberal democratic principles, the Khilafat component of the mass movement of 1920–1922 was totally unconcerned with constitutional issues. It had strong anticolonial overtones, but its primary object was to safegaurd the caliph's suzerainty over the places holy to Islam. Insofar as the Khilafatists were in support of the demand for *swaraj*, a term that Gandhi himself refused to define precisely, they had a conception of India under *swaraj* totally alien to all notion of a modern state. They envisaged a political future in which India would be a federation of autonomous communities and the Muslims would live by the Islamic law as interpreted by the divines. An echo of this premodern ideology was heard in the early days of Pakistan when a section of the *ulama*, as the interpreters of the *shariat*, claimed a monopoly over legislation.

At least three other strands within the anticolonial movements were ambivalent toward or unconcerned with constitutionalism. The tradition of revolutionary terror, which goes back to the first decade of the century, not only rejected constitutionalism and nonviolence, but projected no model of the future polity. One militant leader, known to have had a close relationship with the revolutionaries, definitely rejected the Westminster model as unsuitable for India; in his political autobiography, Subhas Chandra Bose offered a blueprint for the future constitution that, in his own words, drew on what was best in fascism and communism. Turkey under Ataturk was probably the model he really had in mind. By the early 1930s, the Communist Party of India was very much a part of the anticolonial front. The stated ideal of the dictatorship of the proletariat of course implied a rejection of democratic forms. But the policy of alliance with the bourgeois nationalist forces precluded any overt opposition to the ideals of liberal democracy. A bourgeois democratic not a proletarian revolution was the ideal to which the party was committed.

The third strand that deviated from constitutionalism has been mentioned already. The unlettered masses who responded to Gandhi's call interpreted his message about the future in a variety of ways. The structure of the polity does not feature in any of these constructions. The masses saw in Gandhi's *Ramarajya* (the reign of Rama, a mythical golden age of moral perfection) a millenial promise of an end to their economic misery and social degradation. Even the lesson of nonviolence did not sink in deeply. In the spontaneous rising of 1942, resort to violence came easily and naturally.

Nationalism's Acceptance of Constitutional Framework

Until 1920 there were criticisms in mainstream nationalism, but no basic rejection, of either the constitutional framework or the constitutional initiatives of the Raj. The latter were described as inadequate in relation to the level of expectations at any given point in time and each constitutional initiative did generate a flurry of activity and representations. The nationalists claiming to represent the entire population did not stay away from these constitutional efforts. Before 1920 the line of demarcation between patriots and collaborators or between nationalists and representatives of communal interests was far from clear. To understand the Muslim representation to the Viceroy in 1906 seeking protection of Muslim interests in the proposed Councils Act (of 1909) as an act outside the orbit of Indian nationalism would be a mistake. The Muslim League, established as a part of the same initiative, soon had members who were honored leaders of the Indian National Congress as well. The resolution of mutually competing expectations of different groups within a constitutional framework was a major challenge to the nationalist forces. This was one important reason why the Indian National Congress repeatedly had to engage in constitutional dialogues with the colonial power. The Raj was not a party to all the exchanges between the INC and the representatives of particular communities, for a prime object of nationalist aspiration was to secure a consensus and to face the rulers with demands to which all major elements in the political nation agreed; the INC–Muslim League pact of 1916, which accepted the principle of separate electorate for Muslims and agreed to some weightage in their favor in the provinces where they were in a minority, was the one successful attempt at such mutual accomodation; the pact assumed the existence of future legislatures in an India expected to be autonomous in some unspecified way. The All Parties Conference of 1928, dominated by the INC, was convened to draw up a draft constitution for the future domain of India. By then, however, Muslim political aspirations had moved too far in the direction of autonomy and exclusive political rights to be accomodated within some universally acceptable formula.

The INC, The Rowlatt Bill, and Nationalism after 1920

The INC, as the main forum of the nationalist forces, was inevitably involved in exchanges with the colonial government on issues affecting constitutional change. Some shifts in attitudes naturally occurred in this continual dialogue, and, of course, there was a range of opinions. At first, the 1917 British declaration promising progressive realization of responsible government in India was not treated with undue suspicion in nationalist circles. There were no reasons to suspect in 1918 that in a year's time the INC would call for noncooperation with the proposed reforms. The circumstances that caused the change and the debate on the questions are of relevance to the present discussion. The political mood turned sour when the Rowlatt Bill was proposed in 1919, empowering the government to detain political suspects without trial. Intended to deal with the threat of revolutionary terror, it was meant to be an extension of the special powers that the government had assumed during the War. Indian political opinion had found the suspension of civil rights during the war perfectly acceptable. Its continuation in peace time was universally rejected by moderates and extremists alike. These facts indicate a deep involvement of the indigenous politics with the values and processes of constitutional democracy. The unanimous opposition to the bill in the central legislature was followed up with the first countrywide agitation of an extraconstitutional character the same year.

So far as the initiator of that agitation, Gandhi, was concerned, it was extraconstitutional in a fundamental and innovative sense. The anti-Rowlatt Bill *satyagraha*, or nonviolent resistance, was perceived and projected by Gandhi, not as a blow for civil liberty, but as noncooperation with moral evil; it was launched in a spirit of loyalty to the Raj. The mode of protest he suggested had resonances of Hindu purificatory rituals, that is, fast and purificatory bath.

A perceptive observer has suggested that rather than bringing religion into politics, as is commonly supposed, Gandhi brought politics into religion. His first action on a pan-Indian scale supports this statement. His political career, beginning in South Africa, had the character of a moral crusade, not a moral effort to gain specific ends. Constitutionalism can fit into such concerns only as a marginal issue and the Mahatma was never entirely at ease when it came to constitutional dialogue. Further, Gandhi's own emphasis on the economic autonomy of the villages based on the revival of handicrafts and his deep misgivings about both industrialization and the modern centralized state also imply a political vision out of tune with constitutional democracy. His personal preference, it appears, was for a political utopia where the state would have a minimal role. The individual, living in virtually self-governing villages, would be free to pursue self-abnegating goals of moral perfection with the least possible interference from any authority outside the village. This particular ideal had, however, very little impact on the political thought of nationalist India.

The INC and Constitutional Dissonance

But for the events in the Punjab and the notorious massacre of Jallianwalabagh in 1919, and what was seen as British attempts to condone butchery, the Congress, and Gandhi would have been willing to give the new reforms a try, though they were critical of them. The constitutionalist moderates who broke away from the Congress to form the Liberal Party continued to seek a constitutional solution to the impasse between the government and the militant nationalists. The more moderate element within the Congress remained willing to settle for a firm declaration promising dominion status in some foreseeable future. More important, the *Swarajya* Party within the INC decided on Council entry, ostensibly to expose the fraudulent character of the reforms. The willingness to use representative institutions to challenge the colonial regime itself indicated a penchant for constitutional maneuvers. Many *swarajists* who entered the Council evidently liked what they saw and stayed on.

Again, on the eve of the decision to launch the civil disobedience movement in 1930, the INC had prolonged debate as to whether the Congress should aim at dominion status or full independence. It also participated briefly in the Round Table Conference with Gandhi as the sole representative. The result of that Conference, the 1935 Act, which granted a measure of autonomy in the provinces, was partly accepted and the Congress went on to form ministries in the majority of the Indian provinces. During the war, the Cripps Mission, sent to secure the cooperation of political India failed, not through any intransigence on the part of the Congress, but because Churchill and Linlithgow had decided to sabotage it.

The nationalists had to focus on constitutional issues through a more compelling imperative as well. The Muslims in the Muslim majority provinces had a vested interest in the combination of provincial autonomy and communal electorates introduced by the reforms opening the way to partition. The Muslim political aspirations that nationalists had tried to accomodate outside the formal structure of constitution making now emerged as a specific constitutional demand. An answer had to be found within the terms dictated by this imperative. The 1928 conference aimed at this objective ended in failure as did the effort to avoid partition.

Conclusion

Certain concerns and assumptions emerge from the constitutional exchanges in which nationalism in India was perforce involved. The organizational record of the INC provides further data that helps to fill in the picture. The Congress as organized in 1920 created a structure of command from the working committee at the top through the provincial, district, and the village committees; ostensibly elections at each level were by members at the next lower level. In other words, the formal structure was based on the democratic-representative principle, and meant to represent a federation of regional interest; in practice, however, the party was an oligarchy led by a leader who often kept out of the formal organization but did not tolerate opposition when it came to basic decisions. The pattern was repeated at the provincial level. The INC was formally a democratic structure under an oligarchic leadership that had a popular mandate.

The constitutional concerns of the nationalist movement can be derived from all these facts and circumstances. On the one hand, it was based on a commitment to representative institutions and democratic values. On the other hand, it accepted submission to a popular leadership whose authority often went against the democratic principle. The movement was aware of the tensions inherent in a plural society and the inevitable competition between different regions. Federalism was the formal solution for the problems arising therefrom. The real solution lay in the authority and effective powers of arbitration vested in the leadership. Where this authority did not apply, the federal solution failed and the country had to be partitioned.

The dissonance between the formal and real political structures was inherited by the polity of independent India. And as the quality of charisma in the top leadership has waned over time, so has the legitimacy of the real political structure. Another inheritance of the colonial era also plagues contemporary India. The legitimacy of individual and group action in challenging the colonial state in extraconstitutional ways was never in doubt before independence. That heritage adopted at times for less savory objectives is a major threat to the democratic processes in an independent country. This is a problem not peculiar to India alone.

The political behavior of the Indian masses in independent India and Pakistan reveals a concern for the preservation of democratic rights. Perhaps it would be correct to trace some of that concern to the struggle for independence that was understood at least as a fight against tyranny. Popular resentment against the emergency in India and, more recently, against the dictatorship of the army in Pakistan is in a way informed by the same democratic impulses as manifest in the movements for the attainment of national independence and the establishment of Pakistan.

The nature and circumstances of the nationalist movement thus created a perpetual tension between constitutional and extraconstitutional concerns that has been inherited in a somewhat unwholesome form by the post-colonial states in the subcontinent.

Note

1. There are no secondary works dealing directly with the subject matter of this chapter. Raja Rammohan's ideas discussed here are based on his English letters (S. D. Collet, in Dilip Kumar Biswas and Prabhat Chandra Ganguli, eds., *The Life and Letters of Raja Rammohan Roy* 3rd ed. Calcutta: Sadharan Brahmo Samaj, 1962). The best introduction to Indian political thought in the colonial era is Bimanbihari Mazumdar, *History of Social and Political Ideas From Rammohan to Dayananda (1821–1884)* (Calcutta: Bookland, Allalbad, Patna, 1966). Surendranath Banerji, *A Nation in Making: Being Reminiscences of Fifty Years of Public Life* (London: Oxford University Press, 1925) documents inter alia the attitudes of a founding father of Indian Nationalism. For the shifts and tensions in the nationalist discourse *vis-à-vis* constitutionalism, see *Congress Presidential Address: Second Series 1911–1934* (New Delhi: AICC, 1975). The standard source for Gandhi's ideas is the *Collected Works of Mahatma Gandhi* (Delhi: Publications Division, Ministry of Information and Broadcasting, Government of India, 1964–1973). Especially relevant to the subject under discussion are his *Hind Swaraj* and *An Autobiography or My Experiments with Truth*. For the nationalist perceptions of major constitutional issues, see J. Nehru, *Unity of India, Collected Writings* (London: Lindsay Drummond, 1937–1940), Vallabhbhai Patel, *On Indian Problem* (Delhi: Publications Division, 1949), and Rajendra Prasad, *India Divided* (Bombay: Hind Kitab, 1947). For a very different perspective see Subhas Chandra Bose, *The Indian Struggle 1920–1934* (London: Wishart & Co., 1935). Of the vast amount of secondary literature on the Indo-British political encounter and Indian Nationalism, the following are particularly

relevant: R. Coupland, *The Constitutional Problem in India 1933–1935* (London: Oxford University Press, 1944); R. J. Moore, *Crisis of Indian Unity 1917–1940* (Oxford: Oxford University Press, 1974); B. R. Tomlinson, *The Indian National Congress and the Raj 1929–1942* (London: Macmillan, 1976); Bipan Chandra, *Nationalism and Colonialism in Modern India* (Delhi: Oxford University Press, 1970); Sumit Sarkar, *Modern India 1885–1947* (New Delhi: Macmillan, 1983); D. A. Low, *Congress and the Raj: Facets of the Indian Struggle 1917–1947* (London: Heinemann, 1977); C. H. Philips and M. D. Wainright, eds., *The Partition of India: Politics and Perspectives* (London: George, Allen and Unwin, 1970). For the "Cambridge thesis," see J. Gallagher, G. Johnson, and A. Seal, eds., *Locality, Province and Nation* (Cambridge: Cambridge University Press, 1973); D. J. Baker and D. A. Washbrook, *South India, 1880–1940* (Delhi: Macmillan, 1975). The nature of mass political consciousness is discussed in the papers published in R. Guha, ed., *Subaltern Studies*, Vols. I–V (New Delhi: Oxford University Press, 1982–1987) and D. Hardiman, *Peasant Nationalists of Gujrat: Kheda District 1917–1934* (New Delhi: Oxford University Press, 1981). For discussions of Muslim politics, see Mushirul Hasan, *Nationalism and Communal Politics in India* (Delhi: Oxford University Press, 1979); P. Hardy, *The Muslims of British India* (Cambridge: Cambridge University Press, 1972); A. Jalal, *The Sole Spokesman: Jinnah, The Muslim League and the Demand for Pakistan* (Cambridge: Cambridge University Press, 1985).

IV

INSTITUTIONAL ARRANGEMENTS

13

Reconstructing Political Space: Militarism and Constitutionalism in Africa

Eboe Hutchful

It is probably safe to say that most postindependence constitutional initiatives in Africa have been associated with military regimes. It is estimated that between January 1956 and the end of 1985 there were 60 successful coups,[1] many (or probably most) of these resulting in some form of new constitution. This link between militarism and constitutionalism may at first appear paradoxical. Why would military usurpation, the epitome of constitutional illegality, become the predominant avenue to postindependence constitutionalism in Africa? At one level this "paradox" is more apparent then real, since the objective of most military-sponsored constitutions was to legitimize and civilianize military rulers rather than to restore constitutional life as such [e.g., the Zairean constitutions of 1965 and 1974, the Congo (Brazzaville) constitution of 1973, and the constitutions adopted in Rwanda and Burundi in 1978 and 1981, respectively]. Nevertheless, some constitutions initiated by the military did lead to a real restoration of the rule of law and civilian participatory activity, although such situations have been, as a rule, short lived. The Ghana constitutions of 1969 and 1979, the Nigerian constitution of 1979, and the constitution under which Sudan returned briefly to civil rule between the two coups of April 1985 and June 1989 are examples of this temporary restoration.

All military-sponsored constitutions, however, whatever their proclaimed rationale, belong to a common class of phenomena. They have the objective of reorganizing or modifying the legal and structural context of national political life. This reorganization may be undertaken for specifically political reasons: the need to avert the threat (real or preceived) of political disorder or collapse, as in Nigeria in 1966 or in Zaire in 1965; it may also be undertaken to limit what is seen as the ruinous effects of politics on the economy, as in Ghana between 1967 and 1969 or in Nigeria now. Each national case involves different political problematics as individual national and historic contexts determine the actual preoccupations behind military constitutionalism.

Nevertheless, military coups in general function politically as "charismatic moments" in their dissolution and reconstruction of political structures and relations. As used in this context, the concept of "charismatic moment," adapted loosely from Weber, contains two elements: the first, the delegitimation and loosening of pre-existing structures and relations of power and authority, which is the result of the general questioning of political and social realtions in Africa and of the failure to resolve embedded problems; the second, the opportunity to extensively reorganize these relations, which is a specific creation of the military coup. Mass disillusion may pervasively undermine the efficacy and credibility of existing power structures in Africa, but only the military has possessed the actual capability to overthrow incumbent regimes and initiate a process of reorganization or reform of political structures. This capacity helps to explain the variety of political architectural schemes in which the *military* finds itself involved.

The defining characteristic of the charismatic moment is its appearance of a "new beginning" in national political life, signified by the usual rhetoric of revolution. This "new beginning" gives the military coup its appearance of a "national reformation," and its apparent ethical dimension. More realistically, such periods are ones of "rethinking" of politics, an opportunity for overhauling existing structures and advancing novel solutions. In specific cases the moment even assumes a genuine not rhetorical, revolutionary aspect as an eruptive liberation of popular politics or (depending on the context) of society from the "tyranny" of politics, and an historic opportunity for political outgroups to participate in the reshaping or refounding of the state. We may witness a temporary recovery of the effective element and even the relegitimation of the state under the command of a new ruling fragment; popular participation and mobilization may be reawakened and furnish the resources for political and economic reorganization. A new constitution embodies the logic of this recreative moment. In this way the military acts constantly to redefine the *formal* context and space within which politics may be practiced, and to inject the state with reserves of legitimation.

The ability to stage coups is not of course a sufficient explanation of the self-identification of the military with this constitutional engineering role or its acceptance by significant sectors of the civilian population. The military sees itself, and is frequently seen, as the only organization sufficiently removed from political partisanship to be able to claim an arbitrating role and to set common rules of political discourse. Its relative autonomy (constituted formally, mythically, through the constitution and its "nonpolitical" status, and substantively through corporate practices and ideologies emphasizing the social exclusivity, political neutrality, and institutional separateness of the military) promotes this self-conception within the military and grants it varying degrees of legitimation within society as a whole. More relevantly, only the military possesses the coercive power to assign places within the political structure and to impose rules of contestation where these are the object of bitter dispute; this power, however, is not (as our analysis will suggest) unlimited or uncontested, particularly as its exercise requires legitimation in some way. In reality, of course, the military is far from being only self-interested or strictly nonpartisan, even in those situations where constitutionalism implies complete civilianization of politics. How to establish general and impartial rules of political procedure in which the subjective interest and preferences of the military are nevertheless embedded is one of the abiding dilemmas of military constitutionalism, which we shall attempt to explore in this chapter.

Military constitutionalism has been essentially reactive in origin, simulated by a variety of structural and conjuctural problems and crises. Its agenda too has been varied: to transform governmental conduct and performance, to reinforce the system of authority, to routinize politics in accordance with some prescribed scheme, even occasionally (and much more ambiguously) to open up the political process to deprived groups (including those in the military itself), and through these avenues to improve the ability of the state to address economic and social problems. (In this sense constitutionalism may be seen very much as the "dependent variable" in the military's program, and may help to account for the opportunism that often characterizes its approach to this issue.) The inability of the military to carry out this agenda in any definitive fashion and to resolve inherited problems of state, society, and economy accounts for the persistence of charismatic moments and political remodeling exercises in many African countries.

Problems of Political Structure

While emphasizing once again the contextual nature of military coups and the differences in the specific directions taken by military constitutionalism in individual African countries, we must note that the very persistence, frequency, and pervasiveness of these schemes of political architecture would seem to suggest certain common problems of political structure and process in Africa, the origins of which may be traced in various degrees of colonialism.

The Problem of State–Society Relations

The primarily administrative and extractive relationship between the colonial state and society, emphasizing the element of coercion and command, left large areas of state–society relations undefined. The transfer of the modern state form was both institutionally and culturally selective. The institutional unevenness was evident in the lopsided development of the state's apparatuses, with representational bodies emerging last, often only on the eve of decolonization, in the preponderance of criminal over civil law (much of which is relegated to the residual area of customary law), and so on. In particular, the colonial state failed to instill ideas of the legitimate purposes and limits of state action, of acceptable procedures for gaining and maintaining power, and of the place and rights of the individual in the political system, all notions and practices firmly entrenched within traditional African political systems; nor did the colonial state elaborate effective-symbolic supports for state authority based on concepts of the utility, relevance, and distinctiveness of the state. The reason for these failures, of course, was that the colonial state was not a "political" state in the normal sense of deriving its sense of legitimation and authority from society or being concerned with the representation and pursuit of a "national" interest.

The lack of an organic and elaborated connection between state and society created a large area of vacancy and ambugity in their relations. Late-colonial and postindependence constitutionalism may thus be seen as a process of "filling in" these spaces, of defining the proper relationship between the two spheres and developing appropriate linking mechanisms between state and society. The effect has been to install constitutional experimentation and innovation as a principle in most postcolonial polities.

Various reasons account for the failure of earlier constitutional activity to resolve satisfactorily the problem of state–society relations. The bourgeois constitutional formula had limited relevance for African social formations. It assumed nationhood and national sovereignty when both were problematic. It sanctioned parliamentarianism, a democratic practice for which there was no experiential basis in colonial or precolonial society, as the dominant articulating mechanism between state and society. At the same time, it delegitimated or submerged other linking mechanisms with a traditional basis in African society; in this way it drove a wedge between the formal and the much more extensive "informal" political sphere, which included the entire political substratum of chieftaincy and traditional authority relations, norms and values that were depoliticized and consigned to the realm of civil society. Parliamentarianism established a privileged political discourse with normative prescriptions accessible only to a small minority of the population; its political selection mechanisms similarly excluded large strata of the population. The effect was to perpetuate rather than bridge the separation state and society and to drive large areas of the political sphere "underground."[3]

The liberal constitutional model was inappropriate for other reasons. Its emphasis on formal legal and political rights to the exclusion of social and economic rights, on negative rather than positive liberty, was offensive to the ideological agenda of African nationalism; its endorsement of elaborate judicial safeguards and constraints on government contradicted the nationalist emphasis on the state politics as the site of transformative practice. Bourgeois rights inhere in individuals and not in collectivities; individual property rights received constitutional recognition, while the collective property rights fundamental to traditional social organization were ignored. Liberal individualism and its assumption of social homogenization, of the equivalence of individuals and social conditions, could not easily accommodate or reflect cultural and social diversity. The "social diversity" of liberalism lay rather in the right of the individual to be different; the individual was, for this purpose, the unique appropriator of a "legalized space," prescribed, defended, and bounded by the state, which none might violate. "Cultural rights" were mystifying if not regressive and obscurantist. Nor did liberalism recognize social distinctions, such as age and sex, vital to the foundation of traditional authority; equality of voting rights thus had a corrosive effect on patriarchal and gerontocratic institutions.

Therefore, liberal constitutionalism proved unable to accommodate the effects of the colonial and nationalist activation of African society, which expressed itself in the assertion of ethnic, cultural, and religious distinctiveness, in the questioning of the terms of participation in the state and its spatial arrangements, and in associated demands for sectional sovereignty or autonomy. Ironically, the roots of this distinctive "pluralism" grew from the encouragement given to colonial subjects to identify with and participate in parochial rather than national political structures; the sudden introduction of a *national* political life converted these parochialisms into vehicles of political competition. At the same time, the colonial state was unable to provide the "arc of solidarities"[2] required to bond together culturally fragmented and historically autonomous communities.

The result was the "overflowing of the social" (to borrow the suggestive terminology of Ernesto Laclau and Chantal Mouffe) relative to the inherited political order. This was apparent in the great variety of politicized groups and demands, the plural contradictions and points of struggle, and the many opportunities for evading the state. It also appeared in the inability of the formal political mechanisms (including their existing territorial definition) to accommodate the diversity and relational complexity of African society, requiring a network of extraconstitutional supplementational mechanisms, often based in much more indigenous norms and practices and replicating the functions of the formal political sphere. The "legal–rational" state, as a constitutionally sanctioned ensemble, confornted, articulated with, and was eroded by a vast subterranean political field defined by clientage and by partimonial, patriarchal, and gerontocratic relations.

Constitutional activity and the constant modification and readjustment of state–society boundaries may be seen as an attempt to bring these two levels into some form of equilibrium. Given the state-centric character of this enterprise, the essential objective of African constitutionalism has been a constraining one: the recapture and entrapment of the social. Its preoccupation has been to strengthen the political as the level of consolidation of fragmented social formations. The military regime itself, with its enforced depoliticization of the population and its banning of political organizations and activity, is the quintessential example of the closure of political space and the expulsion of social diversity from the surface of politics. Some of this arbitrary closure carries over into the era of constitutional formation; the military dictates the terms of constitutional discourse and the setting of the agenda. For instance, in 1978 General Olesegun Ogansanjo intervened to summarily order the Nigerian Constituent Assembly to cease a debate on Shairia'a law; in 1988 Rear-Admiral Augustus Aikhomyu of the Armed Forces Ruling Council (AFRC) again intervened to close a similar debate on the new constitution on the grounds that it was "divisive." Over a decade after the original debate, the shari'ah issue remains banned as far as constitutional discourse is concerned. The present Assembly had earlier, this time on its own initiative, dismissed without debate a proposal to entrench women's rights in the constitution (frivolous, they said).

In spite of much rhetoric by drafters.of the constitution, little effort has been made in postindependence constitutionalism to correct these earlier deficiencies and to indigenize the state and constitution in order to reflect the diversity and pluralistic basis of African society.[4] The narrow conceptual basis and insitiutional rigidities associated with African constitutions continue to contrast with the variety, vigor, and heterogeneity of society.

Intrastate Relations

Ambiguity also describes the internal relations between the constituent elements of the state apparatus, in particular, between the political executive and the bureaucracy, between the hypertrophied executive and bureaucratic organs and the legislature and judiciary, and between the central and regional and substate organs. These relations are constituted neither logically nor merely through constitutional sanction, but through ideological and historical practice; here again, colonialism provided little guidance in defining the relative domains of these institutions or their proper articulation. Thus, internal imbalances characterize the state apparatus, most obviously in the form of excessive executive dominance, centralization, and atrophy of local and regional organs, and so on. Military–civil executive relations have been a particularly sensitive area; neither the notion of the political supremacy of the civil authority nor that of the nonpolitical character and institutional autonomy of the military appears to have been well grounded. The constant juggling and redefinition of the *internal* relations of the state apparatus, vertical as well as horizontal, shows these structural imabalances to be a key constitutional issue in their own right.

Political and Legal Dualism

A third problem is that of political and legal dualism, which exists in the dual frameworks of law and political action in the uncertain articulation between traditional African authority systems and the formal political system. In many African political systems the question of the constitutional status of chieftaincy (whether it is regarded as a political or merely civil institution) persists as a problem defying definitive solution, and one to which constitution drafters constantly (and often spuriously) return. The political and legal strata coexist as almost hermetically sealed levels, animated by different norms, values, and symbolisms, deriving their energy, relevance, and weaknesses from contrasting sources. Phoenix-like, traditional political institutions arise again and again out of ashes to which modernization, politicians, and constitution drafters in turn would consign them, increasing their influence and efficacy at the expense of the formal political sector.

The Problem of State Decline

More recently a disturbing new problem with vast implications for political redesign in Africa has appeared in the political literature. It is variously referred to as "state decline," "political decomposition," "political recession," and so on. C. Young and T. Turner, in their work on Zaire, describe this problem in terms of the "shrinkage in the competence, credibility, and probity of the state." The state in Zaire, they argue, has "progressively lost its capacity to relate means to ends, bringing about a loss of belief, within civil society, the state can be expected to perform its accustomed functions."[5] N. Chazan elaborates in her study of Ghana where she draws striking attention to the loss of state legitimacy, authority, and autonomy, the "deflation of state power and its reallocation," and the "dispersion of social, economic and political life away from the state and towards more enclosed, self-reliant local and horizontal entities."[6] These and other studies point out the severe erosion of the *de facto* reality of the state in many African countries even while their *de jure* existence survives intact on the international plane.[7]

This tendency to state decay is a cumulative result of the structural and other problems of the colonial and postcolonial state noted above, and the failure of successive constitutional and other modifications to solve these problems and thus consolidate statehood in its various crucial dimensions. As Chazan, Young and Turner, and others have shown, it is also the result of new problems and processes confronting the African state, in particular economic stagnation and shrinkage in the resource base of the state. State debilitation has further complicated the task of political reconstruction and thrown into stark relief the limits of constitutional engineering. It is increasingly clear that nothing less than the reconstruction of the entire economic, social, and normative foundation of the state is required, a task that goes much beyond constitutional engineering. The tendency for the military in a number of African countries such as Ghana, Burkina Faso, and Ethiopia to abandon constitutional experimentation and to resort to radical political schemes outside the framework of the liberal and colonial experience is one indication of this.

It is not surprising that so many fundamental problems of state, society, and economy have "overloaded" the constitutional agenda in African countries. We refer to the diversity of fundamental demands (of a social, economic as well as political nature) directed at the state and the range of social objectives and values to which various groups attempt to commit the state through the constitution. In Africa this problem appears particularly acute, partly because much constitutional activity is of post-facto legitimation of the extensive interventions of the state, and partly because of the absence of ingrained conceptions of the legitimate limits of state acivity. But this overloading of the constitutional agenda is actually characteristic of postliberal constitutionalism as a whole, the product of the expansion of the state and the effacement of the boundaries between the political and the economic and between the political and the ideological. Liberal constitutionalism was founded on the assumption that the boundaries between the state and civil society could be delineated with reasonable certainty. The objectives of constitutionalism were by nature limited; they specified the political and legal rights of citizens, the functions and limits of government, and the formal rules of political contestation. Liberal democracies inherited their constitutions at a time when it was still possible to so delimit the sphere of the political. Since then the changes in the ideological character of liberalism (from "negative" to "positive" liberty) and the growing social and economic penetration of the state has made it much more difficult to define the limits of the political. Within the liberal democracies, much of this growth in the sphere of the state has occurred outside the constitution and "overflowed" its limits, a development marked by the increasingly difficult judicial decision that the courts are being called on to make in the areas of the family, abortion, and reproductive rights, and the environment, to mention just a few. These developments have transformed the terrain of constitutionalism; inherited constitutions are no longer a reliable guide to the nature of the state and the extent of its power and activity.

Military constitutionalists have responded to pressures to recognize and entrench the social obligations of the state in various ways. A fascinating contrast may be drawn for instance between the response of the Constitutional Commission in Ghana in 1968 and the Constitutional Drafting Committe (CDC) in Nigeria in 1976. The Ghanaian drafters refused demands to include a "social charter" in the constitution, arguing that the Constitution "should be a legal document"; the ostensible justification for this conservative position was the great difficulty of securing "general agreement on a meaningful statement of the aims of the state in the field [sic] of education, family relationship, ownership of the means of production, distribution and exchange, religion and international relations." This was an allusion to the fact that the most heated areas in the constitutional debate in Ghana at that time had concerned the role of the state in the economy and in development. The drafters felt that to include such statements in the constitution would render in inherently unstable.[8] Conversely, in Nigeria the Constitutional Assembly accepted the inclusion of "fundamental Objectives and Directive Principles of State Policy" in the constitution. These were incorporated in sections 14 to 22 in the 1979 constitution and committed the Nigerian state to a number of social, political (including foreign policy), economic, and cultural objectives. These "objectives and principles," however, were not justiciable.[9]

Problems of Military Constitutionalism

The military's emphasis on constitutionalism as a method of effecting political change and routinizing political processes itself raises questions. In Africa, as in most of the Third World, the exaggerated philosophical significance attached to constitutions must appear clearly at variance with their marginal impact on the organization of political and social life, particularly given the wide range of instrumentalities available to the state and politicians to evade constitutional provisions. The limited treatment of constitutionalism by African jurists and constitutional experts has usually involved legalistic discourses that divorced the study of constitutions from the analysis of power structures and political processes. Social scientists, on the other hand, have almost completely ignored constitutions.[10] Most important, the restricted audience for constitutional discourse must place obvious limits on the extent to which constitutions can be used to influence political behavior or to condition political futures.

Nevertheless, there appear to be a variety of reasons for the faith placed by the military in constitutionalism. First, the military has few other instruments, short of perpetuating its political rule, to influence political futures in a legal manner. In a more fundamental sense, this faith is the result of "systems" approach to politics that stresses the efficacy of formal structures and institutions, and believes that politics can be influenced through manipulation of its legal and institutional parameters. There is a profound sense in which this focus emerges from genuine (if naive) desire to routinize political processes and confer on the political a *public* character, to purge from politics its informal, subterranean, and, as the military sees it, devious and corrupt character.

The result of this rigid "systems focus" has been the failure to penetrate and influence the informal networks and normative structures of African politics, and naive expectations of what "systems engineering" can accomplish. As General Ibrahim Obasanho, reflecting on the failure of the Nigerian constitution of 1979, ruefully admitted:

> Until 1979, I was by virtue of my training and upbringing, what you might call a systems man. I believed that if a system was good and well-founded, any person with average ability could make it work. I changed my belief after watching the rapidity with which the system was perverted and destroyed and the depth to which rot set in within a short space of time.[11]

This belief in "Systems engineering" is in larger part the reason for the selective approach to political reform, which stresses the implantation of "appropriate" institutional structures but, beyond fitful campaigns against "corruption" and "indiscipline," ignores the inculcation of positive political values. Only in Ghana did the regime of the National Liberation Council attempt (with far from certain results) such a program of education, establishing a Centre for Civic Education in 1967. More recently, Babangida has attempted something similar in Nigeria with the establishment of the Mass Mobilization for Social and Economic Recovery (MAMSER) in 1986. Generally, the military has sought to instill probity and accountability into the political process through particular constitutional provisions, such as the requirement, in the 1969 Ghanaian and the 1979 Nigerian constitutions, for senior public servants and politicians to declare assets; in both cases this was ignored by politicians.

Antipolitical Bias

If anything, the military has brought to constitutionalism a profoundly antipolitical orientation. Discussing the attitudes with which the Zairean army approached constitutional reform after the 1965 coup, Young and Turner argue that

> from colonial days through the initial years of the Second Republic, a militantly apolitical—even anti-political—orientation had been inculcated among the troops. Politics and politicians were a veritable cancer on the body politic; the army, higher custodian of the nation, was to remain far from this sordid fray.[12]

Nigerian military leaders have been particularly consistent in their suspicion of "politics" and rejection of ideologies. General Mohamed Buhari defended his abolition of political activity after the 1983 coup by describing politics and "politicking" as distracting and "unproductive."[13] General Tunde Idagbon, Buhari's lieutenant in the governing Supreme Military Council, was even less compromising, arguing that the military was not interested in "propounding theories of capitalism, socialism, or other 'isms,'" diminishing the possibility of any national ideology which goes beyond "Nigeria First."[14] This antipolitical and antiideological attitude characterizes even the so-called mobilization military regimes in countries such as Ethiopia, Burkina, and Ghana, although in a much more elaborate way. The primary objective of military constitutionalism has thus often been to "chain the political," to limit, through a variety of devices, what it sees as the "disruptive effects" of politics.

This restrictive approach to politics and ideology has been apparent in the military's use of constitutionalism to redesign political space and relations. Military political reformers have targeted political parties, the dislike of which has sometimes assumed a virtually pathological intensity (the latest example is the fulmination of General Omar Bashir against the "depravity and corruption" of the Sudanese parties). Military regimes have imposed restrictions on the number of political parties, banned certain types of parties (such as ethnic, religious and regional parties), imposed official parties, "national movements," and "popular organizations," and advocated "nonparty" systems. To deradicalize politics they have also sought to manipulate electoral systems, imposing modes of indirect elections, electoral colleges, proportional representation, single candidacies, restrictions on political compaigning, even raising the voting age. Military regimes have often attempted to impose ideological restrictions, including a ban on the advocacy of certain ideologies. Finally, the military has sought to prevent the emergence of popular political coalitions by separating local from national politics and political structures and by civilianizing and "democratizing" local politics while keeping military control over national politics.

Its Abstruse Nature

It would also be naive not to see in the class-bound discourses of constitutionalism an element of mystification. Certainly in Africa, the abstruse legalism that defines constitutionalism suggests less an interest in promoting popular empowerment than in evading it through legal–institutional provisions, especially since it is the more conservative military regimes that have tended in the past toward liberal constitutionalism. The writers of constitutions seem more concerned to shape and control the parameters of intraelite contestation than to guarantee the political rights and access of the masses, to whom the prevailing discourses of constitutionalism are largely meaningless. A member of the Nigerian Constituent Assembly spoke for the masses of Africa when he complained to his collegues: "This is a country in which more than eighty percent of the population do not read or write and certainly do not speak the language of political discourse. What meaning could their protracted and elaborate debates have for this national audience?"[15] In this remark can be found the reason for the frequent dismissal of constitutionalism as a "bourgeois indulgence" by ordinary Africans as well as political activists on the left. The unfortunate impression has thus been created that constitutionalism is an elite device to mystify the people and ignore their real concerns. This should explain the drastic decline of popular interest in constitutional issues in postcolonial Africa, even though the struggle for constitutionalism had formed a major objective of the mass mobilization for decolonization in many African countries.

In military constitutionalism the state, in effect, elaborates its own relationship both with society and with itself; it is a state-conditioned and dominated process, an intrinsically different enterprise from earlier liberal experience, where the initiative was taken by groups from outside the state apparatus with a primary interest in limiting state power or in redefining its distribution. The fact that in the cases discussed in this paper constitutional experiments have been undertaken or sponsered by elements *within* the state suggests that only limited readjustment of state-society relations and the state sphere may be excepted. In this sense the "charisma" generated by military coups occurs within narrow and carefully circumscribed limits.

Constitutionality and Inflexibility

The limited perception of constitutionalism, often in contradiction to its vast ideological pretension, is not peculiar to the military variant; it characterizes African constitutionalism as a whole. African constitutional traditions and practices have given selective and uneven emphasis to the range of themes usually associated with liberal constitutionalism. We are sometimes apt to forget that modern constitutionalism incorporates a diversity of themes, philosophical traditions, and political and legal objectives, not all of which are necessarily logically related to or in harmony with each other. Thus we find that African constitutions stress (1) the "constitutive" function, which establishes the (postcolonial) state as national in scope, sovereign, and legitimate, and defines its formal-legal structures; (2) the establishment of rules of (elite) political contestation; (3) the demarcation of rival spheres of competence within the state apparatus itself; and (4) values of "positive" rather than "negative" liberty. These concerns are in general state-enhancing. On the other hand, African constitutionalism, in theory and even more so in practice, has been notably weak in its conception of and concern for civil rights and due processs, in placing limits on executive power and competence and ensuring participation in and control over political and decision-making processes. H. W. O. Okoth-Ogendo[16] describes this lopsided approach to constitutionalism as "constitutions without constitutionalism," as *constitutionality* rather than constitutionalism. A compounding factor is that in many African countries the legal and administrative codes (supplemented by various executive decrees, emergency powers, special courts and tribunals, and other instruments of military and authoritarian regimes) rarely reflect the constitution with complete fidelity. One can thus understand why this type constitutionality is prefectly consistent with unfettered growth of the state power, and how the African state (or at least its executive core) can emerge from successive redefinitions of its constitutional parameters with its substantive powers intact.

One common feature of military constitutionalism finally deserves mention:

the failure of the military to initiate innovations in its own constituency, in the institutional structure of military forces and in civil–military relations. No country has produced a satisfactory constitutional formula that gives substance to the concept of "civilian control" or "military autonomy," although the possibility exists of secret understandings, negotiated between departing military leaders and incoming civilian politicians. A related difficulty is the failure to solve the problem of the form of incorporation of military forces into the political process. A few novel solutions have been advanced, but, with the probable exception of Tanzania, none of these formulas appears to have been successful.[17] Civilian constitutionalists resisted successfully alternative proposals to grant some form of constitutional recognition to a military veto or to the military coup as a political succession mechanism, despite some evidence of popular support for the idea. On the other hand, radical military regimes, such as that of the late Thomas Sankara in Burkina Faso, have denied that a problem exists; the soldier is also a citizen, and like all citizens has a right to politics.[18]

Comparative Military Constitutionalism: Ghana, Nigeria, Zaire

It would be dangerous, however, to generalize about the attitudes of the African military to constitutionalism. Although we have so far stressed the common elements in military constitutionalism, there have been significant differences in the approaches of various national militaries (or competing strata or functions within them) to the task of establishing a particular brand of constitutionality. In Ghana, the military has proposed a variety of constitutional, political, and ideological models within a consistently unitary framework, without succeeding in resolving the underlying political and economic difficulties of the country; we may distinguish between the "legalist" National Liberation Council (1966–69), the "corporatist" Supreme Military Council (1975–1978), and the "populist" Provisional National Defence Council (December 1981 to present). The first of these regimes (made up of senior military officers) established a conventional liberal constitution; the second (comprised of senior and middle-level officers) proposed to modify this with a "Union Government" arrangement that would have allowed the military and civilians to share power; the third (comprised of junior officers, other ranks, and radical civilians) initially rejected parliamentary democracy as a "sham" and attempted to institute instead a "popular democracy" based on "defence committees" and other "revolutionary organs," including a system of judicial tribunals. Thus, it is difficult to isolate a consistent "military approach" to constitutionalism in Ghana. Conditioning these changing perceptions of constitutionalism were changes in the nature of the dominant military strata, in the political equation within Ghanaian society (the emergence of new and previously excluded social and political forces), in the articulation of the military and civil strata, in the perceived character of the national crisis, etc.[19]

The contrasts are also sharp between the political and constitutional responses of the military in Nigeria and Zaire to similar challenges of rampant pluralism and ethnic diversity. Nigeria has responded by entrenching federalism, progressively increasing the number of states from 3 to 21 between 1967 and 1987 and adopting a policy of "federal character" (by which indigenes of all state receive equitable representation in all federal offices) to give expression to ethnic diversity. Various constitutional and extraconstitutional modifications (such as the change from a parliamentary to presidential system) have also strengthened the federal center relative to the states.[20] Zaire has moved in the opposite direction, from federalism to unitarism and from administrative decentralization to hypercentralization. The first military-sponsored constitution in 1967 reduced the number of provinces from 21 to 9, abolished parliament (until 1970) and the office of the Prime Minister, and increased the powers of the presidency. The provincial assemblies were first demoted to advisory councils and then abolished, and the provincial governors became cetnral government functionaries. The Zairean state itself was formally absorbed by the ruling single party, the Popular Movement for the Revolution (MPR), acting in turn as the personal vehicle of Mobutu Sese Seko.

Both Zaire and Nigeria blamed political parties for political chaos and instability. Nigeria has retained a competitive party structure while progressively modifying it to ensure that parties function more as vehicles of national integration and less as instruments of ethnoregional interest. The 1979 constitution implicitly banned ethnic and regional parties by requiring a national distribution of party support; the new constitution adopted by the Babangida government further restricts the number of recognized parties to two. Zaire banned political parties for 5 years after the 1965 coup; in 1974 the constitution legalized a *de facto* single party system by sanctioning the MPR as the sole national political party; advocating the formation of any other party became a criminal offence. The single-party system has been combined with a strong personalization and patrimonialization of the power structure and the cooptation and/or suppression of rival political factions.

The reasons for these contrasting responses are complex and should be sought at a number of levels: in differences in colonial political and constitutional frameworks and experiences, in the nature of ethnic units and boundaries, in the relationship between ethnic and political units, and in the character of class structure and consciousness. The precolonial and colonial processes in Nigeria solidified three core ethnic identities (Hausa-Fulani, Yoruba, and Ibo), each identified with a particular region and a major political party. The limited number (three until the creation of the Mid-West in 1962) and the large size of the regions, each with a distinct ethnic core, and the relative stability of their boundaries, not only provided stable parameters within which ethnic identities, alliances, and hegemonies could be nurtured, but also meant that ethnicity could establish itself at a more incorporative substate level. Political parties developed within this context (compared with Zaire over a relatively longer time frame) and were able to play a more aggregative role as ethnoregional vehicles.

Particularly important was the Nigerian emphasis on both the federal system and constitutionalism as instruments of ethnic engineering and bargaining. By independence federalism had been accepted as the appropriate formula by most of the power elite, at least for the foreseeable future. In addition to a relatively rich postwar constitutional experience and strong legalist tradition (at least in western Nigeria) the explicit use made of the constitution after 1950 to mediate and entrench ethnoregional interests gave the constitution a political saliency unusual in Africa. The imbalances built into the original independence constitution—between north and south, between majority and minority ethnic groups, and between the location of political power (which lay in the north) and economic power (located in the south)—continued to focus attention on the constitution as a major arena of contention. Finally, Nigeria possessed, in the west and the north, particularly large professional commercial and traditional aristocratic strata whose different groups had highly developed fractional conciousnesses, which led to considerable intraelite conflict. Before 1966, these weakly articulated ruling strata concentrated on developing vertical links of solidarity with ethnic compatriots and consolidating regional bases from which to confront each other and to bid for control of the federal power structure. The trauma of the civil war, accumulation opportunities opened up by oil, and military tutelage reoriented the ruling strata to the construction of horizontal linkages and class alliances. "Federal Character" and the "zoning" practices of the National Party of Nigeria (NPN) and the major political parties after 1979 were partial evidence of this.

In Zaire, for various reasons, ethnicity and political parties could not play the same incorporative roles but rather tended to exert dispersive and fragmenting effects. Zaire lacked a constitutional history right up to the precipitate grant of independence in 1960, and participatory spaces opened up much later and much more abruptly than in Nigeria. While this favored the use of ethnicity as a mobilization and competitive vehicle, it did not provide a similar opportunity to solidify ethnic consciousness and alliances. Rapid changes in political context, such as the increase in the number of provinces from 6 to 21 in 1962–1963, led to a major redefinition of ethnic identities and alliances. While Nigeria was able to sustain a three-party system almost until 1966, over 300 parties emerged to compete for the national elections in Zaire in 1965. The emotional debate between "unitarism" and "federalism" preceding independence and again in the 1963 elections showed that there was little consensus regarding the spatial and structural dimensions of national politics. Finally, the severe underdevelopment of the Zairean bourgeoisie and army accounted for the low level of ruling class consciousness and the tenuous links between the army and the class, for the sense of autonomy that was to lead the army to attempt to displace this "ruling" class, and for the reality of institutional fragility that was to permit this army to be displaced, in turn, by Mobutu.

Dilemmas of Legitimation and Control

Finally, a word about how the military approaches the constitutional remodeling exercise. Where the military does take a constitutional route it will attempt to design or manipulate constitutional provisions so as to realize specific objectives and exclude particular possibilities. In trying to use constitutional reform to influence political structure and outcomes the military faces important dilemmas.

It cannot afford to abondon control over the constitution-making process altogether, but attempts to control overtly constitutional choices stand to prejudice the future legitimacy of the constitution. At least three problem areas can be identified. The first concerns the choice of personnel to be entrusted with the development of a new constitution. Reasons of legitimacy suggest that the process of drafting and adopting the constitution incorporates the widest possible consensus and representation, preferably through elections; but elected representatives may be hard to control and, confronting self-appointed military leaders lacking a popular mandate, may raise difficult problems of rival legitimacies. The usual procedure adopted by the military has been to appoint a drafting body of constitutional experts and eminent civilians to work with a constituent assembly comprised primarily of elected representatives and members nominated by the government. Elections to the Constituent Assembly have also been a useful political bellwether, indicating to the military government the nature of the emergent civilian political forces and providing possible evidence of the degree of influence exercised by *ancien regime* politicians.

A second problem concerns the definition of the constitutional agenda. In September 1975, the Supreme Military Council of Nigeria spelled out the constitutional agenda for the Constitution Drafting Committee, and so defined (or imposed, if you wish) the basic parameters and limits of constitutional reform. By contrast, the Ghanaian National Liberation Council in 1966 granted the Constitutional Commission *carte blanche* to determine the constitutional preferences of Ghanaians, specifying merely that the constitution give adequate protection to individual rights and include, "so far as is consistent with good government," a separation of powers.

A third problem involves the process of approval and adoption of the constitution, i.e., its legitimacy. In Nigeria and Ghana a controversy arose between the military government and the Constituent Assembly as to who would approve the promulgate the new constitution. In Nigeria the military government adopted the position (similar to that of the Ghanaian authorities) that the role of the Assembly was limited to making "recommendations," which would be considered for adoption by the government; the Assembly argued that as the elected representatives of the people, it possessed "a legitimacy superior" to that of any other body, including the military government.[21] The Constitutional Commission in Ghana adopted an identical position. Although both military governments "won" the argument, the reaction demonstrated the sensitivity of the problem, which beyond the immediate question to wider issues of the legitimacy of the government. In Nigeria the military also altered the finished work of the Constituent Assembly by adding 22 modifications designed to "strengthen the constitution."[22]

Conclusion: Return to Constitutionalism

Regime after regime in Africa is currently reinstating multiparty democracy or committing itself to democracy and constitutional rule.[23] In some countries political liberalization has caused regime regroupment and renewal rather than a political revolution; in Benen, Cape Verde, Sao Tome, and Principe it produced the defeat of incumbent regimes. Nevertheless, there is no mistaking the extent and rapidity with which the movement to democracy and constitutionalism is reshaping the political map in Africa. Democracy, constitutional rule, and human rights halve also been endorsed by various official and international bodies [among them the Organization for African Unity (OAU), the Economic Commission for Africa (ECA), multilateral institutions, and donor governments[24]] as the solution to Africa's malaise. Clearly, however, the major impetus for democratization has come from popular movements determined to wrest power from the existing regimes and to make the state accountable. We need to learn more about these movements; they do appear to be broad and socially diverse, if predominantly urban, in their composition, drawn from virtually all siginificant social strata; students, professionals, labor and community organizations, peasants and urban employed who are activated by the economic crisis, by the abuses of human rights and political exclusion, and encouraged in their struggles by external pressures for democracy and the political transitions in eastern Europe.

The "constitutionalism from below" characteristic of these movements must be distinguished in spirit and intent from the "constitutionalism from above" identified with military regimes; groups outside the state apparatuses are now taking the initiative to demand the redistribution of political power and a redefinition of the terms of political engagement. This trend is closer to the classic tradition of movements for constitutionalism. These movements have forced a reopening of political spaces, enabling the reassertion of popular claims (ethnic, religious, gender, and class), the relegitimation of forbidden political ideas and language (the subversive discourse of democracy and constitutionalism), and the rediscovery of proscribed political vehicles (the political party). The social (to revert to the terminology of Laclau and Mouffe) has liberated politics from the confines imposed by the state. Perhaps, far from being a new phenomenon, these movements are a recovery of the popular, antiauthoritarian spirit of constitutionalism that characterized the earlier independence struggles.

What visions of democracy and constitutionalism are embodied in these movements? Although we have much to learn in this respect, what does appear striking (at least to external observers) is their emphasis on traditional liberal political values—multiparty systems, rules of law, human rights, and the independence of the judiciary and the return to liberal constitutionalism that this suggests. However, to read this emphasis as another example of the "triumph of liberal reasoning" would be misleading. First, these movements incorporate but also transcend liberalism in their effort to combine the values of negative and positive liberty; political liberals are not necessarily economic liberals.[25] Second, democratic advocacy in Africa today is complex and varied in content and context. It draws on indigeneous traditional, communitarian, populist, and collectivist notions of democracy. The primary values of these notions are consensus, cooperation, and community needs, not political competition and individualistic rights. From the rich struggle between the many meanings of democracy may emerge new and distinctive permutations in Africa.

Nevertheless, I think I detect in these democratic movements a new and greater appreciation for the values of negative liberty, those that protect the person from injury by the state and external forces and less emphasis on the values of positive liberty, which view the relation between and democracy in terms of the fulfillment of human needs and potentialities. As argued earlier, the latter set of values predominated in African political discourses, defining the nature of the social compact and informing the drive to state preeminence. There are several explanations for this current shift in emphasis. The record of African states in assuring the fulfillment of positive rights has been abysmal and will remain so in the foreseeable future. Citizens are therefore diversifying their survival strategies by loosening their dependence on the state and seeking the satisfaction of needs through nonpolitical channels. Further, the dangers of endowing the state with virtually unlimited power have become obvious. Citizens, therefore, are less inclined to see the state as an enabling entity; they insist instead on the need for protection *from* the state.

As in eastern Europe, the process of liberating civil society and politics has resurrected old social divisions previously suppressed by state authoritarianism. Their first manifestation is the resurgence of ethnic and national chauvinism. Another is the rise of religious fundamentalism as a potent electoral vehicle in countries such as Algeria and the Sudan. The third is the appearance of conditions of ungovernability—multiplicity of parties, unstable coalitions, civil disobedience, and popular violence. These social divisions in turn threaten the collapse of economic austerity programs that had depended on political authoritarianism and discipline. Democracy and constitutionalism in Africa are thus confronted by an accumulation of crises: national fragmentation, state delegitimation and collapse, and acute economic decline.

To survive, constitutionalism and democracy will have to pose fundamental questions (evaded or suppressed in earlier forms of constitutionalism) about the nature of social diversity and the terms of political and social cohabitation in Africa. This new thinking must begin with the recognition of the problematic character of nationhood itself; constitutionalism will be required to constitute not only the state and state–society relations, but nationhood as such, through its attention to the rights of nationalities. Earlier constitutionalism tried to proscribe the subterranean social diversity from African politics; pluralism and diversity will have to be the foundation for the new constitutionalism (only Nigeria, its motto "Unity With Diversity," has tried to accomplish this). The incidence of separatism and sectarianism following political liberalization shows that achieving this new basis will not be easy (indeed in countries such as Somalia and Ethiopia a fundamental reshaping of the spatial boundaries of state and nation may be required); nevertheless, working out social, cultural, and political differences in an atmosphere of give and take is the only way to transform African societies from state-nations to nation-states. Closely related to this need is the necessity for the new constitutionalism to explore seriously how to root the state in indigenous structures, beliefs, and practices, and to draw strength from them. As long as the "ideological contradiction" exists between the institutions and practices of the modern state and those of the traditional systems in Africa, political alienation and instability will continue.[26] Constitutionalism will also have to develop and incorporate a broader conception of rights appropriate to Africa's distinctive diversity, which will include protection for the rights of national, religious, and cultural minorities as well as workers, women, and children.

What will be the military's role and future in this process? Three crucial developments have affected the political power of the military in Africa. First, the popular movements for democracy have discredited military-backed regimes. With the exception of Nigeria (where the military has managed to retain control over the pace and direction of democratization), the military and the democratic movements have found themselves on opposite sides of the barricades. Second, the end of the Cold War has deflated the geopolitical significance of armies and threatens to sever African military forces from the external resources that formed in important basis for their power and autonomy. Third (and most ominously), the devastating defeat of conventional armies by armed irregulars in Uganda, Liberia, Somalia, and Ethiopia has serious implications for the prestige, political influence, and legitimacy of professional armies as well as for the state. These defeats have undermined not only the claim of the military to an effective monopoly on violence, but also the whole system of perceptions that has underpinned and rationalized the social and political power of the standing army in Africa and its prodigious claims on resources. We may expect this undermining to have profound effects on the relationship of the military with both civil society and the state, particularly in terms of its ability to dominate the two spheres. Further, it poses a challenge to the state formations that have attempted (rather arrogantly) to claim a monopoly over politics and authority on the basis of their exclusive control over the instruments of force.

Nevertheless, while the military may appear for the moment to be in political decline, the problem of the military has not gone away. On the contrary, it is more urgently necessary than ever to find means to create viable civil–military relations and achieve constitutional and democratic control of military forces. These objectives cannot be divorced from the need to evolve a national military or defense format that *appropriately* reflects indigenous traditions and institutions, rather than an entirely alien structure, and is *sustainable* from both economic and organizational points of view. The urgency of the situation emphasizes once again the need to define an acceptable political role for the military. These are crucial issues that have not been resolved in the democratic transitions in Africa. Should democratic governments in Africa fail to adress their urgent problems (including their relationship with their military forces) and/or the international environment becomes less supportive to democracy, we cannot discount some kind of predatory return by the military.

Notes

1. Pat McGowan and Thomas H. Thompson, "Sixty Coups in Thirty Years—Further Evidence Regarding African Military Coups D'État," 24(3) *Journal of Modern African Studies* 539–546 (1986), p. 540.

2. Oscar Ozlak, "The Historical Formation of the State in Latin America," XVI(2), *Latin American Research Review*, 3–32 (1978), p. 6. The original phrase is O'Donnell's.

3. For instance, the 1968 constitutional proposals in Ghana claimed to have extracted their recommendations from values "animating our traditional social institutions." but are in fact replete with quotations from Locke, Mill, and Plato. Ghana, *The Proposals of the Constitutional Commission for a Constitution in Ghana* (Accra: State Publishing Corp., 1968), p. 3

4. This theme has received excellent treatment in Naomi Chazan, *An Anatomy of Ghanaian Politics* (Boulder, CO: Westview Press, 1983), pp. 346–360. In a similar discussion Maxwell Owusu argued that the "ideological contradiction" between the traditional and the inherited postcolonial political structures is the "basis of much of the crisis of political instability and legitimacy in African countries." Owusu goes on to see military coups as "rituals of rebellion" aimed at reasserting the "jural postulates" underlying tradition authority. "Customs and Coups: a Juridical Interpretation of Civil Order and Disorder in Ghana," 24(1) *Journal of Modern African Studies* 69–99 (1986), p. 72.

5. Crawford Young and Thomas Turnal, *The Rise and Decline of the Zairean State* (Madison: University of Wisconsin Press, 1985), p. 45.

6. Naomi Chazan, *An Anatomy of Ghanaian Politics*, note 4, pp. 331–353.

7. Robert H. Jackson and Carl Rotberg, "Sovereignty and Underdevelopment: Juridical Statehood in the African in the African Crisis," 24(1) *Journal of Modern African Studies* 1–31 (1986) and "Why Africa's Weak States Persist: The Empirical and the Juridical in Statehood," 35(1) *World Politics* 1–24 (1982).

8. Ghana, *The Proposals of the Constitutional Commission*, note 3, pp. 14–15.

9. E. Michael Joye and Kingsley Igweike, *Introduction to the 1979 Nigerian Constitution* (London: Macmillan, 1982), pp. 48–65.

10. H. W. O. Okoth-Ogendo, "Constitutions Without Constitutionalism: Reflections on an African Paradox," a paper presented at the African Regional Institute on Comparative Constitutionalism, Harare, May 22–25, 1989, p. 2.

11. Quoted in John A. A. Ayoade, "States without Citizens: An Emerging African Phenomenon," in D. Rothchild and N. Chazan, eds., *The Precarious Balance: State-Society Relations in Africa* (Boulder, CO: Westview Press, 1988), p. 116.

12. Crawford Young and Thomas Turner, note 5, p. 69.

13. Quoted in Eboe Hutchful, "New Elements in Militarism: Ethiopia, Ghana and Burkina Faso," XLI(4) *International Journal* 802–830 (1986), p. 805.

14. *Ibid.*, p. 806.

15. Quoted in E. Michael Joye and Kingsley Igweike, note 95, p. 141.

16. H. W. O. Okoth-Ogendo, note 10.

17. For an account of the "dyarchy" debate in Nigeria, see Henry Bienen, *Armies and Parties in Africa* (New York: Africana Publishing, 1978), pp. 256–259.

18. Thomas Sankara, Interview with Nii-K Bentsi Enchill, *West Africa*, 20, February 1984.

19. The best account of political restructuring by the present military regime in Ghana is Emmanuel Hansen, "The State and Popular Struggles in Ghana 1982–86," in Peter Anyang Nyong'o, ed., *Popular Struggles for Democracy in Africa* (London: Zed Press, 1987), pp. 170–208. See also Don Ray, Ghana: *Politics, Economics, and Society* (London: Frances Pinter, 1986), pp. 30–73; Z. Yeebo, "Ghana: Defense Committees and the Class Struggle," 32 *Review of African Political Economy* 64–71 (1985); and Eboe Hutchful, note 13.

20. For a discussion of these measures and the problems associated with them see

John A. A. Ayoade, "Ethnic Management in the 1979 Nigerian Constitution," *Canadian Review of Studies in Nationalism* XIV(1) pp. 122–141 (1987); A. H. M. Kirk-Greene, "Ethnic Engineering and the 'Federal Character' of Nigeria: Bone of Contentment or Bone of Contention?," 6(4) *Ethnic and Racial Studies* pp. 457–476 (1983); and J. Iswa Elaigwu and V. A. Olorunsola, "Federalism and the Politics of Compromise," in Donald Rothchild and Victor A. Olorunsola, eds., *State Versus Ethnic Claims: African Policy Dilemmas* (Boulder, CO: Westview Press, 1983), pp. 281–303.

21. E. Michael Joye and Kingsley Igwekie, note 9, pp. 46–47.

22. *Ibid.*

23. Among those countries that have already made the transition to multiparty democracy are Gabon, Ivory Coast, Benin, Cape Verde, and São Tomé and Principe. Among those contemplating it are Nigeria, Angola, Ghana, Zambia, Togo, Zaire, and Mozambique. Kenya is the best known holdout. Before 1990 the only functioning electoral democracies in Sub-Saharan Africa were Botswana, Senegal, Zimbabwe, and Mauritius.

24. The most official declarations in favor of democracy and human rights in Africa include the African Charter of Human and Peoples' Rights (OAU, 1981), the African Charter for Popular Participation in Development (Economic Commission for Africa, February 1990), the Declaration of the Heads of State and Governments of the OAU Concerning the Political and Socio-Economic Conditions in Africa (OAU, July 1990), the Challenge to the South (Report of the South Commission), and *Sub-Saharan Africa: From Crisis to Sustained Growth*, published by the World Bank (November 1989). Since these are in many cases the same governments and organizations that have provided support for authoritarianism in the past, the value of these declarations should naturally be taken with some skepticism.

25. This poses an important problem for the relationship of these democratic movements to market-oriented economic reform, in that these movements are not, in the main, a *consummation* of market liberalization (as wrongly assumed by liberal governments and donor institutions), but a protest against it.

26. The quote is form Maxwell Owusu (see note 4). In a much cited article Peter Ekeh has pointed to the existence in Africa of "two publics," one constituted by the formal state sphere of colonial origin and the other by the traditional kinship organization, arguing that it is the latter rather than the former that is the object of civic loyalty. See Peter Ekeh, "Colonialism and the Two Publics in Africa: A Theoretical Statement," 17(1) *Comparative Studies in Society and History* 91–112 (1975).

Narrowing the normative gap between the two publics implies not the abolition of kinship or clan organization or ethnic and cultural distinctiveness (as assumed in modernization theory) but rather an emphasis on shared values, customs, and traditions (of which there are many) as the basis for nationhood and for a common political discourse or civic culture. The many notions of traditional democracy would be a good starting point on which to base such a civic culture.

14

Providing for the Common Defense: What Latin American Constitutions Have to Say About The Region's Armed Forces

Juan Rial

The countries of Latin America, with the exception of Mexico, retain constitutions that resemble those found in the liberal states of the west; in fact, these early documents were based on European conceptions of constitutionalism, implying ongoing legislative control over the actions of the executive as well as a lasting commitment by the legislature to administer order in such a way as to prevent the violation of its rules.[1] The approach to constitutionalism in Latin America is based on the European theory of the *état de droit* and the practice of the German *Rechtstaat,* which differs considerably from the Anglo-Saxon tradition of rule of law.

Constitutions imply the existence of territory within which a state exercises its sovereignty. Thus, a military is needed to protect the state in the event that conflicts with foreign threats arise. However, armed forces are not always the loyal public servants that liberal theorists envision; the military can disrupt the normal functioning of government by bringing its coercive force to bear against civilian decision makers. Liberal constitutions have, in fact, always had difficulties with the military. The liberal state must maintain sufficient military strength for protection, but not enough to be overthrown by it.

Speaking about the armed forces in *Democracy in America,* Alexis de Tocqueville underscored the contradiction between equality and the army, an institution that, he contended, cannot be democratic for reasons of efficiency. Because of the inherent authoritarian nature of the military, there is, in democratic countries, ongoing concern that permanent forces, such as the officer corps, will grow large enough to threaten the internal political stability of these nations. Civilian policy-makers also hope to prevent this sector of the military from becoming detached from the rest of society, a situation that is brought about by the military's development into a "total institution."[2]

When Latin American countries were formulating constitutions in the nineteenth century, decision makers had to decide whether to institute a permanent armed force. During the breakdown of colonial rule, those fighting for independence created military forces to fight against Spain. Brief times of peace followed periods of war. Those involved in the army quickly found themselves engaged in a "revolutionary career";[3] this situation mandated that these military chiefs play a principal role as political actors. The first problem of civil–military relations is, thus, to square the ideological principles of liberalism with political practices common to Latin America. This challenge is accompanied by questions of whether to create a permanent military force.

Armed forces defend the social and political orders that created them. In Latin America, the independence revolutions engendered an order based on democratic liberalism and market economics.[4] The initial constitutions of these countries contained provisions that empowered the legislatures of these nations to establish a military, detailed its characteristics, and, in some cases, stated the period of their existence. It was understood that these legislative bodies would authorize the existence of only a small corps with a limited budget, to be controlled by civilian policy-makers. The legislature also had the constitutional power to build up nonpermanent military personnel (e.g., militias and national guard units). These constitutions were based on the liberal model. The United States Constitution was emphatic about civilian control of the armed forces. The U.S. Congress had, and has, the final say on most of the larger policy questions relating to the military, while individual states enjoy the right to regulate their militias. The 1791 Second Amendment recognizes the right of individuals to possess and carry weapons within the context of state militia activity. These same provisions were discussed during the 1813 Constituent Assemblies of the United Provinces of the South during the search for a suitable constitutional system. However, civil wars following the wars of independence leading to the creation of Argentina, Paraguay, and Uruguay, precluded the right to bear arms and the possibility of limiting military despotism.

In the nineteenth century, breakdowns in the political processes of these countries led to modification in their constitutions. Today, all Latin American constitutions, except that of Costa Rica of 1948, prescribe the existence of an armed force. Most constitutions assume that the armed forces exist as a separate component of the political system. The provisions in many of these documents refer to the armed forces as an entity whose existence precedes that of the constitutional order.

Although current constitutions authorize the legislative branch of governments in Latin America to create militias, national guard units, or other reserve forces, such services do not exist as auxiliary troops: they are often under the command of the armed forces. Some constitutions [e.g., Chile (1980), Ecuador (1986), and Brazil (1988)] categorize state, provincial, and military police forces as parts of the armed forces. These constitutions grant the armed forces a monopoly on state violence, although in some cases reserve or police forces also enjoy this power. They also set forth duties regarding national defense and the maintenance of the preexisting institutional order.

The Development of Military Professionalism and Corporate Autonomy

Since the last quarter of the nineteenth century, Latin American countries have not directly experienced large-scale international conflicts. Since 1879, no Latin American capital, nor any major city in the region for that matter, has been subjected to aerial attack or has been occupied by a foreign military force. Mobilizations involving significant numbers of citizens are unknown to Latin America. When wars did occur, they involved only small sectors of the population or marginal territories.

The absence of war between countries in Latin America did not, however, diminish the activities of the military forces, which actively intervened constantly in internal political affairs, actions prohibited by the legal order. There were, in short, many revolutions, civil wars, and "pronunciamientos."

In the nineteenth century, the army chiefs and civilian leaders, both drawn from the middle classes, were the major protagonists in the construction of South American states and society; they were supported by the country's budget. Most members of the armed forces, however, were nothing more than civilians mobilized for short periods of time. Many officers combined handling of the sword with their civilian activities: farming, cattle breeding, and trading. For these *caudillos*, military activity was simply another form of political involvement. Slowly, as the formation of these nation states progressed, military professionalism made its appearance.

The officer academies were established at the beginning of the twentieth century to form professional military corps based on European models. Specialties were differentiated and specific rules for military careers were set forth. Patriarchal military forces organized around a *caudillo* became professional forces that were commanded by officers who had been trained in specialized academies. During this period of transition, between 1870 and 1900, the political participation of the army dropped substantively. The focus of their efforts was the building of a professional entity.

Professionalism was achieved at varying times. Countries in the southern cone and Brazil adopted a more professional configuration at the turn of the century, with the creation of an officer corps and a military staff, and with greater differentiation between service branches. In some cases, forces were dismantled and recreated, as was the Mexican army after 1910. In Central America and the Caribbean, the United States, after several interventions, created military forces, the *Guardias Nacionales*. These forces were to maintain internal order in this cluster of countries. Most of these units were annihilated after subsequent military defeats or weakened by revolutionaries in the 1960s and 1970s. Other forces in the Latin American region professionalized later; Venezuela, for example, did not do so until 1940.

Civilian elites actively participated in this process of professionalization. They supported the idea of an army serving the entire nation, subordinated to civilian elites who would lead the modernization process. These elites also regarded professionalism as a means of overcoming the problem of the constant anarchy caused by idle *caudillos* and their armed civilian contingents. That both civilian and military sectors of society shared the objective of professionalization in the armed forces was but one of the factors responsible for achieving this goal. However, when the fear of external conflicts that had motivated many to support the professionalization process failed to materialize, many civilian elites ceased their oversight of the military, encouraging their autonomy. The military developed into a corporation with the ability to intervene in the domestic politics and to break institutional frameworks during times of crisis. The major constitutional implication of this development was that though the armed forces were supposed to deal with external confrontations, they assumed the role of the main guarantors of the internal political and social orders.

The Military as Political Actor

In the twentieth century, the professionalized armed forces of Latin America, as they defended the order that had created them, began to function as the moderator in the political life of these countries. The place that the military found for itself can, in fact, be easily compared to the niche carved out by the armed forces of Spain's First Republic.[5] This institution sought to maintain the stability of existing economic, social, and political systems, and intervened only to prevent crisis, to separate various competing factions, and to restore, to the greatest possible extent, the prior situation.[6] In many cases, this status quo resembled the Roman concept of dictatorship.[7] It was often true that the disputants were inside the military institutions, and usually acted as party factions with strong links to civilian groups. With further professionalism, this "moderator" role of the military began to erode. The institutional interests of the armed forces gained priority. New forms of political intervention were found expressing the forces' own interests. These interests were, it should be noted, always aligned with higher concerns for the nation or the motherland. Often the civilian sector supported the military chiefs by proclaiming that the "hour to take sword" had arrived. Soon, however, the military began to take action on its own initiative, as in Argentina in 1943.[8]

By various means and pretexts, the elite of the officer corps, which functioned as the main military corporation in Latin America, became increasingly autonomous political actors. Authors such as José Nun sought to explain the high degree of military intervention in this region by focusing on the coincidence of interest between the middle class sectors of society and the military.[9] This approach also stresses the middle strata origins of military officers. It also should be noted that in the 1960s and early 1970s, revolutionary movements led by elite middle-class groups worked for socialist governments by mobilizing the subservient sectors of society. A majority of these governments were ultimately defeated. The main opponent of these reform efforts was another elite middle-class group, the officer corps of the armed forces, which was able to mobilize the entire middle class.

In the nineteenth century, military and civilian policy-makers had acted as partners in the development of the state. One hundred years later, these two sectors of society traveled their separate ways. The military became a professional force in the majority of countries in the southern cone. Its core, the officer corps, isolated itself from the rest of society as well as from the state. However, when the armed forces, especially the army, realized that the state was in danger of destabilization by revolutionary movements, it decided to rule the country with the support of its civilian allies.[10]

Since the 1960s, most Latin American countries have been in the initial stages of attempts at socialist revolution. The founders and supporters of these reform efforts hope to replace the traditional socioeconomic order based on market relationships with one characterized by centralized planning and significant state participation. These attempts, made by elitist groups self-appointed as the avant garde of society, also propose a political dictatorship based on the Leninist model. The first triumph of this movement occurred in Cuba in 1959. The achievement of this goal required the defeat of a National Guard army. Subsequent attempts had different fates. A popular urban insurrection in Santo Domingo in 1964 defeated the National Guard; only direct intervention of U.S. military forces prevented this country from plunging into a socialist revolution. Attempts at insurrection were defeated in other countries, such as Venezuela in 1966 and Guatemala in the 1970s and 1980s. The focal points of insurrection in Peru and Bolivia were destroyed in 1967. However, Ernesto Che Guevara's insurrection in Bolivia had important symbolic value for the whole Latin American revolutionary movement. More spectacular than these rural rebellions were the urban guerilla movements whose actions received much press attention. In Brazil, the movement was quelled by the end of the 1960s. Though the movements in both Argentina and Uruguay were defeated in the 1970s, the wounds which they caused are still open.[11] The second triumph of socialism took place in Nicaragua when the Sandanistas took office in 1979, after the defeat of the National Guard. It should be noted that this regime was not made up entirely of socialists. Despite the Sandanistas' loss in the 1990 election, socialism has by no means died in that country. El Salvador has been experiencing a civil war since the 1960s. The *Farabundo Marti de Liberacion Nacional* (FMLN) has launched four big offensives without success and is currently involved in peace talks with the government. Colombia has dealt with 50 years of revolutionary movements and other forms of violence; much of the recent strife involves the narcotics trade. The government authorities in Peru are fighting another type of rebellion. This one involves the *Sendero Luminoso*, a Maoist group that calls for class struggle and feeds on the social resentment created by racial stratification. The movement was formed in 1980.

For insurrection to triumph in these countries, revolutionaries had first to defeat the armed forces. The threat of such a defeat caused Latin America's armed forces to adopt as their overriding purpose the destruction of insurrection. Thus, military corporations used the threat of revolution to justify their existence and growth, protected by their constitutional monopoly on the authorization of violent force. They developed into political actors when they proposed to intervene in daily matters of government. Often they did so in the name of the modernizing rationality needed to overcome the crisis of the traditional forms of domination. At other times, however, they acted as moderators. The "arbitrator role" presupposes that the army accepts the existing social order and that its task after a coup is to reestablish stability by settling civilian political disputes, installing an "acceptable" government, and returning to barracks. However, in the 1960s and 1970s, the break of Latin America with the capitalistic system and with semiliberal political structures led to a new form of military–political action.

In recent decades, the confrontation between the armed forces and the revolutionary sector, or those considered by the military to be allied with so-called subversive groups, has extended military action in internal conflict. This factor, together with influence from abroad, mistrust toward the traditional political leadership, the government's lack of will to grapple with continued destabilization, the social unrest protagonized by the labor unions, the perception of a deep economic crisis and corruption, facilitated the intervention of the armed forces as a corporation in politics. The varying military ideologies and histories of each country, as well as different weights placed on counterinsurgency doctrines, determined the approach.[12] Authoritarian governmental institutions supported by the armed forces appeared in the majority of Latin American countries and disrupted the existing constitutional order. *Coups d'état* were commonplace during the late 1960s and 1970s; they took place in Argentina, Bolivia, Chile, El Salvador, Guatemala, Honduras, Peru, and Uruguay. Panama was under military rule from 1964 until the U.S. invasion of 1960. General Alfredo Stroessner controlled Paraguay from 1954 to 1989. In Brazil, Chile and Uruguay, there were attempts to create states in which the military would be a political actor with rights incorporated into the formal constitutions; under such systems, the armed forces would be consulted in certain basic decisions relating to those political or socioeconomic subjects that the military felt affected "national security." In Chile, this subject has been at the forefront of ongoing negotiations since 1988; in Uruguay, an institutional role for the military failed after a plebiscite in 1980. Today, constitutions once again have a more liberal orientation in Latin American countries. In some cases, however, the wording of these documents assumes that the armed forces exist as an integral component of the political system; the 1988 Brazilian constitution, which gives the military power for certain limited forms of intervention in politics, lends this contention added credibility.

The Military Budget

The original Latin American constitutions provided that military budgets would have a defined form, with the purpose of limiting the existence and resources of the armed forces. They often exerted pressure on various members of the legislatures to obtain funding increases. This military direct intervention in politics did not always increase their budget allocation; the legislature often responded by citing the high level of corruption in the services. The armed forces nonetheless sought to increase the officers' salaries. In the twentieth century, especially after the military had ruled most Latin American countries for some time, the legislatures relaxed their control of the military budgets. The executives took the initiative and the military continued to throw its weight around in the funding process; hence, in legislatures from Caracas to Santiago, the budget is rarely an item of debate. Recent constitutions do not refer to military budgets; the military budget is allocated within the state budget and the figures are accrued. In reality, the autonomy of the armed forces gives them limited control of their future expenses. The military merely amasses its own income, leaving little room for legislative control. Even in countries such as Venezuela that consider themselves democratic and possess stable relationships between their civilian and military sectors, the budget is approved in its accrued from. The institute that controls governmental accounts excludes the defense budget from legislative control.

The most controversial and preponderant items of these military budgets usually relate to the salaries, pensions, health services, and other social benefits of the personnel of the armed forces, particularly of the officer corps. Public opinion, which senses the existence of unfair privileges, is highly responsive to this issue. The armed forces usually argue that their exclusive dedication to the task of ensuring national security prevents them from engaging in other remunerative tasks; therefore, they must be appropriately compensated for their contributions to the well-being and stability of the nation. The legislative branches negotiate the precise size of the budget with other governmental representatives who represent the interests of the military and exercise pressure on civilian decision makers.

Since the beginning of the twentieth century, European military equipment and technological innovations have encouraged the armed forces in Latin America, particularly those based in the larger countries of this region, to increase their war material inventory. After World War II, the United States was the principal source of this area's military equipment. In the 1940s, the Argentinean armed forces created their own military–industrial complex. It functioned well during Juan Peron's time and into the 1970s, when it experienced periods of acute crisis. Its existence caused a marked expansion in the scope of activities undertaken by the Argentine military. The development of a military industry in Brazil in the 1960s took a different course. Promoted by a military bureaucracy which actually headed the government, military production was entrusted to private industrialists. In the 1980s, Chile chose to follow the Brazilian model. Other countries such as Colombia, Peru and Venezuela have smaller military–industrial subsidiaries. However, the smaller these entities are, the more dependent they are on foreign countries for their equipment. Their ability to pay for items, to make political arrangements to obtain military aid, or to secure long-term loans are crucial variables.

The military in Latin American generally informs the executive branch about their acquisitions and investments, but they have the initiative. The executive approves or vetoes their course of action, and rarely informs the legislature about these activities; these budgetary decisions take into account the interests of each service in the armed forces. In general, there is no unified military security police;

consequently, the different parts of the armed forces form a confederation in which each component retains a semisovereign character and seeks to outmaneuver the others. In the larger countries of Latin America (Argentina, Brazil, Chile, and Venezuela), keen competition for limited resources exists between the army and such lesser services as the navy and the air force. In the smaller countries of the region, the army receives the largest portion of the funds.

Military Institutions and Their Command

All Latin American constitutions establish a presidential or rather, semipresidential system of government, in which the executive is normally the commander-in-chief of the armed forces. Under the older constitutions, the executive also had the power of operational command of the armed forces in times of war. Sometimes he even had a formal position in the army or was empowered to nominate officers; however, for the appointment to be binding, he had to gain the consent of one of the chambers of the legislature, a task that often fell to the Senate. The creation of military schools at the end of the nineteenth century and the increased professionalization of the army changed the relationship between the executive and the armed forces; it could be argued that these schools gave their students careers that were sheltered from the manipulations of civilian authorities. Executive rules eventually put an end to the discretional power of the president. Only the breakdown of the constitutional order disrupted this process of career bureaucratization. When this occurred, as it did in Argentina during the 1950s and in Guatemala during the 1960s, military officers, to advance their careers, took partisan positions in internal conflicts and worked to eliminate those who competed with them for promotions.[13] In other countries, the reverse held true; the bureaucratic structure was increased substantially to avoid internal crisis and legal authorization was given to those in the high ranks of the military in Venezuela during the 1960s, in Uruguay in the 1970s, and in El Salvador during the 1980s.

This greater professionalization resulted in the military exercise of the main controls on the nomination of military personnel. Only at the higher levels do the civilian political leadership and those in the legislative branch of government have any control and they, it should be noted, exercise it only subjectively.[14]

The Organization of Military Institutions

Under Latin American constitutions, the organization of the military force is the joint duty of a country's legislature and of its executive. The legislature or parliament issues general laws; the executive issues instrumental laws through regulations and administrative resolutions. Throughout the entire region, the military structure is fragmented and decentralized, a reflection of the fear in many parts of Latin America that a unified force would be more likely to intervene in the political realm. A minister of defense is responsible for the political coordination of military security. The ministries under this person's direction do not become deeply involved in military policy-making and rarely make up the true structure of the command of the armed forces. Generally, the ministries handle the military's budget and function as social welfare and auxiliary support entities; even the police forces report to the Ministry of Internal Affairs, although in a crisis, they frequently are under military command.

From a judicial point of view, the military structure is a confederation of sovereign organizations in their normal operations. Little coordination exits between the different branches of the military. Internal conflicts between the services and among branches of one service are common; generally the army predominates. In the most part, factional agreements resolve disputes over areas of influence and turf battles about coastal zones and archipelagos. The armed forces are, however, strongly unified in their political views. It is precisely this unity of political views that makes civilians perceive the military as a single corporation. Because they are separate from the rest of society, the armed forces in Latin America have a value system that is based on an organic ideology[15] or a professional ideology;[16] consequently, this sector of society is clearly distinct from the civilian components of Latin American countries. Because of its unique structure and almost absolute authority, civilian sectors see the armed forces as a separate entity.

If the political leadership in Latin American countries had a clear military policy, it would be more possible for civilians to take advantage of the military's fragmented structure and to exert their authority. If these nations had a bureaucratic apparatus headed by a permanent, strong leader and if their hierarchies were independent of political waverings and capable of resisting pressures and modifications during political crises, civilian control would be more assured. Such is not the case in Latin America.

Civilian control is made even more difficult by the presence of intelligence services. In the larger countries of Latin America, a state information service emerged, first as a functional speciality and then as an independent entity. In general, military or quasimilitary governments created institutions based on this model. These information systems duplicate the intelligence services of the armed forces and those of the police. The military establishment and its civilian elites consider intelligence work to be highly significant, particularly in view of perceived internal threats, supposedly derived from revolutionary movements. These entities carry on extensive research of the activities of citizens or organizations; when a perceived conspiracy against national security arises, the services can act. On paper, the executive branch of government controls these intelligence-gathering entities. In reality, however, the president is rarely involved with the on-going operations of these units. The legislatures do not have the power to oversee these intelligence activities and the judiciary does not act as an arbitrator of conflicts over human or other liberal rights as it does in the United States. Nor do Latin American countries possess an equivalent to the British tradition of "honorable men" in their intelligence organizations.

The Deployment of the Military

The deployment and configuration of the armed forces is in theory, the primary responsibility of the legislative power, to be implemented by the executive authority. Over time, military organizations have proposed their own organizational forms; the executive powers sanctioned their proposals and legislative involvement disappeared.

The only Latin American military forces that exist outside of the boundaries of their native countries are peace-keeping units (e.g., in Kashmir and in Cyprus). Deployment occurs internally, and generally on territorial principles. As there is not usually a unified command, the three different services coexist uncoordinated. Legislative decision makers play no part in any facet of their deployment.

In the colonial era, to ensure the security of large, empty spaces, the urban centers were the predominant base of the armed forces. This practice was continued into the twentieth century because social conflicts in the cities required the availability of repressive forces. After the 1960s, a decade in which motor transportation became more prevalent, the use of these units became unnecessary. Despite this reality, most Latin American countries still rely on this strategy of stationing troops in urban settings. The military stays close to cities to remind the political leadership and the rest of society of its power. Officers in the armed forces also live the comfortable life of an urban existence; normally, high-ranking members of the army and other military services function as part of the urban elite and enjoy the possibility of a higher social status than do their counterparts in the west who must often live on isolated bases (only the air forces have attempted to base themselves in accordance with functional criteria). This organizational system reinforces the autonomous character of each service and reflects patterns of political culture created by the military corporations and the political leadership; it does not reflect the influence of a constitutional system.

As we have seen, the military principle of unity of decision and command and sole liability tends to crumble at the top. Various military chiefs share responsibility; constant negotiations take place between them. In periods of civil rule, they must share part of their duties with civilian policy-makers. This means, in reality, that they must form a sort of partnership with the executive authority. Hence, many authoritarian cooperative governments have, of late, supported the existence of military colleges that exercise supreme command. They are supposed to function as "substitute parties,"[17] and prevent the emergence of *caudillos* such as Chile's General Augusto Pinochet, who controlled the military structure. The military regimes in Brazil (1964–1984), in Argentina (1976–1983), and in Uruguay (1973–1984) also provide graphic illustrations of this tendency.

The Armed Forces and Their Behavior in Times of War

Practically all Latin American constitutions empower the legislative branch of government to declare war or to authorize the executive to take this course of action. In general, these constitutions also establish certain ways for the judiciary to deal with internal problems. With the declaration of a "state of siege," a "state of emergency," a "state of national defense," or the need for "security measures," the armed forces may be used to control internal order. Constitutions in Latin America are ambiguous about this point; more recent ones (Brazil, 1988) tend to increase the control of the legislature over the armed forces' intent to employ coercive tactics to restore stability.

Although these constitutions give the power to declare war to the legislature, in only a few cases has war started with this formality. Normally, after an incident on one of the many borders in this region, the executive makes the decision. As the most frequent conflicts are internal, the enemy is defined as inside the country. During these periods, the constitution is in abeyance and remains so for the duration of the crisis. When emergencies are endemic, constitutional guarantees become extremely fragile or simply illusory. The prevalent political culture in Latin America gives the executive the benefit of the doubt in times of crisis and severely restricts the decision-making capacities of the legislature. The executive must impose its views during these periods of instability because some factions in the legislature will support those who seek to change the social order, or will adopt sometimes semiloyal, if not frankly disloyal positions.[18] If the executive is not successful in suppressing this dissent, all civilian decision makers must confront the possibility that the armed forces will step into the picture and resolve the situation by themselves. Their solution usually takes the form of a coup.

All wars occasion a conflict between the need for effectiveness and the necessity of legitimacy. When the conflict is internal, the difficulty of the dilemma is compounded. Secrecy and the autonomous centralization of command favor efficiency. Legitimacy has its basis in political support for the war, and sometimes implies a certain degree of open information and limits on military operations. It also assumes that war is a last resort for a democratic regime. Latin American constitutions are, however, unclear on this matter. This reality has led these civilian elites to resist calling internal conflicts "war." As civilians normally lack the knowledge to refute the arguments of the military, they are generally unable to propose alternatives to what the armed forces offer as solutions to domestic strife.

The Members of the Armed Forces and Their Position Vis-À-Vis Society and State

As we have seen, the first constitutions in attempting to limit permanent forces also tried to curtail the possible pressure by the military on the political leadership by establishing a militia or national guard. For these permanent, or front, forces, as they were often called, additional limits were set to curb their political activity. Policy-makers suspended the civic status of troop personnel, enlisted or contracted, during the period of their service. Military officers attempted to outmaneuver these restrictions; they simply discharged their forces a few days before elections and the soldiers reenlisted a few days after. With the creation of the professional army in Latin America in the beginning of the twentieth century this situation changed. The constitutions of this period expressly stated that military service was an important civic duty. These documents stressed the virtues of service as a means of achieving social integration, the leveling of class differences, and as part of the process of forming national identity. In reality, however, the poorest sectors of society supplied most of the recruits for the rank and file of the armed forces. Many noncommissioned officers also came from the lower socioeconomic strata; the officers of these militaries were men with middle class origins. Policy-makers chose not to institute a draft system because they could not accept the notion that sons of wealthy landowners or industrialists might be mere privates; they also feared that it would be difficult for members of the lower class who became officers to control subordinates who were wealthier.

Currently, rank and file members in the Latin American armed forces lose their civic rights during their time of service, which lasts between 1 and 2 years. The few countries in which basic personnel enlist permanently have recently granted these soldiers the right to vote. Many Latin American constitutions limit the social rights of the officers corps as well; they can only vote. In general, military personnel are expressly forbidden the right to exercise any political activities; they cannot join political parties or engage in proselytizing activities. The military has no right to petition the state collectively nor can it make political demands on governmental agencies. Recent constitutions (e.g., Chile, 1980, and Brazil, 1988) expressly prohibit the formation of unions of military members. Following France's 1791 constitution, armed forces are forbidden to participate in deliberations with other sectors of society. Some of the Latin American constitutions allow a military officer to declare candidacy for office; however, when an officer takes this course of action, his military status is suspended, and in some countries, he must retire. Usually, however, military officers do not enter the political arena as candidates in the first place. To compensate for these limitations, Latin American constitutional law does establish a set of privileges for the military. Their status, protected by certain rules of discipline and by honor courts, allow members of the armed forces to pursue careers safeguarded by the state. A special military judicial structure exists to deal with crimes covered in military codes.

These safeguards against the military's interference in domestic politics have led to the alienation or separation of the military from the rest of society. As has been pointed out, a professional armed force, particularly the officer corps, isolates itself from society and state.[19] In recent decades in Latin America, those who desired to maintain current social and economic conditions often saw the military as an institution that preserved the existing order; radicals and revolutionaries, who wanted to change the existing fabric of society, saw the armed forces as a barrier to change. The indifferent mass of people desired peace and denied the cost of the repression needed to maintain it. They viewed the armed force as a potentially dangerous institution, separate and distinct from the mainstream of society. The armed forces, whose legitimacy depends on their ability to defend the internal order as no credible external threats exist, responded to these attitudes by using their autonomy and the political space, which they have gained as shields for protection.

In the authoritarian regimes of the 1970s, especially in those in the southern cone, the military has had difficulty in overcoming its isolation from the rest of society. The armed forces in Chile and Argentina saw their legitimacy questioned. Though the armed forces acted repressively and suppressed a wide range of liberal freedoms, the military believed that it was acting in the name of democracy.[20] Although the military subdued the populations, it failed to convince most that to save the state, it was first necessary to wreak havoc on it. Because the civilian segments of these countries refused to subscribe to the military's logic, the armed forces eventually negotiated an exit from the business of governing.

Constitutional provisions in Latin American countries tend to reinforce the isolation of the military from the political sphere, denying its role as a political actor. Recent history tends to disprove this view. The military is a key participant in Latin American politics. As the civilian and military sectors of Latin American societies look to the future, they must reconcile the constitutional prohibitions on the activities of the military with its actual everyday participation in internal political affairs.

Conclusion

Latin American constitutions are notoriously ambiguous in their definitions of the social and political roles of the armed forces. Despite rules governing the creation, development, and command of the military, payment and civic activities of the armed forces, decision makers have continually construed these documents so as to confirm the political practices that favored the autonomy of the military and allowed it to assert itself as a power broker in internal confrontations. More recently, the armed forces have enlarged their role in domestic strife and have become one of the principal actors in these struggles. Armed interference in the political life of Latin America has become one part of a complex reality in that region. This active role in internal politics is rare in North Atlantic countries.

The military's problematic tendency to shape the outcomes of domestic politics is rooted in the predominant political culture of the region. Civilian elites fail to understand the problems of military corporations; their separation and isolation from the rest of society will persist as will the threat of continued military intervention. Many members of the armed forces will continue to mistrust civilian policy-makers, who, they believe, in moments of crisis may abandon their defense of the traditional social underpinnings and allow subversive forces to destroy the existing order. With the Soviet Union, eastern Europe, and Cuba in crisis, the threat of subversive movements is low. However, violent reform efforts are still quite alive: the *Sendero Luminoso* and the *Tupac Amaruc* in Peru, the *Farabundo Marti* in El Salvador, the *Cordinadora Simon Bolivar* in Colombia, and the UNRG in Guatemala. Latin American armed forces also contend that new types of guerilla uprisings could appear even without the traditional support of external forces that the military in this region has labeled the "international Communist movement."

If the trend toward democratization that exists in eastern Europe and the Soviet Union emerges in Latin America, the possibility exists that the content of the constitutions of the region might coincide with what is actually practiced on a daily basis. When such a day arrives, these legal texts will support a liberal democratic framework and civil control of the armed forces, who will no longer sit in their barracks suspiciously watching the political processes swirl about them.

Notes

1. Alain Rouquie, *Pouvoir Militaire et Société Politique dans la République Argentine* (Military Power and Political Society in the Argentinean Republic) (Paris: FNSP, 1978).
2. Erwing Goffman, "Characteristics of Total Institutions" in M. R. Stein et al., eds., *Identity and Anxiety* (Glexoe, IH.: Free Press, 1960).
3. Tomás de Iriarte, *Memoires* (Buenos Aires: Fabril, 1961).
4. Juan Rial, *The Armed Forces: Are Soldiers/Politicians the Guarantors of Democracy?* (Montevideo: CIESU-CLADE-Ebo, 1986).
5. Samuel H. Finer, *The Man on Horseback: The Role of the Military in Politics* (London: Pall Mall, 1962); 2nd edition enlarged (London: Penguin Books, 1975).
6. Alfred Stepan, *The Military in Politics: Changing Patterns in Brazil* (Princeton: Princeton University Press, 1971).
7. Phillipe C. Schmitter, *Speculations About the Prospective Demise of Authoritarian Regimes and Its Possible Consequences* (Washington: The Woodrow Wilson Center, Working Papers No. 60, 1979).
8. Alain Roquie, note 1. Also Robert A. Potash *The Army and Politics in Argentina, 1928–1945; 1945–1962* (Stanford: Stanford University Press, 1969/80).
9. José Nun, "The Middle-Class Military Coup Revisited," in A. Loewenthal and S. Fitch, eds., *Armies and Politics in Latin America* (New York: Holmes & Meier, 1986).
10. Juan Rial, note 4; Also Alain Roquie, note 1; Alfred Stepan, note 6. Also Augusto Varas, Felipe Aguero and Fernando Bustamante, eds., *Fuerzas Armadas y Democracia.* (Santiago: Fiacso, 1981).
11. Carina Perelli, *To Submit or Convince. The Military Topic* (Montevideo: CLADE-EBO, 1987).
12. Genaro Arrigada, *The Political Thinking of the Military* (Santiago: CISEC, 1981).
13. Rosendo Fraga, *The Army: The Derision of Power (1973–1976)* (Buenos Aires: Planeta, 1988).
14. Samuel P. Huntington, *The Soldier and the State: The Theory and Politics of Civil-Military Relations* (Cambridge, MA: Harvard University Press, 1957).
15. Amos Perlmutter, *The Military in Politics in Modern Times* (New Haven: Yale University Press, 1977).
16. Jacques Van Doorn, *On Military Ideology* (Rotterdam: Rotterdam University Press, 1971).
17. Juan Rial, note 4.
18. Juan Linz, *Crisis, Breakdown & Reequilibration* (Baltimore: Johns Hopkins University Press, 1978).
19. Samuel Huntington, note 14; Morris Janowitz, *The Professional Soldier* (Glencoe, IL: The Free Press, 1960); Gerke Teitler, *The Genesis of the Professional Officer's Corps* (Beverly Hills, CA: Sage, 1977).
20. Juan Rial, note 4.

15

Parliamentary Democracy in Europe 1992: Tentative Questions and Answers

Joseph H. H. Weiler

In December 1990, the governments of the member states of the European Community (EC) opened two Intergovernmental Conferences representing a new stage in the process of European integration. One conference will deal with the move to full economic and monetary union and the other witn further steps toward European political union. Thus, the community is planning its post-1992 destiny, after the achievement of the single market. Central to the discussion of institutional change in this post-1992 destiny will be the question of the powers and functions of the European Parliament and the democracy deficit of the community.

Undeniably, the European Community suffers from a democratic deficit in the operation of its decision-making process. Few disagree that this deficit is a serious defect in the process of European integration. It is an embarrassing blight on a community that insisted that democratic structures and processes were conditions precedent for admission of new member states and that is moving now, in the context of the 1992 process, to a further stage in achieving "an ever-closer union among the peoples of Europe," as stated in the Preamble to the Treaty of Rome. The single most glaring cause of this deficit is the weak position of the European Parliament in the community political structure. Any attempt to close the deficit must involve a greater role for the European Parliament. It is thus surprising that all progressive discussion about the community institutional structure calls for increased power for the European Parliament. (By "progressive," I mean those views broadly favorable to the continuing process of European integration.)

In this chapter I shall raise questions regarding these basic premises. I shall do this with the hope of enriching the debate about the future institutional structure of the community. The essay is deliberately a *polemical exercise* because it seems to me that in the current academic debate there are only two principal voices: one that is deeply concerned about the future of the community and thus eloquently and persuasively musters all possible arguments for an enhanced role for the European Parliament; the other has two positions. One is that of the "pure" antimarketeers to be found even in the European Parliament itself; they are opposed to an enhanced role for the Parliament, but their opposition is part of a general oposition to European integration and the European Community.[1] Others accept these aforementioned premises but claim that the proposals for a greater role for Parliament are "unrealistic" or politically unviable.

Largely missing from the debate is an explication, from a point of view sympathetic to European integration, of a principled argument for an increase in the powers of the European Parliament. This chapter is therefore an attempt to construct the strongest possible case, what I call a revisionist view, opposing the progressive view. It will be for the reader to construct the final synthesis, or perhaps even to refute, point by point, my arguments. In either case the cause of a more democratic community will be served.

The structure of the chapter is simple. After a brief recapitulation of the traditional view of the place of the Parliament in the community structure, which I will call the progressive view, I shall review, equally briefly, the principal strategies and tactics that, based on the progressive view, have been suggested over the years for increasing the capacity of Parliament to exercise its control and legislative functions in the community decision-making process. I shall then reexamine the key concepts of democracy and legitimacy and their relationship to the process of integration. This reexamination will depart from the mainstream discourse in the European literature. Using these reexamined concepts and placing my neck squarely on the block, I shall suggest more expansively, and in a deliberately polemical fashion, alternative interpretations of the place of Parliament in the European construct. This view will be called the revisionist view. By its nature a revisionist view is backward looking, not a comfortable position to espouse, but one that I accept following the polemical strategy of this chapter.

At the outset I wish to state my awareness that some of my characterizations of the progressive view will be extreme and may perhaps misrepresent many of the more nuanced and subtle constructs in the literature. I hope this tactic will be understood as part of my attempt to polarize the positions in the interest of sharp differentiation.

The Progressive View

Democracy Deficit

It is the custom to start an analysis of the place of the European Parliament in the governance structure of the community by a recapitulation of the existing democracy deficit in EC decision making. It is this deficit that has informed, animated, and mobilized the drive for change in the powers of the European Parliament. To the extent that the governments of the member states have responded, weakly and grudgingly, to this drive, it is surely because even they have recognized the compelling power of the democracy deficit argument.

According to the progressive view the European Parliament is the only (or at least the principal) repository of legitimacy and democracy in the community structure. The phrase most typically used in this context is democratic legitimacy. The commission, the progressive view points out, is an appointed body of international civil servants; the Council, by definition, represents the executive branch of government, which has, through community structures, legislative powers which the executive lacks at the national level. Thus, the Council, a collectivity of ministers, on a proposal of the Commission, a collectivity of appointed civil servents, could, and in some instances has to, pass legislation that is binding and enforceable, superseding conflicting legislation passed by national parliaments without their scrutiny and approval. Indeed, it could pass the legislation in the face of European parliamentary disapproval. This happens with sufficient regularity that the point is not simply theoretical. What is more, the Council can legislate in many areas that were hitherto subject to parliamentary control at the national level.

According to this view, the powers of the European Parliament are both weak and misdirected. They are weak in that the legislative power (even after the Single European Act) is ultimately consultative in the face of a determined Council,[2] the budgetary powers, though more concrete, do not affect the crucial areas of budgetary policy: revenue raising and expenditure on compulsory items. The power to reject the budget in toto has not always been effective, although in 1984 the budget was ultimately amended in a direction that took account of some of Parliament's concerns. The possibility of denying a discharge on past expenditure lacks any real sanction. Those powers that are real, the power to dismiss the Commission, to ask questions of the Commission, and to receive answers, are illusory at best and misdirected at worst—illusory because the power to dismiss is collective and does not have the accompanying power to appoint, and misdirected, because the Council is the villain of the piece in most parliamentary battles. It is all these well-known factors taken together that constitute the elements of the democracy deficit and create the crisis of legitimacy from which the community allegedly suffers.

The Decision Malaise

Although the democracy deficit is prominent in parliamentary rhetoric, historically the daily complaints about Parliament were not about a too vigorous community legislator (the Council) that violated democratic principles, but rather about a community legislator (the Council) that failed to act vigorously enough and incapacitated itself and the entire community by abandoning Treaty rules for majoritarian decision making; it did so by giving a de facto veto to each member state government in the form of the 1966 Luxembourg Accord, which asserted a "national vital interest."

This veto power arrogated by the member states produced another facet of the democracy deficit: the ability of a small number of community citizens represented by their minister in the Council to block the collective wishes of the rest of the community. The point would be driven home most dramatically if we imagine a blocking veto (1–11) by, say, a Danish Minister representing a minority government and thwarting the wishes of 320,000,000 citizens. The lawyer will add that the matter is particularly acute in an exclusive area of community law (fisheries, common commercial policy) or in an area where the exercise of community powers preempts member state action (aspects of agriculture, environment, etc.), In these cases, the effect of the minority veto is to prevent action both at Community level and at member state level. This aspect of the deficit was largely removed by the Single European Act, which restored majority voting in most areas where the Treaty itself provides for such a vote.[3]

The Remedies of the Progressive View

Most parliamentarians claimed that both facets of the malaise could be corrected by institutional changes that would unblock the Council by restoring majority voting and would also significantly increase the legislative and control powers of Parliament. This is the view of most academic literature as well. It has become virtually an article of faith.[4] Increased powers to the Parliament, directly elected by universal suffrage, would, so it is claimed, ipso facto substantially reduce the democratic deficit and restore legitimacy to the community decision-making process. The point seems so obvious that it receives little critical analysis.

With respect to the decisional malaise, Parliament has, so the progressive view claims, boasted over the years a *Communautaire* spirit that would, if given effective outlet, transcend nationalistic squabbles and introduce a dynamism far more consonant with the declared objectives of the Treaties. The large majority accorded to the Draft Treaty Establishing the European Union is often cited as a typical example of this dynamism.

For a long time, however, parliamentarians have split on the best strategy to achieve these transformations. Some favoured a step-by-step approach; others, a more radical one. In its most recent resolutions in the context of the preparation for the Intergovernmental Conferences that opened in December 1990, the radical approach won the internal parliamentary battle. Parliament's proposals call for the recognition of Council–Parliament as colegislators with equal weight and prerogatives in the legislative process.[5] As the Intergovernmental Conference is unlikely to accept this notion of colegislator in the full version advocated by Parliament, the debate about Parliament and its role is likely to remain within the above parameters.

Democracy, Legitimacy, and Integration

To establish a framework for understanding of the revisionist view, I must burden the reader with a set of conceptual distinctions and relationships. I shall discuss first the difference between democracy, formal legitimacy, and social legitimacy. I shall then discuss the relationship between integration of polities and democracy. I shall then try to show how these clarified concepts and relationships affects, in my view, some of our hitherto unquestioned assumptions about the community and its governance.

Democracy and Legitimacy

Very frequently in discourse about Parliament and the community the concepts of democracy and legitimacy are presented interchangeably. In fact, they do not necessarily coincide. A stark example may drive the point home. Germany during the Weimar Republic was democratic, but the government enjoyed little legitimacy. Germany under National Socialism ceased to be democratic after Adolf Hitler rose to power, but the government continued to enjoy widespread legitimacy well into the early 1940s.[6] I think that today it would be difficult in the west for a nondemocratic government structure or political system to attain or maintain legitimacy, but it is still possible for a democratic structure to lack legitimacy, either in toto or in certain aspects of its operation. In other words, although the existence of democratic structures surely influences the legitimacy of governance structure, it does not guarantee it.

Formal (Legal) Legitimacy and Social (Empirical) Legitimacy

So far I have treated legitimacy as a unitary concept. It will be helpful to break it into the categories of formal (legal) and social (empirical). To refer to the formal legitimacy of institutions or systems connotes that in their creation all requirements of law were observed. (It is a concept akin to the juridical concept of formal validity.) Clearly, in today's Europe (and generally in the west) any notion of legitimacy must rest on some democratic foundation loosely stated as the people's consent to power structures and process. But, we can still speak of formal legitimacy if we can show that the power structure was created following democratic processes and with the people's consent. Thus, I would simply point out that the treaties establishing the EC, which gave such a limited role to the European Parliament, were approved by the all national parliaments of the founding member states and, subsequently, by the parliaments of six acceding member states. Proposals for change that would give more power to the European Parliament have failed, for a variety of reasons, to complete the democratic process in the member states.

This definition of formal legitimacy distinguishes itself therefore from simple "legality." It is legality understood, however, in the sense that the law on which it is based (in our case the Treaties) was created by democratic institutions and processes. In this formal sense, then, the existing structure and process of the EC could be said to rest on the formal approval of the democratically elected parliaments of the member states; yet, undeniably the community process suffers from a clear democracy deficit.

Social legitimacy connotes a broad societal (empirically determined) acceptance of the system. An institution or a system any be socially legitimate even if broad sections of society do not favor its specific composition, program, or operation. For instance, in the last elections in Great Britain only a minority of the electorate voted for the current Conservative government. But that government enjoys, beyond any doubt, social legitimacy because most people accept the rules of the game according to which a minority of the electorate may end up with a large parliamentary majority. Many other factors contribute to this legitimacy, which has an additional *substantive* component. Legitimacy is achieved when the government process displays a commitment to and actively guarantees values that are part of the general political culture such as justice and freedom. The importance of this further refinement will be made clear below.

Now we may explore the relationship between the two types of legitimacy. An institution or system or polity will in most (but not all) cases have to enjoy formal legitimacy in order to enjoy social legitimacy. This is most likely the case in western democratic traditions. But a system that enjoys formal legitimacy may not necessarily enjoy social legitimacy. Most popular revolutions (from the French Revolution onward) took place in polities where the government and the system were formally legitimate but had lost social legitimacy.

Integration and Democracy

Let us now turn to the more delicate problem of the relationship between integration or unification of polities, and democracy.[7]

No modern polity aspiring to democracy can govern itself today like the Greek *polis* or the New England town. Representative (parliamentary) democracy has replaced direct participation. Nonetheless, one yardstick of democracy is the closeness and responsiveness to, and representativeness and accountability of, the governors to the governed. Although this formula is vague, it is sufficient for present purposes.

Let us now assume three polities, each independent and each with a democratic representative form of government. To simplify matters, let us further assume that each government in these polities enjoys legislative and regulatory power in the fields of education, taxation, foreign trade, and defense. Therefore, in relation to each of these functions the electors can directly influence their representatives (through elections, etc.) on the polity's education policy, its level of taxation, the type of foreign trade (protectionist or free), and the nature of its defense forces and policy. Let us further assume that for a variety of reasons the three polities decide to integrate and to "share their sovereignty" in the fields of taxation, foreign trade, and defense. If within each of the three polities this decision was democratically reached, the integrated polity will certainly enjoy formal legitimacy.

What about democracy? By definition there would intitially be a diminution of democracy in the new integrated polity. Why is this so? Because prior to the integration, the majority of electors in polity A would have had a controlling influence over their level of taxation, the nature of their foreign trade policy, and the size of their army and its posture. Under the integrated polity the electors of polity A (even a huge majority) could be outvoted by the electors of polities B and C. This would be the case even if the new integrated polity has a perfectly democratically elected "federal" legislature. The integrated polity would not be undemocratic but it would be, in terms of the ability of citizens to influence policies affecting them, less democratic.

We see this idea, in reverse form, when a centralized state devolves sovereign power on more or less autonomous regions as in Italy, Spain, and, in recent years, to some extent in France. Regionalism is, in some respects, the opposite of integration. One of the prime motivations for regionalism is to enhance democracy in the sense of giving people more direct control of areas of public policy that affects their life.

To suggest, as I have, that in the process of integration there is a loss, at least in one sense, of democracy, does not condemn the process of integration. There usually would have been formidable reasons that prompt the electors in polities A, B, and C to choose integration, despite this loss of some direct control in the larger polity. Typically, the main reasons would relate to size and interdependence. By aggregating their resources, especially in the field of defense, their total welfare may be improved despite the loss of the more immediate influence of each government's policies. Similar advantages may accure in the field of foreign trade; further, there may be phenomena such as multinational corporations that, escaping the control of any particular polity, can be taxed effectively, say, only by an integrated polity. In other words, the independence and sovereignty of the single polities may be illusory in the real interdependent world. Nonetheless, the ability of the citizens of polity A, B, or C directly to control and influence these areas would diminish with integration.

It is true that even within each polity (A, B, or C) the minority had to accept majority decisions. So why am I claiming that in the enlarged integrated polity, where an equally valid majoritarian rule applies, there would be a loss of democracy? This is the toughest aspect of all democratic theory. What defines the boundary of the polity within which the majority principle should apply? There is no theoretical answer to this question. It is determined by long-term factors such as political continuity, social, cultural and linguistic affinity, and a shared history. No one factor determines this boundary, but the interplay of some or all. People accept the majoritarian principle of democracy within a polity to which they see themselves as belonging. How convincing do you think it would be to tell the Protestant majority electorate of Northern Ireland that in a United Ireland, where they would suddenly be a minority within a Catholic majority, they would enjoy perfect democratic rights? The whole nature of their polity would change despite their electoral rights.

The process of integration, even if decided on democratically, brings about, initially at least, a loss democracy in its actual process of governance. Despite this loss of total control over the integrated areas by each polity, what becomes crucial for the success of the integration process is the social legitimacy of the new integrated polity.

The next question is what factors would contribute to this increased social legitimacy?

There are two principal answers. The first would be the visible and tangible demonstration that integration raised the level of the total welfare of the citizenry. The second would be the guarantee of the democratic structure of the new integrated polity, itself within its new boundaries. But more important still would be the granting of, for a time at least, a stronger voice to the separate polities. It is not an accident that some of the most successful federations that emerged from hitherto separate polities, the United States, Switzerland, and Germany, enjoyed, prior to unification, a period as a confederation. This does not mean that one has to have a confederation prior to a federation. It simply suggests that in a federation created by integration, rather than by devolution, there would have to be a period of adjustment during which the political boundaries of the new polity became socially accepted as appropriate for the larger democratic rules whereby the minority would accept a new majority. From the political point of view (though not in its legal architecture)[8] the EC, despite the important changes brought about by the Single European Act (SEA),[9] is in fact confederal in nature. The big debate is therefore whether the time is ripe for a radical change toward a stronger federal structure, or whether the process should be allowed to continue in a more evolutionary fashion.

Sadly, these two answers can be at odds with each other. Giving a stronger voice to each polity may impede the successful attainment of the goals of integration. Denying sufficient voice to the constituent polities (allowing the minority to be overridden by the majority) may bring about a decline in the social legitimacy of the polity with consequent dysfunctions and even disintegration. An example demonstrates the difficulty of balancing these two interests. The American confederal structure, which gave a telling voice to each individual state (not unlike the Council of Ministers in the Community), debilitated itself to the extent that it failed to exploit the benefits of size; hence, the impetus that resulted in the adoption of the new federal constitution. (Incidentally, the Convention and the adopted Constitution were in violation of the Articles of Confederation. In the strict legal sense, the American federal polity is based on an instrument, the Constitution, whose formal legitimacy was flawed.)

Be this as it may, in terms of democratic theory, the final objective of a unifying polity is to recover the loss of democracy initiated by the process of integration. This recovery is complete when the social fabric and discourse are such that the electorate accepts the new boundary as defining the polity and then accepts totally the legitimacy of being subjected to majority rule in a such larger system comprising the integrated polities.[10] But this process can take a long time. The social legitimacy of the federal government in the United States was not consolidated until well into the nineteenth century after the bloody Civil War, triggered by the slavery issue, but really fought on the issue of the rejection by the old southern slave-holding states of the federal discipline. They simply would not accept as legitimate the democratic decisions taken in a Congress dominated by a Northern majority.

Obviously there is no risk today that the member states of the community would resort to armed force to solve any of their problems. The single biggest success of the communities, from a long-term historical perspective, has been making the idea of war not only impossible but unthinkable. It is less clear that a radical change in the political architecture of the community would not introduce serious destabilizing forces.

The Revisionist View

We will now explore the ways in which the revisionist view works itself out in the context of the European Community, with particular reference to the

European Parliament. We will subject the progressive view to a critical examination in the light of the above conceptual clarifications.

Integration, Democracy, and Legitimacy in the European Community: The European Community's Crisis of Legitimacy

As stated above, the progressive view premised that the community suffers from a crisis of legitimacy. Is the absence of legitimacy formal? Surely not. The community, including its weak Parliament, appointed Commission, and unaccountable Council, enjoys perfect formal legitimacy, as we have seen.

If there is a crisis of legitimacy it must therefore be one of social (empirical) legitimacy. What is the nature of this crisis? The progressive view is that the absence of legitimacy is rooted in the democracy deficit. And, as stated above, the implication is that any increase in the legislative and control powers of the European Parliament at the expense of Council will contribute to an elimination of this legitimacy crisis.

It is possible to question both this premise and the conclusion. Clearly, in the face of the democratic deficit, Parliament should be given enhanced powers. But I think that it is at least questionable whether this will necessarily solve the legitimacy crisis. It may even deepen it. The legitimacy crisis is generated by several reasons. The primary reason is because arguably the European electorate (in most member states) accepts only grudgingly the notion that crucial areas of public life should be governed by a process in which a national voice becomes a minority one that may be overridden by a majority of representatives from other European countries. In theoretical terms there is still no legitimacy to the notion that the geographic boundaries of this decision making process must now be European, not national.

At its starkest, the revisionist view would claim that in terms of social legitimacy no difference exists between a decision taken in the Council of Ministers and a decision taken in the European Parliament. Both present themselves to the electorate as legislative chambers with representatives of the member states. In both cases, until this dimension of legitimacy is resolved by time and other factors which I shall discuss, the electrorate of a minority member state may find a majority decision of a redefined polity hard to swallow and could consider it socially illegitimate.

From the point of view this revisionist premise, the single most legitimating element (from a social point of view) was the Luxembourg accord and the veto power. To be sure, the cost was huge in terms of efficient decision making and progress. But it was this device that enabled the community to legitimate its program; the legislation for it provided both an ex-ante "insurance policy" to the national electorates that nothing could get through without their voice having a controlling say, and it presented a postlegitimation as well in that everything that the community did, even those things that were not popular, had to be passed with the assent of national ministers. To the extent that the output of the community decisional process was legitimate, it was so at least partially because of the knowledge that it is controllable in this way.

I do not with to be misunderstood here. I am not suggesting through the above analysis that the restoration of majority voting in the community was a negative development. But I am saying that this course of action may exacerbate legitimacy problems and that even a beefed-up European Parliament (which also operates on a majority principle) will not necessarily solve that legitimacy problem, as in my analysis the legitimacy crises does not derive principally from the accountability issue at the European level but from the very redefinition of the European polity.

Where is the evidence for these contentions? There are no decisive empirical measures for legitimacy;[11] I am rather skeptical about public opinion polls that show that in the abstract the European electorate is in favor of more European integration. These things can only be tested in the crucible of real life. The community is now in a phase of transition in which it is difficult to get clear indications. On the one hand, there are still instances of considerable political capital gained in some member states by national politicians "standing up to the community." This is particularly so in Britain, Denmark, and Greece. But it is also in strong evidence in many of the older member states. Even after the conclusion of the Single European Act (championed by France) assurances had to be given that the abhorrent Luxembourg Accord remained intact.[12] On the other hand, strong arguments have been put that the effect of the new "information society" has been to break down national boundaries and diminish the member state as the principal referent for political legitimacy.[13] The community might even be in the peculiar situation where neither the member states nor the community can any longer fulfil that legitimating function; if so, the situation suggests an enquiry into other loci such as regions, corporations, and the like.[14]

Finally, let me go back to the notion of substantive legitimacy alluded to above. Our principal objection to the regimes in Greece under the Colonels, and in Spain and Portugal prior to democracy was not simply an abstract one to a nondemocratic process, important as that may have been. Objection was critically tied to the regime's content, characterized by an oppression of individual rights and by a fundamental lack of liberty and due process of law.

By contrast, the British model of democracy has many perplexing structural features. Britain has an electoral system that regularly gives large majorities in the House of Commons to parties for which only a minority of the voting electrorate cast their vote. The millions who vote for the liberal party, and more recently, for the Social Democrats, have been practically disenfranchised. A majority of members of the House of Lords are there by hereditary right. The highest judge in the realm, the Lord Chancellor, frequently sits in judgment as a member of the highest court and is an active member of the government; and finally, there is no bill of rights that protects individuals and minorities (or indeed the British majorities) from any dictate of Parliament. As a text model the British system would fail many of our basic notions of democratic legitimacy. Yet we rightly, despite discreet criticism, continue to regard Britain as a bastion of democracy. We do so for several principal reasons. Despite these structural defects, the operation of the system is respectful of minorities and individuals;

there are government changes; and fundamental liberty is de facto usually protected. Further, the rule of law is truly respected.[15]

Why this is important emerges from the following consideration regarding the European Community. It is true, of course, that structurally the European Community suffers from a democracy deficit. But we can point to only a few cases in which the Council, in terms of content, has adopted rulings that take advantage of its lack of accountability and subvert basic values. And the rule of law in the community, though not perfect (where is it perfect?), has reached, because of the Court of Justice, a level that is enviable by the standards of any other trans-national venture.

Usually, though not always, what we complain about in substance about the democracy deficit (i.e., going beyond the abstract principle) is that the Council is not proceeding vigorously enough in the process of European integration, contrary to the wishes of the electorate as expressed through the European Parliament. If I am right in this last contention, two points emerge. First, it shows that the outcry about the democracy deficit is at least in part fueled by a different agenda, furtherance of European integration. And, more crucially, the query arises whether the current position of the European Parliament favoring a stronger process of integration is self-evidently an expression of the people's will.

I am not suggesting that the European Parliament has not got a mandate for its call. But in dualistic systems electorates quite happily give conflicting mandates to differently elected organs. In the United States, the House of Representatives, the Senate, and the President are all popularly elected by universal franchise; each claims a mandate from the people; frequently these mandates conflict; often they are diametrically opposed. We see similar phenomena in France and on occasion in Germany. It is at least arguable that the collective wish of national parliaments, indicated at least by inaction, is to leave the Community structure as it is. This would be an equally authentic expression of a popular mandate.

The Decision Malaise

I stated previously that a first way to enhance the legitimacy of an integrating polity would be by a demonstration of a tangible gains in welfare that integration brings about. It is the prize one gains for giving up national control. Ultimately the success of integration depends on such a demonstration. I also suggested that this demonstration is at odds, sometimes, with another condition of first stage integration, namely, an enhanced voice to the constituent polities.

Nowhere is this dialectic more evident than in the community. As argued above, the Luxembourg Accord and veto power actually contributed to the social legitimacy of the community. At the same time, it is fairly certain that this development was the single most important factor that has prevented the community from realizing the huge and promising potential inherent in European integration. In this sense then, the Luxembourg Accord has prevented the growth of social legitimacy and has powerfully contributed to the legitimacy crisis.

The question today, therefore, is whether the substantive gains the community may achieve with its new majoritarian principle will outweigh the potential destabilization inherent in the redrawing of the political boundaries for purposes of the decision making.

Given that the Council has shifted in most (though not all) of its decision making to majority voting, the specific issue now is whether Parliament should, as it demands, become a true colegislator. In terms of reducing the democracy deficit, this is an unassailable demand. What is often overlooked is the impact of greater powers on the style of Parliament itself. At present the desire to be reelected has little impact on members of Parliament; because Parliament is so weak, what a member does or does not do in Parliament matters only in a limited way the prospects of reelection. As the powers of Parliament increase, the demands of reelection will increase correspondingly. The experience of the U.S. Congress is that party affiliation is only one, and often not the most important, predictor of legislative behavior.

The trend I predict is that an increase in parliamentary powers will cause a significantly greater coalescence, across party lines, between the behavior and positions adopted by ministers in the council and those of MEPs from the same member state in Parliament. This will not necessarily produce the same kind of blockages that now exist in the Council (because of the operation of the veto). But it could well bring about a significant reduction in the overall *Communautaire* spirit now prevailing in Parliament. At the moment the Parliament, despite many divergences among its members, acts alongside the Commission as a kind of conscience of the community and its ideals. If my analysis is correct, this feature will diminish considerably in a clientalistic Parliament. Again, this argument must not be taken as a prescription against increasing the powers of Parliament, but simply as an element in a more realistic prediction of some of the consequences of such a move.

By way of conclusion I would like to deal briefly with the issue of the legitimacy of specific institutions and, in particular, that of the Commission. The Commission has usually been an easy target, attacked as lacking in "democratic legitimacy." I dissent, at least in part, from this characterization. We have seen that, in terms of formal legitimacy, the Commission credentials are impeccable. If it has legitimacy problems, these would be of the empirical type. (By contrast, the European Council, before the Single European Act, was a good example of an institution that lacked formal legitimacy but enjoyed impeccable social legitimacy.)

It is claimed instead that the Commission lacks democratic legitimacy. Although its democratic accountability is not perfect, it is still formidable. It is appointed by elected representatives (governments of the member states answerable to national Parliaments) and it is removable by the European Parliament. Cabinet ministers in many democratic governments are no more accountable than the Commission as a body. Thus, in my view, the claim that it lacks democratic legitimacy is vastly overstated.

To the extent that the Commission lacks legitimacy (and I have never seen hard evidence for this), I think it derives, if at all, from a different source, from a radiation effect of the federal legitimacy crisis of the community as a whole.

The Commission, much more than any other institution, is associated in the public mind with "Europe." It is the public repository for all manner of frustration with the community, exacerbated by the mythical imagery of an overblown bureaucracy (a wildly exaggerated claim in comparison to any national administration) and by the European life style (high salaries, etc.).

But this very analysis also demonstrates the huge potential for the social legitimacy of the Commission. Any European success story will rub off first on the Commission (even if strictly speaking it is only one actor in the Community process). The success of the community is also the key to the legitimacy of the Commission. The major problem of the Commission, which is felt throughout the community, is not then one of formal accountability and "democratic credentials." It is the question of the responsiveness and the kind of system of governance that emerges in the community. The community is in many ways a technocratic and fragmented system with its own functional dynamic (single market), one in which input and influence may be perceived to be highly elusive to its individual subjects.

Strangely enough, the European Parliament itself may not be perceived as closing this gap. To discuss the legitimacy of the European Parliament itself is something of a taboo. After all, in what sense could the legitimacy of a directly elected chamber be called into question? I believe this can be done in two ways. In strict legal terms the formal legitimacy of the European Parliament is based on the Treaties. In a more formal sense the European Parliament has no mandate to seek to perform functions or to exercise powers that are not stipulated in the Treaty. In a strict legal sense it was not set up to do so and the electorate did not vote for it to do so. Unlike national parliaments, it is decidedly not, from a legal point of view, the repository of community sovereignty.

In terms of social legitimacy, I believe that the European Parliament enjoys less social legitimacy than at least some of its members believe, partly because it lacks substantial powers. It is difficult for an organ with only limited relevance to gain social legitimacy. (Think of the Parliamentary Assembly of the Council of Europe that has even less social legitimacy.) The relatively low turnouts in elections are evidence of this. Another possible reason exists. The public does not see Parliament as a watchdog of the community, but only as part and parcel of the community bureaucracy. Its stand over the years on many issues alongside the Commission, counter to the position of the Council has had the same unfortunate result that has afflicted the Commission. Any public dissatisfaction with the community as a whole rubs off not only on the Commission but also on the Parliament. Strange as it may seem and wrong as it is, the public eye views the Council of Ministers as often standing up to the "faceless Eurocrats," the real watch dog of the community.

Conclusion

I suggested earlier that the purpose of the revisionist view was not to replace the progressive view but to complement it and to enrich discussion of possible future paths of development for constitutional democracy in the community.

The community is poised to take a further step on the road to European union. Clearly any such step must be accompanied by a strengthening of its democratic structures; central to this process would be an increase in the powers of the European Parliament. Nonetheless, it would be foolhardy to imagine that this step alone would eliminate problems to legitimacy in the community. Awareness of the dangers will, one hopes, be helpful in addressing and redressing them.

Notes

I am drawing on my "Parlement Européen, Intégration Européenne, Démocratie et Légitimité," in J. V. Louis and D. Waelbroeck, eds., *Le Parlement Européen Dans L' Evolution Institutionnelle* (Brussels: Editions de Université de Bruxelles, 1988). I am indebted to Professor Jean-Victor Louis of the University of Brussels, Dr. Roland Bieber of The European Parliament, Professor Frederick Schauer of the Kennedy School, Harvard, and Professor Ann Marie Burley of the University of Chicago Law School, who, responding to my request, offered a series of biting criticisms of the first draft of this chapter. They have saved me from many factual errors and weaknesses of opinion. On some points I have remained unrepentant.

1. See J. H. H. Weiler, "Attitudes of MEPs towards the European Court," 9 *E. L. Review* 169–175 (1984), which includes survey data of MEPs toward, inter alia, proposed increase of powers to the European Parliament.

2. The new Cooperation Procedure established by the SEA certainly does give the European Parliament more leverage over the other institutions, but not in the face of determined and unanimous opposition. See generally, R. Bieber, J. Pantalis, and J. Schoo, "Implications of the Single Act for the European Parliament," 23 *CML Review* 767–792 (1986); Richard Corbett, "Testing the New Procedures: The European Parliament's First Experiences with Its New 'Single Act' Powers," 27 *JCMS* 359–372 (1989).

3. Article 100a of the SEA provides for majority voting for "the achievement of the objectives set out in Article 8a," which in turn defines the objective of achieving an internal market comprising "an area without internal frontiers" There are some exceptions to the principle of majority voting. See Article 100a (2).

4. See, e.g., report being drawn up on behalf of the Committee on Institutional Affairs on the democratic deficit in the European Community (Toussaint Report), PE Doc A 2-276/87.

5. See Resolutions of Parliament of 12 July, 1990 (Martin Report).

6. See generally, G. A. Craig, *Germany 1866–1945* (Oxford: Oxford University Press, 1987), especially Chs. 15 and 18.

7. In this section I have been considerably helped by, and have drawn in particular on, the following works: Robert A. Dahl, "Federalism and the Democratic Process," in J. Roland Pennock and John W. Chapman, eds., *Liberal Democracy*, XXV Nomos (New York: New York University Press, 1983), pp. 95–108; L. Henkin, *Constitutionalism, Democracy and Foreign Affairs* (New York: Columbia University Press, 1990); Th. M. Frank, *The Power of Legitimacy Among Nations* (New York: Oxford University Press, 1990); L. Brilmayer, *Justifying International Acts* (Ithaca, NY: Cornell University Press, 1989); J. Habermas, *Legitimation Crisis* (New York: Beacon Press, 1975). My own synoptic presentation cannot do justice to the richness of the works cited.

8. See J. H. H. Weiler, "The Community System: The Dual Character of Supranationalism," 1 *Yearbook of European Law*, 267–306 (1982).

9. Of the immense literature on the 1992 program and the Single European Act I have found particularly useful: J. De Ruyt, *L'Acte Unique Européen* (Bruxelles: l'Université Bruxelles, 1989); R. Bieber, R. Dehousse, J. Pinder, and J. Weiler, eds., *1992: One European Market* (Baden-Baden: Nomos, 1988); George A. Bermann, "The Single European Act: A New Constitution for the Community?" 27 *Columbia Journal of Transnational Law*, 529–587 (1989); R. Dehousse, "1992 and Beyond: The Institutional Dimension of the Internal Market Programme," 1989/1 *Legal Issues of European Integration* 109–136 (1989); H. J. Glaesner, "The Single European Act: Attempt at an Appraisal," 10 *Fordham International Law Journal* 446–502 (1987); H. J. Glaesner, "The Single European Act," 6 *Yearbook of European Law* 283–312 (1987); H. J. Glaesner, "L'Article 100A: Un Nouvel Instrument Pour la Realisation du March Commun, 5–6," *Cahiers de Droit Européen* 615–626 (1989); Claus-Dieter Ehlermann, "The Internal Market Following the Single European Act," 24 *CML Review* 361–410 (1987); Ehlermann, "The 1992 Project: Stages, Structures, Results and Prospects," 11 *Michigan Journal of International Law* 1097–1118 (1990); Andrew Moravcsik, "Negotiating the Single European Act: National Interests and Conventional Statecraft in the European Community," 45 *International Organization* pp. 19–56 (1991).

10. L. Brilmayer, note 7, especially Chs. 1 and 3.

11. Cf. Alan Hyde, "The Concept of Legitimation in the Sociology of Law," *Wisconsin Law Review* 379–426 (1983).

12. See, e.g., statements by French and British foreign ministers before their respective parliaments on presentation of the SEA. Both ministers insisted that the Luxembourg Accord, allowing a veto power to the member states, remain intact. Hansards Vol. 96, 1986, 23 April [European Communities (amendment) Bill at p. 320; *Journal Officiel de la Republique Française*, 1986, No. 109 [1] A.N. (C.R.) 21 November 1986 at p. 6611 (debate of November 20].

13. See, e.g., J. Ostrom Moller, *Technology and Culture in a European Context* (Denmark: Handelshojskolens Forlag, 1991).

14. *Ibid.*

15. See generally, Ralf Dahrendorf, "A Confusion of Powers: Politics and the Rule of Law," 40 *Modern Law Review* 1–15 (1977).

V

CONSTITUTIONAL CONUNDRUMS IN EUROPE

16

The Necessity and Impossibility of Simultaneous Economic and Political Reform

Jon Elster

In eastern Europe, including the Soviet Union, many countries are currently trying to establish economic and political regimes that will guarantee individual rights, ensure popular participation in decision making, and generate equitable economic growth. Within a few years, China may try to follow the same path. Although disagreement may arise over the precise institutional design that would best promote these goals, there is a broad consensus concerning the basic ingredients that will have to go into any such system: constitutional democracy, competitive markets, and a welfare state. My concern here is not to discuss the issue of optimal design. Rather, I want to discuss a question that, from the practical point of view, must be prior to that issue: assuming that we identified the optimal system, how could it be brought about? Or, in other words, how to get from here to there?

In the first part of this chapter I shall make a systematic case for the conclusion that we cannot get there. *All* regimes that are minimally satisfactory when evaluated in light of the three basic goals are unattainable. Needless to say, I do not want this conclusion to be true. Nor do I have a high degree of confidence in its truth. It rests on seven distinct premises, each of which is certainly open to question. But the issue at hand is not so much whether the premises are true without exception, as whether one can identify, ex ante, the exceptions that would ensure a feasible path to a minimally satisfactory regime. My chapter, therefore, will have served its purpose if it can focus attention on this issue. The arguments, as will become apparent, are highly stylized. Vital distinctions among the various countries are ignored. For some purposes it may be ridiculous to treat China and the Czech and Slovak Republic within the same framework. Yet I believe that all of these countries have some dilemmas in common, if we define them at a sufficiently high level of abstraction. To discuss exceptions and solutions, however, one would almost certainly have to use concepts of finer grain, and look at each individual country.

In the second part of the chapter, I proceed toward the same conclusion, albeit in a less systematic manner. In addition to the basic structural dilemmas discussed in the first part of this chapter, the countries in eastern Europe will meet a number of other obstacles on their path. These include the relations to the old elite the demand for rectification and retribution the demand for welfare goods beyond what the economy can support and problems of the constitutional process. As in the first part of the chapter, the arguments are deliberately left in a sketchy state that leaves much to be filled in. Before we can come to grips with details, we must establish a framework.

An Impossibility Theorem

The countries of eastern Europe are now undertaking a double reform process, which involves the simultaneous transition to constitutional democracy and a market economy.[1] This is not a totally unprecedented process. Many Latin American countries have been faced with similar double challenges. As a participant in a conference in Buenos Aires in November 1988, on human rights and democracy in Argentina, I met with former president Raoul Ricardo Alfonsin. Argentina is a fragile democracy. It has just emerged from a particularly brutal military dictatorship and, for reasons discussed below, elected an old-style Peronist president. Economically, it is in very bad shape. Around the time of World War I the Argentine per capita product was more than five times that of Japan; today the proportion is four to one the other way around. All sectors and groups in the economy enjoy huge subsidies and other special arrangements. In this country with 30 million inhabitants, there are only 30 thousand taxpayers, individuals and corporations included. To get rid of the monopolies and protected sectors, a move to a competitive market economy is vitally necessary; yet each sector has strong political representatives that guard its privileges jealously. With this background in mind, the question I put to Dr. Alfonsin when my turn came, was the following: "In light of the events taking place in eastern Europe and China, do you think a strategy of joint economic and political reform is feasible?" He eyed me sternly, and said: "I know what you are suggesting. But let me tell you, in Latin America the strategy of implementing economic reform before political reform has been tried over and over again. It has never succeeded." If a successful reform includes an equitable distribution of income, he was right; otherwise, recent Chilean history may provide a counterexample.

The dilemmas of double reform are uniquely acute in eastern Europe, however. The step from an oligopolistic to a competitive economy is short compared to the transition from central planning to a market system. Unlike most Latin American countries, many of the communist or formerly communist countries have no prior experience with democratic modes of government. Under certain conditions, these apparent handicaps might turn into assets. We can imagine, for instance, Albert Hirschman making a strong argument to this effect. The question, once again, is whether these conditions can be identified ex ante: and here, again, I am skeptical.

As I see them, economic reform and political reform in the communist or formerly communist countries have two components each. On the economic side, both price reform and ownership reform are needed. Price reform—letting prices be determined by supply and demand, with no attempt by the state to set prices—is needed to ensure that prices reflect the real scarcity of resources, and that investment, expansion, and contraction occur in the right sectors. Ownership reforms are needed to ensure that managers have incentives to perform efficiently. Now that goal may be achieved by reforming management without changing the ownership form. The state enterprises in South Korea, for instance, are said to face hard budget constraints that create incentives for efficient behavior. It is doubtful, however, if that solution could be adopted in societies where managers and officials alike have taken it for granted that if a firm gets into trouble, the state will come to its rescue. In this context, the joint-stock form seems to be the only reliable tool.

On the political side, both democracy and constitutional guarantees for individual rights are strong desiderata, in themselves and as prerequisites for economic reform. I shall not here consider the argument that rights and democracy are values in themselves, but consider them only from an instrumental perspective. I want to point out, though, that the instrumental point of view may not provide a sufficient motivation. Tocqueville seems to have got it right when he stated:

> Nor do I think that a genuine love of freedom is ever quickened by the prospect of material rewards; indeed, that prospect is often dubious, anyhow as regards the immediate future. True, in the long run freedom always brings to those who know how to retain it comfort and well-being, and often great prosperity. Nevertheless, for the moment it sometimes tells against amenities of this nature, and there are times, indeed, when despotism can best ensure a brief enjoyment of them. In fact, those who prize freedom only for the material benefits it offers have never kept it long.[2]

I now proceed to argue that the double reform process is fraught with difficulties. I shall do so by stating seven interdependencies that cannot be obtained simultaneously.

1. To be efficient, ownership reform presupposes price reform. To allow private entrepreneurs in an economy with administered prices would encourage arbitrage, at the expense of productive activities.[3] Also, profit could not be used as an index of efficiency. Since bankruptcies would not necessarily reflect inefficiency, support measures would be introduced and, inevitably, extended to inefficient firms.

2. Conversely, to set prices free while relying on bureaucracy-cum-bargaining for the allocation of capital and labor would blunt the impact of market forces. Prices would not reflect the scarcity of resources but, ultimately, the distribution of political clout.

3. Political democracy excludes price reforms, if they lead to the worst-off being very badly off. Free price setting will certainly lead to inflation; if combined with ownership reforms, free prices will also create bankruptcies and unemployment; in China there might even be starvation. If workers have political

influence, through parties or trade unions, they will use it to stop or reverse the process. The argument that hardships necessary during transition will be no part of the steady-state system that finally emerges, may carry some weight with them, but not much, and not for very long.

4. Ownership reforms are also incompatible with political democracy, if they lead to the best-off being very well off. Private ownership leads to income inequalities that are unacceptable to large segments of the population. In eastern European societies, economic emulation has degenerated into envy, because of the lack of nonpolitical channels of upward mobility. By a twist of history, the workers of China and the Soviet Union now brandish the egalitarian ideology as a weapon against the regime itself, as they did until recently in Hungary. In doing so, they find natural allies among the conservative bureaucratic forces who want nothing more than the failure of the reforms. Although by now everybody knows that nobody believes in Marxism, the regimes that still officially subscribe to it are hard put to defend themselves against claims that are based on it.

5. Ownership reforms demand legal stability and constitutional guarantees. To ensure the willingness of economic agents to make investments that take time to mature, property rights must be respected, and retroactive legislation made impossible. In China, the absence of a stable legal system creates a very short time frame for economic agents. Even where private initiative has been allowed, as in agriculture and parts of industry, profits are used to construct private homes rather than reinvested in production. In eastern Europe, foreign investments will be hard to attract unless there are credible guarantees against confiscation and nationalization.

6. Credible constitutional rights presuppose democracy. This proposition might appear to be vulnerable. Constitutional monarchy, after all, worked in a fashion; why not a constitutional dictatorship? The difficulty is that the strength of the dictator is also his weakness: he is *unable to make himself unable* to interfere with the legal system whenever it seems expedient.[4] Constitutional monarchies were kept in line by strong intermediary bodies, whereas in modern dictatorships the society is largely atomistic. Power must be divided to ensure that the constitution will be respected.

7. Conversely, democracy without constitutional constraints is ultimately impotent; it can make decisions, but it cannot make itself stick to them. Even if individual preferences do not change, turnover among citizens and their representatives makes simple majority rule vulnerable to unstable oscillations between 51 and 49%. For another, preferences often do change for no good reason, in the heat of passion or under the influence of demagoguery.

These relationships can be summarized in a diagram. Here an arrow from X to Y means that X, to be effective, requires Y. A blocked arrow means that X is an obstacle to Y.

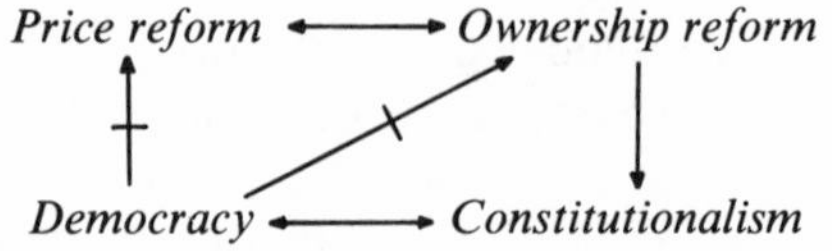

If these premises are true, full scale reform is impossible. Given the direction of the causal arrows, political reform without a transition to competitive markets might appear to be possible. In the long run, however, democracy will be undermined if it cannot deliver the goods in the economic sphere. Calls for an authoritarian regime will be made, and ultimately heard.

Now, each of these seven propositions might be contested. Fine tuning and incrementalism by the authorities, and willingness in the population to accept temporary hardships and inequalities, might sustain a feasible path to a stable market democracy. There may, to be sure, be a path that is economically and politically feasible; but how can one find it? Would eastern European workers accept an economic dictatorship that might last for a decade or more? There is no theory to guide the reformers, and no earlier experiences on which to draw. The lessons of experiments will be invalidated by the fact that people behave differently, in particular, their time frame is shorter, when they know that the current policy is an experiment than when they believe it to be definitive. In this state of radical uncertainty, the population would find many good reasons to oppose policies of hardship and abdication, in addition to the obvious bad reasons. In a country such as Poland, the leaders might solve the problem by handing over power to the International Monetary Fund, so as to be able to say credibly to the population, "Our hands are tied." But it is hard to imagine the Soviet Union going into receivership. Reports that the Soviet Union might sell off the family silver (their gold reserves, actually) to finance imports of consumption goods during the turbulent transition to a self-sustaining economy seem implausible; cautious leaders would hardly use this high-risk strategy.

Some Additional Problems

There are additional difficulties. Political culture—a factor no less important than it is elusive—might prove an obstacle. The double reform will not succeed unless the military stays out of politics and unless economic transactions are constrained by elementary norms of honesty and trust. In societies where the army has been political to the core and where hypocrisy and distrust have been indispensable for survival, these values will not emerge overnight. A delegation of Soviet legal scholars recently visited the University of Chicago to learn about the mechanics of compliance with the law. "We have excellent laws," they said, "but we do not know how to get people to obey them." It would have been tempting to answer, "Wait a few hundred years." The fact that some of the reforming countries are now trying to compress into decades or years what in the west took centuries, and to do intentionally what in the west came about largely as the unintended result of decentralized decisions, may prove a fatal difficulty.

One cannot take it for granted that the people are unanimously for democracy. Once again, I draw on evidence from Argentina. The participants in the conference I mentioned earlier also met with Antonio Cafiero, the chairman of the Peronist party, who told us how he used his power in a way that undermined his own position. After the collapse of the military regime, he undertook to inculcate respect for democratic values in the party. As part of this reorientation, he organized the party itself along more democratic lines. Traditionally, the Peronist candidate for presidential elections was chosen by the top leaders of the party, without concern for the opinions of the rank and file. As contender for the candidacy, Mr. Cafiero could just have selected himself, but this he decided not to do. He could also have opted for a limited democratization, by having the candidate chosen by the party congress, in which process, he said, he would have beaten by ten to one the other contender (and current president), Carlos Menem. He preferred, however, to have the selection made by the more than 3 million party members, who chose Mr. Menem by a narrow margin. Although Mr. Menem is much closer to the traditional Peronist mold, he had stronger popular support than the contender who wanted the candidate to be chosen by popular vote. I am not repeating the story for its historical accuracy, about which I know nothing, but to suggest that a problem of this kind may arise in the Soviet Union. Gorbachev's striking policy of reform through preemption of popular claims rather than by response to them means that democracy has largely been introduced from above. It remains to be seen whether, in genuinely free elections, the candidates that stand for constitutional democracy will be chosen. The reactionary (i.e., nondemocratic) and populist (i.e., nonconstitutional) strands in Russian culture suggest that they might not be.

To ensure a smooth transition, it may be necessary to ensure that the former elite does not lose too much, partly because their active cooperation will be needed to run the country in the future, and partly because they may obstruct, delay, or sabotage the change if they stand to lose from it. Thus the peaceful Polish transition was an important model for East Germany, by showing that it was possible to "live quietly in the new society" (a remark attributed to the East German ambassador to Poland). The difficulty, however, is that there is no guarantee that autonomous democratic institutions will respect private deals made with former oppressors. Again, the Argentinean experience is instructive. After several unsuccessful military uprisings, President Alfonsin promised the officers that he would stop prosecuting them for atrocities committed during the military regime. He then issued a directive in December 1986 that any further accusations would have to be made before the end of January 1987, knowing the judiciary usually goes on summer holiday at that time. Angered by this attempt to manipulate them, the prosecuters went on working through the vacation and probably brought more cases than they would otherwise have done. We do not yet know which deals, if any, were made with army, party, and security force leaders in Romania, East Germany, and Czechoslovakia; nor, if such deals were made, whether they will be respected by democratic institutions; nor, if they were made and are not respected, do we know whether these leaders have the power to reverse or delay the reforms. Looking to the future, the difficulty of making promises on behalf of emerging democratic institutions may also turn out to be an obstacle to a move toward democracy in China.

On the other hand, it may also be necessary to ensure that the former elite does lose its privileges and, more specifically, that it is punished. If the eastern European populations are asked to endure hardships, they will not accept the emerging trend of letting former party functionaries buy up the newly privatized enterprises. Economically, this trend may be the best solution, since there is probably nobody else who can run these firms with a modicum of competence. Politically, the trend may prove disastrous. In addition, strong claims for backward-looking justice are being made. One issue is that of rectification: the restoration of confiscated property to the original owners and their descendants. If implemented, the policy might destabilize the new regimes by recreating the large landed properties. Failure to implement, however, might have the equally destabilizing effect of alienating small landholders.

Another even more burning issue is that of retribution, not simply of criminal acts such as torture, but for illicit economic gains and political collaboration with the Soviets. In most eastern European countries, the new governments want to draw a veil over the past. As firm believers in the rule of law, they are sympathetic to the perverse claims of the gangsters from the old regime that they should not be condemned for acts that were legal at the time they were performed. (Since the laws were extremely vague and open-ended, this covers a great deal of behavior.) At a conference on constitutionalism in eastern Europe, a former Hungarian minister of justice observed that since the mid-nineteenth century 14 Hungarian prime ministers had been executed or forced into exile, adding that it is time to break with this tradition. He also mentioned that in Hungary a commission had started looking into the sources of the wealth of high officials; about 4,500 dossiers were opened, but, after a while, the investigations died out. In his opinion, these investigations were clearly anticonstitutional. I predict, however, a conflict between this appeal to the principle of legality and the equally intelligible demand that justice—real justice—be done. Whichever path is taken, it will be fraught with dangers.

The punishment of the military and the security police raises a special problem. Harsh punishments can be justified on both retroactive and forward-looking grounds, as constituting both proper retribution for the guilty and deterrence for anyone who might be tempted to violate the constitution in the future. The signal sent to the future might, however, boomerang. Although it is true that an expectation of severe punishment makes a coup less likely, it also ensures that if a coup nevertheless does occur, the leaders will not leave power peacefully.

Consider, finally, the form and substance of the constitutional processes now taking place in eastern Europe. The main difficulty seems to me to be that of finding a format that ensures legitimacy for the constitution that is finally adopted. It is clear, for instance, that the current Polish parliament does not have sufficient legitimacy. Being largely a creature of the 1989 roundtables with large Communist participation, the Sejm has a guaranteed communist representation that has no democratic grounding. Largely because of recognition of this defect, it now appears that the elaboration of the new constitution will be entrusted to the parliament that emerges in the next free elections. That solution, too, may be fragile, since a main task of a constitutional assembly is to strike the proper balance of power between the legislative and the executive branches of government. A legislative assembly that writes itself into the central place in the constitution may not enjoy sufficient legitimacy. A variant of the same problem exists in Hungary. Here, recognition of the fact that the governmental apparatus is too contaminated by the past to be trustworthy has led to a constitutional bias in favor of the legislative. But this creates another dilemma. Either the constitution is supposed to last indefinitely, in which case future generations will be saddled with a system designed for the period of transition, or the constitution is supposed to be merely transitory, in which case it will not have its intended beneficial effects on private long-term planning.

On the substantive side, the main conflict may turn out to arise over the issue of positive rights in the constitution. Two models converge to create a strong and perhaps irresistible pressure for a right to work or, at least, to unemployment benefits at a high level. On the one hand, the peoples in eastern Europe look to the welfare states in western Europe, which offer substantial unemployment benefits. On the other hand, the communist regimes have a tradition of security of employment that has been effectively contrasted with the irrational and inhumane practices of the west. If positive rights are included in the constitution, in a form that makes them into more than programmatic clauses, they could easily cripple economic development.

Notes

1. Perhaps it would be more appropriate to talk of a *triple* reform process, adding the creation of a welfare state to the economic and political transitions. Below I briefly touch on some of the additional tensions that arise when this goal is included.

2. *L'Ancien régime et la révolution*, in Alexis de Tocqueville, *Oeuvres Complètes* (Paris: Gallimard, 1952), p. 217.

3. When traveling in China in April 1988, I visited a city with private banks whose shareholders got a return of more than 30% on their investment. Normally, one would expect this to generate competition. Some banks would offer lower rates of interest on loans, while simultaneously raising the rate of interest on deposits to attract the capital to finance the loans. This does not happen, however, as the state sets an upper limit to the rate of interest on deposits. The limit is made necessary by the artificially low and politically determined rate of interest on loans from state banks to state enterprises. Since the state banks have to finance interest on deposits out of the interest they earn on loans, the low level of the latter constrains the former to be low.

4. See Jon Elster, *Solomonic Judgements* (Cambridge: Cambridge University Press, 1989), pp. 196ff.

17

Parliamentary Crisis and How to Strengthen Democracy

Klaus von Beyme

Constitutionalism and Parliamentary System: Post-1945

A crisis of parliamentary systems occurred between the two world wars. The new post-1945 constitutions were reactions and sometimes overreaction to this crisis. The founding fathers of the new republics in France, Italy, and Germany constitutionalized the parliamentary system that had developed under the old regimes (Belgium 1831, Netherlands 1815, Norway 1814, Sweden 1809, Italy, Statuto Albertino of 1848) despite their more dualistic constitutions, which did not recognize the supremacy of parliament.

France

The new constitutions were obsessively concerned with avoiding the inter-war crisis of parliamentarianism and incorporated some of the theories on the "rationalization of parliamentarianism" that had been discussed in many countries on the continent since the old debate on the authentic (e.g., British) and phony (e.g., the French) forms of parliamentarianism. France did not share this obsession; it produced in the Fourth Republic (1944–1958) a more liberal and democratic replica of the Third Republic (1871–1940). Only with deGaulle's access to power did an extreme rationalization of parliamentarianism take place in France. René Capitant and Michel Debré had developed the French version of a rationalized parliamentary system under the Fourth Republic. It took shape in 1958 without a major involvement of parliament, in a process completely dominated by de Gaulle's executive; the communication was between the executive and the people, rather than between the traditional two major powers in the parliamentary system. This process, which led to the Fifth Republic of France, was the result of the only major crisis of parliament that occurred in postwar Europe (with the exception of that of Greece in 1967). But the parliamentary crisis was only a minor aspect of the system's crisis, its inability to cope with the problem of decolonization. It is most likely that de Gaulle, with the solution of the Algerian problem, could have governed with the constitution of the Fourth Republic, although he might have preferred the post of President of the Republic with much less power than under the constitution of 1958. The crisis of 1969 showed, however, that even the power of a president under the semipresidential system of the Fifth Republic was rather limited. In France there remained alive a certain nostalgia for the "true parliamentary system" of the Fourth Republic, but it gradually withered away (François Mitterrand, once a forceful opponent of de Gaulle's system, was aptly using it for his own purposes. He completely abandoned the former concept of his Socialist Party for reparliamentarizing the system).[1]

De Gaulle's return to the semidualist system was inspired less by the presidential system than by an Orleanist preparliamentary constitutional dualism. De Gaulle's claim on a monopoly of representing the nation occasionally led to the sort of phenomena that had once made politics difficult in constitutional monarchies: for instance, when the majority in parliament felt itself to be in opposition. In a pure parliamentary system, the sort of opposition that the president of the Senate, Gaston Monnerville, tried to organize in 1962 would be scarcely conceivable.

It was not until the parliamentary election of March 1986 that there was once again talk of a new crisis in the semipresidential system. The Union Democratique Française (UDF) and Rassemblement pour la République (RPR) together wanted to do a "Macmahon" on Mitterrand; they threatened that in the event of their victory, he would have to *se soumettre ou se démettre* (yield or resign). The "cohabitation" of different majorities would be impossible right at the outset because individual components would refuse to cooperate in a coalition. This announcement caused the beginning of a renewed discussion of the possibility of transforming the Fifth Republic into a full presidential system, precisely what earlier experts regarded as impossible. No less an authority on France than Stanley Hoffmann regarded as more likely a move back toward a parliamentary system. Others put forward the "internal logic of the system" as an argument in favor of "presidentializing" it. The 1981 change in power appeared to have halted this latter development. In 1964, Mitterrand had branded the gradual expansion of the powers of the President as a "permanent coup d'état."[2] Since 1974, this candidate of the left has adjusted one step at a time to the presidential idea and the supremacy of the President.[3] Since 1981, he has even reacted in a more Gaullist fashion than de Gaulle himself over certain issues. With the eventuality in mind of hostile presidential and parliamentary majorities, even the Socialists are, once again, beginning to reopen the discussion on complete "presidentialization" of the system. Without showing any enthusiasm for the American system, Guy Mollet had, in resignation, once suggested removing the hybrid element by letting the people choose between the two models, parliamentary and presidential[4]—a well-meaning proposal but one that could certainly have demanded too much of the people and could, under certain circumstances, have left the decision to short-lived majorities. The left wing, as represented by Pierre Mauroy,[5] is still strictly against a full presidential system.

The electoral reform of 1985 (a return to proportional representation in parliament) could be seen as a step toward parliamentary government, but the decision was revised after the victory of the Gaullists during the next elections.

Other Western European Countries

In all the other western European countries more or less traditional forms of parliamentarianism took shape. Some systems modernized their constitutions rather late (Sweden 1971 and 1975) to diminish the power of future monarchies. Others saw a debate on modernization and rationalization; in Italy the Socialists demanded reform of the electoral law, a unicameral system (as introduced by Denmark and Sweden after 1945) and the popular election of the President of the Republic along the French model.[6] The critics[7] did not hesitate to show that these propositions mainly furthered the interest of the smaller coalition partner in government, such as the Socialist Party under Bettino Craxi. As they are neither in the interest of the two major parties (Communists and Christian Democrats) nor in the interest of the minor parties such as Republicans, Liberals, and Social Democrats, the debate will continue without effective results and constitutional amendments.

All the other parliamentary systems have introduced minor changes in the rules between the powers of parliamentary systems. One of the largely overrated attempts to rationalize a parliamentary system was the German constructive vote of no-confidence, imitated by Spain in 1977. This provision was a typical reaction to the problems of the Weimar Republic without knowledge of the forthcoming problems of the Republic of Bonn. When this mechanism of the constructive vote of no-confidence was used to topple a government (in 1972 unsuccessfully against Brandt, successfully in 1982 against Schmidt) it showed its detrimental sides; it forced the coalition partner who wanted change to conspire behind the back of the acting Federal Chancellor, and it contaminated the climate among the coalition partners. At best, its use was superfluous because of the considerable concentration of parties in the system. Both Germany and Spain ended up with four major parties, in spite of much fragmentation at the fringes of the party system and the new social movements.

Constitutional rationalization of parliament proved to be unnecessary, because the shifting parliamentary majorities can no longer topple most of the governments. The author has demonstrated that from 1947 to 1983 only 20 governments in Europe fell because of a vote in parliament.[8] The major reasons for cabinet disintegration were in 143 instances election and in 81 instances change of coalitions. Parliamentary systems since pre-World War II times have democratized. Elections, as they should, are now the main reason for governmental change. Parliamentary oligarchies still exist, but are less powerful. Governmental stability, always endangered in the early periods of parliamentarianism, has increased.[9] Only extremely fragmented multiparty systems such as the Finnish and the Italian (and the ethnically conflicted Belgian) show government in stability of about the one government per year (Belgium one and a half); the average duration of a government is about 30 months.[10] The most important developments diminishing the potential for crisis in parliaments in the postwar years are not the constitutional arrangements for limitations of the parliamentary principle, but the change in the party power structure of parliament.

The Changing Power Structure within Parliaments: The Parliamentary Groups

Some constitutions, especially those of Lutheran countries such as Denmark and West Germany, explicitly state the representative principle to defend deputies against inperative mandates. This defense, directed against mass pressure in the constituency and lobby pressure from organized interests, did not apply to the pressure from the party outside parliament, able as well to encroach on the free conscience of parliamentarians.

In the days of the older parliamentarianism, prior to World War II, since Maurice Duverger,[11] the assumption had been that the number of parliamentary groups outside of parliament depended on the genesis and social background of the respective party: bourgeois parties developed within parliament knew a hegemony of the parliamentary group; Socialist parties, on the other hand, a preponderance of the Weltanschauungs' Party outside of parliament. These differences have disappeared. In Socialist parties parliamentary groups gained in power. In bourgeois parties (especially among the Christian Democrats, less so among conservative parties) the growing importance of members, party conventions, and party democracy has strengthened the party outside.

The Development of *Parteienstaat*

The development of the *Parteienstaat* or *partitocrazia* may have weakened parliament as a whole, but it has strengthened cabinet stability and the capacity for continuous state intervention on the lines of a coherent program. To answer the question of how to strengthen democracy we must know the internal power structure in the parties and parliamentary groups that streamlines parliamentary decisions. Experts suggest that the proper units of analysis are not parliament as a whole or even parliament minus the government, but these party groupings and/or combinations of them.[12] In modern parliamentary systems very few decisions are made on a nonparty basis, such as "free votes" in the House of Commons,[13] or "nonparty," or all-party committees of one sort or another (where the backbencher behaves more like an American congressman, for whom the executive–legislative dimension is sometimes more important than the party dimension). In those rare committees the backbencher may feel free of party bias and able to confront the government: "you can get the minister and grill him—grill him in all-party atmosphere."[14] In general, however, the partisan dimension is the most important unit of analysis of behavior in parliaments. There are now few parliaments in which individuals, minorities, or even parliament as a whole have considerable importance vis-à-vis the government, and where the centers of parliamentary decision are dispersed to the extent, say, of the Italian parliament.[15]

Democratization of parliaments developed along with party dominance in legislative assemblies, resulting, in most cases, in the increasing influence of the parties outside of parliament on parliamentary decisions.

The development of the *Parteienstaat*, which according to some German theories made the old system of liberal representative democracy an obsolete form of the parliamentary system,[16] has indeed shifted the balance of power in all modern mass parties. This shift is more marked with the concentration of the party in the postwar period, and with the bourgeois parties having become modern "catchall parties," not restricting themselves to certain social or religious groups. The most notable example of such a party is certainly the CDU in Germany, which can be called the first authentic *Volkspartei* in western Europe.

Development of Social Democratic Parties

This shift in the power balance also owes something to the development of social democratic parties in northern Europe, from the ghetto of working class subculture to the modern catchall party that attracts more and more groups from the middle class and the intelligentsia. Again, Germany is frequently noted as having the most outspoken "tweedledee-tweedledum" party system. A comparison of the statutes of the two biggest parties there shows that the internal provisions for the relationship between party and parliamentary groups are almost identical: the Social Democrats make the parliamentary group responsible to the central institutions of the party only in a very indirect way (Section 20) and the Christian Democrats appear only slightly more in favor of the autonomy of the parliamentary group: "resolutions of the party conventions and the program are the basis of the work of the CDU parliamentary group."[17] The statutes of most other social democratic parties contain similar statements.

In northern Europe one sometimes finds greater differences between the rules of bourgeois parties and those of social democratic parties. The precarious equilibrium between party and parliamentary group, attributed to a middle stage of development in Duverger's typology, finds formal expression in party rules such as those in the statutes of the Finnish Centre Party, which prescribe "common deliberations of party delegations and the parliamentary group on the governmental policy."[18] In Switzerland the Conservatives emphasize the complete autonomy of the parliamentary group; since 1966 the Social Democrats have provided only a certain autonomy for the parliamentary group within the general resolutions of the party congress of the party leadership.[19]

In the postwar period, one observes a clear global tendency toward the parliamentarization of formerly antiparliamentary groups, though one still finds mental reservations about the majority principle of parliamentary government in the programs of some conservative Christian parties (such as the Christian Historical Union in the Netherlands). The socialists have adapted to parliamentary government step by step, via the "ministerial socialism" of individual socialists in bourgeois government, until the complete socialist takeover of governmental responsibility. Parliamentary socialization has integrated even the more radically minded socialists into governing socialist parties; surveys among the younger rebels in the parliamentary groups show that these either dropped out of the parliament or gave up certain ideas about the direct realization of the "public will" as formulated by groups in the electorate outside parliament.[20]

The Parties and Information Systems

Recent surveys of parliamentarians indicate that to some extent Duverger's typologies are still viable. In a polarized party system such as that of Italy, the Communist deputy is party oriented in activities and attitudes; the Christian Democratic deputy looks towards parliament and his parliamentary group.[21] Bourgeois parties are not, however, completely concentrated on internal parliament information systems; surveys in other countries demonstrate that their channels of information are less closely connected with the extraparliamentary party than with interest groups and administrative agencies. Empirical inquiries show that the representatives of bourgeois parties usually demand greater independence from the parliamentary groups (not only from the party outside), and tend to emphasize the "free mandate" more than do the Social Democrats.

Nevertheless, occasional surveys cannot verify once and for all the global typologies concerning the relations between parties and parliamentary groups. Clear changes mean these typologies are less useful; the hypotheses need further differentiation. For instance, the figures for Italy indicate that there must have been greater variation in the use made there of the different political parties as primary sources of information when the Communists were still a party that reluctantly participated in parliament, and when the predominance of small cliques of Christian Democrats was so unbroken that the mass mobilization of the party outside parliament seemed to be less necessary.

The more evident orientation toward the party of deputies of workers' parties may, in many cases, cause frustration and disenchantment. In Britain only 18% of Labour deputies (as against 80% of the Conservative party) considered their party head office as a major source of information; the remainder were considerably dissatisfied with the information service and research support.[22] Nor is it likely that the help given to Conservative deputies is superior; conservatives simply expect less, and are therefore less often disappointed.

Surveys of other parliamentary systems show more emphasis given to the hierarchical structure of information. In multiparty systems, such as in the Netherlands, the smaller parties have so little help from their head offices that they must rely to a greater degree on private sources and interest groups. Party specialists, who depend heavily on a few extraparliamentary actors and on expert knowledge, run the larger parties.[23] Some "incentive studies," which explain political behavior in terms of "strong inner needs," overlook this hierarchical structure of information and activity.[24]

The question of how to strengthen parliament implies among other things the pluralization of information, which has certainly increased since the development of new social movements. Deputies under pressure of party discipline also communicate more with groups outside the parties proper. Within the party the tendency to form wings and opinion groups has increased as well. This tendency is clear in all the major catchall parties in the 1980s, most strikingly in the German Socialdemocratische Partei Deutschland (SPD).

Oddly enough, the ecological parties have tried to impose the most rigorous restrictions on the individual behavior of their deputies by the devices of rotation in office and of limitation on income. The result has been to strengthen the collective bodies enormously and to give the parliamentary group considerable power over their members because the deputies are more dependent financially and organizationally on their party than deputies in traditional parties.[25] This practice has, however, generated countervailing forces within the ecological parties; *correntocrazia* and internal party strife develop more disintegrating force than in other groups.

Democratization of Parliamentary Systems by Oppositions

The conditions of the party state doomed to failure the hopes of many liberals, radicals, and libertarian socialists to democratize parliaments by strengthening the individual deputy. The "decline of parties" did not take place. Although the parties lost members in some countries, and party identification did decline in many places (though less strikingly in Europe than in America), they were able to strengthen their roles through elite recruitment and policy formulation. Both functions predominantly take place in parliament.

Not even referenda, except in Switzerland which has no parliamentary system, were able to break the power of party machines. Italy is the most striking example. In the 1970s and 1980s the people in most referenda voted as they were told by their respective parties. Attempts to kill progressive parliament bills (e.g., with respect to divorce and abortion) failed. Even unpopular institutions such as public subsidies for the parties were not revoked by popular decision. Hopes for counterlegislation by the people failed to materialize.

The only way to democratize parliament and the dominating parliamentary majorities and governments has been to increase responsiveness to popular demands from below. Extraparliamentary oppositions and new social movements have been more successful in this respect during the 1970s and 1980s than ever before in the history of parliamentarism.

New oppositions, even when they think of themselves as fundamental dissenters, now have more impact on parliamentary decision than in the early periods of parliamentary government. For instance, the party establishment harassed the Greens by petty impediments when they first entered parliament; nevertheless they integrated fairly quickly into the system. In cases where vital issues were at stake they entered informal coalitions; on the German Länder level they have twice entered a formal coalition.

The opposition's ability to influence legislation can sharpen its ideological zeal. This potential is least developed in the Westminster model of a winner-takes-all situation. A landslide victory of the government party, such as Mrs.

Thatcher's in 1983, can demoralize the opposition. Labour attendance in the Commons these days is so poor that it is beginning to worry even the government Whips, and Labour Whips appear to have difficulty in finding speakers.[26] Loose talk about "postparliamentary democracy" starts only in countries with a weak opposition. Fortunately, the British public still rates Parliament highly because it does not differentiate between the formal and the real powers of the House.[27]

Opposition Tactics in Parliament

To study the impact of ideological orientations our analysis must concentrate on program realization in parliament. As in the electoral arena, oppositions tend to concentrate on a couple of issues dear to them. (Specialization in debate has been studied for Denmark,[28] but the results in a multiparty system with a high degree of fragmentation can hardly be generalized as the Danish party system encourages parties to concentrate on a few issues per se.)

The high degree of issue specialization also serves opposition parties' interests *vis-à-vis* the electorate. Emphasis on more than six or seven issues does not mobilize the electorate as much as it creates confusion;[29] this observation is also more or less true for the opposition's parliamentary behavior. It less adequately describes the exercise of control powers, in which the opposition parties can use all available issues to inquire, to investigate, and to try to mobilize by criticism of the government. In most parliaments, however, the oppositions give away a good deal of control power because of their tendency to expand issues to general discussion, as demonstrated in the debates on the annual budgets; therefore, the bureaucracies responsible for the accounts are increasingly more effective in controlling the governments than are the oppositions. There is not much leeway on this issue anyway because oppositions are also handicapped by the fact that 95% of most budgets are not open to annual changes, even if the oppositions win the arguments. Another handicap of oppositions manifests itself in France, where too-centralized a distribution of parliamentary seats exists. The French "*parachutés*" (candidates that have been imposed by the party leadership) sometimes strengthen local aspects of the debate to gain a higher profile in their constituencies. The general powerlessness of parliament also affects the local interests of opposition parties, which fail to control government in its major policy orientations.[30]

In times of modernization euphoria in the mid-1970s, wide discussion of the participation of parliament in expectative planning took place. Oppositions benefitted because of the lack of implementation of all of the ideas for a parliamentary involvement in planning. The exercise of the legislative powers of oppositions demands a greater concentration on a few issues, simply because they can undertake only a limited amount of work and because the help of parliamentary staff cannot substitute for the direct and indirect help that the bureaucracy gives to the parties in power. The party system and its structure are important intervening variables here. In a quasi-two-party system or in one where there is a net division of the political arena into two political camps (Scandinavia, the former West Germany; Austria is an exception), the opposition usually has greater incentives to introduce counterproposals than they do in the consociated climate of a multiparty system with its blurred boundaries between the ruling coalition and the temporary opposition.

The more ideologically minded the opposition is, the more it tends to apply a "holistic" strategy of counterproposals, which are alternative in every aspect, as the SPD did under Kurt Schumacher. With its growing integration into the political system, the zeal of the SPD for using legislative initiatives as an instrument of opposition weakened. During their time in opposition, the Christian Democrats (CDU) preferred to use their power to initiate calculated inputs by amendments to SPD bills and, especially during the phase of the decline in Chancellor Helmut Schmidt's majority after 1980, did so with remarkable success, usually concentrating on projects in economic and social policies.

Cooperative Opposition

Sometimes the opposition has to be cooperative, however, even in the use of its amending power. Usually, to avoid the blame for the failure to resolve an urgent problem it does not press so many amendments as to force the government to abandon the project.

Especially with regard to the legislative function, cooperative opposition is a widespread phenomenon—a fact that renders the older dualist typology of cooperative and competitive oppositions irrelevant. The great majority of all bills in parliaments pass unanimously or almost unanimously. In Germany, bills whose contents are close to the ideological core beliefs of the parties (e.g., the distribution of wealth or additional rights of participation) can expect less opposition cooperation. Even those oppositions dubbed "unfair" by Giovanni Sartori, like the Italian Communists, have joined ranks with the Christian Democrats to support some there-quarters of legislation.[31]

Is this "irresponsible" opposition? In many parliamentary systems highly competitive opposition parties show traits of "parliamentary cogovernment" in crisis: in Italy during the time Aldo Moro was held prisoner by terrorists and in Germany from the time of the building of the Wall to the Schleyer incident.

In multiparty systems the differentiations between oppositional attitudes are much more difficult to identify. Even parties in government are partly in opposition on some issues. In a political system with proportional government, as in Switzerland, issues structure areas of conflict. Sometimes occasional governmental opposition attitudes are found only by studying the behavior of the parties during the referenda in the various cantons.[32] What has been dubbed the "helvetic malaise" is partly caused by the two ways to initiate legislation by parliamentary initiative and by popular referendum, which encourages the blurring of opposition and government parties, and invites occasional oppositions on many levels.

Oppositions in the postmodern parliamentary system (postmodern being a recent term for nonhegemonic systems with power dispersed)[33] are more quickly integrated into the system than in earlier periods. What they lose in thrust towards rapid change they gain in influence.

New parties acquired *Koalitionsfähigkeit*, the ability to form coalitions, sooner than older ones. To achieve this capability took the Communist and right-wing parties decades. The German Green Party has been partly accepted on the *Land* level after only a couple of years. Even though the new oppositions (for example, the Greens) were initially discriminated against by denial of their fair proportion of committee seats or by application of the whole rigor of parliamentary rules rarely evoked in cases of poor discipline by deputies of the established parties, they have become candidates for coalitions in a much shorter period of time than used to be the case. Political systems learn with regard to new oppositions: some SPD members claim that a coalition with the ecologists is necessary for sociotherapeutic reasons, that is, to further an integration process.[34] Considerations of this kind apparently motivated Mitterrand to accept the Communists in the new government coalition in 1981, though he did not need them for a parliamentary majority. In spite of a lot of noise in some European parliaments, oppositions have broadened and have become more rapidly integrated. All the forcasts prophesying transformations of the political systems have proven premature, even in cases where national party systems did not gravitate back to normalcy (e.g., in Denmark in contrast to Norway).

Conclusion

The constitutionalization of parliamentary systems was primarily a response to the crisis of parliamentarianism between the two world wars. This crisis of parliamentarianism and the occasional constitutional crises in the postwar period accompanying changes in regimes (in France 1958, in Greece 1967) were not caused by the parliamentary crisis.

Social scientists increasingly abandoned the legal zeal to rationalize parliamentarianism to make it workable. Parliamentarianism became workable not because of new rational constitutional devices but through its acceptance by all the relevant parties, including the Communists. Party concentration in many countries, most strikingly in Germany, France, and Spain, overcame former deadlocks in the system. Highly fragmented systems, such as Belgium, Finland, and Italy, compensated for this weakness by oligarchic *partitocrazia*.

Some countries recognized a crisis of the system, which they perceived as a crisis of the party system, hardly as a crisis of the parliamentary institutions. The changes being discussed, in the 1990s in Italy, for example, do not touch the core of government/parliament relations. Most countries have little inclination to imitate a semipresidential system, such as de Gaulle created in France, to streamline the parliamentary system.

Shifts in the power structure of parties, not the individual institutions forming part of the parliamentary system, create changes in parliament. The party state penetrated the parliamentary systems; individual deputies are more subject to party discipline than ever before. Differences in the degree of independence in the information system of the deputies still exist between bourgeois and worker's parties. Even the Green parties, in spite of their libertarian outlook, have made their deputies more dependent on the parliamentary group and party conventions than have the conventional political forces.

Democratization of parliamentary groups did not occur through the strengthening of the individual deputy and the securing of his constitutional independence. The attempt to break the power of party machines in parliament via referenda as a type of counterlegislation failed; where the instrument is used frequently the majorities in the referenda largely reflect the majority in parliament (with the exception of Switzerland).

The greater impact of new oppositions is the most effective way of strengthening democracy. They more quickly integrate into the systems than before, and use opposing, amending, and cooperative strategies.

Despite many prognoses that parliament and the established parties in it would be weakened, parliament remained the most important arena for decision making, although most of the decisions first take form at the level of party conventions, coalition agreements, and later in cabinets and ministries. But modern parliamentary systems are no longer judged by the model of separation of powers. They are an interlinked system in which government has the predominant position—as long as it commands a parliamentary majority.

Neither corporatism and the big interests nor the social movements have made parliaments superfluous. Many of the theories on the crisis of parliament start from too simple a theory of representation and overlook the multitude of forms of participation, representation, and governance in a modern society.

Notes

1. Klaus von Beyme, *America as a Model* (New York: St. Martin's, 1987), p. 56; François Mitterrand, *Le côup d'état permanent* (2nd ed., Paris: Juillard, 1984).
2. François Mitterrand, note 1.
3. Oliver Duhamel, *La gauche et la Ve République* (Paris: PUF, 1980), p. 279.
4. Guy Mollet, *Quinze ans après. La Constitution de 1958* (Paris: A. Michel, 1973), p. 150.
5. Pierre Mauroy, *A gauche* (Paris: A. Michel, 1985), p. 14.
6. Guiliano Amato, *Una Republica da Reforma* (Bologna: Il Mulino, 1980).
7. Gianfrano Pasquino, *Degenerazioni die partiti e riforme instituzionali* (Bari: Laterza, 1982).
8. Klaus von Beyme, *Political Parties in Western Democracies* (New York: St. Martin's, 1985), p. 329.
9. Figures in Klaus von Beyme, *Die parlamentarischen Regierungssysteme* (München: Piper, 1973), p. 875.
10. Klaus von Beyme, *Political Parties in Western Democracies* (New York: St Martin's 1985), p. 331.
11. Maurice Duverger, *Les partis politiques* (Paris: Colin, 1977).
12. Anthony King, *British Members of Parliament: A Self-Portrait* (London: Macmillan, 1974), p. 13.
13. P. G. Richards, *The Backbenchers* (London: Faber, 1972).
14. Anthony King, note 12, p. 101.

15. Guiseppe Di Palma, "Institutional Rules and Legislative Outcomes in the Italian Parliament," 1 *Legislative Studies Quarterly* 147–179 (1976), p. 150.

16. Gerhard Leibholz, *Strukturprobleme der Modernen Demokratie* (Karlsruhe: C. F. Müller, 1967), p. 93.

17. Ossip Flechtheim, *Die Parteien der Bundesrepublik Deutschland* (Hamburg: Hoffman & Campe, 1974), pp. 360, 364.

18. J. Nousianinen, *Finlands politiska partier* (Helsinki: Schildt, 1969), p. 36.

19. Erich Gruner, *Die Parteien in der Schweiz* (Bern: Francke, 1969), p. 205.

20. Bernhard Badura and J. Reese, *Jungparlamentarier in Bonn. Ihre Sozialisation im Deutschen Bundestag* (Stuttgart: Fromann–Holzboog, 1976).

21. R. Leonardi et al., "Institutionalization of Parliaments and Parliamentarisation of Parties in Italy," 3 *Legislative Studies Quarterly* 161–186 (1978), p. 173.

22. A Barker and M. Rush, *The Member of Parliament and His Information* (London: Allen & Unwin, 1970), p. 234.

23. M. P. van Schendelen, "Information and Decision Making in the Dutch Parliament," 1 *Legislative Studies Quarterly* 231–250 (1976).

24. O. H. Woshinsky, *The French Deputy: Incentives and Behaviour in the National Assembly* (Lexington, MA: Heath, 1973), p. 3.

25. H. Fogt, "Die Grünen in den Parlamenten der Bundesrepublik," 14 *Zeitschrift für Parlamentsfragen* 500–517 (1983).

26. Margaret von Hattem, "The State of Parties in Parliament. The Labour Party's Second Term in Opposition," 55 *The Political Quarterly* (1984) 364–372.

27. Philip Norton, *The Commons in Perspective* (Oxford: Martin Robertson, 1981), p. 245.

28. Erik Damgaard, *Folketinget under Forändring* (Copenhagen: Samfunsvidenskabeligt Forlag, 1977), p. 205.

29. Ian Budge and Dennis J. Farlie, *Explaining and Predicting Elections* (London: Allen & Unwin, 1983), p. 15.

30. Pierre Birnbaum et al., *Réinventer le Parlement* (Paris: Flammarion, 1977), p. 34.

31. Franco Cazzola, *Governo e opposizione nel Parlamento Italiano* (Mailand: Giuffré, 1974), p. 99.

32. Henry H. Kerr, *Parlement et société en Suisse* (Saint-Saphorin: Georgi, 1981).

33. Richard Rose, *The Post-modern President* (London: Chatham House, 1988), p. 2.

34. Bernd E. Heptner, *Politik als Therapie. Warum die hessische SPD am Bündnis mit den Grünen festhält, Frankfurter Allgemeine Zeitung* 12 (4 Oct. 1985).

18

Iberian Case Study: The Constitutionalism of Democratization

Jordi Solé Tura

The notion of an "Iberian Case" is a somewhat eccentric one. Of course, Spain and Portugal are geographically close and, at first glance, their similarities are marked: both countries were subdued by dictatorships through the same periods of the present century, both experienced important processes of transition from dictatorship to democracy in basically pacific modes and in the same decade, and both entered the European Economic Community at the same time. Further, the modern political history of both countries demonstrates an astounding set of parallelisms: the source of the first Portuguese Constitution (1822) is the first Spanish Constitution of 1808; the nineteenth-century civil wars between absolutists and liberals are parallel processes; the dictatorship of General Primo de Rivera in Spain corresponds to the military dictatorship in Portugal before the *Estado Novo* of Oliveira Salazar; and the "revolution" of April 1974 in Portugal and the Constitution of 1976 are immediate precedents of the beginning of the transition and the constitutional process in Spain.[1]

Beneath these similarities, however, significant differences between the two countries are important. The first is that historical events have produced strong mutual feelings of distrust, even of hostility. Portugal developed early as an independent political entity at odds with the Spanish kingdom of Castile. After a short period of political union under the Spanish King Philip II at the end of the sixteenth century, Portugal became an independent country in the seventeenth century. Since then, Spain has nourished fears of certain forms of Portuguese nationalism; and Portugal has seen Spain as the only real threat to her independence, something similar to the foreign enemy that haunts and sustains all kinds of nationalism. In fact, even today both friendship and mistrust characterize the relationship between Spain and Portugal. Politically and culturally, Spain tends to look toward northern and central Europe and Latin America rather than toward Portugal; Portugal still fears the danger of Spanish hegemonism.

The second significant difference is that because of differences in social structure, until recently Portugal has been both a colonial power and a metropolitan agrarian society, with internal zones of underdevelopment and backwardness. Spain has, of course, marked inequalities between developed and undeveloped zones, but its industrial economy and its tertiary sector are more developed than Portugal's. Finally, because the development of and the results of their respective transition processes to democracy have been so different, so have been the resulting political and institutional structures, even if later developments tend toward greater similarity.

Thus, to refer to an "Iberian Case" is to reduce its complexity. Reviewing parallelisms and differences, we can speak of two processes of transition from dictatorship to democracy, close in space and time, but fundamentally different in their origins, their causes, their developments, and their constitutional solutions. For illumination of these differences, I shall deal with these three topics from a comparative perspective.

The Roots of Democracy

In Portugal, the transition to democracy began on April 25, 1974 with a military coup. The transition in Spain developed as a complex civilian process after the death of General Franco on November 20, 1975. Each of these events was preceded by long dictatorships and unique historical developments.

Portugal

The Portuguese dictatorship began in 1926 with the military coup of General Gomes de Costa: later, under the rule of General Antonio Carmona as President of the Republic and Oliveira Salazar as Prime Minister, it developed as a "civilian" dictatorship, the *Estado Novo*, largely inspired by the Catholic corporate system promoted by the Vatican in the 1930s and by Italian fascism. It was, of course, a one-party system, the *Uniao Nacional*; all civil and political rights were suppressed. The dictatorship was neither "industrialist" nor "developmentalist" in character; under Oliveira Salazar's rule, Portugal was immobilized in its internal economic and social structures and in its relation to its colonial territories.

Portugal was itself an undeveloped country whose economy depended largely on the exploitation of colonial resources by a monopolistic group of financial and commercial corporations; the paradigmatic example was the *Companhia Uniao Fabril* (CUF). These Portuguese ruling groups were themselves largely subordinated to British capital; and in fact, the Portuguese colonial empire was a subsystem of the British African empire. When political movements for self-determination and independence began in Africa, and Great Britain and France moved to other systems of relationships with former colonies, Portugal remained locked in old schemes of colonial domination; it used military repression and colonial wars to deal with independence movements in Angola,

Mozambique, Guinea-Bissau, and Cape Verde. A deep financial and social crisis resulted (which occurred simultaneously with the general crisis of the seventies in Western countries), accompanied by an increasing feeling of uneasiness and rebellion in the colonial Army and followed by the military defeat in Africa and the breakdown of the national economy. These circumstances were the immediate cause of the military uprising of 1974.

The Portuguese colonial Army was the main protagonist of the fall of the dictatorship. This crucial fact implies two others: first, the army itself had the capacity, in its contact with colonial realities, to develop in its own ranks a quest for democracy; second, the Portuguese people were too unorganized, socially and politically, to be able to take the main initiative against the dictatorship. Both facts were decisive for the development of the transition process, a process in which the Army had a key position as a leading force.

Spain

The historical background and the actual development of the transition process in Spain differed significantly. Portugal remained a colonial power until the 1970s; Spain had lost the remnants of its colonial empire in the last years of the nineteenth century, after the humiliating war with the United States. Portugal became a Republic in 1910; the Spanish political system remained a centrist, militarist, authoritarian, and clerical Monarchy, closed to political reforms and extremely hostile to liberal and left-wing movements, as well as to bourgeois nationalist movements. Every attempt to implement democratic reforms under the Monarchy resulted in a radical clash between the Monarchy and the republic. This clash was the main dividing line in modern Spanish political history; after unsuccessful attempts to establish and stabilize a Republic, the clash exploded in 1936 into the bloodiest civil war in all of Spain's history.

In 1923, in the Monarchy of Alphonso XIII, Spain knew its first military dictatorship, that of General Primo de Rivera, largely inspired by Italian fascism and similar to the Carmona–Salazar *Estado Novo* in Portugal. The fall of this dictatorship in 1930 opened the way to the Spanish Republic in 1931; the King, refusing to abdicate, was outlawed and fled the country. The period of the Republic was a time of social and ideological turmoil; it raised great hope and promised long-awaited social and political reforms. In fact, it was the great opportunity to fight underdevelopment and to modernize Spain, politically and culturally. But the rebellion of the Spanish Army, headed by General Francisco Franco, put an end to all hopes and expectations; after the defeat of the Republic in 1939, a bloody repression inaugurated 40 years of military dictatorship.

This long and ruthless dictatorship did not end as did Portugal's as a result of a colonial crisis or of a military uprising, but by the conjunction of several factors. The first, obviously, was the death of General Franco, and the inability of the dictatorship to exist without him or to face the unresolved contradictions of Spanish society, accumulated throughout the 1960s and 1970s. The second involved the new conditions created by Spanish society in a European context, which made impossible the continuity of the nondemocratic institutions, practices, and ideas imposed by the Franco regime after the Civil War in a country then politically and economically isolated. The third conjunctive factor was the painful but effective reconstruction of the democratic political and union vanguards destroyed by the repression after the Civil War. The fourth was that, notwithstanding this reconstruction, the anti-Franco opposition did not succeed in transforming itself into a vast popular movement, able to defeat and overthrow the dictatorship.

Consequently, the transition to democracy in Spain began and developed as a succession of clashes and agreements between the "reformists" of the Franco regime itself, who understood the ineluctability of change and wanted to control it, and the groups of the democratic opposition, progressively united in a quest for democratic change without limitations or exclusions.

The overall result was the achievement of democracy, the drafting and promulgation of the democratic constitution of 1978, the restoration of democratic liberties and civil rights, the free activity of political parties and unions, the establishment of a federal kind of system of political autonomies, and the opening of the country to the European Community. But this result was strongly nuanced by the continuity of the main institutions of the Franco state that remained untouched: the armed forces and the security forces, the judicial system, the public administration system, the public corporations, and the privileges of the great private corporations and the Catholic Church.

Therefore, the fundamental problem of the transition to democracy was to consolidate the new system, to strengthen its supports, to solve the great inherited historical problems, such as the conflict between the Monarch and the Republic, the conciliation between Spanish national identity and the pluralism of national and regional identities, and, at the same time, to incorporate into the democratic system, without traumas or new civil conflicts, the institutions of the previous regime. The awareness of this need was the underpinning of the consensus that marked and led the transition process to democracy in Spain.

The Developments of the Democratic Process

Portugal

Oliveira Salazar ruled Portugal from 1933 until 1970. After his death, his successor, Marcelo Caetano, sought to balance minor internal reform and the maintenance of the dictatorial rule. He failed; change became inevitable. After unsuccessful attempts of some military conservatives to control the change, the military coup of April 25, 1974 installed in power a junta of seven officers from the *Movimento des Forças Armadas* (Armed Forces Movement or MFA). This movement was predominantly left-wing, blanced between radicals and moderates, all of whom were deeply influenced by their experience in the Portuguese colonies and clearly sympathetic with anticolonialist movements.

The military coup restored political liberties and civil rights; political parties became active; but the leadership remained with the MFA. Some radical measures were taken; the political police forces were dissolved and many of its members jailed. The conservative and rightist forces, compromised along with the fallen regime, were unorganized; the party balance shifted clearly to the left, where the Communist Party was highly influential and had close links with some of the military leaders. A unitarian provisional government was formed, under the direction of the MFA and with the participation of political parties, all of which were weak except for the communists. Communists appeared to be very strong in the new unions, and communism became a major issue as, with the restoration of democratic liberties throughout the country, a great wave of political, social and economic demands, particularly for agrarian reform, arose.

In *Time and Chance*, James Callaghan sums up this situation: "Initially, these two groups (the MFA and the Communist[s]) were perhaps the only bodies sufficiently well-organized to be able to step into the power vacuum. In a country starved of political, social and cultural freedom since the 1930s, the coup was greeted enthusiastically."[2]

A different political framework emerged from the first general elections for a constituent Assembly. Despite some significant oscillations, this framework has remained stable: at left, a dominant Socialist party, with contending trends in its ranks, gathered around Mário Soares; a hardline but minority Communist Party; at center-right, a consistent *Partido Popular Democratico* (PPD), later transformed into the *Partido Social Democrata* (Social Democratic Party, or PSD), with contending internal trends, under the leadership of Sa Carneiro; at right, the *Centro Democratico Social* (CDS). This party scheme has only been partially modified by the brief life of the *Partido Renovador Democratico* (PRD), headed by the former President of the Republic, General Ramalho Eanes. The transition process in Portugal was characterized by the difficult relationship between the leading MFA and the political parties and by the changing balance of power between all these forces in a society that, after the first period of radical demands and reforms, looked for moderation and stability as the basis for new internal equilibriums.

The Portuguese constitution of 1976 expressed the hopes and expectations of the parties and the balance of power of the first period. It is a constitution marked by an overall socialist orientation, both in its general aims and in its concrete goals, e.g., collective property. Its most specific feature is the constitutional role of the Armed Forces, which became something like the highest institution of guarantee and control, functioning in a complex interaction with the President of the Republic, the Government, and the Parliament.

The main role of the Socialist party was to ensure a "civil" development of this original impulse. In 1976, the Socialists won the majority, although not an overall majority; its leader, Mário Soares, formed the first constitutional government with General Ramalho Eanes as President of the Republic. The provisional period was over, but the great problems of Portuguese society emerged in all areas; the Socialist Party was unable to retain its majority. Since then, the building of Portuguese democracy has developed around three major issues: the reduction of the military role in the constitutional system, the definition of a workable system of political alliances between the major parties, and the economic development of a country that changed abruptly from the immobility of the Salazarist system to a new and extremely mobile competitive system, without the resources of the colonies and within the framework of the European Economic Community. The problem of alliances has been a major one, as the Communist Party is excluded, or excludes itself, from any possible majority. The Socialist Party has shifted from minority governments to alliances with center parties and has paid a high price for the shift in terms of internal homogeneity and of electoral support. Finally, the center-right party, the PSD, under the leadership of Anibal Cavaco Silva, won the absolute majority in the last general elections; for the first time since 1974 a single party stable majority governs the country.

Spain

In Spain, the transition to democracy began, not with a military coup, but with the ending of military rule at the death of General Franco in 1975. According to plan King Juan Carlos succeeded Franco; confronted with the alternative to continue the *franquist* system, or to advance toward democracy, he chose the latter way, with the help of all the political forces, those coming from *franquism* and those coming from underground opposition.

The end of *franquism* coincided with the worst economic crisis in recent Spanish history. Further, the building and implementation of a democratic system had to be dealt with in the context of the inheritance of the state apparatus of Franco's regime. The only way to cope with this situation democratically was to count heads and to establish a clear line between those who wanted democracy and those who wanted a return to dictatorship. Every political force had to make a difficult complex decision about this dividing line, a decision about some of the most intractable unresolved historical conflicts (e.g., that between the Monarchy and the Republic, that of national identity, and that of pacific separation between state and church). The decision was also conditioned by memories of the recent past. The Franco regime had maintained the memory of the Civil War as the basic source of its own legitimacy and as the basis of the general distinction between winners and losers; the Civil War weighed on the collective conscience of the immense majority of Spaniards as a trauma that must not be repeated. Finally and significantly, the Spanish society of the 1970s was a society of new generations, a society that wanted to be rid of dictatorship but wanted to achieve democracy without any major conflicts, in peace. All the significant political forces understood these issues; all became aware that the only way to proceed with the establishment of democracy and consolidation was by consensus.

The achievement of consensus was not easy. Differing political forces emerged after Franco's death. Inside the Franco regime developed a reformist movement or, more precisely, some reformist movements. The first one that managed to take the lead in the post-Franco government was the group headed by the former Minister of Information, Manuel Fraga Iribarne; he intended a limited reform, that would include the Socialist Party but exclude the Communist Party and the rest of the left. Failure soon followed such a limited democracy in which the "accepted" democratic forces would be compelled to complicity in the restraint of democratic rights. It failed also because emergent social movements soon overflowed the limits set by the government.

The second government of the new post-Franco monarchy was headed by another former Franco minister, Adolfo Suarez. Mr. Suarez himself understood that the only way to create a democratic process was to allow it to develop without the limitations that had caused the failure of the previous attempt. At the same time, the opposition forces succeeded in establishing a unique and unitarian platform, including all the significant groups from Christian Democrats to Communists. These political alignments were the basis of the final agreement between the *franquist* reformists and the opposition. General elections were held on June 15, 1977, with free participation of all the political parties.

Two facts emerged from the political constellation that resulted. First, the victory of the political forces that wanted democracy was overwhelming; in the elected Parliament, there was not a single partisan of the Franco dictatorship. The way was open to a constituent process. Second, no single political force was able to lead alone or to implement alone the constitutional reforms and the consolidation of the new democracy. The consequence was obvious: consensus was needed to draft the constitution, to implement the reforms and to cope with the more urgent problems, especially the economic ones.

The Spanish Constitution of 1978 was drafted by a group of seven deputies elected by the first democratic Parliament, the *Congreso de los Diputados*; the seven represented the elected political alignment. Three of them represented the *Union de Centro Democratico* (the UCD), the party headed by Mr. Suarez and formed of *franquist* reformers, Christian Democrats, liberals and social-democrats, which won a majority; one represented the Socialist Party, one the Communist Party, one the little group, *Alianza Popular*, and one the nationalist parties of Catalonia and the Basque Country. This group of seven, popularly known as the "Founding Fathers," was charged with the material task of drafting the text of the constitution; it also became the center of all the political compromises between the parties. The aim was to draft a constitution that could be accepted by all the democratic forces and that could be then submitted to popular referendum with a unanimous positive vote recommendation. That result was attained.

The most important issue at stake was, obviously, the consolidation of the emerging democracy. Consolidation meant more than agreement about the constitution and parliamentary institutions; it also meant finding solutions for the serious problems that were at the root of the tragic experiences of the past, particularly those of the Monarchy and of national identities and nationalism. In 1977 the Socialist Party, the Communist Party, and all the forces of the left, as well as some nationalist groups, were republicans and opposed the Monarchy. This opposition was not ideological, but the consequence of the Monarchy's traditional belligerency to the left and the peripheral nationalism. The split between the Spanish political forces over the issue "Monarchy or Republic" was radical. It even involved divisions about the symbol of the national flag and the national anthem.

However, the Spanish transition began with an existing monarchy, restored by Franco on a legal basis that the great majority of citizens rejected and that the new democracy set out to modify.

In that initial moment, with weak democratic forces and with the major institutions of the Franco regime still intact, it was obvious that a strong stabilizing element was necessary. Only the Crown could serve this purpose. The majority of the army, the security forces, the public servants, and the judicial system accepted, many reluctantly, the legitimacy of democracy and the democratic process only because the King himself accepted it, not because of the leadership of new political parties. Thus, the issue "Monarchy or Republic" had the potential to become a rallying cry for those who were for Monarchy and against the Republic. Finally, the Crown itself needed a *democratic* legitimacy; its alternative was the perpetuation of the legality of the Franco regime, its own original source of legitimacy, and the closing of the door to democracy. An agreement was necessary to break the hold of the past's spiral of political confrontations between the Crown and the republicans, so that both would be free to confront the new problems. The constitutional compromise was the parliamentary Monarchy. The Crown and the Monarchy as a system obtained a new democratic legitimacy; the left obtained a system of democratic liberties, of territorial autonomies, and of parliamentary institutions that until then could have been achieved only through the Republic and the overthrow of Monarchy. When in 1982 the Socialist Party won the general elections with an overall majority, for the first time in Spanish history the left governed without problems under a monarchy. This historic compromise allowed the democratic forces to gather against the partisans of dictatorship, without secondary divisions that would have weakened the whole process of transition to democracy.

Constitution Making: A Focus on Spain

Self-Determination and National Identity

A constitutional solution was also found for the other bloody conflict of modern Spanish history, the conflict about national identity, which had pitted authoritarian centralism against the quest for autonomy of the most developed zones of Spain, especially Catolonia and the Basque country. When nationalism began to develop in both regions at the end of the nineteenth century, the Monarchy and the central ruling class had ordered the army to fight nationalism in the name of Spanish national unity and of Spanish central nationalism; the army thus became the armed depository of the integrity of the Spanish nation and the centralist Monarchy against all internal opposition. The Republic of 1931 tried to solve the problem by opening the way to regional autonomies. The clash became especially violent under Franco's dictatorship, which persecuted and suppressed all the identity signs (institutions, languages, cultures) of Catalonia and the Basque Country and stressed Spanish national identity as the old Spanish nationalism linked with centralism and authoritarianism. By 1977, the issue of regional nationalism was not only a problem of political organization but also an ideological problem. In Catalonia and the Basque Country, in Galicia and other parts of Spain a strong collective feeling of nationality had developed which was difficult to integrate into the wider collective feeling of the Spanish nation, after Franco's strong regime of ultrarightist Spanish nationalism.

The constitutional compromise resolving this conflict is stated in Article 2 and Title VIII of the new constitution. Article 2 defines the concept of the Spanish nation. It states that Spain is a true united and indivisible nation, formed by "nationalities" and "regions," each one having a right to political autonomy, recognized and guaranteed by the constitution itself; the link that unites this new Spanish nation is "solidarity." From a theoretical point of view, Article 2 seems an odd combination of heterogeneous elements, the result something like a "nation of nations." But Article 2 is not a theoretical exercise; it is an attempt to find a political solution to one of the most serious and bloody conflicts of the Spanish political history. The constitution opens the way to a radical reorganization of the Spanish centralist state into a federal kind of system of political autonomies.

The Process

The constitutional resolution of these profound conflicts expresses the deep spirit and commitment of the Spanish transition to democracy. Other important issues, namely the implementation of civil rights and political liberties, the separation between the state and the Catholic church, the abolition of the death penalty, and the full recognition of political pluralism, were resolved in the same spirit.

The constitution was the work of consensus, which prevailed in the first period of the transition, until the completion of the constituent working groups at the end of 1978. The second general elections of 1979 confirmed the political framework created by the first ones. The UCD was again the main political force, but again was not able to attain an overall majority. The new government, led again by Mr. Suarez, chose to govern alone, putting an end to consensus; the Socialist Party became the main challenger. The UCD government, confronted with the implementation of democratic reforms in all the state institutions, with the implementation of regional autonomies and with the fight against the economic crisis and inflation, began to divide into factions and to break down. After the dismissal of Mr. Suarez and the failed military coup of February 23, 1981, the crisis in the UCD was open. It had been deepened by the results of the first local elections of 1979 in which Socialists and Communists obtained the majority in the more important Spanish towns, especially Madrid and Barcelona.

The general elections of October 28, 1982 changed the political framework. The Socialist Party (PSOE) obtained more than 10 million votes and an absolute majority in both Houses of Parliament. The UCD disappeared, the Communist Party fell abruptly to 5%, and *Alianza Popular* became the main conservative force and the second-ranked group in Parliament. In Catalonia and the Basque countries, the nationalist parties confirmed their positions and in the subsequent elections to their regional Parliaments became the majority forces. The general elections of 1986 confirmed this general framework. The Socialist Party retained its absolute majority, and a new party, the *Centro Democratico y Social* (CDS), led by Mr. Suarez, began to emerge as a center force. Predictions about future political developments are difficult. Spain has become a dynamic country; changes are abrupt and deep; new generations take the field. Spain finds itself still between past and future with the same problems of other more developed European countries and with historical problems not fully resolved, especially those of basic economic structures and of public administration. But the main political phantoms of the past have vanished, and the main challenge of 1977 has been fulfilled. Democracy in Spain in a stable system and it works.

The Institutions of Democracy in Iberia

The different processes of transition to democracy in Portugal and Spain led to substantial differences in their constitutional and political frameworks. In more recent years, however, the actual working of the institutions and of the political forces has led to increasing similarities.

The Portuguese Constitution of 1976 emerged in the political wake of the April 1974 uprising. It is a syncretic constitution, but its overall inspiration is more radical than that of the Spanish Constitution. Some of the main principles of the 1976 Portuguese Constitution are the collective appropriation of the main means of production and of land and natural resources, and the elimination of monopolistic corporations and of *latifundia* in the general perspective of a "transition to socialism" (Article 89.1). A significant main feature of the constitution is the constitutional role granted to the Armed Forces through the "Council of the Revolution," one of the key institutions of the constitutional system.

The 1986 constitutional revision reflected an important change in the original internal logic: the feeling of "transition to socialism" disappeared, despite a remaining mention of socialism in Article 2; the role of the military and the "Council of the Revolution" was eliminated. The whole constitutional system has evolved into a closer parallel with other systems in Western Europe.

Under the 1986 constitution, Portugal has a semipresidential republic, or what one could call a mixed presidential–parliamentary system. The President of the Republic, for the first time a "civilian" President with the 1986 election of the socialist leader Mário Soares, is elected directly by the voters; he has no executive powers, though he has a limited veto power and the power to dismiss the government and to dissolve the Assembly of the Republic. Due to his direct election, the President has an important political role as a stabilizing factor and as a mediator; the importance of this role increased after the constitutional elimination of the military "Council of the Revolution," whose role conflicted with that of the President. It is interesting to note that in all the presidential elections held up to now, the majority has not coincided with the party majority in the Parliament. At present, with an overall majority in Parliament of the center-right PSD, the President was elected with the support of the left.

The system works as a parliamentary government with a single chamber, the Assembly of the Republic, elected by direct popular vote under a proportional system. As in all the modern parliamentarian systems, the center of gravity has shifted to the government and party politics predominate; this situation became marked after the general election of 1987, which gave a single party, the PSD, the overall majority. The party system has evolved toward a system of equilibrium, similar to those balances of political forces existing in other western countries and in Spain. The balance is not the same in Portugal and Spain, but the party system shows increasing similarity.

The Portuguese constitutional structure is a centralized or unitarian one, which does not allow for regional autonomies. But Article 6 of the Constitution ensconces the principle of autonomy of the local governments; it establishes two autonomous regions in the archipelagos of the Azores and Madeira, each with a regional Assembly, a regional government, and a president appointed by the representative or minister of the republic in the islands. Each autonomous region has its own statute, drafted by the regional Assembly and approved by the central Parliament, the Assembly of the Republic.

The main difference between the Portuguese constitutional system and the Spanish one is, obviously, that Spain is a monarchy. More precisely, Spain is a "parliamentary monarchy," in which the King reigns but does not rule. The King has no veto power, cannot dismiss the President of the Government nor any Minister, cannot dissolve the two chambers of the Parliament (the *Cortes Generales*), and, although he is the nominal Chief of the Armed Forces, cannot dispose of them, as only the government can decide on military affairs.

In this sense, the Spanish system is a purer parliamentarian regime than is the Portuguese one. The undisputed political leadership lies in Government and Parliament. The Parliament, or *Cortes Generales*, has two chambers: the *Congreso de los Diputados*, elected by direct vote with a proportional system, and the *Senado*, elected in part by direct vote with a majority system (each province elects four Senators), and in part by indirect vote (the Parliament of each autonomous region elects Senators proportional to its population).

The structures and the implementation of the parliamentarian system are similar to those of other parliamentarian countries, with a specific regulation of Parliament's control of the Government in the "constructive" sense of the former German Federal Republic system. In Spain, too, the center of gravity has shifted to the Government and political parties, especially after the overall majority obtained by the Socialist Party in 1982.

Another main feature of the Spanish constitutional structure is the creation of the federal-like system of Autonomous Communities. Seventeen Autonomies now exist in the territory of Spain, with the exception of the two North African cities of Ceuta and Melilla. Each Autonomous Community has its own constitution or statute, its own Parliament, and its own government. The structure and the actual working of these autonomous institutions are parliamentarian, even if the office of President and that of Prime Minister coincide in the same person. Each Parliament is elected by direct vote through a proportional system; the President is elected by the Parliament and is reponsible to it; the statutes were drafted at the initial stage by the representatives of the Autonomous Community in process of formation and finally approved by the *Cortes Generales*. Competences and financial resources vary among these 17 Autonomous Communities. Catalonia, the Basque Country, Galicia, and Andalusia are autonomies of a higher level, but the logic of the system is that all the existing Autonomous Communities will evolve to a similar degree of autonomy. Moreover, in those regions that have specific languages, like Catalonia, the Basque Country, Galicia, Valencia, and the Balearic Islands, the languages are coofficial with Spain's official language, the Castilian or Spanish.

From this general perspective, we may conclude that beyond these specific features and differences and beyond the historical conflicts and mistrust, it seems obvious that Portugal and Spain are evolving largely along in the same path and in the same direction. We may assume these similarities will increase in the future as both countries are now integrated in the same process of European unity.

Notes

1. Revista de Estudio Politicos (R.E.P.), *El Sistema Politico y Constitucional Portuguel, 1974–1987* (Madrid: Centro de Estudio Constitucionales, num. 60–61, 1988), with extensive bibliography.
2. J. Callaghan, *Time and Chance* (London: Collins/Fontana, 1987), p. 260.

Bibliography

Aja, E., J. Tornos, et al., *El Sistema Politico de las Comunidades Autonomas* (Madrid: Ed. Tecnos, 1985).

Aja, E., J. Tornos, et al., *Informe sobre las Autonomias* (Madrid: Ed. Civitas, 1988).

Ballbe, M., *Orden Publico y Militarism en la España Constitucional (1812–1983)* (Madrid: Alianza Editorial, 1983).

Callaghan, J., *Time and Chance* (London: Collins/Fontana, 1987).

Carr, R. and J. P. Fusi, *De la Dictadura a la Democracia* (Barcelona: Ed. Planeta, 1979).

Clark, R. P., "Spain's Autonomous Communities: A Case Study in Ethnic Power Sharing," 2.1 *European Studies Journal* 1–16 (1985).

Clark, R. P. and M. H. Haltzel, eds., *Spain in the 1980s. The Democratic Transition and a New International Role* (Cambridge, MA: Ballinger, 1987).

Gomes Canotilho, J. J. and Vital Moreira, *Constituição de Republica Portuguesa Anotada* (Coimbra: Coimbra Ed., 1984).

Gomes Canotilho, J. J., *Direito Constitucional* (Coimbra: Coimbra Ed., 1986).

Gunther, R., G. Sani, and G. Sabhad, *Spain After Franco: The Making of a Competitive Party System* (Berkeley: University of California Press, 1985).

Linz, J. and J. R. Montero, eds., *Crisis y Cambio: Electores y Partidos en la España de los Años Ochenta* (Madrid: Centro de Estudios Constitucionales, 1986).

Miranda, J., *Constituicao de 1976, Formacoa, Estrutura, Principios Fundamentais* (Lisboa: Liv. Petrony, 1978).

Miranda, J., *Revisâo Constitucional e Democracia* (Lisboa: Ed. Rei dos Livros, 1983).

Peces Barba, G., *La Elaboración de la Constitución de 1978* (Madrid: Centro de Estudio Constitucionales, 1988).

Revista de Estudio Politicos (R.E.P.), *El Sistema Politico y Constitucional Portuguel, 1974–1987* (Madrid: Centro de Estudio Constitucionales, num. 60–61, 1988), with extensive bibliography.

Rokkan, S. and D. W. Urwin, *Economy, Territory, Identity, Politics of Western Europe Pepripheries* (London: Sage, 1983).

Seco Serrano, C., *Militarismo y Civilismo en la España Contemporánea* (Madrid: IEE, 1984).

Torres Murillo, J. L., *La Europa de las Autonomias* (San Sebastian: Caga de Ahorros Provincial de Guipuzcoa, 1985).

Solé Tura, J., *Nacionalidades y Nacionalismos en España* (Madrid: Alianza Editorial, 1985).

Solé Tura, J. and E. Aja, *Constituciones y Periodos Constituyentes en España (1808–1936)* (Madrid: Ed. Siglo XXI, 1984).

Wheeler, D. L., *Republican Portugal: A Political History, 1910–1926* (Madison: Wisconsin University Press, 1978).

19

The Role of the State: Contradictions in the Transition to Democracy

Lena Kolarska-Bobinska

The evolution in east European countries is usually analyzed as a movement on an axis with the market and democracy as one of its poles. That analysis places the transition period on that axis and perceives its solutions as functional to the goal. I shall argue, however, that this period has a dynamic and logic of its own, which evoke tendencies contradictory to the logic of the market and democracy.

This issue is of critical importance for the creation of the new constitution in Poland. If the period of transition is marked by logic and requirements different from, and often contradictory to those of the period to follow, then will the constitution be of the transition period, or will it envisage a system correlative with the goal? If the latter, who is to determine the future system now that the political scene is unstructured, social interests remain uncrystallized, and the Polish parliament has not been elected in free elections?

This chapter will explore the contradiction between the constraints and solutions of the transition period and those of the goal of the changes—the market and democracy, with reference to the role played by the state in the transition period.

The transition from a socialist system to a market economy assumes that the role the state plays in every sphere of social life will change. Grass roots entrepreneurial initiatives, spontaneously organized groups, and autonomous, self-governing local units will replace the organization of the economy and social life from above. These initiatives will fill the gaps left by the state administration. Indeed in Poland the withdrawal of the state from the economy and other fields is one of the crucial points of the program of transition to a market-oriented economy.

As yet, only general terms describe this program; the role of the state is as vaguely defined as is the model of the social order to which Poland aspires. Tadeusz Mazowiecki, the former Prime Minister, spoke in 1989 of a "social market economy" for the country, without saying what this might actually mean. Leszek Balcerowicz, a Deputy Premier and the author of Poland's stabilization program, has repeatedly stressed that Poles lack time to experiment with a "third road" somewhere between socialism and capitalism and must imitate patterns well-tested in the west.

However, which of the western European countries is to serve as a model and to what extent are still unknown because of the lack of a more specific program for the reconstruction of Poland's economy. One of the consequences of this vague vision of Poland's social and economic order is the absence of any conception of the role the state should play in social and economic life, besides a very general call for the reduction of its role. Thus, conflicting factors shape the role of the state, the neoliberal ideology, the constraints, and contradiction of the period of change.

The result is that, in spite of the general premise about the need to reduce the role of the state, it plays an essential part in the transition from socialism to capitalism.

Government Role in Transition

In the first period after the communists lost their power, political liberalization paved the way for economic change, but it was too fresh to be in a position to define the trend and the character of that change by intergroup negotiation; the various political options within society were not yet crystallized and the structure of interests and attitudes still functioned as it had been shaped in the preceding period. Accordingly, the trend of economic change was defined by a group of professionals formerly connected with the opposition, who became members of government. They intended to prepare a plan of transformation to reach capitalism by the shortest way without going astray and engaging in unnecessary experiments. Thus the government, not any political party or social movement, is the author of the program of economic change now being implemented. These changes will have a crucial impact on the whole structure of society.

A good example of the importance of the government's role is the privatization program prepared by the Privatization Ministry, established particularly for that purpose. The type of privatization (the sale or free distribution of shares, its principles, which groups are to receive, how much, etc.) may result in the emergence of new and unexpected economic divisions, not to speak of their more indirect impact on participation in such goods as political influence, power, and prestige. Thus it is the state administration that is introducing a new social order creating new sources of wealth and prestige, and new inequalities and class division. As Deputy Premier and Minister of Finance Balcerowicz has stated: "In our conditions the state is responsible for the construction of a new economic system."[1] And for a social system, one may add. In western states, as C. Offe writes, "due to the constitutional arrangements that we find in liberal democracies, the state is not even allowed to pursue any substantive ends other than those that constitute the preconditions for universal commodity relationships."[2] In the west the state does not change the character of the system but merely functions as a harmonizing and supportive force to protect the existing exchange relations. In Poland the state is creating an entirely new socioeconomic system.

The social consequences of privatization will become visible only after a longer period has passed. The Polish government, however, has made decisions that differentiate employees and have caused considerable dissatisfaction. A special tax (commonly referred to by its Polish slang name *popiwek*) collected from those enterprises that pay their employees' salaries and wages above a certain fixed ceiling was intended to act as a hedge against inflation by slowing down the rise of salaries and wages. Introduced as an element of the economic transformation, the so-called Balcerowicz plan functioned effectively for more than a year, influencing all institutions without exception. Because of the necessity to speed up privatization the government made use of this tax to encourage employees to privatize their enterprises. As of January 1, 1991, those enterprises that had declared their intention to turn private are free from the tax, which means the freeing of the wages and salaries of their employees from administratively set limits.

Then many people began to wonder why those employed in the state-owned sector should be handicapped while those in the private sector are privileged, and why it was the state authorities who introduced such an unjust division. The decision has proved unfortunate on the whole because it visualized the truth, denied by the representatives of the government, that salaries and wages depended not on the invisible hand of the market but on the decisions of the authorities. The state is the employer and pressure has to be exerted on the state authorities. The last Communist cabinet tried to extricate itself from direct conflicts with employees by adopting the position of an arbitrator; it did not succeed. Nor did the first non-Communist cabinets, which started the transformation of the system. As Michal Boni, Minister of Labour, Salaries and Wages, said in February 1991, he had "to act as a fireman who must extinguish fires," that is, as negotiator called on by striking employees.

Some contradictions of the transition period result from the fact that the central authorities, by methods that C. Offe would call contradictory to the logic of exchange relations, are introducing a market economy, which is based on the interplay of interests and on the organization of groups. Some authors suggest that a "revolution from above" is taking place in Poland.[3] There are several causes of this state of things.

Predictability versus the Uncertainty of Market Reform

The creation of a market economy is a goal obtainable only in the long run. Short-term tasks consist of the quickest possible activation of grass roots mechanisms and of the forces driving change at the lowest level of the economy. The race against time is important in view of the social moods: society was prepared for sacrifices and deprivations, but believed that the new system would, after a short period, bring about a rise in living standards. Therefore the new market system should start working and producing results before the patience of the public is exhausted, a condition that could block the reform.

If we define the goal as the creation, as soon as possible, of market economy mechanisms, then we must adopt those measures that most fully guarantee the attainment of the goal, minimizing uncertainty and the risk involved in that process. Even if the Minister of Finance, Mr. Balcerowicz, does not want to "experiment with the third road," he is experimenting with introducing the market to a formerly socialist economy and society. The effort to reduce the uncertainties resulting from the introduction of a market economy, and to eliminate spontaneous unpredictable factors that may appear during that process, strongly influences that behavior of the decision makers and their strategies. Capitalism and democracy are based on certain procedures, but their outcome is uncertain. The striving for the certainty that the creation of market institutions and mechanisms will be attained quickly and effectively results in the recourse to bureaucracy, administrative decisions, and the apparatus of the state, in the hope that they can reduce the possibility of the development of spontaneous and uncontrolled processes that would disturb the change, its character, and intentions. This reaction is a major part of the explanation for the strong centralization of privatization in east European countries. As A. Sajó wrote about Hungary, "a tiny government body (the Fund) controls or will control an enormous sector of the economy."[4] Some think that the enterprises in Hungary are under stronger state supervision during the transition period than they were under the communist system[5] and that their managers are losing the independence they won at the close of the communist rule.[6] The opinion of its Economic Council assessed the government plan for the commercialization of enterprises in a similar way in 1990.

The unpredictable effects of some mechanisms were observable during the first year of the implementation of the economic reform in Poland. The purpose of the tight budget constraints and cuts of subsidies to state-owned enterprises, which formed part of the Balcerowicz plan, was to threaten those enterprises with bankruptcy and so bring about a change in managerial practices. Yet managers, instead of dismissing employees, gave them paid or unpaid leaves; instead of changing the products, they stored them, etc. They resorted to various adaptive measures to enable the enterprises to survive for a relatively long time in an unchanged form. Some 18 months after the adoption of the Balcerowicz plan, the number of bankruptcies has been minimal. This experience may undermine the state administration trust in and reliance on general rules and their automatic regulatory functions. And, as time presses, there will be a tendency to replace regulations and rules by centralized administrative decisions. Thus the striving for quick and certain effects does not favor the introduction into a state hitherto so far centrally planned and from the top of the market system, whose essence consist in spontaneous grass roots entreprenurial initiatives, decentralization of decisions, and economic mechanisms.

Democratic procedures do not yield certain results; they also take a relatively long time to take effect. In some cases this may create a tension resulting in a conflict between democracy and efficiency.

The Need for Legal Change versus Efficiency

The formation of a market economy requires the establishment of some preconditions. The creation of these preconditions in eastern Europe necessitates, among other things, a change in many regulations and in the ways in which the system of law functions, a modification of the functioning and structure of state administration, the breaking of monopolistic structures that mark many fields of economic and societal life, the preparation of a banking system, and a change in the structure of ownership. Changes of this magnitude in these areas are neither spontaneous nor automatic and hence the role of the state in reorganizing the institutional structure is enormous. In western countries changes are important too, but that task cannot be compared to the one in a country in which a large part of the legal and institutional structure was intended to support a completely different system.

The necessity to change the law, including the constitution and many regulations so that they do not hamper the development of the new relations and can adjust to them, creates a specific tension during the transition period. It is the tension between legalism and effectiveness that frequently requires quick reactions not bounded by legal regulations. As Andras Sajó put it, regulations in east Europe are modified at a relatively slow pace because formalistic legalisms fascinate the new parliaments.[7] And the modified regulations after some time prove inadequate and require subsequent modifications. "We live in a situation in which regulations lag behind the requirements of life," one of the representatives of public administration has said.[8]

The relatively slow change in regulations breeds the temptation to evade them, and to act outside or above the law in the name of speed and efficiency. In this way the point of gravity tends to shift from legislative to executive authority. In Poland the deputies to the Parliament frequently comment on how burdensome is the incessant need to amend or change the law, while the cabinet emphasizes the fact that the Parliament lags behind the requirements of the time and binds the hands of the government.

The constant making of new legislation, including the constitution, gives the impression that the law is fully flexible. This intensifies the conviction, common under the socialist system, that the law serves an instrumental purpose.[9] This writer was present at a discussion in the Polish Parliament on the political status of one of the parliamentary groups. One of the deputies, interested in a political change in that group, claimed that the discussion had an informal, friendly character and those who thought otherwise "wanted to settle the issue by resorting to regulations. The law is to serve us, to be for us. It is not so that we are to serve the law. We are the makers of the law, and not its slaves." His opponents called for respect of law and suggested that "it could be seen who is hampered by the law."

The making of a new legal order requires not only the formulation of adequate regulations. Equally, if not more important, is the necessity for a change in attitude toward the law of both its makers and ordinary citizens. This process is a long one and requires democratic relations, even at the cost of effectiveness.

The State and the Social Vacuum

Several tensions arise because the need for change runs counter to the need for a stable set of circumstances necessary for the development of the new economic system.[10] Persons and institutions who want to invest, in particular foreign investors, need stability—of economic parameters, of rules of the game, and of the political situation. The as yet unformed political system and the changing legal system are now not in a position to offer such guarantees. Therefore, the state gives them, further increasing its role during the transition period.

Another precondition of the market economy is the existence of forces and groups interested in the implementation of that system. Yet in the transition period the market, a system whose essence consists in individual and group interest, has to emerge in a society without clear-cut groups connected with that reform by their interests. Although it is true that the noncommunist governments enjoy broad public support, that people are convinced of the necessity of painful changes, and quite universally declare their liking of the market economy, it is also true that in Poland no social group that could be the agent of the change is directly interested in its introduction.

The functioning of the myth of the market as a solution good and advantageous in every respect did not change the fact that once the market was introduced, several groups feared that they would lose rather than gain.[11] E. Mokrzycki wrote about the contradiction between the theoretical position (everyone supports the idea of the market) and the real interests (the market threatens group interest).[12] Moreover, the introduction of the market in the first phase meant deprivations joined to a lowered standard of living. For this reason, and also because the market was not linked to social interests, the government had to appeal to patience, forbearance, sacrifice, and patriotism, motives totally unrelated to the logic of the market.

A lack of social forces directly interested in the introduction of the market economy contributed substantially to the increased role of the state. Its structures and employees had to bear the burden of reform and of convincing people of the necessity to change their ways of thinking, habits, and interest. As a result, the state is the basic institution implementing the change.

These factors, and in particular the decline in living standards and the restriction of privileges, have resulted in a situation in which society's low level of activity and its passive consent to the change were in the interest of the authorities. Nor did the organization of groups always mean active support of the reforms; in many cases, it took the form of defending interests threatened by the change. Many causes influence the slow and reluctant organization of like-minded people in society; one of them is the by-product of changes—social anomie.[13] Without full discussion here, it can be said that a paradoxical situation arose in Poland in which a social order to be based on grass roots initiatives and groups' self-organization was introduced from the top downward with the passive consent of a part of society. J. Staniszkis, describing the mode of thinking of the new political elite (she addressed her comments to the Mazowiecki cabinet, of which she was very critical), stated that the elite was strongly statist minded and treated society and its demands as a potential barrier to change. In the long run "that means a contradiction between the dilemmas of building democracy in a poorly developed civil society and the necessity of the state's introduction from the top of new structural solutions, social roles and interests."[14]

The collapse of the communist rule in Poland coincided with a deep economic crisis and high inflation. In that situation only the state authorities could undertake adequate measures to combat the inflation. The authorities, in thwarting inflation, fixed and changed in short periods a number of the basic financial parameters and, at the same time, strove to enforce a change in the ways of thinking and in the behavior of both consumers and managers of industry. By using for that purpose a tight financial corset, the authorities tried to force industry to change its structures. Those measures, unpleasant by their very nature, were perceived as restrictive and as coming from above, from the central authorities. In this way the perception of the center as the main actor is still obtained. Many people think that since the government fixed such a high interest rate, it is to be blamed for their troubles. Customers do not buy our commodities because the government has frozen salaries and wages. And so the state is still seen as the agent who determines the rules of the game, as the addressee of various expectations, and as the source of conflicts. The central authorities maintained their image of persons adamantly carrying out their program by declaring on TV that should inflation recur, the interest rate would be again raised as much as necessary; the government would not abandon its program.

Antiinflation measures created a serious recession in Poland. The rise in prices of many commodities and the limitation of consumption, with the resulting limitations on production, meant that the road to a contemporacy market economy based on consumption, spending, and investments led through a period characterized by restraint, by limited expenses, by the impossibility of investing, and the unavailability of "expensive" credits and great difficulties in promoting entrepreneurship. To people at large this state of affairs appears to be contradictory to a market economy.

Ambivalence and the Welfare Role

Social attitudes toward the welfare role are very important in determining people's perception of the state. From the beginning of the transformation with the introduction of the Balcerowicz plan and throughout 1990, the state declared that it would reduce its role in the welfare sphere, and that self-help groups, local initiatives, and community actions should substitute for the overprotective state and its inefficient administration.

That reduction of the state's role in the welfare sphere has been announced during a period when the living standard of many groups is drastically falling, the sphere of poverty is widening, and the danger of unemployment is becoming very real. The economic reform, which in its initial period (whose duration can hardly be estimated) will adversely affect many spheres of life, is being carried out in Poland 10 years after the beginning of the economic crisis; the standard of living has not risen for 10 years, and economic problems have intensified.

The attitude of society toward the state and its protective functions is now ambivalent: the universally accepted government, for many "the cabinet of the last hope," claims that these protective functions must be limited; the situation, however, calls for their intensification.

A series of opinion polls conducted by a group of scholars from the Polish Academy of Sciences showed that, in 1988, 72% of the respondents thought that the state ought to give more help to those people who could not cope with their difficulties. In 1990, that percentage rose to 80.[15] Eighteen months after the beginning of the introduction of the market-oriented reforms, 53% thought that the workplace should take care of the welfare problems of its employees; 27% are opposed. Also particularly interesting is the fact that 66% of the Poles are in favor of state-controlled prices, and 67% favor the full employment policy; in 1988 that policy was supported by 58% and in 1984, by 53%.

Even though the acceptance of privatization is growing in Polish society, people are convinced that the state should help the needy. The definition of that category, which is the key problem, is, however, unknown. It may be supposed that the respondents would include the unemployed in it, especially since the fear of unemployment is increasing.

In October 1988, 25% of the respondents considered it likely that they would lose their jobs; in November 1989, that percentage rose to 46. In the opinion of 74%, it is the government's duty to secure new jobs for all those discharged, and 87% of them think that the state should secure opportunities for retraining.[16] All respondents had a clear opinion on that matter; there were exceptionally few answers, "it is hard to say."

These attitudes toward the state must be examined in light of attitudes the society has had for years. Until recently the overlapping of the political, the economic, and the social spheres had two results: society developed different attitudes toward the different spheres of the state's activity, and its attitudes shifted from one sphere to another.

The former was expressed in the acceptance of the state's welfare activities and the simultaneous rejection of its efforts to control political and economic behavior. As Pawel Kuczynski wrote:

> the ambivalent attitude towards the state is expressed, on the one hand, by demand put upon it, and on the other, by resistance to the all-encompassing monopoly of the state. In other words, the slow change of the attitudes towards the state is manifested by the belief that the state should secure and take care of employees' social security and standard of living and restrain itself from interfering in the liberties of the individual.[17]

The myth of the market mentioned above developed because the market was perceived as a means of limiting the political and economic functions of the state. The resistance to the social consequences of the market was a result of the belief that social benefits were valuable and due to the populace.

Accompanying the tendency to reduce state control over the economy for political reasons and those of efficiency was the fear that the welfare state would completely withdraw from the economy; deteriorating living conditions reinforced these findings.

Moreover, the expectation of the various benefits provided by the state combined with a resentful attitude towards the state. J. Korchewicz wrote about the "unfriendly" world of institutions.[18] The research project "Poles 84" demonstrated the belief that well-being and earnings depended on decisions made at the top was combined with a negative assessment of that fact.[19] The dislike of the political system, or, more specifically, of the ruling Communist party, shifted to the state and its institutions. Now the attitude toward the state should change gradually because it is finally "ours." But unexpected reactions can result from the fact that the state, on which millions of people depend in one or another way, although beginning to be friendly, at the same time disclaims firmly its various earlier duties. What if, at the time when it should play an essential role in planning and preparation of protective measures in the various spheres of societal life, it exhorts the citizens to organize self-help and charitable activities?

Contradictory signals also come from comparing the propaganda slogans averring the state administration's withdrawal from many spheres with an observation of facts. The critics of the government program emphasize that although the state has withdrawn various subsidies from, for example, the housing cooperatives and reduced them significantly for cultural projects, it continues to play the key role in setting limits to salaries and wages. Can then one rely on the state or not? What is its true role now? As the state is carrying out the stabilization plan and the reforms, it is perceived as the author of change. It is the state that raises and lowers taxes and interest rates, and declares that it will block further rises in the price of bread if they became too high. Many examples confirm the belief that the state continues to be present in some spheres of daily life while withdrawing from many others; and one can hardly grasp the logic of those decisions.

This clash of state declarations with social expectations and with the observation of old as well as new practices produces a complex situation. One might risk the hypothesis that with time a different kind of "unfriendliness" of institutions could emerge, based not on this resentful attitude toward the political and economic activities of the state but on the refusal to accept the way in which it performs its protective functions. Perhaps that change of perception will be conducive to the emergence of a civil society, which in the field of social welfare would really resemble those in western Europe.

Conclusions

This special and imprecise role of the state in the introduction of a new social order, during a time of economic crisis, creates several dilemmas and has different consequences. The state and its agencies are becoming the main actors in the social conflict, even as they strive for uninvolvement. Under real socialism the state administration, linked to the ruling Communist party, was the principal distributor of many resources and goods, the main conflicts were between a given group and the central administration identified with the state.

In this period the state plays the key role on the social scene as the main owner of means of production, as the source of resources that it does not distribute, and also as the creator of the new social structure, of changes whose result will be that some group will lose and others will gain. Moreover, the perception of the state as the author and promoter of change will mean that society will ascribe to the government responsiblity for the various features of the present condition of the country and situation of particular groups, even remote ones not linked to the essence of change. In this way the state may become an important actor in the social conflict, especially since all other actors and structures are weak.

A journalist in an interview with M. Boni, the Minister of Labour, Salaries and Wages, made the comment that nothing has changed; people stretch their hands to the central authorities, put pressure on the government, which then distributes the means, and the Minister negotiates. Minister Boni replied:

> Today the causes are different. The managers of the enterprises are weak, their possibilities are limited. The manager does not enjoy the power of authority. The weaker he is the more willingly he hides behind the laws, especially *popiwek* (the tax restricting the rise of salaries and wages). That is why the trade unions want to discuss matters directly with the government. The lack of the partners to the dispute who would negotiate at lower levels makes controversies political and shifts them to the level of controversy between the authorities and society.[20]

The involvement of the state as a party to basic social conflicts may account for the fact that the role of the state has become the subject, not of debate, but of a political game.

The importance of the state administration gives rise to many problematic questions. Can the old bureaucratic structures implement change in the social order to the extent necessary to bring about a system that is a result of negotiations among various interests and social forces? There has been no essential change in the personnel in the state administration at lower levels because of a lack of experts and professionals. How many persons, and in what posts, must be replaced if the bureaucracy is to be inspired with a new spirit? The state authorities, while preparing the change and implementing it through the governmental agencies (e.g., the Ministry for Privatization), must themselves redefine their role and that of their apparatus. Can this requirement be included in the constitution without resulting in the necessity of frequent amendments? And above all, will the state authorities be capable of redefining their role, and will society be interested in such a change? It may be supposed that the solutions adopted during the transition period as a result of various necessities and constraints will last, significantly influencing the future system in east European countries.

These constraints and contradictions discussed here account for the fact that during the transition period the role of the state is particularly essential and undoubtedly different from that played by the state in a stabilized market system.

The importance of the role of the state raises a question of whether the transition period requires the application of different methods and special measures to overcome the resistance of the old system and to facilitate the implementation of the new one. Is the recourse to such undemocratic means justified by considerations of efficiency and speed? Will not the use of means whose logic is contradictory to the nature of the system that is the goal deform the shape of its solutions? Should that be sanctioned by the constitution? Undoubtedly the constitution will be a result of many contradictory tendencies, various authors' ideas, political compromises, established transition period practice, etc. On the one hand there is "the assumption of the authors that the future constitution is to guarantee to the government a strong position and vast prerogatives which would enable it to take effective actions. The authors of the draft also intend to define a strong position of the prime minister."[21] But the solutions of the constitution will also be influenced by facts and institutions established in the meantime, such as the election of a definite president. L. Walesa is greatly expanding his office staff and intends to play the first fiddle in controlling the transformations. This fact may influence parliament's voting preferences for a presidential rather than a parliamentary system.

J. Staniszkis[22] recognizes the need for strong state authorities during the transition period, but suggests the inclusion in the constitution of a guarantee of the self-limitation of the state after a short period of the implementation program. I do not think this is a feasible option because the end of the period would be difficult to foresee; one cannot impose a temporal frame on such unpredictable processes as the changes in eastern Europe.

The constitution will certainly bear the mark of the fact that it is being written during the transition period. B. Geremak, Deputy to Parliament and the chairman of its constitution committee, says as much when he says that the constitution ought to define "the model of the state and political system which best suits the period of transition to democracy and which guarantees a safe future to the latter."[23] Thus the main task of the constitution, besides defining the socio-economic system and the model of the state, is to guarantee the possibility of attaining the goals of transition to democracy and to a market economy. If that is to be possible, changes must take place in society's attitude toward the role of the constitution and the law in social and political life. This is a long and complex process and one of the essential aspects of a systemic transformation.

Notes

1. L. Balcerowicz, "Quicker in the Same Direction," *Gazeta Wyborcza*, January 10, 1991.
2. C. Offe, *Contradictions of the Welfare State* (London: Hutchinson, 1984).
3. J. Staniszkis, "The Dilemmas of the Transition Period: Case of Poland," *Tygodnik Soldarnosc*, June 1, 1990.
4. A. Sajó, "Struggle for Ownership Control: New Contents of State Ownership in Hungary" (unpublished paper, 1990).
5. M. Csanadi, comment made in a personal conversation, Warsaw, November 1990.
6. A. Sajó, "Struggle for Ownership Control: New Contents of State Ownership in Hungary" (unpublished paper, 1990).
7. A. Sajó, "The New Legalism: Law as an Instrument of Social Transformation"

(paper presented at a Conference on Constitutionalism and the Transition to Democracy in Eastern Europe, Pécs: Hungary, June 18–20, 1990).

8. I. Morawska, "The Education of the Plaincloth Guard," *Spotkania*, February 27, 1991, pp. 22–23.

9. A. Sajó, "The New Legalism: Law as an Instrument of Social Transformation" (paper presented at a Conference on Constitutionalism and the Transition to Democracy in Eastern Europe, Pécs: Hungary, June 18–20, 1990).

10. L. Zienkowski, discussion on a meeting of Economy Council, January 1991.

11. L. Kolarska-Bobinska, "The Myth of the Market and the Reality of the Reform," in S. Gomulka and A Polonsky, eds., *Polish Paradoxes* (London: Routledge, 1990), pp. 160–180.

12. E. Mokrzycki, "The Legacy of Real Socialism. The Search for a New Utopia" (paper presented at a congress of Polish Sociological Association: Torun, 1990).

13. L. Kolarska-Bobinska, "Civil Society and Social Anomy in Poland," 4 *Acta Sociologica* 277–287 (1990).

14. J. Staniszkis, "The Dilemmas of the Transition Period: Case of Poland," *Tygodnik Solidarnosc*, June 1, 1990.

15. W. Adamski, I. Bialecki, K. Jasiewicz, L. Kolarska-Boniska, A. Rychard, and E. Wnuk-Lipinski, *Polacy 90/Poles 90* (Warsaw: Institute of Philosophy and Sociology, 1991).

16. CBOS Research Center for Public Opinion, Polish Academy of Science, "Public Opinion about Unemployment," materials of CBOS, 1989.

17. P. Kuczynski, "Political Attitudes of Workers: Between Modernization and Normalization," in W. Morawski, ed., *Economy and Society* (Warsaw: Warsaw University, 1986).

18. J. Korolewicz, "Obraz spoɫeczeństwa a poczucie dyskomfortu psychicznego" ("The Image of Society and the Psychological Discomfort"), in E. Wunk-Lipiński, ed., *Nierowńosci i upośledzenia w swiadomości spotecznej (Inequalities and Injustice in Social Consciousness)* (Warsaw: Polish Academy of Sciences, Institute of Philosophy and Sociology, 19), pp. 63–111.

19. W. Adamski, K. Jasiewicz, and A. Rychard, eds., *Polacy '84: Dynamika Konflicktu Konsensusu* (Warsaw: Warsaw University, 1986).

20 M. Boni, "Hand pulled out to the Centrum," *Zycie Warsazwy*, March 4, 1991.

21. *Zycie Warszawy*, November 21, 1990.

22. J. Staniszkis, "The Dilemmas of the Transition Period: Case of Poland," *Tygodnik Solidarnosc*, June 1, 1990.

23. B. Geremek, "Non Circumstantial Matter," *Rzeczpospolita*, December 8–9, 1990.

20

Perspectives on the Current Constitutional Situation in Poland

Wiktor Osiatynski

Today all the countries of central Europe have many problems in common; each of them, however, has taken a somewhat different road away from Communism. In Poland where political transformations started first, changes seem to occur at a slower pace and without the spectacular successes in overthrowing the Communist system as have taken place in the other countries. On the other hand, Poland's prolonged struggle based on compromises has resulted in a greater political maturity of society and its leading elites. Moreover, the Poles seem to have already experienced a good deal of the disappointments and revaluations necessary to the process of departing from Communism.

This chapter concerns the problems of post-Communist constitutions, specifically from the viewpoint of the current situation in Poland.[1] Since December 1989, the Polish Parliament (Sejm) has changed the Constitution a number of times to delete Communist slogans and to make it an instrument of the transformation toward a capitalist market economy. These changes, often introduced in haste, resulted in an inconsistent structure, which was rather poorly adjusted to the new reality and hindered the process of reform. The legislators were well aware of the need for the new Constitution. No fewer than two constitutional commissions were appointed, one in the Sejm (which was elected according to the quotas accepted at the Round Table agreement between the Communists and the Solidarity opposition, giving a majority to the Communists and their allies) and the other in the Senate (which in free elections secured 99% of the seats for the Solidarity-linked opposition).

Both commisions began to work on a new Constitution without delay, determined to adopt a new document on May 3, 1991, a bicentennial of the first modern constitution in Europe adopted in Poland in 1791. However, major parties emerging from the Solidarity movement as well as a number of members of the Parliament soon challenged the very legitimacy of this Sejm to prepare a Constitution. Moreover, the conflict between the commissions in the Sejm and the Senate deepened steadily, to the point of a breach in cooperation and communication between them. As a result, on May 3, 1991, the Sejm adopted its own draft of the Constitution, after the Senate's adoption of its own version in April. Now, both projects are to be submitted to public discussion, but the final adoption of the Constitution will, most probably, be left for the new Parliament elected in the fall of 1991.

These developments in Poland since 1989, as well as the constitutional proceedings in both houses, have raised a number of problems clustering around fundamental attitudes relevant to the process of writing a Constitution during the transition from Communism. Before we consider some of them, a brief summary of the constitutional tradition of Poland is in order.

Constitutional Traditions in Poland

The tradition of Polish constitutionalism is similar to that found throughout continental Europe, where constitutions were a specific privilege granted to the people by rulers rather than a social contract on the basis of which authorities were appointed with clearly limited competences. In Poland, constitutions were a "grant of freedom given by power rather than a grant of power given by freedom." In fact, nobody ever questioned that interpretation of constitutionalism.

Three of the six Constitutions in the history of Poland (Grand Duchy of Warsaw, in 1807; Congress Kingdom, in 1815; and Polish People's Republic, in 1952) were imposed by foreign powers, usually with an active participation of a part of the Polish political elites with collaborated with those powers. The two Constitutions of the period between the two World Wars were passed under pressure of contemporaneous interests and fears. In 1921, fearing a strong President, Marshal Josef Pilsudski, the Legislative Diet adopted a model of the parliament's supremacy, unduly limiting executive authority. When, in 1926, many conflicting parties splintered parliament's authority, and the powerless Government and President could not act efficiently, Pilsudski staged a coup. Constitutional amendments then introduced, followed by the new Constitution of 1935, granted full authority to the President, who was to be responsible before nobody but "God and History." Thus the principle of separation, and above all of balance of powers was never consolidated in the tradition.

What is more, the principle of balance of powers seems to be hardly comprehensible to Polish politicians and constitutionalists. As a result of manipulations of Pilsudski's followers who described the 1935 Constitution as an adjustment of the U.S. model to Polish conditions, the U.S. Constitution is misinterpreted in Poland as embodying nearly unlimited Presidential authority rather than as a mechanism to balance separated powers. The constitutional models that are most frequently considered are the French ones, the discussions usually concerning the choice between the parliamentarianism of the Third Republic and the presidential supremacy of the Fifth Republic. What is more, in Poland constitutionalism was not usually understood as a limitation of democratic and parliamentary authority; Poland lacked the traditions and mechanisms of submitting parliamentary acts to constitutional review, and the traditions of administrative and constitutional courts were just as weak.

Nor did the tradition of a limited state take root in Poland. This failure was partly a result of poor memories of the days of democracy and privileges of the nobility when the weakness of the state contributed to the fall of Poland and was partly due to the fact that during the period of the country's partitions, and afterward under the German and Soviet occupations, the lack of a state was tantamount to the Poles deprivation of their basic rights: to freedom, to property, to cultural identity, and even to life. Hence, the Polish people appreciate the need for a strong State, provided it is their own, benevolent and democratic.

An important trait of the Polish political consciouness has been a combination of democratic traditions and a strong leadership, and sometimes even a trust in a savior who would secure freedom, democracy, and prosperity for the nation. Nor should a good leader be unduly limited when fulfilling his mission. The Polish tradition is therefore one of a benevolent paternalistic authority figure that grants favors to the people rather than one in which people enjoy inalienable rights and have claims on the authorities based on those rights.

In this conception of power and the state, found in the traditions of both Christian social ethics and the pre-Communist Social-Democratic Left, civil rights are closely related to duties toward society and state. Those traditions attached an incomparably greater weight to the social rights than to liberties. What is more, they understood a strong state to be the instrument to provide social welfare; the Constitution, in turn, was to create that very instrument.

This interpretation of state and constitutionalism was a logical effect of the modern Polish history: the history of a weak state situated between two hostile powers; the history of a powerless society composed of a small class of lords and of masses of indigent peasants, without a strong middle class; the history created not by capitalists but by the intellectual elite derived from *declassé* nobility who aimed at retrieval of lost power and influence by political means.

The present social discredit of the vision of a strong state as the means to achieve the general welfare is probably the weightiest effect of the decline of Communist rule in Poland. At the same time the situation today obligates the Poles to verify most of their political beliefs and adopt new principles with which to think about the public life, the role of the state, and the individual's role in society and in the state. This task involves the resolution of many problems that spring from fundamental attitudes in Polish society and affect the choices to be made during the writing of the new Constitution. We will now look at these.

The Nature of Political Elites in Poland

The rerforms enjoy a broad social support, but elites formed in the year of oppositional activities play a decisive role. In Poland today, for that matter, pluralism is mentioned more often than democracy; underlying this emphasis is a correct intuition that pluralism is primarily a "democratic" competition of many elites. The problem is, what nature will those elites have? Today, they are mostly political elites seeking a social base. At the beginning of the "pluralization" of Solidarity, its leader Lech Walesa himself was creating new groupings by giving some authority and power to new people. Later new parties emerged as a result of personal conflicts, animosities, and ambitions, rather than differences of ideas, programs, or interests.

Is this to be the chief way of creating the leading elites in Poland? It is a rather hazardous one to the extent that purely political elites often tend to compete with one another, using as their weapons abstract programs, and even more frequently, the ambitions of their leaders. Elites that represent specific economic interests of producers, investors, capitalists, and workers are more apt to seek a compromise than are the elites run solely by abstract values or the ambitions of their leaders to articulate economic interests in political life. How can interests be represented in the constitutional mechanism of division and balance of power? This uncertainty also attaches to the very process of preparing the Constitution. Is it to be created by "intellects," or by "interests?" Who will play the decisive role in the preparations: intellectuals, lawyers, and the other experts with university education, or people who represent different economic and social interests? Experience shows that theoretical constitutions tend to fail in practice; therefore, the problem arises of how various groups of interests, including those that now have no parliamentary representation, can secure influence on the process of preparing the Constitution. Some thought should also be given to whether the Constitution is to solve specific social and political problems, or should create the mechanism for their solution in the future.

This last question is rooted in the Polish tradition. To what extent will the new Constitution be influenced by the current arrangements of coalitions within the elites in power, by personal strifes, fears, and conflicting ambitions? Will its contents be influenced by Parliament's apprehensions about Walesa's power, as was the case with Pilsudski in 1921? Will the conflicting ambitions of the Sejm and the Senate influence the Constitution? Or will the authors of the new Polish basic statute be able to rise above personal interests, prejudices, and fears?

Attitude of Reforming Elites toward Local Democracy

Another group of problems concern the very attitude of the reforming elites to local democracy. Though democracy of elites may well exist in a centralized form, it is impossible to build from the top a democracy based on participation of the people. It has to be built from the base up, from local governments. The local and municipal elections of May 1990 helped change the former arrangements of local Communist cliques; but the actual liveliness and responsibility of local democracy will depend on the Constitution. This responsibility requires that the local governments be granted independence and secured specific competences on which state authority cannot encroach. Some have suggested that those spheres reserved for local governments should include care for the social problems of the inhabitants; state authorities would thus be relieved of the welfare duties that sometimes clash with the aims of economic reform toward a market economy and of political reform. The question here is would reforming intellectuals within the parliament and those connected with the government be willing to trust local governments and relinquish the desire for control over all issues and reforms in the State?

Necessary to the promotion of the autonomy of local governments is their financial independence. This issue caused a bitter controversy between President Walesa and the Parliament during the budget debate in early 1991. The President criticized the government and the Sejm for allocating so little money to local governments that they were unable to fulfill their responsibilities. Budget constraints made it clear that the financial independence of local governments depended on granting them the right to levy local taxes. What has proved more controversial, particularly in light of the requirements of the economic reform, is the question of the local governments' possible profitable economic activities. The Act on Local Governments of 1990, which granted the right to carry out these activities, has met with criticism with respect to all forms of state property: How to secure the economic effectiveness of that property and prevent infringements of competition by the local government-owned companies and firms, less efficient by their very nature?

The question we asked about the system of power in the State as a whole also concerns local governments. What mechanism should be created to identify and surface conflicting interests and to reach compromise on a local level?

System of Separation of Powers

As we have seen, the principle of separation, and particularly of balance, of powers is not part of the Polish tradition. During numerous discussions in the Parliament, in the drafting Constitutional Committees and among the leaders of emerging parties, two different visions of the balance of powers emerged. One was a model of parliamentary democracy in which the prime minister is appointed and held responsible by the parliament and the president is an umpire, mediating between the legislature and the government as well as between other conflicting interests. The other vision tends to vest more independent power in the executive: the President, selected by popular election, would appoint the Prime Minister and the government; the responsibility of the government to the Parliament would be much more limited. Also, it should be noted that in the latter case the legitimacy of the entire executive branch (including the government) would derive from presidential rather than parliamentary elections.

Related to this discussion is the question of the nature of parliamentarianism in Poland. The rapid process of emergence of many small parties causes fears that the Parliament might be transformed into a bazaar with many parties of little influence, a circumstance that might lead to the kind of government instability notorious in the period between the two World Wars. Hence the suggestions that the Constitution should include a specific system of electoral representation, either proportional or single mandate according to the British model, which would offer incentives to a multiplicity of parties in society to establish two or three large party blocs within the Parliament. However, in the bitter struggle for the electoral law, the majority of the Sejm supported the idea of proportional representation, paving the way to the Sejm for many small parties.

Range and Nature of Polish Democracy and the Protection of the Rights of Individuals and of Minorities

The notion of democracy traditionally appeals much more strongly to the Poles than do freedom or the principle of limited government. Almost immediately after the replacement of the Communist government, new dangers surfaced: intolerance towards minorities, and paralysis of the authorities when faced with infringements of the rights of minorities or of individuals by a crowd or by groups of rioters. What served as a litmus test of democracy was the attitude of local communities towards HIV carriers; in several instances, without any action on the part of the authorities, the crowd forced the infected to leave town. In one case, the local legislative agency gave a certain date by which the AIDS patients were to leave; then, it turned out that, in the Polish legal system, such an unconstitutional resolution can be appealed only to a people's council of a higher level. The individual whose rights have been infringed cannot appeal against this decision to any other court or tribunal.

This situation is related to the problem of *guarantees of individual rights* in the new Constitution. There has never been a strong tradition of individual rights in Poland; during the last few decades those rights were treated first of all as limits to totalitarian authority. Can we now accept the fact that human rights limit all authority, including (and perhaps in particular!) the democratic one? History demonstrates that democracies, particularly the local ones, are not too sensitive to the rights of minorities and of individuals who think differently. Thus the greater the powers of local governments, the more important it becomes to mark the exact limits of their power, that is, the rights that no authority may infringe.

Individual rights seem to be particularly needed today for still another reason. The odds are that the Poles will learn democracy in the practical lessons of their own mistakes. The problem is to prevent those inevitable mistakes from taking too heavy a toll. The limits of social experimentation should be set by human rights, which cannot be violated even for future benefits of the society. Therefore, human rights should receive an explicit formulation in the Constitution, which must also provide for a mechanism through which all citizens can vindicate their rights. The Polish traditions in this respect can hardly be called excellent. Before World War II and in the 1952 Constitution human rights received but a declaratory treatment; further, they were subject to various restrictions by force of legal acts of a lower rank, and there was no provision for individual remedies in cases of infringements of those rights.

What is more, human rights have gone hand in hand with duties in the modern history of Poland, a tradition that still seems rigid today. All studies show that the Poles perceive duties as the conditions of rights; the only concession to a liberal interpretation of rights is an occasional admission that an individual has rights in relation to the state, and duties in relation to society.

Conflicts between the Economic and Political Reforms and the Aspirations for Social Equality and Safety

A group of problems related to Constitutional concerns are those involving conflicts between the economic and political reforms and the aspirations to social equality and safety. The relatively simplest problem here is the squaring of the inviolability of property and transactions with the social sense of justice. A large part of society would want the members of the Communist *nomenklatura* to return the wealth appropriated while they were in power, even if this would weaken the much needed process of the privatization of the economy and the creation of a capitalist class. Among others, the delicate problem arises here of invalidating the so-called *nomenklatura* companies, particularly those that have already formed joint ventures with foreign capital which expects regard for ownership and contracts.

A more serious problem is the squaring of contradictory economic and social values. A rather distinct conflict exists between the changes of the political system and reforms aimed at the market economy on the one hand and the trend to secure economic and social safety on the other hand. One possible way to soothe that conflict would be the separation, already mentioned above, of responsibilities between state agencies and local governments, e.g., to transfer welfare matters to local governments with a simultaneous grant of financial means necessary to perform such tasks. But the problem of the sense of social and economic security is not limited only to the issue of centralization versus decentralization of the decisions in such matters.

Social rights have always been the focal point of both the Leftist and the Christian tradition of human rights in Poland. The 1921 Constitution declared what was probably the broadest set of social rights in Europe. If, however, we are to treat human rights seriously today, we cannot grant rights in the Constitution that we will not be able to secure. Most certainly, today's Poland cannot afford a state guarantee of the right to work or the right to rest, and perhaps not even the right to free medical care. If such vain declarations were to be included in the chapter on civil rights, it would result in a depreciation of all rights, including political rights and liberties. On the other hand, a removal of social rights from the Constitution would be an abandonment of the entire Polish social tradition.

The Constitution will have to effect some sort of a compromise in this sphere. One possible solution would be to include in the preamble a declaration to the effect that the guarantee of social rights is the future goal of the society. Another possible solution goes somewhat farther: the creation of a mechanism to provide for means to solve social problems in the future. For example, that mechanism might be a constitutional provision stating that in the future a given percentage of growth in the national income, or in the state budget and/or the local budgets, should be reserved for implementation of social and economic rights. The historical experience of developed countries shows that before they reached the level of development necessary to implement social rights, strong political and economic elites in all those countries resisted redistribution, because they themselves did not need such rights. The creation of a mechanism of future redistribution would be a serious attempt to provide for the rights that most citizens seem to be most particular about today.

The Rank of the Constitution

Poland has never had a strong tradition of constitutionalism that limited parliamentary authority; the expectation for the administrative and constitutional courts has been just as weak. There is not even a national consensus about the fundamental values of constitutionalism. What will the new Constitution be? As it was in the past, a mere plan of organization of power and a charter of privileges granted by the authorities? Or a truly supreme law, binding on the citizens and on the authorities, including the Parliament? Will it create a mechanism to secure review of the constitutionality of statutes? What specific mechanism of such review are the authors of our Constitution going to choose?

Connected to the question of the Constitution's rank is the very procedure of its passing. Obviously, society should participate in that process, the more so as the present Sejm and Senate were not elected but are the result of a political compromise negotiated during the "Round Table" conference. Anyway, no parliament should have the right to decide single-handedly about the Constitution by which it is granted a greater or smaller amount of power. The Parliament's decision on this matter requires social approval.

What does seem controversial is the actual form of expressing that approval. Most deputies and senators seem to favor a national referendum. Another option proposes ratification of the Constitution by independent local communities; it is argued that this solution would encourage the formation of a civic society, which cannot be built from the top, that is by the Parliament. The grant of a right to ratify the Constitution to local governments would give those basic units of the civic society a sense of identity as independent and fully legitimate actors in Polish social and political life. At the same time, it would increase the sense of social responsibility and mitigate the severity of the traditional chasm between "us" and "them." Ratification by this means might also provide a mechanism to link political elites with the masses, and an unprecedented opportunity for mass political education.

The problems discussed briefly above are but some of the options for the new Constitution. The difficult choices are the task of the authors of Poland's new Constitution—and of society as a whole. After all, those problems reflect the fundamental questions in Poland today, the answer to which can only be partial in even the best of Constitutions. How can the foundations of freedom be created in a country that lacks a strong class of businessmen independent of the state? And, how can the foundations of democracy be created in a country without a middle class, and where the odds are that further polarization of society will take place?

And finally, how can the sense of responsibility for one's own life be developed in each Polish citizen? The history of Poland has hardly been conducive to the shaping of that sense essential to the building of democracy; joint responsibility for the nations's collective fate. The foundation of responsibility for one's own life is freedom: free choice of one's life path. The Constitutions that the post-Communist countries need today should provide the foundations for that freedom.

Note

1. This chapter was written in April 1990 and was reviewed for inclusion in this volume a year later. In that time, much had happened in Poland, and in the course of the Sejm's and Senate's preparation of the draft constitutions, many constitutional issues were raised. These events basically confirmed the importance of the issues and questions dealt with in my chapter. One issue not raised by me, although it was heatedly debated at the Pecs conference, was the problem of the source of the legitimacy to write the new Constitution.

21

Rule by Law in East Central Europe: Is the Emperor's New Suit a Straitjacket?

András Sajó and Vera Losonci

This chapter analyzes the new legalistic trends developing in east European socialist countries, considering events in Czechoslovakia, in Hungary, and in Poland; it only occasionally refers to Rumania, Bulgaria, Yugoslavia, and the Soviet Republics. Repudiating the earlier system, emerging leaders promise a liberal legal system. It is not clear, however, whether the attempts to create this new legal framework aim at establishing a rule by law or a rule of law system. *Rechtsstaat* and rule of law are used as having separate meanings. *Rechtsstäatlichkeit* is the functional equivalent of the rule in a society such as Germany where the state and its bureaucracy play a more prominent role than these institutions had in the formative period of the rule of law tradition in Anglo-Saxon countries. The role of the judiciary also differs.

By rule of law I mean the continuation of the German *Rechtsstaat* tradition, which played a considerable role in the pre-Communist legal and political culture of the region. The new regimes tend to rely to a great extent on law to define the new societies in order to transform them. It is only a slight exaggeration to state that most of the efforts of social transformation focus on achieving the governance of these societies by impartial laws.

In the turmoil of the recent and ongoing changes and transformations in eastern Europe, the people of this region think of themselves as on their way to becoming central Europeans, which in their eyes equals being accepted or incorporated into a somewhat mystical Europe. This aspiration is particularly strong in Czechoslovakia and Hungary. In that process, emphasis lies on the rule of law and the *Rechtsstaat* legalism both for the protection of society and human rights against an all pervasive state (party) domination, and for the promotion of a market economy, believed to be the ultimate solution to the present economic crisis. However, when it comes to creating a positive legal framework for the functioning of a market economy (a more liberal contractual and property system, bankruptcy law, banking law, mortage system, etc.), the process becomes slow and painful, partly because fundamental constitutional (and social) issues are unresolved.

As will be noted, these dominating ideas are generally simple negations of the former system and the idea of market is generally used as an attractive promise. There is little desire to pay the social price of a market-oriented transformation. I will try to point out that there is a similar reluctance when it comes to taking seriously law and the rule of law. These reluctances are related.

Further, to understand the meaning of "legalism" and the striving toward a market-supportive rule of law system in these countries, two circumstances should be taken into consideration. First, in these societies social oppression was, primarily, oppression by the state. The State and the Party controlled the society through a baised and discretionary legal system and through state ownership of the national economies. Liberation in these countries means the curtailment of the powers of the state and the bureaucracy; it is in this context that rule of law and privatization are to be understood. Second, there are indications within the present transformation of the survival instincts of the former ruling classes, who, in some countries, seek a compromise with new forces representing the "new" legitimate ideologies, for example, those presecular value systems that resisted socialism. Religion and nationalism are particularly important in this respect. In other countries, compromise is out of the question; these presecular forces tend simply to gain control of the old centers of domination. According to this scenario, the bureaucratic and monopolistic systems of social control will survive; the new bureaucrats will be the members of the victorious groups. All this goes on under the banners of national interests and public concerns, but the result will be the preservation of the present social and economic structural arrangements, which may result in further isolation from the leading world market forces. The reluctance to change radically the economic and other (e.g., cultural) monopolies and the easy falling back on concepts of material justice indicate similar tendencies.

The *Rechtsstaat* Tradition and the Underdeveloped Constitutionalism of the Pre-Communist Period

The absence of a constitutional tradition of the pre-Communist period is a considerable factor in the present legal and constitutional transformation process. One of the great problems that the new regime currently faces is that members of the political elite and the judiciary were educated in the Communist system; therefore, little understanding of what constitutionalism entails exists even among members of the former opposition, not to mention the popular masses. Observers are nevertheless struck by the resurgence of prewar behavior patterns and cognitive structures, which may and actually do have institutional implications. A prevailing concept in east central Europe is that after the past 40 years of usurpation, return to the traditional institutional and moral systems represents genuine national values and virtues, and that "return" is to a legitimate constitutional system. The idealization of the past is obviously an expression of national identity, a sense of which played a major role in the resistance to Communism. Modeling society on the traditional institutional and moral systems poses an obvious problem when it comes to the question of private property and redistribution. Aversion to private property, increased pauperization, and egalitarianism make the prewar, often privilege-oriented private property system less attractive. Yet a reluctance to safeguard property dooms all constitutional efforts both politically and socially. The transformation of the legal system can only be partial without a wholehearted endorsement of free market legal institutions.

The Poles are proud of the progressive democratic nature of 1791 and, naturally, there is strong political interest after the election of Lech Walesa in believing that Pilsudski's presidential powers are comparable to those of the Fifth Republic in France, and therefore fully meet modern requirements of democracy. In Czechoslovakia the prewar regime is evaluated according to the letter of the Masaryk Constitution; people equate it with a constitutional reality. Leading Hungarian political forces believe that the unwritten constitution of Hungary—a fragmentary system of medieval laws and liberal legislation that was politically repealed after 1920—represents a genuine liberal constitutional and democratic tradition. There was in fact a strong liberal tradition noticeable among the intelligentsia of the region, but this was never predominant. The political and legal institutions of the period were not particulrly influenced by liberal ideology, since intellectuals as a group, in general, remained outside the ruling elite and the state machinery. The prevailing official ideology reflected the privileged and dominant role of the nondemocratically controlled state. The state had a special role in the attempts at economic modernization of the east central European periphery, resulting in a special bureaucratic legal tradition that is mirrored in the concept of rule by the law.

The prewar state bureaucracy was controlled by laws that gave some protection to the individual without the assertion that the individual had endowment or rights, except in strictly private relations with other citizens. As Hans Kelsen, the founding father of the Austrian Constitution, put it: "Subjective rights are only reflexes of the protection given by courts and through the courts by positive law." [1] This seems to have been true even in Czechoslovakia where the Austrian legal tradition survived under the Masaryk Constitution. Reliance on the rule by law tradition is, of course, attractive to all social and political forces that have an interest in maintaining some kind of an etatist system after the collapse of socialism. All this is not to say that a rule by law system would not be a major step forward in the region, or that a *Rechtsstaat* would not be the most realistic optimum given the social and political realities of the region.

Legality under State Socialism

According to the now defunct official ideology of the eastern European socialist states, law serves the building of socialism. To be an effective means of building socialism, law must conform to the ideals of socialist legality. The socialist systems of eastern Europe were legalistic societies to a surprising extent, although the meaning of law may have been quite different from what one generally conceives under this notion.

Legal scholars claimed that in eastern Europe law is also a generalized system of commands (though there were some serious but hidden problems with the generalization of these commands that often came from unrecognized sources). With respect to the protection of (individual) rights, the socialist theory boasted of the "superior nature" of socialist law precisely because it was not based on the concept of individual rights. Theory claimed the law to be a collective interest-oriented system that emphasized the reciprocity of rights and obligations, with social obligations as the source of rights.

One cannot deny that given the bureaucratic system of social dominance, and the great concern about centralism (etatism), there has always been some interest on the part of rulers in a formal uniform command system. Lenin himself, in his struggle to regain central control over society, emphasized the importance of socialist legality. He defined socialist legality as a uniform country-wide application of the central commands versus the autonomous and capricious decision making of local bodies, including the revolutionary tribunals applying the standards of the revolutionary consciousness of the worker-judges. To promote the central control a former Czarist institution, the military organized *procurata*, received extended powers to review various decisions for the purposes of conformity to the law. This was an extraordinary power because it meant that no court decision was immune from review. The *procurata*'s powers were discretionary. As laws were extremely loosely worded, therefore, nearly all decisions could be reviewed for reasons of nonconformity with the law.

A second feature of the socialist legal system emphasized by Lenin is the predominance of public law over private law. ("We do not recognize anything private. For us all is public.") The statement clearly prioritizes public interest, understood as party and state interest.

In eastern Europe socialist law was interpreted as a system closely following the example of Soviet law. Nevertheless, because of the different legal traditions and the lesser degree of centralization of society, the legal systems of the people's democracies are much closer to the western, civil law tradition. There was some independent legal thinking both in legal reasoning (legal dogmatics) and in substantive terms of rights. It would be an error, however, to overestimate the importance of these features, especially if one takes into consideration the amount of discretionary power built into the flexible texts of the laws, and the lack of sufficient and independent judicial review.

Law was understood as instrumental to social and economic planning; its legislative role was negligible in comparison with its regulatory function. Regulation by governmental decrees, some secret, was present to varying extents in all countries. An equally serious distortion concerning the participants in the legal system is noticeable. Judges and courts acted as bureaucrats, and fulfilled the expectation that they would promote centrally determined public interests. The courts were declared independent; however, the career of the judges was bureaucratic as was their remuneration and evaluation; all were based on political loyalty.

Lawyers were existentially dependent on the legal system. They played a subservient role in exchange for the privilege of *numerus clausus*. Their university education and legal training were subject to party control. Their socialization made them vulnerable to external, nonlegal values and interests. They conceived their role as directly related to general social concerns and legal texts offered little possibility for independent action. Lawyers became increasingly dependent on their superiors and on political forces. The prestige of the legal professions declined. Under these circumstances not even the relative simplicity of access to justice and the relatively low cost of litigation are attractive to the public, since the achieved justice does not protect their interests (not to mention rights).

A closer look at the contents of laws and regulations reveals further consequences of the instrumentalist approach. Laws were intended to achieve set targets, partly by strict orders and partly by prohibitions and hidden constraints. In this area the law was hair-splittingly keen on precise details; in many other areas one cannot find any reasonable rule. The law promoted privileges simply by failing to regulate relations openly. The wide gap left to administrative discretion was filled by secret regulations granting privileges to the state and the members of the *nomenklatura*. In many cases no rules were set, but those who applied the law knew which departments of institutions, offices, local party organizations, and other local notables were to be obeyed when it came to decision making.

The system created for itself the advantage of keeping most of its participants (including the decision makers) in a dependent position. This dependence resulted from imprecision and the insecurity stemming from it. Anyone could be summoned to account under many pretexts; this possibility increased dependence and obedience to informed commands. On the other hand, the system managed to disguise under its legalistic facade a great number of built-in inequalities and modes of domination.

Modernization in eastern Europe depends to a great extent on the state's use of its laws to promote it. Because of systematic efforts by the Communists, very few institutions remained independent. In reality all actions had to originate from the state, and, therefore, had to have some appearance of legality. Consequently, law was bureaucratic and purposive; it denied individual rights, as rights might have resulted in independent social action. Social reliance on the state increased; independent organizations were considered suspect or were simply not tolerated. The state initiative remained the only or, at least the only admitted, active force in society. Projects of the central government were often arbitrary as they were based on external models of socialist modernization.

As the system did not tolerate self-interest, not even in its most enlightened version, it assumed that all participants in the realization of a centrally determined and therefore legally prescribed project should be controlled; law was to a great extent understood and used to control and supervise people who would have been otherwise unmotivated to comply. In the economies of shortage the motivation to cheat existed to meet the unrealistic centrally planned goals and the people's modest needs.

The legal system was further distorted by the influence of the Communist

Party, though this was generally informal and/or to a certain extent illegal. The ways and means of the influence of the Party varied from country to country, but it was far-reaching everywhere with respect to the contents of the legislation and personnel policies. The Party often made the actual decisions of the local public administration, and the legal system was obscure and discretionary enough to allow for the protection of the privileges of the *nomenklatura*.

Lasting Consequences of the Socialist Legal System

In the Weberian sense, the legal systems of eastern and central eastern Europe were open to demands to substantive justice. This was, of course, determined by etatist centralism and Party influences, and, therefore, affected by egalitarianism, which only served to disguise privileges. However, in Poland, Hungary, and perhaps in Czechoslovakia, the ideas behind law making and application of the law were not contrary to legal formalism. Undermining this modest formal virtue of the legal system was, however, the nonlegal determination of the *Rechtsträger*—lawyers, legal scholars, and legislators; therefore, foreseeability was not expected of the system. Politically, the law became an overt means of repression of the political opposition. The general public was skeptical about the nuclear and unprotective legal system, an obstacle to be outmaneuvered for survival's sake.

The attitudes of the elites and the general public toward law will play an important, perhaps crucial role, in the shaping of the new legal and constitutional system. These attitudes were contradictory. Generally, the opposition in the east European countries felt that they were persecuted by the existing legal system. Their criticism was based less on the technical concepts or models of western constitutionalism and rule of law than on universal human rights. This position related to a tactical possibility offered by international conventions on human rights. Some east European countries ratified them or at least voiced their support for human rights to create a direct confrontation between the existing legal practice and the officially accepted standards. This position also resulted in a strange "legalism" by some opposition groups, which made attempts to force the authorities to take "their law" seriously. On the other hand, by rejecting the existing political system the opposition emphasized the importance of civil society. The autonomous bodies of civil society presuppose a legally bounded state, a kind of rule of law over the state.

The New Legalism

Legalism as Legitimation

Reformative and revolutionary forces considered the legal system one to be sued and conquered for their purposes. In Hungary, and to a certain extent in Poland, and in a different way in the Soviet Union, Communists were partly responsible for the beginning of reform or, at least, some of the Communists tried to control reform processes. In these countries, the transformation of the legal system was considered a proof of the good intentions of the reformists. It was an often-stated belief that a modernized legal system, which observed constitutionalism and promised a calculable legal environment for business, including a gradual transition to market economy, would grant legitimacy and credibility to the reform process both inside and outside the country. Furthermore, it was hoped that a system with more open rules would increase the efficiency of that system. The ruling elites hoped that once their system became constitutional, it would also be acceptable and, therefore, would continue to survive.

Given the nature of the system, the interests of the participants and the transition process, this proved to be a somewhat naive illusion. The results were contradictory, and certainly far from the expected with respect to the quality of the legal system. In the Soviet Union, Mikhail Gorbachev's rule partly destroyed the old inefficient but working network of illegal relations without replacing it with a system based on the rule of law. In Poland and Hungary, the spectacular changes in the public law contributed to democracy, but failed to instill respect for constitutionalism or to create the rule of law.

Both in the reform process and after the more or less revolutionary victories by the masses, the creation of a constitutional legal system with western types of liberal/formal solutions was a high priority. For the public this ideology was not self-legitimating. Religion, anticommunism, nationalism, and consumer values seem more important now to the masses. In any event, it was never made clear what was constitutional; nor were the fundamental differences between the American and the *Rechtstaat* model taken into consideration. There has only been a minimal common acceptance of the liberal tradition. Agreement exists on the importance of human rights, on the separation of powers (interpreted as denial of one-party rule), and on independent judiciary; but there is still no position of principle on welfare rights or on public interest priorities, in particular *vis-à-vis* private property. This level of acceptance obviously reflects the present political struggle for the control of the state, and more generally the slow emancipation of society from centralism.

Democratic legislation was thought to be a remedy for the malaise of the previous system. In this respect the east European transformation process follows the general pattern of revolutionary legal change: it is a denial of the previous solutions. The replacement of these solutions is, however, a matter of choice; there are many ways to part with the past. One group of possible choices is offered by the available western models (which are often little and selectively known or misunderstood, and are too sophisticated to be adapted). Another major choice consists of the pre-Communist legal solutions, which present linguistic barriers, and which are attractive because they can be legitimized as genuinely national solutions. The problem is that these solutions are often outdated; they did not meet criteria of democracy 50 or 60 years ago. Nor were these central European societies particularly modernized before World War II. One should keep in mind, however, that nationalism and religion were important sources of resistance, and important conservative voices among the emerging leaders in the society supported this solution.

If the new ruling classes and elites manage to convince the population that they are offering them rights through the new legal system, their legitimacy will increase. This is not an easy task, as economic hardship and political instability make it imperative to pass unpopular measures through law. The inherent formalism of a legalistic system will be unpopular, too. The possibility exists (some manifestations of it are discussed below) that the new political elites will seek popular support by disregarding legal formalism, its own "creation," claiming that it supports only the unjust *status quo ante*. The investigative special procedures against the former leaders aid in their discrediting; with these, however, the rule of law concept becomes fully instrumental or nonexistent: special tribunals are set up and retroactive force is acceptable. The extreme case is Rumania where due process is irrelevant when weighing needs for punishment and revenge.

At the moment, however, the great bulk of the legislation is certainly in line with western standards. Laws are enacted by the former opposition with the clear intent to repeal the source of the formal party–state system and some of the most discriminative and oppressive rules of the former regime, especially in the field of criminal law, by decriminalizing civil liberties (e.g., the abolition of restrictions on free speech, the right to freedom of association and to leave one's country).

To abolish and repeal seems relatively easy. The difficulties arise when it comes to safeguarding and promoting liberties. We will explore some persuasive evidence for this statement.

Different Uses of Law

Constitutions

One of the first steps of the social and political transformation taken in all former socialist societies was the amendment of the Communist constitutions. These amendments abolished the privileges of the Communist Party. Moreover, in the case of Hungary, they institutionalized the protection of human rights and separation of powers. Nevertheless, in every case the amendments were the result of an elite agreement with the former Communist leadership. They were not intended to be expressions of the "will," values, or demands of the masses who to varying degrees participated in the process resulting in the collapse of Communist rule. The amendments, openly intended to be revised, reflected the provisional arrangements; revisions became routine procedures as new conflicts emerged. Such confrontations surfaced over presidential powers in Poland, Bulgaria, and Hungary, over federalism in Czechoslovakia, and over the constitutional powers of the executive (government) in all the countries of the region.

From the point of view of a rule of law system or any system that takes law (i.e., the meaning of words) seriously, utilizing the constitution to rewrite political agreements is counterproductive to the goal of creating respect and belief in constitutionalism. If a constitution is easy to amend it loses its majestic special role. The Hungarian Constitution of 1989 was amended six times in the first year of its existence; the changes amount to one-third of the text. Issues of constitutional amendment aimed at settling conflicts absorb a considerable amount of time in parliamentary debates in Czechoslovakia and in Bulgaria. In that process law, including the text of the Constitution, easily becomes a matter of technicality. For instance, after the Hungarian Constitutional Court ruled unconstitutional an article of the Election law, the Parliament the next day amended the Constitution so as to make the article in question conform to the Election Law!

Public Interest Legislation

Legislation is still understood as a means to protect the public interest with the consequence that wide discriminatory powers are granted to public authorities. The amendment of the press law in Hungary is a typical case. The amended Act on Press established practically complete freedom of the press, a somewhat redundant act insofar as a limiting regulation of the government had been repealed earlier. But the fascination of legalism constrained the Parliament to have the existing system sanctioned. The change was, however, limited in its spirit. Freedom of the press did not include an understanding of what free speech means. In the case of libel, the journalist must pay a fine to the *state*, and not to the injured party (who would have to go through a civil process for damages). Notwithstanding the resistance of the Minister of Justice and a leading opposition MP, the overwhelming majority of Parliament accepted a further provision which states that the libel fine applies in case of harm to *public morality*.

The extremely slow and contradictory process of privatization is also illuminating in this respect. After much hesitation, Hungary, Poland, and Czechoslovakia have committed themselves to some kind of privatization, and some kind of reprivatization. Rumania expressly denied reprivatization in the industrial sector, and discourages the reprivatization of land. Even where privatization appears to be a governmental policy, it is not construed as a legal question or as a constitutional issue. Public interest concerns prevail, resulting in the creation of new state bureaucracies or in the extension of the powers of the already existing bureaucracies, which can control privatization without judicial review, public liability, or a limit to administrative discretion. Xenophobia, nationalism, or simple government (bureaucratic) interests result in discriminatory measures against foreign investors, which is of course counterproductive. Economic dissatisfaction, on the other hand, results in granting to the government extraordinary unconstitutional power to deal with the economic hardships.

Some scholars do take Frederic Hayek more seriously and would limit government intervention to a minimum (after the destruction of the monopolies and regulations). Notwithstanding the popularity of Hayek as a brand name, most people are too afraid of the unforeseen consequences of liberalism. On the other hand, one can easily predict the consequences of public interest protection through regulatory agencies where there is no countervailing market force and where public interest protection means only the protection and survival of existing bureaucracies.

Given the predominance of public interest concern with obvious political overtones, it is hardly surprising that in Hungary there is little willingness to rely on impartial abstract rules operating within an independent judiciary. The Act on the Prosecutor's Office of 1953 often gives the public prosecutor special rights to review cases, although these rights are clearly part of the Stalinist legacy. Parliament sets up almost on a daily basis "independent" investigative commissions with undefined powers and without procedural rules.

Juridification

The earlier-mentioned strong tendency to neutralize political conflicts by turning them into legal issues coexists with the contrary trend of impatience with solutions offered by the legal system, and insistence on "legal solutions" directly dictated by political considerations. In this respect it is worth mentioning that the wiretapping of former opposition leaders by the Hungarian Ministry of the Interior as late as 1989 is seen to a great extent as an issue of the constitutionality of the secret rules on wiretapping conferring authority on the Ministry, rather than as a breach of the Round Table agreements.

The contradictory nature of juridification is perhaps most obvious in the role attributed to the recently established Hungarian Constitutional Court. Citizens have a basically unlimited right to petition the Court, and the Court itself may refer cases to its own jurisdiction! In the first 60 days of its existence more than 50 laws were referred to the Court for nullification. The Government tried to use the Constitutional Court as a means to avoid politically embarrassing decisions. For example, the Prime Minister tried to avoid a conflict within the government coalition by asking the Court to give a preliminary advisory opinion on the restitution of private property confiscated by the Communists. When the Constitutional Court in May 1991 later declared unconstitutional the government's reprivatization Act, leading members of the majority parties started a campaign to curtail the powers of the Court. The Dred Scott case is an extreme, but in all respects instructive, example of the possible consequences of the juridification of politics.

Activism

Obviously, rule of law is not a system based on any kind of active interference, and certainly not on the active role of the judge. Of course, if there is enough time and initiative in a society to let autonomous forces develop reasonable solutions, Bentham's point about the judge who waits until his dog does something wrong to punish him makes perfect sense. Quite understandably, however, one might expect active intervention and shaping of liberal institutions in a society on the verge of economic collapse whose faculty of self-determination has been systematically destroyed. Although this activism is not, however, acceptable as part of the judicial attitude it does make sense to state that at least some of the elementary systems and institutional frames to promote market relations in such a society have to be created by the government. The theory of modernization through law offers arguments in favor of this approach and I am not going to repeat those. It seems reasonable to regulate legally companies limited by shares if you want foreign investment or domestic transfer of capital, and some positive evidence exists to support governmental creation of stock markets. A great bulk of the east European legislation takes that direction.

However, a closer scrutiny of some of the market-creating laws yields controversial findings. Most of the laws concern organizational matters, regulating extensively the hierarchical relations. Evidence suggests that one of the crucial aims of these laws in Hungary was to make the head of governmental agencies (generally someone who served the Communist Party) unremovable. The laws creating the agencies do not set forth rules to govern their activities; there is only a general clause about protecting public interest and promoting the establishment of the market. The law creating the Agency for State Fund provided internal rules for the composition of governing bodies, but, notwithstanding repeated warnings by the World Bank and some domestic agencies, failed to set forth either clear policy criteria or due process requirements. The rule of law issue is settled simply by granting judicial review, without offering criteria for that review. In all countries, and in Poland in particular, there is a growing dissatisfaction with the existing business law structures, which seem only to guarantee in private business the privileged positions of the former Communist bureaucracy.

Political Justice

A major blow to the *Rechtsstaat* principle is expected from the "legalization" of political justice, intended to be used against former communist leaders. The scope, sanction system, and retroactivity of these tribunals vary from country to country, depending on the level of hatred, the legal culture, the number of supporters of the Communist Party, and the need for finding scapegoats. These tribunals are not yet established at the time of writing, but elements of unfairness are easily noticeable in the Ceausescu and Honecker cases.

Judicial Review and the Judiciary

Although judicial review in the German tradition (i.e., in cases where actual individual decisions affected individual interests and rights) was to be the cornerstone of the new legalism, it meets considerable resistance. Rumania rejects it outright and relies on the French tradition of administrative review by the *Conseil d'Etat* (which, of course, is a quasijudicial review in a country where the government respects the independence of the Council members). In Hungary, the Parliament failed to enact a law that would have institutionalized judicial review as required by the Constitution; the Constitutional Court declared administrative decisions concerning the fundamental rights of citizens to be subject to appeal, but there are simply no courts to review these appeals.

As we know, the east European judiciary was trained in a bureaucratic tradition open to extralegal considerations (the public interest) and with little interest in independence, though most of the judges believe that what they have is independence indeed. Practically all county court presidents in Hungary openly declared that they saw nothing wrong in summoning young judges who were about to pass sentence, as these "youngsters are not well prepared and thereby unfair and illegal decisions are avoided."[2] In some countries judges are also the worst paid members of the legal field, and a decreasing number of judges have to handle a growing number of cases, different from those litigated under the socialist system. Moreover, some of the judges and prosecutors were politically compromised by administering political justice or by simply having used their discretionary powers unfairly against the victors of today. Reactions to this reality differ from country to country. In the GDR, agreement was reached to dismiss, though not try, 10 to 15% of the former judges. In Hungary, a handful of compromised judges was quietly asked to retire. In Poland, however, there was a major replacement of judges with young lawyers who were partly schooled by Solidarity.

Changing the judiciary, even for a "good cause," is particularly problematic because it represents a departure from the idea of judicial independence. Nor is there trained personnel to replace judges in most of these countries. Mediation and other alternatives to justice are unpopular because of earlier abuses of informality; informal justice contradicts the strict legality that is to be reestablished.

In response to the demands of rule of law in Hungary, judges hurried to support the suggestion of the anti-Communist opposition at the Round Table talks that judges be barred from membership in any political party in exchange for an informal grant of immunity. Parliament and the Ministry of Justice also promised them self-government, which may maintain for their lifetimes the positions of Communist Party appointees. The contradiction is obvious: if you support judicial self-government as part of creating the *Rechtsstaat*, you will be aiding the position of people who seem to be unresponsive to ideas of fairness, are unfamiliar with judicial independence, and resist responsibility for creative precedents.

On the other hand, as is usual after revolutions, judges are not much trusted. And after so many years of imposed will, the doctrine of popular sovereignty identified with parliamentary majority rule fascinates the people. They would like to have all authorities, including the courts, subjected to laws insofar as is possible. This attitude is, of course, rather far removed from the rule of law doctrine, and might become functionally rigid and unresponsive in a rapidly changing complex society.

Little help can be expected from the bar. The lawyers enjoyed the privilege of *numerus clausus* and became wealthy partly through illegal activities or other privileges (in Hungary, real estate agency monopolies). Their interest lies in the preservation of the present system. Formal entry barriers to the bar will probably disappear, but the lawyer will not automatically become an active supporter of a rights-based litigious system. (Criminal defense lawyers are something of an exception because of their constant frustration during their meetings with the police.) Lawyers are not interested in upgrading the judges' position either. The present system, which expects an active judge, is rather comfortable for the lawyer, especially as the determination of the most important and lucrative issues takes place outside the court.

Evaluation and Conclusions

It is certainly too early to make a definitive evaluation of the nature of and results of the changes in these societies from the point of view of rule of law or of a market-oriented liberal–democratic legal system. Before any evaluation, it should be stressed again that the differences among the countries discussed are enormous and nothing conclusive has been achieved.

First, under socialism, the role of law was understood in its relation to the state. Its purpose was to discipline people and create some kind of bureaucratic consistency in the administration of state affairs. Contrary to Weber's bureaucratic law model, this legal system was not predictable; bureaucratic discipline and the rules of jurisdiction served the irrational or only the Party-dictated politically rational decisions of the moment.

After the collapse of state socialism contradictory tendencies emerged. Party of the intelligentsia, which opposed Communism and now has some influence on legislation, supported the liberal tradition and maintained that law should be used to limit and govern government action. They considered the judiciary a key element in case of a state breach of its legal mandate *vis-à-vis* the citizen. In the short run, this assumption will be so exaggerated as to lead to the juridification of politics. No doubt this tendency is partly a result of the lack of confidence in traditional political organizations and private agreements. Further, with the collapse of other normative communication systems, law as communication has become particularly important.

The new political mechanism and the emerging power elite share this interest in legalism. The new governments hope to achieve internal and external (international) legitimation by making their actions more legalistic and basing their legalism on attractive formal criteria. They use law, and legislation in particular, as a symbolic means to create the *Rechtsstaat* system. The formal regulation of social relations, even if often accomplished in a liberal manner, presently does not have the dignity of law. Dignity of law in this respect requires built-in mechanisms that make the law relatively unalterable and self-reflecting. Since legislation plays a primary role in the process of creating a rule of law, or at least a rule by law system, and has extensive legitimizing functions, much less importance is given to the internal characteristics of law, or to use Lon Fuller's approach,[3] the morality of law. Procedural legitimation, including both the democratic making of law and judicial review by constitutional courts, prevails over the internal structural components of the rule of law system, such as retroactive laws and the responsible use of and definitions as a protection against discretionary power.

These important elements in legislation and in the political culture, however, are not favorable to constitutionalism (in the rule of law tradition). In this connection we have already mentioned the *Rechtsträger* and other groups of former privilege. Too, the emerging sentiments of nationalism and religion are not particularly tolerant of some of the formal "impartial" criteria of law and constitutionalism. Other elements relate directly to the interests of the freely elected governments in maintaining the role of the state sector in the economy and perhaps in the welfare sector as well. Social groups for whom the reduction of the state sector means unemployment and poverty support these tendencies. The same social groups have less interest in and comprehension of individual rights and their protection through courts as their education, in a paternalistic tradition, has alienated them from law. Paternalism, in this context, means that they accept their role as clients and as more or less obedient servants of an uncontrolled state welfare system.

Political power factors also make the emergence of constitutionalism difficult. In all these societies at least part of the present ruling elite was involved in one way or another in the Communist system. Revision of the past through retroactive laws (political justice, revision of privatization decisions, reprivatizations, and indemnification of the economic and political victims of Communism) became crucial in one respect or another in all the countries of the region in 1990. Obviously, this is not the best education in constitutionalism. A contradictory situation emerged. "Rejecting the embourgeoisment of the old elite jeopardizes economic liberalism, but accepting it jeopardizes political liberalism .... Accepting the embourgeoisment of the nomenclature, however, allows liberalism to be perceived as representing the interests of the Communists."[4]

Forms of intolerance, in addition to anti-Communism, present problems for constitutionalism. In general, there is little tolerance for minorities, and protection of them is not high on the priority lists of political organizations capable of shaping constitutions. Political forces do not incline to undertake the commitments necessary to write a constitution for the future that would require a firm stance on constitutional values that are unpopular or still debatable. Constitution making is taking the form of a major power struggle in Czechoslovakia in relation to the federalism issue and in Bulgaria. In Poland, in light of an increasing personal presidential power and an antiliberalism reflected in the pending antiabortion legislation, religious school education by ministerial decree, and nonprivatization, a new constitution may well not be a major contribution to constitutionalism.

The emerging elites and the lack of constitutional legal culture are not the only factors responsible for these conceptual insufficiencies. Communist rule and the lack of a capitalist society and a civic culture contributed to the passive acceptance and mistrust of law. On the other hand, as the emergence of civil society and a nonstate ownership system that would make personal independence a possibility is very slow, there is little actual interest or urge to have a rule of law system. Of course, the failure to develop a constitutional framework and an impartial legal system will make the formation of a constitutionalism-hungry society extremely painful if not impossible in the coming years. There are social groups advocating their interests in the new-corporatist structures, which are ready to promote concepts of material justice. If there is not enough time left for the consolidation of formal structures, the inevitable result will be the maintenance of the present imperfect legalism where the law has mainly symbolic and legitimating functions.

Notes

An earlier version of some parts of this chapter has appeared in "New Legalism in East Central Europe: Law as an Instrument of Social Transformation," 17 *Journal of Law and Society* 3 (1990).

1. Hans Kelsen, *Reine Rechtslehre* 2 (Vienna: Deutike, 1960), p. 4.
2. Quotation from a National Conference of County Court Presidents, held in Miskole in 1989.
3. Lon Fuller, *The Morality of Law* (New Haven: Yale University Press, 1965), p. 27.
4. David Ost, "Post-Communist Society and the Obstacles to Democracy in Eastern Europe" (paper presented for delivery at the International Conference on democratization in Europe and Latin America, University of Guadalajara, Mexico, 1991, p. 10).

VI

REFLECTIONS ON CONSTITUTIONALISM

22

Latin America: Constitutionalism and the Political Traditions of Liberalism and Socialism

Atilio A. Borón

Latin American Historical Legacies

Constitutions without Constitutionalism

It is impossible not to be shocked by the wide gap dividing Latin America's history of constitutions and the weakness of its constitutionalist tradition. In this sense I would say that the concrete operation of constitutionalism in Latin America has largely been a fraud. The record on the continent since independence is layered with constitutions tailored to please the ambitions of the powerful and marked by the utter inability to provide for the establishment of a vigorous constitutionalism.

This land of constitutions is also one that violates and subdues them as in few other regions of the world. In this sense I do share the pessimistic vision of H.W.O. Okoth-Ogendo, who considers the existence of constitutions without constitutionalism to be "an African political paradox."[1] Unfortunately, his felicitous formulation describes as well the Latin American record.

This proliferation of constitutions and weakness of constitutionalism force us to enlarge our theoretical perspective so as to emphasize the formative processes of Latin American societies and the structural fractures that created a type of capitalism particularly unfit for democracy and constitutionalism. It could be argued that the hidden secret of constitutionalism lies in the particular type of society required to ensure its successful operation. Many Latin American countries successfully imitated the U.S. Constitution; what proved impossible to reproduce in societies built on *latifundia* were the social and economic structures created in the United States by a capitalism based on free farmers (notwithstanding the slave-owning enclaves in the south) and urban industrialists.

Here it seems appropriate to recall Hegel's views of the liberal constitution imposed on Spain in 1812 by Napoleon; it remained a dead letter and was replaced by its predecessor after the collapse of the Napoleonic regime. Commenting on these events, Hegel wrote that

> A constitution is not . . . manufactured; it is the work of centuries, it is the Idea, the consciousness of rationality so far as that consciousness is developed in a particular nation . . . . What Napoleon gave to the Spaniards was more rational than what they had before, and yet they recoiled from it as from something alien, because they were not educated up to its level.[2]

It is not necessary to share Hegel's political theory to agree with these views;[3] constitutions do reflect the level of development reached by a given society at a certain period in history. If an artificial creature does survive, it will become a caricature of itself, as Latin American presidentialism has become a mockery of the presidentialism of the United States.

But the metaphysical nature of much of Hegel's argument condemns individuals' and social groups' passivity and immobility, as they wait for the dialectics of history to fulfill its tasks. His comments are undoubtedly pessimistic ("every nation has the constitution appropriate to it and suitable for it"[4]) and forcefully argued. His historical fatalism is entirely unacceptable, but his warnings could play a positive role in ensuring a balanced view on the prospects of the diffusion of constitutionalism and democracy around the world.

After all, both constitutionalism and democracy as a set of ideas, institutions, and political practices have proven difficult to transplant. After the collapse of the so-called "real existing socialism," capitalism as a mode of production reigns supreme, but we have learned that only a few of the types of social and economic structures associated with the predominance of capital in modern societies are compatible with democracy and constitutionalism. Last but not least, democratic capitalism has been a *rara avis* outside the rather limited borders of the OECD countries. Today we are entering a new era, in which capital democracy and constitutionalism appear to be emerging in some of the most advanced segments of the periphery, especially in Latin America. It is too soon to pass judgment about the fate of these processes, but we can understand the historical legacies in which they are rooted.

The Political Legacy of Oligarchy

Constitutionalism in Latin America has been a fraud because its banners were raised by a social alliance of landed upper classes and mining interests closely linked to the export trade, and the representatives of foreign capital, whose political domination was marked by invocations of liberalism, constitutionalism, and political democracy, as frequent as they were empty. This "political formula" was a convenient guise to cover the staunch defense of elite interests. The practice of the oligarchic state was not in the least consistent with the genuine promotion of the values of constitutionalism; it failed to secure fundamental civil, political, and social rights. The separation of powers is still, today, after almost two centuries of independence, a goal to be achieved; in "democratic" governments as well as in consolidated dictatorships, the congress and the judiciary have been docile agents of the executive.

The absence of constitutionalism, despite many attempts to impose its political institutions and culture, is certainly related to the effect of the weight of the terrible political legacy of oligarchism on the citizenry of Latin America. In the political culture (a substratum where constitutionalism sometimes finds a favorable soil for its roots) a set of ideas, beliefs, and attitudes is now so ingrained in the mass consciousness that it is more of a mentality than a conscious ideology. This mentality is extremely cynical and suspicious, permeated by a mistrust that also extends to the public institutions and the rule of law. Falsely evoked for decades, civil rights, public freedoms, representative government, etc., became hated symbols of the old rulers when the oligarchies gave way to populist governments. In the name of constitutionalism, Latin America endured arbitrary governments, the supremacy of the executive branch, press censorship, and the minute curtailment of every single individual freedom granted, on paper, by the Constitution. This mentality is profoundly antagonistic to the kind of universalistic or altruistic arguments needed to create a democratic state and to ensure the rule of law.

The net result has been the corruption of civil society, with its attendant obstacles to the constitution of solid democratic regimes throughout Latin America. Words and promises were—and still are—seen as empty because the facts of life deny each one of them. No pacts or compromises are possible or likely to endure because the minimum of good faith and the basic consensus on fundamental values required to seal a pact are absent. Political actors are necessarily treacherous and disloyal, and belief in their discourses would be a mortal trap. Thus, politics was downgraded to the law of the jungle. The oligarchic history of Latin America has taught our people, in Simon Bolivar's words, that "treaties are paper, constitutions books, elections battles, liberty anarchy, and life a torment."[5]

As Bolivar's words of the early nineteenth century indicate, this political cynicism had deeper roots. In colonial times, the dissociation between normal and practical behavior was institutionalized. The "double discourse" of the ruling oligarchies reinforced it throughout the nineteenth century until the Great Depression of 1929.

The Iberian Cultural and Political Legacy

What was the source of Bolivar's desperate words? This failure of constitutionalism was the result of the early failure of the "liberal projects" pushed by the urban elites—the commercial interests settled in the principal cities of the fragmented Spanish and Portuguese empires—and by the Europeanized intelligentsia dazzled with the progress of "civilization" in Europe and North America. For Latin America, the vanquishing of liberalism and of enlightenment ideas behind these "liberal projects" and the reassertion of the traditional corporatist tradition, with its strong antidemocratic and antiliberal implications, was tantamount to the vengeance and revival, in a modified fashion of course, of the obscurantist ideas fiercely struggled against by the leading members of the generation of independence and their successors.

Octavio Paz has suggested that one reason for the weakness of democracy, and we may add constitutionalism, in Latin America is the fact that we did not take part in the great moral and intellectual revolution of the eighteenth century that occurred in some European countries. Latin America, as well as the old Russia, remained outside of this unprecedented revolution, subjected to autocratic rulers exceedingly zealous in protecting their domains from what they regarded as vicious ideas and practices that were undermining the moral foundations of the west. Deprived of these experiences, Latin America remained alien to that intellectual, philosophical, and moral tradition. In Paz' words:

> There is a similarity, little explored so far, between the Hispanic tradition and the Russian one; neither we nor they have a critical tradition, because neither we nor they had something really comparable to the Enlightenment and the intellectual movement of the Eighteenth Century in Europe. In addition, we had nothing similar to the Protestant Reformation, that great seed-planter of freedoms and democracy in the modern world. Thus, the failure of the democratic tentatives in Spain and her ancient colonies. The Spanish empire disintegrates, and with it went our countries. In front of the anarchy that ensued the dismemberment of the Spanish order, we were left with none but the barbarous remedy of *caudillismo*.[6]

It must be admitted that Paz's viewpoints can be regarded as slightly manichean, and are not necessarily shared by scholars such as Richard Morse, who has discerned in the Iberian tradition significant seeds of freedom. In a truly fascinating book, Morse established subtle and illuminating connections between the main elements of the western intellectual tradition, providing an alternative reading of Latin America's cultural legacy. However, he does not seem able to support empirically his argument that Spanish political culture contained the democratic and rationalistic components able to respond to the challenges of modernity.[7]

Despite the merits of Morse's book, the argument advanced by Octavio Paz is grounded in vast and solid empirical evidence. Further, a decadent scholasticism ruled our universities until the Second World War; military regimes and their civilian supporters in the 1970s regarded science as subversive, and Darwin's theses on the origin of man were still fiercely contested in most "modern and secular" countries such as Argentina in the early 1980s. Little wonder that Latin Americans considered democracy an equivalent of anarchy or mobocracy, something alien to the proper organic harmony of the society. There was very little room in the Latin American culture to develop a public philosophy that would foster ideas about freedom, toleration, pluralism, secularism, and rationalism, the necessities of a political culture supportive of democracy and constitutionalism. Instead of the "light of reason," Latin America inherited the fanaticism of malevolent passion. Neither the social structure of dependent capitalism nor the Iberian cultural tradition (about which we will speak below) was prepared to lay the foundations of constitutionalism and democracy.

Latin American intellectuals for two centuries have been sensitive to the Iberian tradition's inhospitability to liberal and democratic ideas.[8] Within a generation after Latin American independence, the Argentine poet Esteban Echeverria had been explicit on this point. (We recall Hegel's words about Spain.) Jose Victorino Lastarria, an eminent liberal and positivist Chilean intellectual and politician, wrote in 1885 that the three centuries between Columbus and Bolivár had been just a "black Winter." His opinion represents well the outlook prevailing up to the end of the century among the majority of the intellectuals of the region.

He portrayed the ideological situation of the new nations by saying that

> we are independent but we are not free; the arms of Spain no longer oppress us but her traditions weigh us down. The social emancipation of Latin America can only be achieved by repudiating the heritage bequeathed by Spain.[9]

In the same vein, Domingo F. Sarmiento, prominent intellectual and Argentine president (1868–1874) wrote that the leadership had been "barbarous like Asia, despotic and bloodthirsty like Turkey, persecuting and deriding intelligence like Islam,"[10]

Sarmiento's views on Spain are as forthright:

> I feel called to struggle against the Spanish race so incapable of understanding freedom here as well as in Spain. The Spanish language is an insurmountable obstacle to the transmission of culture... Spain has never had a thinker, not one notable writer, not a single philosopher. Spain has condemned to backwardness the descendants of Europeans in America.[11]

These opinions offer some clues for understanding the cultural and political discontinuities that separated the new prospective elites and the old imperial rulers, whose effect on Latin American society is all too clear. Claudio Veliz makes this point and underlines the fact that when the United State won its independence from Great Britain,

> there was no simultaneous secession from English literature or from the mainstream of cultural and political traditions that use the English language as their vehicle. The revolutionary institutions of the United States, its political philosophies, its attitudes toward freedom and despotism, its style of life and the aspirations of its people all had roots that went into the history of the English-speaking peoples. In 1776 and after, despite the war of 1812, the United States did not reject its British ancestry in favor of other cultural models.[12]

The Iberian Economic Legacy

This discontinuity is precisely why, Samuel P. Huntington maintains, the Latin American independence is "almost exactly the reverse of that of the United States."[13] Huntington argues that at independence, Latin America superimposed on an archaic (he calls it "feudal" but I do not think that the name is appropriate) social and economic structure a set of

> republican institutions adopted from the United States and revolutionary France. Such institutions had no meaning in feudal society. These early efforts

at republicanism left Latin America with weak governments. Liberal, pluralistic democratic governments served to perpetuate antiquated social structures.[14]

Huntington is right when he notes the basic contradiction between an archaic social structure (which, despite its appearances, was not feudal but capitalist), and the republican institutions brought to replace the collapsed imperial ones.[15] But the liberal impulse was too weak, and quite soon the liberals joined forces with the conservatives and reactionaries who were fiercely fighting against modernity, liberalism, and constitutionalism. Nor was pluralism a much-cherished value in oligarchical and exclusive societies; no democratic government appears in a full-fledged form in a Latin American country before the end of World War II. (Argentina, Chile, and Uruguay experienced important political developments at the beginning of the twentieth century, but none of them could seriously be considered a capitalist democracy.[16])

Latin American capitalism developed without a bourgeois revolution, creating a unique sociohistorical amalgam in which ancient modes of production were subdued and adapted to the necessities of capital accumulation but without destroying or dismantling the preexisting "feudal" social arrangements. Therefore, capitalism in Latin America appears within the structure of *latifundia*, a national projection of its nuclear institution, the *hacienda*, the dual society, the ethnic cleavages, the fusion of church and state, the paramount role of the military, the oligarchical politics, and the legacy of *caudillismo*. The old bulwarks of authoritarianism and reaction—the landed upper classes, the church, the oligarchical army, and the patrimonial bureaucracy, true cornerstones of the *ancien regime* and die-hard enemies of democracy and constitutionalism—were standing in the new era.[17]

The *Junker* road to capitalist development, the slow and partial transformation of the structures of the *ancien regime*, is the exact reverse of the farmer road followed by the United States. If the former reinforced the power of precapitalist economic and social institutions, recreating a capitalist society marked by structural class inequalities and radical symmetries, the farmer road created a society anew, suppressing from the outset all relics of a feudal past that in old Europe haunted and besieged capitalism, democracy, and constitutionalism from its origins. This is the profound uniqueness of American capitalism, a society that is "born equal," to use Tocqueville's words. At the same time Latin American capitalism produced, as a result of the secular decay of the old order, a host of extremely unequal societies in which the spirit of constitutionalism and democracy could hardly survive.[18]

Thus, instead of bourgeois-democratic revolution, its countries experienced the bitter outcomes of a policy of conservative traditional accomodation. As a new geological stratum forms on top of the older one, so the advent of capitalism came to rest on the old semiservile society formed by the long decay of the colonial order. Latin American capitalism is then a typical case of a "passive revolution," in the Gramscian sense, lacking the Jacobin–radical component that in some other countries led to the destruction of the old and the founding of a new society.

The Grand Politicophilosophical Traditions of Liberalism and Socialism

At this point, a personal note is in order. Before my involvement in the ACLS Comparative Constitutionalism seminars, I must confess that I had a rather formalistic view of constitutionalism and was doubtful about its relevance to Latin American democratizations. Because of my participation in two seminars, I think I have improved both my own understanding of the meaning of constitutionalism and of the possibilities of democratic consolidation in Latin America. My thoughts that follow on the relationship today of the traditions of liberalism and socialism reflect my new understandings.

During the 1980s, as never before, democratic ideals mobilized with great strength the expectations and desires of the Latin American masses. But the economic crisis and the consequent "adjustment" policies of a neoliberal economics have created a new type of capitalist society in the periphery. This society, characterized by unprecedented mass impoverishment and cultural and ideological alienation, is precisely the opposite of what the consolidation of a democratic society requires.

What then is the future of these new hopes for democracy? Today in Latin America the destiny of constitutionalism seems inexorably linked to the future of democracy, and is inevitably bound up with the great liberal and socialist traditions of the west. In Europe, however, most states became constitutional and "liberal" before having to solve the challenges of democratization and the integration of the lower classes. This is not the case in the Third World, nor in Latin America where we are confronted with a double and urgent task: the passage from military despotism to constitutionalism and the rule of law, and the transition from autocracy to democracy. Given the unhappy history of liberal ideas in this continent, it behooves us to ask a peculiar question: to what extent is it possible to talk today about a "nonliberal" constitutionalism in societies whose structure created a dependent capitalism particularly unfit for democracy and constitutionalism?

Constitutionalism is a chapter in the history of western liberalism. Its distinguished exponents have some differences among themselves, but, as Walter F. Murphy has written, "with some justification constitutionalism has been called 'Liberalism's political theory'"[19] Constitutionalism has also been defined as the techniques of liberty that guarantee the preservation of individual rights and the rule of law.[20] These techniques vary according to the historical moment and the national tradition, with the appropriate legal and institutional solutions to specific problems evolving with time.

To reach a true comprehension of the scope of modern constitutionalism, it is of utmost importance to stress the continuities between liberalism and socialism. In a seminal article on Norberto Bobbio's political theory, Perry Anderson wrote that

> Liberalism and Socialism have long been conventionally understood as antagonistic intellectual and political traditions, and with good reason by virtue of both the apparent incompatibility of their theoretical starting points—individual

and societal respectively—and the actual record of conflict, often deadly, between the parties and movements inspired by each.[21]

However, Anderson points out that after the events of 1848, John Stuart Mill dramatically reversed his assessment of socialism and began to regard himself as a liberal and socialist. Anderson also notes similar theoretical transformations later in Bertrand Russell, A.Hobson, and John Dewey, and thinks, "It is timely to recall these illustrious examples today, because after a major interval we are seeing a significant new range of attempts to synthesize liberal and socialist traditions."[22]

I would like to add that an analogous movement beginning at the socialist end of the political axis was made by Edouard Bernstein in *Evolutionary Socialism*. This book, published in 1899, produced a tremendous debate within the ranks of the European labor movement and the Second International; however, the overwhelming majority of Bernstein's critics (Lenin, Kautsky, Rosa Luxemburg, Trotsky, among the most important) concentrated on his diagnosis of the economic transformations of *fin de siècle* capitalism and paid little attention to his analysis of the capitalist state and bourgeois democracy. About the latter, Bernstein asserted that social democracy labors rather incessantly at raising the worker from the social position of a proletarian to that of a citizen, and thus to make citizenship universal. It does not want to set up a proletarian society instead of a civic society, but a socialist order of society instead of a capitalist one.[23]

His recommendation is forceful.

> Finally, it is to be recommended that some moderation should be kept in the declaration of war against "liberalism." It is true that the great liberal movement of modern times arose for the advantage of the capitalist bourgeoisie first of all, and the parties which assumed the names of liberals were, or became in due course, simple guardians of capitalism. Naturally, only opposition can reign between these parties and social democracy. But with respect to liberalism as a great historical movement, *socialism is its legitimate heir*, not only in chronological sequence, but also in its spiritual qualities.[24]

Although I do not agree with Bernstein's exaggerated formulation because it neglects the radical discontinuities that separate these two theoretical traditions, it is nonetheless true that in some issues—civil rights, public freedoms, governments by consent—the elements of continuity are of paramount importance. (Immediately after the outbreak of the Russian Revolution, Rosa Luxemburg wrote a premonitory article in which her position moves closer to Bernstein.) These early efforts to synthesize liberalism and socialism failed. New attempts are being made now when the collapse of the "existing socialisms" is forcing the progressive parties to face the catastrophic legacies of Stalinism and to put, once again, on the agenda of socialism the question of democracy and liberty. Anderson is right when he asks, "Who could wish for an illiberal socialism?"[25]

The question, then, is to establish the extent to which the doctrinal and practical instruments of liberal constitutionalism are likely to transcend the framework of liberalism. This is not a rhetorical question; it is an eminently practical one associated with the discussions on the current transformation of capitalist societies, the rise of neoconservatism doctrines and policies, and the apparent exhaustion of the liberal project, all of which call for, according to C. B. Macpherson, the establishment of a new conception: the "postliberal" democracy. Macpherson phrased the problem in these terms: "Is there now a post-liberal-democratic theory? The answer is evident. What we have now is not post-liberal-democratic theory, but recessive liberal theory. It would be nearer the mark to call it pre-democratic liberal theory."[26]

From Liberalism to "Liberism"

The question of the extent of the viability of liberalism is critical, not only for Latin America, but for the other areas of the world in which the dissatisfaction with liberal doctrines and policies is widespread. We must also keep in mind our query whether there is such a thing as a "nonliberal" constitutionalism. Our inquiry must begin with the establishing of some distinctions. As Giovanni Sartori has persuasively argued, liberalism is a rather unfortunate word. Coined in Spain in 1810–1811, hardly a propitious land for baptizing this doctrine, the term "liberalism" came to the world two centuries after the "thing" liberalism had started to revolutionize the world.[27] The misfortune Sartori refers to is partly due to the tardy appearance of the name and partly due to the fact that shortly after the word "liberalism" was invented it had to struggle fiercely against democracy and socialism. But the most fundamental reason for this misfortune was that the name was coined at a time when the novelty was not political "liberalism" but economic "liberalism." As a consequence, the label has come to have more of an economic than a political association: liberalism was called "bourgeois" and "capitalist" and its prophets were thought to be Adam Smith, Ricardo, and Cobden. The association has remained so firm that even today many writers (especially those writing in English) still speak of classical liberalism as a *laissez-faire* liberalism—which is to say that they are still confusing liberalism with economic "liberalism."[28]

This unfortunate confusion, Sartori argues, introduced grave distortions into both the political theory of liberalism and the concrete public policies of liberal governments throughout the world, including Latin America.

Locke, Blackstone, Montesquieu, Constant—to mention a few of the real founding fathers of classical liberalism—were not the theorists of a *laissez-faire* economy. To them, liberalism meant the rule of law and the constitutional State, and liberty was political freedom, not the economic principle of free trade or the law of the survival of the fittest.[29]

How was this semantic distortion possible? It is unlikely that it occurred independently of the historical movement of "liberalisms" around the world. One could reasonably argue that after two centuries, only in the United States did political liberalism significantly honor its promises. In Europe, liberalism stumbled over the surviving rigid class barriers, inherited from the *ancien regime* and reinforced in the first stages of capitalist development, and faced the limits of the narrow borders of citizenship of a liberal bourgeois state that was not ready to accept democracy and popular representation. In this regard, I think Sartori's opinion that

> suddenly in 1848, democracy and liberalism are enemies no more: they join forces. His [Alexis de Tocqueville] antithesis is no longer between liberalism and democracy, but between democracy and socialism. *His* democracy was now liberal democracy.[30]

has to be seriously disputed. Precisely, an understanding of the prolonged liberal rejection of democracy might give us a clue to the debasement of political liberalism and its replacement by economic "liberalism." It was the unwillingness of liberal-inspired rulers and governments to accept political democracy that explains the misfortune of both the "word" and the "thing." The liberal tradition remained anchored in a predemocratic world, faithful to Locke's paradigm, well clear of equality, popular sovereignty, direct democracy, and other prickly themes contained in Rousseau's theoretical universe.[31] The historian E. H. Carr perceived the effects of the time–honored disjunction between democracy and liberalism when he wrote that "in England . . . the word democracy long remained in bad odor with the English ruling classes."[32] John Stuart Mill remained a considered opponent of democracy, advocating an exclusivist system of plural votes for the capitalists and their lieutenants "in order to forestall proletarian class legislation."[33] Norberto Bobbio shares Carr's views:

> today we are so used to the expression "liberal democracy" that we have forgotten that pure liberals up to the beginning of this century have always regarded democracy (and even the simple formal democracy) as the open road towards the loss of all liberties, towards the rebellion of the masses against the elites, as the triumph of the 'man-herd' against the herdsman.[34]

In sum, the coincidence of liberalism and democracy is a novelty of our century. In addition, political liberalism failed to protect equally all men and women: it could not do so because the lives, happiness, and liberties of the citizen are not independent of the social relations of production that define their location and life-chances in society, issues on which the liberal formula remains conspicuously silent. In Latin America, it is quite clear that the liberal banners waved to promote *laissez-faire* economy and the free-trade policies sponsored by the oligarchical states. Gramsci's reflections on the process of constitution of the national state in Italy demonstrate that in the backward areas of Europe, as in Latin America, liberalism emerged as "liberism."[35] In the evolution of liberalism as a public philosophy, not in terms of its timeless principles but as a package of concrete policies inspiring a diversity of governments, one can see the progressive abandonment of its political proposals and the growing and overwhelming preponderance of its economic strategies. Liberalism became "liberism," and with this metamorphosis some crucial elements of its revolutionary message were lost.

From the Latin Amrican historical perspective, the reasons for this involution seem clear; liberalism articulated a powerful set of arguments in favor of individual freedoms from the end of the seventeenth century up to the First World War. These principles fitted well with the nature of predemocratic societies, in which only a tiny minority of the adult males had a voice in the conduct of public affairs, and mass politics did not yet exist. Therefore, political liberalism was highly effective in the protection of some fundamental rights in societies marked with sharp class divisions and boundaries, and characterized by the nondemocratic nature of their polities. However, the society that emerged after the First World War, the Russian Revolution, and the Great Depression was entirely different; liberal values alone proved unable to supply adequate responses for societies that underwent the process that Karl Mannheim called "fundamental democratization," that is, the massive incorporation into the state of large sections of hitherto unenfranchised masses. However, it is obvious that liberalism as an ideology did not become obsolete as a result of this structural mutation of old social formations in "mass societies"; but this mutation did introduce a whole new set of values and aspirations that went far beyond the classic agenda and the historical premises of liberalism.

Liberalism cared for the protection of certain individual rights and freedoms, and for the need to protect the individual citizen fron the encroachments of despotic or abusive governments. But individual rights are not metaphysical entities, and it is reasonable to argue that with the development of the process of integration of the popular classes into the state, new rights have emerged, and old ones have been transformed. Human rights, the right to work, the right to a modicum of individual welfare, the right to preserve the identity and autonomy of minorities, the enjoyment of public goods, the conservation of the environment, and the security of the citizens are examples of commonly accepted values, whose concerns are not centered on individuals and markets but on collectivities and societies. It should be noted that most of these values have their ideological origins in a diversity of "nonliberal" and "postmaterialistic" traditions, mostly socialist.

A Mixed Constitutionalist Corpus

In other words, the corpus of late twentieth century constitutionalism contains not only liberal elements but socialist components as well. There is a broad consensus on the necessity considering constitutionalism as a doctrine and a political system that goes beyond a frozen constitutional text. This consensus sees constitutionalism as a living set of values, principles, and institutions, in which the premises of the socialist tradition about fundamental human rights, socioeconomic entitlements, and democratic arguments alien to the liberal tradition have a paramount role.

Modern constitutionalism as a "mixed" system, resulting from the marriage of liberalism and socialism? Surely enough, many will disagree with this formulation, because they still think that these two grand doctorinal traditions of the west are radically discontinuous and mutually exclusive: the progress of socialist ideas can take place only if there is a proportional abandonment of liberal ideas. For others, with whom I identify myself, the relationship is of incomplete continuity.

Why incomplete? Although it is true that some predicaments of liberalism are incompatible with socialism, many others are fully congruent with it. Liberalism's sacralization of individual rights is unacceptable to socialists, because they think collective rights exist and must be protected as well; similarly, socialists reject the superstitious belief in the market because they believe rational regulation and control of the market offer better practical results in terms of equality and justice. But liberalism's vindication of fundamental civil rights, liberty of the person, freedom of speech, thought, faith, and association, and the right to justice, etc., are equally valid for the socialist tradition, and there is nothing in Karl Marx's theoretical argument that could be judged inimical to these fundamental vlaues.[36]

The elements introduced by the socialist tradition, therefore, are fully complementary to some of the central tenets of political liberalism. The socialist project requires the maximum expansion of all public liberties, eliminating their well-known de facto restrictions and curtailments in capitalist societies, in which class inequalities play such a crucial role. Liberalism's child, constitutionalism, is also fully compatible with socialism. How could a socialist theorist reject separation of powers, constitutional rule, checks and balances, and government by consent? What then would be the alternative political model of a socialist democracy? Tyranny, theocracy, or what? The only possible answer is democracy, and a socialist type of democracy can only be conceieved of as building on the tradition of liberal constitutionalism; it could not suppress public freedoms, rule of law, and separation of powers. Should majority rule be considered as a bourgeois political instrument? Should socialists reject universal suffrage? The answer to all these questions is self-evident: some of these liberal tenets—civil rights, separation of powers, limited governments—were crystallized during the ascent of the bourgeoisie in her struggle against absolutist states and decadnent aristocracies; others—the democratic ones, democracy and popular sovereignty, representative government, universal suffrage, etc.—are the guideposts of working class struggles against the bourgeoisie and the capitalist state. A "postliberal democracy" will have to be built on these historical materials, fully developing all their possibilities and suppressing none of them.[37]

Returning to Anderson's question and MacPherson's formulation, it is crucial to understand that socialist doctrine is neither "antiliberal" nor "illiberal," but rather "postliberal." It is of the outmost importance to put as much stress on the continuities between liberalism and socialism as on their ruptures, if a true understanding of the scope and limits of modern constitutionalism is to be achieved. The differences between these two ideological traditions have repeatedly been underlined; however, the intensity of the confrontation has unfortunately blurred the elements of continuity linking liberalism and socialism as separate components of the great western theoretical tradition.

In this regard, few theorists have been more aware and perceptive of these hidden links than Rosa Luxemburg. This is the reason why, after the Russian Revolution, she repeatedly insisted that the creation of a new proletarian state should not be considered as the negation of the "bourgeois freedoms" but as the full extension of all of them to the entire population. She insisted that the historical enterprise started by the Russians should not curtail but should expand the constitutional rights and guarantees established by the liberal constitutionalism in western Europe and stubbornly neglected by the Russian Tzars. In other words, Luxemburg urged the European labor movement to recover the heritage of the triumphant liberalism (both its essential contents and its procedural rules for the peaceful resolution of public controversies), to enrich it with the premises of socialist thought, and "to create a socialist democracy to replace bourgeois democracy."[38]

In recent years the "Bobbio debate" has moved along the same track, ratifying the validity of Luxemburg's contentions and the necessity of reappraising the scope and nature of the hidden links between these two great western politico-ideological traditions. This is certainly the great challenge for the years to come and holds the best possibilities for the chances of constitutionalism in Latin America. Constitutionalism in Latin America must be endowed with ethical contents congruent with the needs of a poverty-ridden mass citizenry whose demands cannot be satisfied by a value system anchored in the "possessive individualism" of eighteenth-century liberalism. And the procedural rules of Latin American constitutionalism must be adequate to govern the complicated, unstable, and turbulent mass societies, which require a more complex institutional design than many advocates of constitutionalism are ready to admit.

Note

1. H. W. O. Okoth-Ogendo, "Constitutions without Constitutionalism: Reflections on an African Political Paradox" (working paper for the ACLS Comparative Constitutionalism Project, September 1988).

2. Hegel, *Philosophy of Right* (London: Oxford University Press, 1967), tr. with notes by T. M. Knox, pp. 286–287.

3. An interesting contemporary example is the American decision to export democracy to the Third World countries. An enlightening discussion of the problems involved in this kind of initiative can be found in Abraham Lowenthal, *Exporting Democracy* (Baltimore: Johns Hopkins University Press, 1991).

4. *Op. cit.*, paragraph #274, p. 179.

5. Simon Bolivar, "Una mirada sobre la America espanola," *Discursos, proclamas y epistola rio politico* (3rd ed., Madrid: Editora Nacional, 1981), pp. 350–351.

6. Cf. Octavio Paz, *El Ogro Eilentropico* (Mexico: Joaquin Mortiz, 1979), pp. 254–255.

7. Cf. Richard Morse, *El Espejo de Prospero* (Mexico: Siglo XXI, 1982), pp. 17–86 and 89–147.

8. A lengthy discussion on these issues can be seen in my "Authoritarian Ideological Traditions and Transition towards Democracy in Argentina," in *Papers on Latin America* (Columbia University, The Institute of Latin American and Iberian Studies, Paper No. 8, 1989). This section of this paper is based on that work.

9. Claudio Veliz, *The Centralist Tradition in Latin America* (Princeton: Princeton University Press, 1980), p. 165.

10. *Ibid.*

11. *Ibid.*, pp. 175–176.

12. *Ibid.*, p. 176.

13. Samuel P. Huntington, *Political Order in Changing Societies* (New Haven: Yale University Press, 1968), p. 135

14. *Ibid.*, pp. 135–136.

15. The literature on Latin American capitalism is considerable, but the debate is already over. The historiographical evidence heavily sided with those who argued that in the nineteenth century the surviving fedual structures were assimilated to the predominant capitalist poles of development.

16. Göran Therborn, "The Rule of Capital and the Rise of Democracy," *New Left Review* 100 (May–June, 1977); Atilio A. Boron, "Latin America: Between Hobbes and Friedman," *New Left Review* 130 (November–December, 1981).

17. Augstin Cueva, *Eldesarrollo del capitalismo en America Latina* (Mexico: Siglo XXI, 1976).

18. Cf. Louis Hartz, *The Liberal Tradition in America* (New York and London: A Harvest/HBJ Book, 1955), pp. 3–32.

19. Walter F. Murphy, "Constitutions, Constitutionalism, and Democracy" Working Paper, ACLS Comparative Constitutionalism Project (September, 1988), p. 28.

20. See Nicola Matteucci, "Constitucionalismo," in Norberto Bobbio and Nicola Matteucci, eds., *Diccionaria de Politica* (Mexico: Siglo XXI, 1981), pp. 388–404.

21. Perry Anderson, "The Affinities of Norberto Bobbio," *New Left Review* 170, 3 (July–August, 1988).

22. *Ibid*, p. 6. On this theme, see also the interesting essay by Jacques Bidet, *Théorie de la modernité* (Paris: Presses Universitatires de France, 1990). In this work, Bidet posed the thesis that the social contract, which has played a key foundation role in liberalism, is also called to play a similar role in the development of a political philosophy of socialism.

23. Edouard Bernstein, *Revolutionary Socialism* (New York: Schocken Books, 1961) pp. 147–148.

24. *Ibid.*, pp. 148–149.

25. Anderson, *op. cit.*, p. 36.

26. MacPherson, *Democratic Theory: Essays in Retrieval* (Oxford: Clarendon Press, 1973), p. 179.

27. Giovanni Sartori, *Democratic Theory* (New York: Praeger, 1967), p. 357.

28. *Op. cit.*, pp. 361–362.

29. *Ibid.*, p. 362.

30. *Ibid.*, p. 359.

31. Boron, note 16, p. 48.

32. E. H. Carr, *The Soviet Impact on the Western World* (New York, 1946), pp. 8–9.

33. Göran Therborn, "The Rule of Capital and the Rise of Democracy," *New Left Review* 193, 3–4 (May–June, 1977).

34. Norberto Bobbio, "Quali alternativa alla democrazia rappresentativa?," In Federico Coen, ed., *Il Marxismo e Vo Stato* (Roma: Mondoperario, 1976), pp. 27–28 (translation ours).

35. Antonio Gramsci, *Note sui Machiavelli: Sulla Politica e Sullo Stato Moderno* (Turin: Einavdi, 1966), pp. 29–37.

36. Marx's permanent recognition of his intellectual debt to Hegel and Spinoza, and the classical political economists (Petty, Smith, Ricardo), is too well known to be repeated

here. cf. *Capital*, Vol. I (New York: International Publishers, fifth printing, 1973), pp. 19–20 and 81. The enormous influence of J. J. Rousseau on Marx's political theory has been documented in a host of books and articles. See, for instance, the enlightening book by Falvano Dell Volpe, *Rousseau e Marx* (Rome: Editori Ruiniti, 1964). Engels also made similar remarks in many wiritings: see, among others, his introduction to *Socialism Utopian and Scientific*, in which he explicitly recognized the contributions of Bacon, Hobbes, Locke, Saint-Simon, and Rousseau to the formation of modern socialist theory.

37. Of course, the argument that Marx would raise is that these political institutions do not operate in the air, but are rooted in particular types of societies, some of which may be more congruent than others with the requirements derived from the political model. All the socialist tradition after Marx has insisted on this point, namely, the lack of affinity—leading to chronic structural tensions and in some cases to aberrant breakdowns like Weimar, Germany, for instance—between the economic and political institutions of capitalist societies. The fact that the universal diffusion of capitalism has not led to the equal dissemination of bourgeois democracy seems to support this view.

38. "The Russian Revolution," in *Rosa Luxemburg Speaks* (New York: Pathfinder Press, 1970), p. 393.

23

Constitutionalism: A Timely Revival

Julio Faundez

The ACLS project on Comparative Constitutionalism has undoubtedly fulfilled the objectives it set out to achieve, that is, to stimulate research, to broaden the scope of constitutionalism, and to provide some practical guidelines based on a wide range of experiences throughout the world. But the contribution made by this project goes beyond these objectives. It has helped to revive and redefine a concept that is potentially capable of providing scholars, public figures, and citizens from different parts of the world and from different intellectual traditions with a common framework to analyze and discuss issues that, for ideological reasons, have hitherto been regarded as beyond the scope of rational debate. Here I will attempt to explore ways in which a revived and updated concept of constitutionalism could provide a new and more fruitful point of departure for both research and policy analysis.

Decline of a Concept

Constitutionalism, a concept that once occupied a prominent place in political theory, has been largely ignored by most practitioners of modern political science. Several related factors explain this development. It is a well-known fact that in modern political analysis there is little room for concepts deemed to be value loaded. Since the notion of constitutionalism, as it has evolved historically, entails a conception about the rightful form of political organization, it is not surprising that modern political scientists should regard it with suspicion. But their dissatisfaction with this concept stems not only from their unwillingness to make normative statements. For the notion of constitutionalism has been generally associated with research that focuses largely on the main organs of the state, and often only from a legal point of view. Hence, it is not surprising that modern political scientists who are committed to discovering laws and regularities derived from actual social behavior should find the notion of constitutionalism both narrow and misleading: narrow, because their concept of political includes a much wider range of social interactions, and misleading, because of the underlying assumption that the constitution and other rules of public law provide the raw materials for the study of politics. The notion of constitutionalism has not, however, been completely abandoned. It retains some popularity among lawyers, politicians, and other professionals involved in advocacy and persuasion. These groups, however, use the concept mainly as a label to praise or to criticize existing political arrangements.

Even as a mere ideological device, the notion of constitutionalism has lost some of its appeal. In some cases this has come about because of the success of existing constitutional arrangements; in others, it is the consequence of their failure. In countries where constitutional arrangements have been relatively successful, public debate often does not directly raise fundamental issues about the organization of the state or government. In some instances, the constitution itself may go largely unnoticed; in others, primarily those in countries that make provision for judicial review of legislation, political conflicts that raise constitutional issues are easily transformed into quasilegal problems capable of yielding a range of outcomes, all of which are generally acceptable to the main political actors. This is of course possible provided that the claims processed through the constitutional mechanism do not challenge the prevailing political system.

In countries where constitutions have little or no durability or where they fail to guarantee a minimum of stability, the issue of constitutionalism is rarely the focus of debate. In these countries, the failure of constitutional arrangements is generally attributed either to technical weaknesses of the constitutional document or to the underdeveloped nature of the economic and social structures. Hence, the solutions offered are either technocratic or fatalistic: that is, either lawyers are brought in to draft new constitutions, or to amend the old discredited document, or the very possibilty of achieving a stable and humane political system is ruled out of order until such time as economic and social conditions are capable of sustaining it. In the meantime, most of these political regimes draw their legitimacy from a vague promise of a future capitalist, socialist, or developmentalist utopia or from the fact that they present themselves to the public as the only alternative to communism, imperialism, religious fundamentalism, or simply chaos.

A Timely Revival

Recent developments in various parts of the world underscore the urgent need for political reform and social change. In several Third World countries, the collapse of authoritarian regimes has opened a political transition process that is attempting to create new democratic forms. A similar process is now taking place in eastern Europe, at a pace that even the most optimistic observers would not have predicted. Meanwhile, in the industrialized countries of the west, the new awareness about the limits of the welfare state has reinforced the belief in market forces and thus prompted the introduction of political and legal reforms destined to have a major impact on the future direction of their political systems.

This global trend of political change has brought about an increase in constitution making and constitutional reforms. This is of course not a new phenomenon. After all, since their independence in the early nineteenth century, Latin American countries have enacted some 200 constitutions and the recent decolonization in Africa and Asia resulted in many new constitutions. In the past, however, constitution making was generally regarded as an issue that only specialist lawyers and a select group of politicians could understand. The situation today is different, the current process of constitution making is backed by greater popular awareness of the need to create viable democratic structures. Hence the renewed interest in constitutionalism both as a common framework for analysis and as a guide for the difficult task of building or rebuilding the political order.

A Common Framework

The need for a common point of departure stems from the fact that the claims for political and economic change from different parts of the world have important affinities cutting across national and ideological boundaries. These claims are for more democracy and greater freedom. Democratic demands involve claims for greater participation in decision making while libertarian demands are framed in terms of the guarantee and protection of individual and group rights. Undoubtedly, these political and legal demands have varying meanings, depending on the contexts in which they arise. The demand for greater reliance on market forces does not have the same meaning in China as it does in the United Kingdom. The pressure to secure workers' rights, including the right to strike, is prompted by different factors in Poland and in Chile, and the outcome of such a struggle will not be the same in the United Kingdom and in South Korea. Likewise, the demand for greater sexual equality in Zimbabwe does not mean what it means in the republics of the former Soviet Union; the call for the protection of minorities differs in Namibia and in the United States. These are all differences as undeniable as they are self-evident. Is it the case, then, that similarities in political demands are purely verbal and that any attempt to treat them otherwise would distort them, yielding, at best, a purely formalistic inquiry having little or no intellectual or policy interest?

It is of course true that political demands framed in identical language often have radically different meaning. This is why the historical perspective—so often neglected by modern social scientists—is crucial. Yet notwithstanding the methodological problems, I would argue that the affinities among the current political demands are not merely verbal. In one way or another they raise the same fundamental issues about the balance between state and society. Thus, as centrally planned economies move toward greater economic and political liberalization, there is undoubtedly much that they can learn from the experience of existing capitalist countries. Likewise, although the welfare state in the west is somewhat discredited, it has not yet withered away and, interestingly enough, has today become a source of inspiration for many political groups in the Third

World and in socialist countries. And much in the experience of some Third World countries merits close attention, for despite the well-known problems, many countries in the Third World have made remarkable progress in creating a sense of national unity without resorting to force. Further, many Third World countries have strong political parties, representing real social interests, that can thus make a positive contribution toward securing stability within a dynamic process of social change.

The range of papers presented at the regional seminars of this Comparative Constitutionalism Project shows that, underlying the worldwide demands for political and economic change, there is a family of related problems that can and should be discussed from a broader comparative perspective. Such an exploration would extend our knowledge, help us clarify our policy objectives, serve as an antidote against parochialism, and, it is to be hoped, make us more tolerant of other political and cultural experiences.[1]

Avoiding Pitfalls

The failure of liberal democracy in many countries of the Third World has been rightly attributed to the fact that the constitutional arrangements introduced in these countries on the eve of decolonization have little or no bearing on the realities of those countries. This point is made, often with great eloquence, in several of the chapters in this volume. The experience of most Third World countries shows that the fundamental principles on which the model of liberal democracy is based cannot fully take effect outside the western European and North American context. In most Third World countries, instead of effective separation of powers, there is an inordinate concentration of power in one branch of government—and often in one person; instead of political accountability, there is almost total political irresponsibility, tempered occasionally by elections or plebiscites, and instead of respect for basic civil and political liberties, there is repression and social neglect, which is all the more offensive as it is generally combined with official patronage and privilege.

It could well be that in some cases the uncritical transplant of the liberal democratic model stems from a sincere belief not only in the virtues of the model, but in the possibility that, with patience and good will, citizens in other countries may learn how to use it. This idea appears to have inspired the recent Democratic Initiative Program launched by the U.S. Agency for International Development. These and similar initiatives seem to be based on the theory that democracy is a technology, like agriculture, with principles and practices that can be easily learned and replicated.

Views of Constitutionalism

The failure of liberal democracy in most Third World countries should not, however, be seen as the failure of constitutionalism. Constitutionalism is not an intellectual commodity that can be used to sell, impose, or transplant political models. This instrumental view draws intellectual support from a conception of constitutionalism as a mere device to control and restrain democracy; this view sees constitutionalism as the embodiment of the antimajoritarian principle that introduces prudence and sobriety into the proceedings of an otherwise unruly electoral majority. This interpretation generally casts the advocates of constitutionalism as wise (and often wealthy), and the unruly democrats as well intentioned, but inexperienced.

My concern here is not with the historical accuracy of this view of constitutionalism, but with its implications for policy. For the notion of constitutionalism as an external barrier to democracy can easily lead enthusiastic policymakers, overzealous national security advisers, and misguided lawyers to the conclusion that constitutionalism is little more than an array of techniques for controlling power.

It is undeniable that the democratic process must be subject to rules and that some of these rules should be designed to safeguard the interests of political minorities and the rights of individuals; these safeguards should not be understood as external to the democratic process, but as part of it. Indeed, the democratic ideal of self-government would be inconceivable without giving full effect to basic rights and liberties. These basic rights and liberties are not a negative force opposing democracy from the outside, but an essential component of democratic process. It must be noted that the failure of democracy in most Third World countries, and in others as well, is not often brought about by the reckless behavior of political majorities acting through legislative bodies. On the contrary, the histories of these countries suggest that, more often than not, it is the majority of citizens who need protection from political elites who consistently frustrate democratic demands in order to protect their interests. Sadly, the negative conception of constitutionalism is often used as ideological cover to legitimize such behavior.

Many of the papers on constitutionalism presented at the regional seminars noted with dismay that in many Third World countries there is a huge gap between the principles and ideals proclaimed in the constituion and the way power is exercised in practice. This phenomenon in Africa led H. W. O. Okoth-Ogendo to the conclusion that constitutionalism will prevail in Africa only when socioeconomic conditions are ripe, after Africa overcomes underdevelopment and social conditions make democracy possible. If western countries had to endure a long struggle to achieve democracy Okoth-Ogendo does not find it surprising that Africa should have to go through a similar painful process. Such pessimism, though understandable, is not justified. Moreover, although founded on a fatalistic interpretation of political development, this conception of constitutionalism is the same negative one that, as explained above, created such great expectations about the possibilities of exporting liberal democracy to the Third World.

It is undeniable as the title of Okoth-Ogendo's chapter, "Constitutions without Constitutionalism," reminds us that constitutionalism is not simply compliance with the rules of the constitution. Such a broad definition of constitutionalism offers no clear normative standpoint to evaluate political arrangements; any behavior in accordance with the constitution would be both constitutional and consistent with the ideals of constitutionalism. The problem in most Third World countries, however, is not that governments do not comply with constitutional rules, good or bad, but rather that, on the whole, governments fail to follow rules altogether.

This problem leads us to the crucially important question of the institutionalization of state power, a process that involves stabilization of practices and requires, among other things, a certain degree of adherence to rules. Although political development scholars have not neglected this issue, policymakers and government advisers consistently fail to appreciate fully its importance. This oversight is all the more remarkable if we consider that the development of liberal democracy in the west cannot be easily disentangled from the process of creating and consolidating nation-states. Democracy is not an appendage to a ready-made nation-state. Therefore, the task of creating stable and efficient institutions in new states should not be seen as separate from the struggle for democracy. The choice and design of state institutions are not technical decisions without relevance for democracy. Constitutionalism is not the culmination of the process of state-building. Constitutionalism must be seen as a process that involves establishing stable institutions within the democratic perspective of securing self-government.

Conclusion

The work done under the aegis of this project suggests at least three lines of inquiry for future research. There is general agreement that constitutionalism is not about the textual study of constitutions and that it involves a multidisciplinary effort. The papers presented at the regional institutes confirm this view, but also suggest that there is an urgent need to study the historical development of constitutionalism within each country. The multidisciplinary approach, which is so effectively applied to contemporary problems of governance, should be applied historically so that we can learn more about the roots of constitutionalism in our respective countries.

It should not be necessary to stress the importance of comparative studies, although many of the papers presented at the regional institutes suggest that knowledge about other countries' experiences is, if not weak, at least one-sided. Intellectuals from Third World countries are generally familiar with European history, but are not often critical enough in their interpretations of it. Indeed, some Latin American intellectuals tend to regard European countries as a more appropriate focus of comparison than countries in their own region.

Intellectuals from industrialized countries, on the other hand, often tend to regard the history of Third World countries as unworthy of serious reflection. Hence, it is not surprising that although they are prepared to regard Hitler as a freak phenomenon in an otherwise civilized political tradition, they tend to regard Pinochet and Amin as endemic to Third World societies.

The third line of inquiry that suggests itself is transnationalism. Recent developments in the world economy have underscored the fact of interdependence. They have also brought about a greater realization that power structures at the international level, both public and private, are today severely undermining the independence and sovereignty of the nation–state. This problem is having a major impact on the development of constitutionalism and cannot be ignored.

Note

1. I would also like to note that by appointing regional committees to organize the respective regional sessions, the ACLS showed genuine interest and respect for cultural and political differences. This is a valuable procedural precedent that ought not to be forgotten.

24

The Crisis of Constitutionalism: South Asian Perspectives

Neelan Tiruchelvam

The South Asian context for their problems of political stability and of institution building is one of extraordinary geographical, political, and socioeconomic diversity. South, in the Arabian Sea, lies an archipelago consisting of sparsely populated coral islands, the Maldives, with a one party republican form of government. On the northern border with China are two land-locked semi-feudal states, Bhutan and Nepal; Bhutan remains a monarchy and Nepal underwent a dramatic political transition to establish a multiparty state headed by a constitutional monarch. Pakistan in the northwest and Bangladesh in the southeast grew out of a bloody partition and a subsequent civil war; in both countries democratically constituted governments have replaced authoritarian military regimes. In the center of the region is India, a federal polity with a long tradition of representative institutions grounded on a strong industrial and technological base. Sri Lanka, off the southeastern tip of India, is an island republic besieged by an insurgency, escalating violence, and the militarization of civil society. Massive economic and demographic pressures further compound their political and institutional problems. The region accounts for a mere 2% of the global income, but must support 22% of the global population. Almost half the population of the region is believed to live below the poverty line without basic needs. The population of the region increases at a rate of 25 million per year, five times the population increase of Organization for Economic Cooperation and Development (OECD) countries.

Despite this diversity and complexity, South Asia is a region with the largest population committed to periodic elections, representative institutions, fundamental rights, and democratic freedoms. It is, therefore, an area of considerable importance in terms of constitutional experimentation, institutional reappraisal, and renewal. Issues of constitutionalism are at the center of its political and intellectual agenda. Nepal has a new constitution based on popular sovereignty, a multiparty state, and enforceable fundamental rights. Bangladesh is in the midst of a debate on its form of government, whether it is to be parliamentary or presidential. In India, revivalist and secessionist movements are challenging the secular foundations of the state and the federal character of the polity. Pakistan is also struggling to reconcile the contradictions of a constitutional framework that sought to graft a Westminster-style government onto a highly centralized Presidential system. Sri Lanka is seeking to reconstruct its Bill of Rights in response to chronic complaints of gross and persistent abuse of the human rights of minorities and political dissidents.

Constitutionalism is viewed in South Asia in three distinct but interrelated ways. First, constitutionalism is understood as a mode of discourse, as a means by which issues relating to political and legal legitimacy and accountability, and the limits of political freedom are conceptualized and articulated within a society. In this sense, a common colonial experience initially shaped the constitutional discourse in Pakistan, India, Sri Lanka, and Bangladesh. This colonial constitutional discourse dealt with questions of limited government, and the struggle for progressive transfer of power to hybrid legislatures with nominated and popular representatives. With the advent of political independence, this discourse shifted to questions of legislative supremacy and the distribution of power between the different organs of government. It presupposed that the postcolonial constitutional arrangements were primarily intended to give effect to the majoritarian principle. As a politically and culturally resurgent majority deployed legislative and executive power to deny equal treatment to ethnic and cultural minorities, a vote in the hands of an intolerant majority was soon viewed as an instrument of oppression. The focus of constitutional discourse began to shift to the need for restraints on the majoritarian principle.

More recently, the discourse has focused increasingly on the constitutional arrangements necessary to preserve the multiethnic character of the polity. These issues relate to power-sharing arrangements, pluralism, secularism, and equalization of opportunities, through the removal of the historic and regional disparities. There are those who challenge the hegemony of the constitutional ideas associated with the modern nation-state and inherited political institutions. The argument is that this form of discourse is no more than an extension of the colonial one, and does not offer any concepts or categories of analysis capable of comprehending the experience of South Asian societies. They contend that this discourse must be extended to accommodate the forces of ethnicity and of nationalities.

These concerns point to the need for new concepts and principles designed to protect ethnic, linguistic, and religious minorities. The protection of such minorities must form a fundamental component of any bill of rights and should primarily be directed toward insulating minorities from any activity capable of threatening their identity or existence. These activities range from genocidal violence or pogroms directed against specific minorities, to policies of assimilation, including state-aided settlement schemes intended to alter the demographic profile of regions where a minority predominates. States need also to be mandated to foster actively and protect the linguistic, cultural, and educational rights of minorities. The discourses of constitutionalism and international human rights jurisprudence have yet to respond imaginatively to challenges that place in jeopardy not merely the nation-state but the very foundations of a constitutional order. These concerns compel reappraisal of the very nature of the nation-state. The entrenchment of the unitary state in constitutional texts often leads to the absurd contradiction of imposing a monoethnic state on a multiethnic polity. The very definition of the state must increasingly reflect the ethnic diversity of the polity, and acknowledge that the state is an aggregation of ethnically and linguistically distinct regions and sometimes of several distinct nationalities.

The discussion of constitutionalism also needs enrichment in the area of the enforcing of fundamental rights. The rhetoric of basic rights and freedoms is based on statist and individualistic conceptions. The ground of support for fundamental rights can be expanded if it is linked to belief systems that have given content and meaning to the social and religious experiences of the people within South Asia. These indigenous, cultural and religious traditions emphasize communitarian conceptions of justice and conciliatory and consensual approaches to the resolution of conflict. Obligations of reciprocity within a family facilitate development of attitudes and values supportive of the right of the child and the needs of the elderly. This approach leads to a more effective protection of social rights than is available in a legal culture that views those issues exclusively in terms of an individual's claim against the state. Another enriching idea is "dharma"; central to the Hindu–Buddhist theory of justice, it defines the moral limits that rulers may not transgress if they are to command the allegiance of their subjects. Little effort has been made to build imaginatively on such concepts to articulate principles of governance and democratic accountability that draw on the language and idioms that form part of the Hindu–Buddhist tradition. Similar attempts are needed to draw the linkages between constitutional values and the rhetoric of rights and the concepts, ideas and institutions central to Islam.

The second view of constitutionalism understands it as an ideal of liberal democratic governance, accountable and answerable to popular will. It is in this symbolic meaning that constitutionalism has been invoked as a rallying cry in the struggle against authoritarianism. During the emergency in India and the struggle for the restoration of democracy in Pakistan, Bangladesh, and Nepal, and in the movements against constitutional authoritarianism in Sri Lanka, this conception of constitutionalism gained ascendency.

The third understanding of constitutionalism arises from the realization that constitutional concepts are fluid; old meanings give way to new interpretations, and new concepts assume priority. In addition to their fluidity, constitutional arrangements are, in the South Asian experience, of a transient nature. Ivor Jennings, the framer of many defunct South Asian constitutions, cautioned us that "Constitutions come like water, and if they don't go like the wind, strange things happen to them which were even beyond the contemplation of their framers." It is in this sense that constitutionalism is equated with the process of value formation, and the effort to build democrative values, civic virtues, and communitarian attitudes on which durable institutions could be firmly grounded.

With sensitivity to the specifications of each national context within which constitutional experiences must be assessed, some general perspectives may be offered that distinguish the South Asian experience with constitutionalism. In the first place, the strength and vibrancy of their institutions such as the party system, the bureaucracy, the judiciary, and the press are partly the result of a long experience with universal adult franchise and competitive political processes. This tradition of political democracy enabled the legal Constitutional order to withstand periodic challenges from insurrectionary movements, *coups d'état*, and subversion of constitutional values and institutions by the ruling elite. This is probably less true of Pakistan and Bangladesh, where there were breaks in the constitutional continuity caused by the forcible seizure of power by the military, but even there the institutional legacy and the legal and bureaucratic culture of the preauthoritarian years retained some resilience and helped mediate the recent transition from authoritarian rule. In comparison, the enterprise of constitutionalism has been more fragile and vulnerable in Africa, in Southeat Asia, and even in parts of Latin America.

Second, despite the apparent resilience of political institutions and processes, South Asia is in the process of a major upheaval in which there is a continuing effort to redefine the nature of the polity and the relationship between the different religious, ethnic communities, and tribal and caste groups. The political compact that followed the transfer of political power provided a framework for the resolution of intergroup tensions. This framework no longer seems to hold and the concepts at its center are being rejected. Concepts such as federalism, secularism, and affirmative equality sustained the balance between different communities differentiated by religion, ethnicity, and caste; the political consensus on these issues soon eroded the inability to agree on alternative arrangements and caused social upheaval and disintegration. Revivalist and fundamentalist forces have also questioned the state's commitments to secular principles. The state, no longer seen as the neutral arbiter between competing religious claims, is increasingly called on to support preferentially the religious beliefs, institutions, and places of worship of a resurgent majority. The realization is growing that there can be no finality in the resolution of these questions and that there will be constant need to renew and reconstruct societal arrangements for the resolution of interethnic and intergroup conflicts. In Southeast Asia, Africa, and Latin America there is less agonizing reappraisal of the basic relationships between groups and the very nature of the polity; the concerns of ethnic and cultural minorities seem less central to the process of constitutional reordering in Africa and Latin America.

The third distinguishing aspect of the South Asian experience is a much greater extent of civic participation, through human rights groups and social action organizations engaged in a creative interaction with journalists and lawyers in the work of redefining the constitutional agenda and the nature of the discourse. In India the emphasis on socioeconomic rights in the enforcement of fundamental rights was partly the result of this process. It is thus clear that constitutional innovation is no longer the sole monopoly of law professionals or party leaders, and that all elements within civil society can play a part in expanding the frontiers of fundamental rights. It is not clear whether such civic involvement in expanding the base of legitimacy of constitutionalism is as pronounced in other Asian and African or Latin American experiences.

South Asia faces the dazzling and yet daunting prospect of defining the frontiers of constitutionalism so as to reconcile the challenges of a reawakened civil society and the disintegrative process of ethnic fratricide with the imperatives of a modern nation state. This opportunity needs to be grasped.

25

Constitutionalism in Africa: Some Conclusions

Samuel C. Nolutshungu

Although all African states attach some importance to their constitutions, as to their national flags and anthems, only very few can be said to abide by them with any consistency. None consider themselves much bound by them on matters such as the limitation of government power, the rights of citizens, the division and separation of powers, or, above all, the objective enforceability of the provisions of the constitutions. Indeed, those elements of the constitutions that place limits on executive power are least respected.

The failure of constitutional government to develop is not the result of popular needs or demands but of governments seeking to escape the constraints imposed by constitutions, laws, and the rights and expectations of citizens. It is true that in some cases, governments enjoyed popular support when they assumed power (whether or not in accordance with the constitutions), or when they set about to weaken the force of the constitution. It is also the case that even when there was no such popular support, there was little protest on constitutional grounds against the usurpation of power. In short, people have supported or opposed particular claimants to power and specific political programs with rather scant regard for the principles and procedures under which these claimants would rule or their aims would be realized.

Where there is, in fact, the potential to resist arbitrary rule, either society is not sufficiently organized politically to challenge it, or the political and legal institutions are too weak, in the quality of their personnel and in their political support from society, to resist or counterbalance executive power. Various aspects of African social structure are directly relevant here. First among them is the fact that the populations consist predominantly of peasants who, by their economic nature, and geographic dispersal, are difficult to organize politically on a lasting basis by any means other than armed revolt. Armed revolt itself does not favor a constitutionalist emphasis in political struggle. Second, the urban classes, workers and capitalists, necessarily have conflicting interests and are each internally divided; they are poorly organized politically. Although some do revolt on questions of civil rights occassionally, as they did in the 1970s against General Kutu Acheampong in Ghana, and recently, against President

Daniel Arap Moi in Kenya, the majority are typically so dependent on the state for their very livelihood that they have a natural reluctance to challenge any government about its use of power.

The central problem is that people lack effective control over their governments and cannot constrain them to act according to law. There is, therefore, a need to democratize politics and society. However, oppositions' weak emphasis on the constitutional questions involved in the governments' abuse of power implies a lack of faith on the part of politically active people, including those with genuine democratic aspirations, in constitutions as important means for furthering or protecting their interest. This itself may be a lesson of their experience.

Clearly, the central issue is the distribution of power and the expectations regarding it: either those who wield state power have enough of it not to have to scruple about the terms under which it may be exercised, or those who seek to replace them also wish to have or believe that they can gain such a power, or they may believe that all previous and existing constitutions are part of the deceptions of the tyranny they seek to overthrow and only a future juster order of power could yield a constitution worthy of defense, in other words, a worthwhile constitutionalism.

What is, however, hardly ever made clear is what the content of such a constitution might be and under what conditions it might acquire general acceptance and binding force.

Material concerns, whether expressed as aspirations for development or for the resolution of social questions of class, nationality, and, latterly, gender relations dominate African reflection on rights, whether applied to institutional design or to specifically constitutional questions. A constitution cannot have much hope of enthusiastic support in the continent if it is not convincingly tied to these preoccupations. Many constitutional documents do indeed contain ringing declarations on such issues, but that has itself fed skepticism in so far as the documents, let alone the subseqent practice of states, have contributed little to alleviate the problems linked to economic and social disadvantage within African societies.

Quite evidently, constitutional provisions proclaiming rights to economic security, improvement, or equality would be hard to enforce by the usual judicial process. What is entailed is not a view of constitutionalism that sees rights as established by the adoption of the constitution, needing only enforcement or clarifiation, or even amplification by the courts. What is required is the notion of a constitution that outlines a desired architecture of social power, represented by the rights it proclaims and the institutions it devises and organizes, but one that can only be realized by subsequent political and economic action rather than by judicial intervention. This constitution would emphasize, not primarily the entrenchment of eternal rights, but the *construction of new power for the weak*. It would not, strictly speaking, be neutral between rich and poor, the weak and the powerful, but would seek equality, being skeptical of any notions of rights or of good government that frustrate that aim.

Conventionally, the pursuit of social justice and economic democracy is seen in terms of giving greater power to the disadvantaged classes, through the control of the power of the public institutions not by its limitation. Various ways have been suggested over the years to achieve such control, ranging from socialist advocacy of a party of workers and peasents that would control the state and realize public ownership and control of the most significant economic processes, to demands for greater decentralization and democratization of decision power. Radical mobilization of workers and peasants would be necessary to enable them to take full advantage of the opportunities thus created. That, however, would be neither easy nor uncontroversial. Attempts to raise popular consciousness and activism in various parts of Africa have often had mixed results. Rarely have such initiatives restrained the concentration of power at the center, or brought it under effective popular control. Generally, they have had their source in the initiative of some benevolent autocrat, civilian or military, so that a certain paternalism characterized the project, whether it was Ujamaa socialism in Tanzania, "people's power" in Mozambique, or people's committees in Ghana or Burkina Faso. These projects have combined, in varying degrees, mass political awareness and local participation with greater surveillance, imposed conformism, and political intimidation.

It is open to debate how far approaches of a conventional socialist kind, based on working class (and peasant) power, exercised through state control of production and redistribution, could in practice be reconciled with populist grassroots activism and participation, or just what forms of economic development each might favor. Although both are radically egalitarian positions, and the ideological rivalry between them is often fudged, these are probably incompatible views of politics and society. No constitution completely dedicated to the one would serve as well for the other.

The two predominating themes of development and economic democracy, though not necessarily expressing the same preoccupations, do share a certain bias toward collective rather than individual welfare. Accordingly, they have in common a certain suspicion of the "individualism" of liberal constitutionalism, even though the "collective rights" placed in opposition to those of bourgeois individualism vary considerably; for some, the collective interest in which rights are construed is that of the "nation," sometimes indistinguishable from the state (as in the OAU Declaration on Human and Peoples' Rights), for others, of classes, and for others still, of national minorities to self-determination. Notions of collective rights might conceivably be applied to a communal habitat and its ecology, to communal land, water resources, and pasture, particularly in those countries where these have traditionally been enjoyed and maintained as collective goods. (Some would add a "right" to development, although the notion of "development" would seem to require rather more precise definition, and the bearers of such a right—state, nations, communities, etc.—would need to be identified in non-arbitrary ways). There may well exist rights of states, relative to other states, in these matters and it would be a nice question how these are reconciled with those of peoples, nations, or communities when they conflict.

Communal land ownership and use are still sufficiently common in many parts of Africa for the idea of communal rights to have real meaning for many people. There are groups of people who live and make their livelihood in contexts that necessitate a communal relation with a specific ecology (e.g., forest people, like the Mbuti) in such a way that the introduction of a regime of private ownership would make their social reproduction and even their mere survival extremely difficult. Indeed, it can be argued that under certain circumstances even the rights of the majority of individuals would be more effectively protected if constraints were placed on the acquisition and alienation of certain ecological assets on the basis of individual ownership. If liberty is linked to property, under certain conditions the alienation of property must also entail a certain loss of personal liberty inconsistent with the idea of free and equal citizenship. In Africa, where the indigency of the overwhelming majority contrasts with the relative superabundance enjoyed by a very few, such conditions may be considered to prevail. (There is a strong tradition that links personal liberty with private property. This is normally advanced in the context of the state versus the individual, but the case of communities and their individual members versus the state also merits consideration.)

None of these concerns, particularly in relation to private property, is unique to Africa, though a case could be made for their special relevance here. Nevertheless, it is by no means clear how substance might be given to the idea of communal or collective rights, or what kinds of institutions might most effectively express and advance them. That is a challenge to the African legal imagination as well as to political theory.

However that may be, even the constitutional protection of communal rights can be circumvented in conditions of extreme economic inequality, and relations of dominance and exploitation can develop within the rights-sharing community. The survival of any rights, individual or communal, depends not only on what is laid down in the constitution but on the substantive ability of persons and collectivities to act to defend or realize those rights. The capacities that are lacking among the African poor cannot be supplied by constitutions but by action elsewhere, in political and economic life generally. The most that a constitution might accomplish is to place as few obstacles as possible in the way of such action.

The proponents of collective rights and of popular empowerment would still confront their opponents, and, indeed, each other and the state, as individuals. They would have to speak, lead, and organize as individuals. For that reason, it is inconceivable that collective or any other imaginable alternative conception of human entitlement could be secured if basic individual rights were not also enshrined in the terms of political association. The resolution of conflict between different notions of entitlement would still require neutral instances to adjudicate, which would, in turn, raise the familiar issues of independent judiciaries and the rule of law. It does not require much imagination to see that this would, in its turn, revalidate traditional principles of constitutionalism regarding the relationships between institutions, such as the division and separation of powers.

Radical alternatives are not all that an African constitutionalism need concern itself about. There have been persistent demands from the opposite ideological direction for both decentralizing and centralizing institutions considered appropriate to "African realities." Sometimes a larger role for "traditional leaders" is demanded. "Traditional leaders" differ greatly from country to country and often within the same country, as do indeed the "traditions" invoked as the bases of their authority; some, evidently, have more solid popular acceptance and support than others. Another variant of the theme of the cultural specificity of African political needs expresses itself in the opposition to competitive politics and is represented in the idea of the one-party state. Leaders of various ideological inclinations have embraced this idea, from African socialists and humanists such as Julius Nyerere of Tanzania and Kenneth Kaunda of Zambia who believed they could realize democracy within the single parties they led, to champions of African "authenticity" such as Mobutu Sese Seko of Zaire and his admirer François Tombalbaye of Chad who, until his death, was also a venal dictator presiding over a one-party state.

Odious as these tendencies may be from the point of view of human rights, they are an undeniable part of contemporary African political culture, and, what is more, they have often been seen, in the initial stages at least, as radical, or progressive responses to the distinctiveness of the continent's people and their needs in state design. What they show beyond any doubt is a widely shared belief that whatever African culture may dictate, it is clearly not comprehended in the idea of organized opposition and political competition. If that belief is true, then democratic constitutionalism would either have no practical application in Africa or would have to be a cultural–revolutionary project in the sense of overthrowing the weight of that aspect of "African culture." As it happens, this view of "African culture," most prevalent in the 1960s and 1970s, was always most firmly held by those who were in power or close to it, and has since come under considerable public criticism.

There is a troubling resemblance between claims that African culture is in some sense incompatible with organized opposition and competition and the view often expressed by colonialists before independence to the effect that Africans were not ready for self-government. One must, however, take seriously the view that some states may be so fragile, in terms of their political cohesion, that they could not survive democracy. Put otherwise, "before it can be democratic, the state must first exist." This latter view is no different from the justification of the supression of liberties and the restriction of democratic procedures in wartime, except that, unlike wartime conditions in democracies, the African emergency is rather less exactly defined and not self-limiting.

Constitutionalism begins with the recognition that the supression of competition and choice by one tendency is little different from its negation by the rival ideological camp, and that the subjective intentions of the parties concerned (one favoring workers and peasants, the other serving the rich and middle classes) are quite beside the point. The point, precisely, is to define nonarbitrary criteria for limiting, and nonviolent means for conducting, competition among these and other classes in society and the corresponding, contending views of politics. Whether African societies are culturally averse to tolerating such competition or to permitting such choices is, to be sure, an empirical matter, which, as luck would have it, can only be determined by the kind of open inquiry possible under conditions of free expression.

It would be a strange idea of constitutional government that provided only for radical choices of basically socialist inspiration, or only for conservative or traditionalist options supposedly based on authentic African culture. If it were argued that certain alternatives, such as dictatorship, should be placed beyond the bounds of legitimate choice, the grounds could only be that these are incompatible with the notions of freedom and equality implicit in the idea of constitutionalism.

By this reasoning, there cannot be a species difference between constitutionalism in Africa and the same beast elsewhere, though local adaptations responsive to deeply felt needs would be indispensable. What matters most is not the document but the principle that makes government and political association generally subject to rights and to accepted rules of procedure in all important spheres and, above all, the will to make it so.

Apart from the demands that constitutional ideas should bend to distinctively African traditions and culture, a line of reasoning generally associated with various brands of conservatism, the issues that Africans typically raise in criticism of liberal constitutionalism are themselves not alien to the West. They involve a tilt in favor of democracy in the balance between it and liberalism, a concept of democracy, participatory rather than pluralist or elitist, that incorporates a substantial commitment to economic equality, and an underlying belief that democracy ought to fight capitalism and foreign economic domination. The critique of liberal constitutionalism is not any more or any less valid in Africa than it is in other parts of the world. It does not, certainly, make a convincing case for "African exceptionalism." However, Africa's present situation increases the unease with conservative notions of constitutional government. The universal belief among Africans that society and culture must change, though the directions of such change are a matter of profound disagreement, focuses debate on the creation of a new social order; this is an essentially radical mission. In these circumstances it is more appealing to envisage the constitution as an expression in legal form of political and other social aims rather than as a set of legal constraints on action to achieve the desired transformations. Given the newness of African states, it may still be possible to think innovatively of institutions and processes and, perhaps, to gain the popular support to enable radical notions of democracy to do rather better here than they have done elsewhere.

Whether any constitution can bear the full weight of all these cares and still stand is uncertain, but what is clearly indicated is the need for political movements that can give substance to these commitments; this can be allowed for in a constitution, but such an achievement occurs through practical politics over a more or less protracted period of time. It may be that the greatest challenge in Africa is to design appropriate institutions that can achieve the enlargement of the idea of rights implicit in some of the criticism of liberal constitutionalism and, at the same time, to provide safeguards for those rights that would be accessible to ordinary people.

In this regard, constitution making is only one of many aspects of state creation. If that is what it always was, the difference now is that what the state judged to be possible, desirable, or needed is one that would take the greater part of the initiative of transforming society and culture, one closer to revolutionary rather than to limited constitutional traditions, to France than to America, to the latter rather than the earlier part of the eighteenth century. The critical question is whether such work of political construction is undertaken within the framework of a cogent rather than a special case constitutionalism (which may amount to not a transcendence of "bourgeois liberalism," but mere special pleading in the face of its stringent demands in the area of rights for those who have different preferences and ideals from one's own).

Beyond the rights of persons or collectivities, there remains a large problem of state capacities. Do modern African states, as such, have the material and human resources to govern at all efficaciously under any general conception of constitutionalism? In this regard, traditionalist arguments may have some attraction in claiming that the "traditional" rulers provide a ready-made extension of administrative and judicial capacity, which may (arguably) impose a lighter burden on state revenues (though not necessarily on citizens from whom they often exact tribute in various forms) than would modern bureaucrats and politicians. This claim has been conceded to some degree in many cases, although never with any noticeable effect on the rate of expansion of the modern bureaucracy, or on its fiscal crises. The response of states, however, to the problem of limited resources and weak authority and power has primarily tended towards greater centralization and concentration of such power as could be mustered. The manifestations of this trend are familiar: the one-party state, civilian, or military unitarist rule, the suppression of ethnic or national minorities, and, in economics, a large role for the state or for a small entrepreneurial class enjoying a privileged relationship with the state. The results have uniformly provoked discontent and alienation from the state.

Material weakness can hardly be made good by the arrogation of powers and the assumption of ever greater responsibility. Latterly, these tendencies have come under criticism. Unfortunately, the revolution has been overshadowed by a limited formulation of the problem in terms of the alternatives presented by international financial agencies such as the World Bank and the International Monetary Fund, or in terms of oppositions such as "the state versus the market," or in social science terms that broaden the issue to "the state versus civil society."

Only rarely has the question been raised whether the unitary nation-state ideal to which African states aspire is not itself a source of weakness and failure.[1] Merely to oppose the unitarist state to equally unitary notions of "the market" and "civil society" does not begin to come to terms with the physical facts and the political–cultural consequences of the dispersal of political communities over vast territories that are costly and difficult to administer, in the context of generally exiguous economies that ensure that the state has often very little to give in exchange for what it takes. It may well be that the precondition of constitutionalism in Africa would be a new kind of state. Just as in Canada and the United States federalism was devised to *cope with* as much as to *allow for* the fact of the dispersal of people and power, so in many African countries new forms of association between geographic localities and between political communities, actual and potential, may be the prerequisite of viable statehood, itself a precondition of meaningful constitutional development. By so doing, African constitutionalism would distinguish itself, not by announcing new principles that depart widely from what has been learned elsewhere, but by an original work of creating institutions appropriate to declared ideals.

There still remains the question of knowing the conditions under which the idea of the constitution might acquire binding significance.

Constitutionalism can arise only out of the practice of politics; it is a result of people asserting themselves in politics and needing to know exactly (or to have confirmed in clear principles) the extent of their entitlement to do so. Classes or fractions of classes that only intermittently articulate their interests in political choices are not likely to produce a constitutionalist discourse and, less still, sustain a costly and protracted struggle under its inspiration.

These facts of political life are clearly linked to underdevelopment as a general condition, with the distinctive political relations it fosters between state and people and among the people themselves. They are particularly associated with the economic crises that permanently characterize these societies and even with the means prefered by both left and right to resolve them. There can probably be no stable, no consensual, and no fair government under conditions of mass poverty and recurrent crises that seem to demand authoritarian solutions.

Here, an ideological element, which is historical, intrudes. Most of the constitutions and constitutional language were not initially adopted under conditions of popular choice or power, nor did they result from an interpretation of the political and constitutional needs of the population. Rather, like the states themselves, they were largely the residues of colonial rule, often the old authoritarian political order in new clothes. They were simply foisted by colonial rulers and their successors on polities structured in ethnic terms that substantially blocked the formation of political alliances based on principles, rights, or interests that could be generalized across "tribal" or ethnic boundaries.

Other constitutions were imposed by military oligarchies or revolutionary vanguards, which more or less directly copied foreign blueprints or merely mocked or dismissed the constitutional ideal. In both the colonial (and neocolonial) and the revolutionary instances, the dominant ideologies reflected an instrumentalism in politics that was indifferent to the means of government and the norms (or social consent) that might govern them.

The historical element is important in another way, also. The constitutions did not grow out of political experience. They were not, except in a superficial way, the embodiment of political realities lived, victories won, and defeats endured, and above all of lessons deeply learned about the costs of arbitrary government and the need to minimize it. Political institutions (in the broad sense that includes associations, parties, and legal institutions) can gain the power to inhibit government and to sustain both the moral force of rights and the rule of law only through more or less prolonged experience of struggle.

But the problem of constitutionalism in Africa, as with the problems of economic development and state formation, is that of guiding and, indeed, forcing the pace of history. That is, undoubtedly a task of education both in the formal sense and in a broader one linked to political activation of the population at large. The latter, however, already involves a challenge to the state and an assertion of rights and is, therefore, inescapably a form of struggle. But it involves a struggle not only against tyrants and refractory oligarchies, but against the cultural reticences and shortcomings of illiterate and often desperately poor people. The poor defer to the rich, the illiterate to those with high attainment in Western education. They are not likely to articulate with confidence their own notions of justice and good order, however well-founded those may be in accumulated experience and wisdom. Equally, material and cultural deprivation restricts the possibility of forming alliances with similarly disadvantaged people across boundaries of language, custom and locality. The political activation of the people is a task for political movements and parties that would be truly revolutionary in scope and consequence, *au fond* revolutionary in overturning the patterns of thinking of the oppressed and obliging them to think of their relief in terms of theories and ideologies that, candidly, are quite alien to them.

Popular acceptance is crucial, but perhaps something more is as well: the belief on the part of all the crucial actors that they would do better for themselves in a genuine constitutional order. This implies more than a cost–benefit calculation, though that too may be consciously invoked. Like state building, coming round to such a view may be the labor of many years, punctuated by partial and ambiguous advances.[2] What seems essential is that constitutional development is essential to the solution of the major problems of public life. The making of the first constitutions was a means to end colonial rule and to resolve contentions between emergent African elites and European imperial power, but it can hardly be said that their making was importantly focused on resolving the barely begun difficulties of the countries concerned. In the postcolonial era, people believed themselves to have alternative ways of resolving their problems: through military seizures of power, in which they did not have to deal with other political forces in the country; through regional rebellions and secession; by withdrawal from the state or by eluding its clutches; and, for some of those who could afford it, through migration. Only occasionally, and fleetingly, have protagonists in large scale conflicts sought to negotiate a general and binding settlement of differences that would also lay down the fundamental terms of political association. In some countries certain ground rules were established that may have laid the foundations for further elaboration in the future (e.g., federalism in Nigeria). In many other countries, however, powerful groups have, quite realistically, judged that they had no problems whose resolution turned on the making of an effective and binding constitution. Sometimes, their interests have been best served by the feebleness of laws and institutions and the existing constitutional void.

Only when the major political forces feel themselves constrained by the power of their rivals can they be expected to prefer durable agreements on the ground rules of political action. Such a recognition itself may be tied to circumstances that may change more or less abruptly as economic and social conditions change. How long the agreements once generated by a favorable balance of power survive the alteration of circumstances and of the distribution of power would depend, in part, on the quality of the agreements themselves; it would also depend on the depth of the impact of the agreement on people's minds: on the historic magnitude of the constitutional moment.

All political struggles have their culminating moments, not all such moments have the same impact on subsequent political consciousness and action. Some moments have a larger historical significance than others, both by what they make possible subsequently and by the magnitude of the break with an evil past that they signify in the minds of contemporaries. For contemporaries, anticipation of the event, in thought and sentiment, adds to its magnification when it arrives. So does the difficulty of the task accomplished, but to accept that the result achieved is proportional to, or crowns the preceding effort, is itself a matter of affective interpretation, of ideology, and of intellectual work.

The conviction on the part of political leaders or, at least, of the political vanguard that the terrain of the constitution is important is necessary if political struggles are to produce a constitutional discourse or culminate in a constitutionalism that matters. Such conviction is, undoubtedly, a product of experience. It is also a result of reflection and debate. This intellection is seldom the outcome of developments within a single country but seems to express the spirit of the times, or an important aspect of it. That was, surely, as much the case with American constitutional ideas in the eighteenth century as it has been with the constitutional skepticism, that has, until quite recently, been a feature of a good deal of contemporary African progressive thinking. Just as states are made possible by world conditions—the creation of modern African states being the most dramatic example—so also are the ideas of statehood and citizenship. In this regard, great constitutional moments for individual countries or regions have often been embedded in great world-historical events as well. The decolonization of Africa was such an event, yet, at the time that it occurred, the dominant political ideas paid rather scant regard to constitutionalism, being focused on the material outcomes of political processes, the empirical behavior of political subjects, and their implications for international politics.

Yet, before there can be any serious and durable commitment to the ordering of political life according to principles whose force inheres in popular acceptance if not consent, there must, to begin with, emerge a positive identification with the project of such a state, a sense of common belonging and destiny as well as a sense of confidence and pride in the political community and the state. In state after state, this subjective element is becoming more deficient, partly because of the misuse of state power, partly because of economic circumstances, but partly, also, because of the facts of international life.

The reality of external dependence undermines the plausibility of the project of independent statehood and nationhood. It is, everyone seems to suspect, somewhere else, outside, that everything that matters is decided, indeed, happens. This realization is corrosive at every level of culture including that of politics. It is not to one's fellow citizens and their possibilities, nor to one's own resources that one looks for the construction of a desirable political order, but to forces outside that cannot be democratically controlled. Concretely, dependence is explicit in the role played by external powers in economic life and, as arms suppliers or as direct interventionists, in internal conflicts, whether these take the form of civil wars or wars of secession. Through most of the 1980s, the most important economic policies adopted by many African states were imposed by foreign creditors, either directly or through the "structural adjustment policies" of the International Monetary Fund (IMF) and the World Bank. In the growth of their indebtedness and in the limited options for resolving the problem, these states were largely the victims of international processes that they could neither influence nor keep at bay. It might be thought, on many issues, it would be as rewarding to seek to influence affairs outside the state as to do so within its corridors of power; or, at any rate, that power within the state was more valuable for what it made possible outside, or in relations with international institutions and powerful states. This high degree of political extroversion of the state (which matches the external dependence of the economy) is difficult to associate with notions of popular sovereignty or with the growth of political responsibility.

In addition, the era of the Cold War and the skepticism within the dominant countries concerning political ideals embodied in their own constitutions did much to undermine the attempt to transplant constitutionalism to the new states of Africa. Rights, legality, and constitutionality were often reduced to mere labels for one side in the Cold War, either affixed to compliant regimes, or worse, waived as the needs of international politics dictated. In the competition between major powers for influence in less developed countries, states were favored over individuals or peoples, and the assistance given to governments encouraged unitarist and centralist tendencies at the expense of political and regional minorities, on the principle that it was better to have a strong government as an ally. For the same reasons both the east and the west supplied the good allies with the means to suppress domestic opponents.

Even when the international response was intended to be more benign (seeking to avoid any accusation of neocolonial interference), it often did much harm by encouraging unlimited toleration of the abuses of governments by the international community, including those countries that bankrolled such abuses, or which, at any rate, sustained the offending governments in power through their aid. Although the principle of noninterference in each others' internal affairs is a sound one for a system of sovereign states, it becomes incoherent when the "internal affairs" are, in large measure, the result of the policies and actions of the other states. In an interdependent world, absolute insistence on the principle of noninterference often turns out to be a cover for other, even more questionable, forms of involvement.[3]

Economic failure, dramatized by the recession of the 1970s and 1980s and growing external indebtedness, has provoked opposition to African regimes, directed particularly against the dominance of the state in economic life and its lack of political accountability. Agitation for democracy has occurred across the continent, on occasion successfully forcing the scrapping of single-party constitutions and the holding of competitive elections. In contradictory ways, this democratic movement, as yet of uncertain depth and durability, has benefitted considerably from international pressures of aid donors and creditors who favor economic liberalization. External criticism has merely underscored internal discontent, but the privatization of public assets, in its own way, reinforces the need felt for greater democracy not merely as a means to constrain the economic excesses of the state or, in prevailing parlance, to strengthen "civil society," but also to democratize political life. Benefitting from externally imposed economic liberalization, the political movement is often animated by radical sentiments that seek to constrain external influence and to bring the process of economic adjustment under popular control. What kinds of constitutionalism may eventually emerge remains uncertain, being part of what is (and may come to be seen to be) at issue.[4]

International relations do not, then, uniformly work against the constitutionalist ideals of even the most dependent countries. Occasionally, they present opportunities for state creation and constitutional development. From the earliest days of decolonization in Africa, Pan-Africanism linked political progress very closely to integration and unity among the emergent states. Many still believe strongly that closer cooperation among African states may enable them to cope with the negative effects of economic dependence. How far cooperation may proceed in the various regions of the continent is impossible to predict, but, in time, it may call into question the inherited boundaries and divisions of people and resources, and, in doing so, give impetus to constitutionalism and a new sense of its possibilities. In Europe, in the last two or three decades, constitutionalism has gained considerably from west European integration in the EEC.

The end of the Cold War has provided not only an opportunity for liberalization and democratization in the Soviet Union and eastern Europe, but the occasion for a revival of intellectual and political interest in fundamental questions of political association. These developments have had some effect on political expectations and rights consciousness in Africa. They have fed expectation in Africa while adding, for what it is worth, to demands that western governments and publics should demonstrate concrete support for human rights movements in the continent.

At the level of ideas, too, developments elsewhere have an impact on the continent's politics. The growing concern in the west about ecology adds a further dimension to African notions of public good that can be the object of collective rights. Similarly, the growth of the feminist movement in the west has helped to draw greater attention to gender issues in African politics than might otherwise have been the case. Needless to say such movements do not always address strictly constitutional questions nor do they express themselves in constitutional terms.

The international climate is, therefore, important for the growth of constitutionalism in Africa. Indeed, if the progressive ideals of constitutionalism regain their importance more widely, they will likely flourish in Africa as well. Here, Mahmood Mamdani's observation is relevant: constitutionalism is inherently a contested field. It is as a contested field that it should come to prominence once more elsewhere, particularly in the countries that set examples, for the real contest to be waged more fully in Africa also. Yet, at the same time, the idea of constitutional government is precisely that of a political struggle that culminates in accommodation and inclusion, one, therefore, that, in its own domain, is not conclusively won by any one particular side, and never exclusively.

Notes

1. The matter has attracted more attention among French-speaking Africanists led by such studies as T. Michalon, *Quel Etat pour l'Afrique* (Paris: Editions L'Harmattan, 1984). See also D. Martin and F. Coulon, eds., *Les Afriques Politiques* (Paris: Editions La Découverte, 1991), passim.

2. Jean-François Bayart makes a convincing case for seeing the project of state formation in Africa as a task of the *longue durée* in his stimulating book, *L'Etat en Afrique: la politique du ventre* (Paris: Fayard, 1989).

3. It is, admittedly, no easy matter to devise satisfactory ways of promoting rights—and constitutionalism—globally. Yet, once the principle is acknowleged it should be possible to begin to think of ways and means of collective action to this end. Of interest on some of these issues, is Charles Beitz, *Political Theory and International Relations* (Princeton: Princeton University Press, 1979).

4. The subject has attracted considerable press as well as academic comment, e.g., Lisa Beyer, "Continental Shift," in *Time*, May 21, 1990; Tom Masland, "A Longing for Liberty," *Newsweek*, July 23, 1990; "The Palms Sway," *The Economist*, June 2, 1990.

Index